Inextricably Bonded

Inextricably Bonded

Israeli Arab and Jewish Writers Re-Visioning Culture

Rachel Feldhay Brenner

THE UNIVERSITY OF WISCONSIN PRESS

The University of Wisconsin Press
1930 Monroe Street, 3rd Floor
Madison, Wisconsin 53711-2059
uwpress.wisc.edu

3 Henrietta Street
London WC2E 8LU, England
eurospanbookstore.com

3   5   4   2

Printed in the United States of America

Library of Congress Cataloging-in-Publication Data
Brenner, Rachel Feldhay, 1946–
Inextricably bonded: Israeli Arab and Jewish writers
re-visioning culture / Rachel Feldhay Brenner.
p.   cm.
Includes bibliographical references and index.
ISBN 0-299-18960-0 (cloth: alk. paper)
1. Israeli fiction—History and criticism.
2. Arabic fiction—Israel—Translations into Hebrew—History and criticism.
3. Palestine in Judaism.   4. Ethnic relations in literature.
5. Zionism in literature.   I. Title.   II. Series.
PJ5029.B74   2003
842.4′3609358—dc21
2003007695

ISBN 978-0-299-18964-8 (pbk.: alk. paper)

For my children, Shelly and Guy,
May love of peace be your guide

Contents

Acknowledgments

I would like to express my gratitude to the various institutions and staff that made the writing of this book possible. I thank the University of Wisconsin–Madison, whose generous financial support aided my research and whose confidence in my scholarship was most reassuring. The primary idea for the book was conceived during my residency as a fellow at the Institute for Research in the Humanities at the University of Wisconsin–Madison. Several summer grants awarded by the Graduate School enabled me to develop my ideas. A Vilas Associate Award made it possible to complete my research in Israel. A substantial portion of the writing was done during my fellowship as Skirball Visiting Scholar at the Oxford Centre for Hebrew and Jewish Studies. An NEH fellowship allowed me to complete the project, and a grant from the Memorial Foundation for Jewish Culture helped with travel expenses. I also thank the University of Wisconsin Press staff for their professionalism and dedication.

The support of friends and colleagues proved invaluable. I would like to express my gratitude to David Sorkin for his interest in my project, his help, and, most of all, his encouragement. My thanks to Gershon Shafir, whose unwavering belief in the value of my work and good advice sustained me throughout the entire process. I am grateful to my friend and colleague Cynthia Miller, who read parts of the manuscript and whose kindness helped me overcome occasional moments of doubt and hesitation. I am most thankful to Rivka Feldhay, whose advice and suggestions helped me to conceptualize this project; her insights enriched this book immeasurably.

Inextricably Bonded

Prologue

Israeli Literatures and Their Presence in Zionist Culture

> Something happens to objects, beliefs, and practices when they are represented, reimagined, and performed in literary texts, something often unpredictable and disturbing. . . . The ability of artists to assemble and shape the forces of their culture in novel ways so that elements powerfully interact that rarely have commerce with one another in the general economy has the potential to unsettle . . . a mutually affirmative relation between artistic production and the other modes of production and reproduction that make up a society.
>
> *Stephen Greenblatt, "Culture"*

Is literature capable of re-visioning the culture in which it was conceived? Are literary texts powerful enough to unsettle the conformist practices of the dominant social discourse? This study examines these questions in the context of literatures produced by Israeli Arabs and Israeli Jews.[1] More specifically, this study probes these literatures in terms of their dissension from the widely accepted ideological propagation of the irreparable antagonism between Palestinian and Jewish national groups. In contrast to the deeply entrenched perception of unbridgeable cultural, social, and political divergences between Arabs and Jews, this study shows that the two literatures affirm a complex yet indissoluble affinity between the two communities.

Israeli Jewish and Israeli Arab communities came into being in

3

the wake of the 1948 Israeli-Arab War, which established the domination of the victorious Jewish majority over the defeated Arab minority. This asymmetrical sociopolitical configuration allowed the
ruling mainstream to carry on the pre-state Zionist politics of separation between Jews and Arabs. The origins of the doctrine that dismissed Palestinian history and ignored the Arab presence in Palestine
can be traced back to the beginnings of the Zionist settlement.

The conceptualization of national literature in the new state perpetuated the exclusionary self-definition of the pioneering Zionists at
the time of the Yishuv (the pre-state Jewish settlement in Palestine).
In its endeavors to construct Israel's cultural identity, the Zionist establishment defined Israeli literature in terms both of its Hebrew
mode and of the Jewishness of its Israeli citizen-authors.[2] Israeli literature was expected to promote the Zionist ideal of the Jewish people
speaking their reborn language in the reborn nation-state. As an artistic refraction of the Zionist separatist discourse, Israeli literature constituted a category of its own; it was meant to represent Israeli culture
as distinct from Jewish Diaspora culture as well as from the Palestinian culture. As it evolved, however, Israeli literature diverged from
the prescribed path. Some Israeli Jewish writers openly addressed the
issue of the suppressed history of the Palestinian Arab population. A
number of Israeli Arab writers told the story of Palestinian suppression in Hebrew. However limited, the phenomenon of Arab writers
who directed their story to the Hebrew-speaking Israeli Jewish majority undermined the ethnic (Jewish) component of Israeli literature.
Even though the controversy over the definition of Israeli literature
has by no means ended, the Arab writers who wrote in Hebrew effectively transformed the concept of Israeli *national* literature, rede-
signing it as a *bi-ethnic* literature.

This study examines the fiction of the Israeli Arab writers alongside literary texts by Israeli Jewish authors. It discusses those Arab
writers who have either written their fiction in Hebrew or published
it in Israel in Hebrew translation: Atallah Mansour (*In a New Light*),
Anton Shammas (*Arabesques*), and Emile Habiby (*The Pessoptimist;
Ikhtayyeh; Saraya, Daughter of the Ghoul*—novels translated into
Hebrew by Shammas). The Arab writers' choice of Hebrew, which
signifies the intention to address the Israeli Hebrew-speaking majority readership, has defined them as Israeli writers. At the same time,

the literary preoccupation of the Arab writers with the tragedy of Palestinian defeat, degradation, and dispossession points to a contiguity with Israeli Jewish writers, who were also preoccupied with the theme of the Arab. My discussion of this theme as represented by Jewish authors focuses on S. Yizhar's "Hirbet Hizah" (a story that depicts the conquest of the Arab village of Hirbet Hizah), A. B. Yehoshua's "Facing the Forests," Amos Oz's "Nomad and Viper" and *My Michael,* and David Grossman's *Smile of the Lamb.*

In his discussion of the inseparability of culture and literature, Stephen Greenblatt maintains that "cultural analysis [of literature] must be opposed . . . to the rigid distinction between that which is within a text and that which lies outside."[3] Indeed, the thematic focus on the Palestinian tragedy in both fictions cannot be dissociated from the Zionist culture that cultivated both separation from the Palestinian Arabs and suppression of their history in the land. There is no doubt that both Israeli Arab and Jewish writings call into question the Zionist exclusionary claim to the land. However, to consider these texts purely in terms of rebellious resistance to the dominant ideology would be to disregard the intricate and highly emotional predicament of the authors who produced the literary representation of the Zionist discourse *and* who are products of the Zionist discourse itself. Not only do the Jewish writers owe their Israeli identity and their language to the Zionist project of revival. The Arab writers' Israeli citizenship and their choice of Hebrew also mark their historically unhappy connections to the Zionist ideological enterprise. From this point of view, it is instructive to consider the conflicted position of the authors with regard to the political and ideological significance of their own writing.

As was already mentioned, the Hebrew language and the authors' Israeli citizenship define this literature as Israeli and its creators as Israeli writers. Ironically, the Israeli literature of dissent owes its existence to the Zionist project against which it reacts so harshly. The writers' highly critical approach to Zionist politics of exclusion and oppression amounts to the denunciation of an ideology that has furnished the tools of their art and, to a large extent, shaped them as artists. The Jewish writers discussed in this work, all of whom are Palestine/Israel born,[4] are proud Israelis quite aware of the fact that the same ideology that propagates the politics of separatism and the practices of Arab oppression—which they have been protesting against—also made them free citizens of their own state. At the same time, the Palestine/Israel-born Arab writers are torn between their Palestinian and Israeli identity,[5] quite aware that their choice to become Israeli writers signals a form of collusion with a regime that defeated them, deprived them of their national freedom, and drove the majority of their people into exile. The affinity between the Israeli Arab and Jewish writers therefore emerges from the complex, difficult, yet inescapable involvement of both sides with the Zionist project of the Jewish state. Despite the disparity between the sociopolitical positions of the majority and the minority, the literary theme that reasserts the Arab presence and reaffirms the history of the Palestinian people reflects a commonality between Israeli Arab and Jewish writers. This linkage of dissension from the Zionist ideological line is, to quote Greenblatt, "unpredictable and disturbing." It unsettles not only the component of *separation* from the histories of the Diaspora and Palestine in the Zionist vision of the "new" Jewish identity but also the component of *imitation* of the West that underscores this new identity.

I have already argued that the prescription for national Israeli literature to be written in Hebrew exclusively by Israeli Jews—a concept undermined by Israeli Arab literary writings in Hebrew—set Israeli literature apart from Jewish Diaspora literatures, as well as from the literature produced by Israeli Arabs. I now wish to suggest that this twofold exclusion not only represented the Zionist separatist trend at large[6] but also defined the limits of Zionist national identity. The Zionist settlement in Palestine—later to become the Zionist state—strove to create a homogeneous Jewish society single-mindedly dedicated to the telos of Jewish national renewal in the land.

To construct a collective identity around the narrative of nation building, other narratives needed to be elided. Two celebrated slogans encapsulated the intentionality of the elision: the *she'lilat ha'golah* (negation of the Diaspora),[7] and the "empty land," a shortened version of the (in)famous catchphrase "for a people without a land [Jews], a land without a people."[8] Both mottoes reflected the intention to eliminate histories that interfered with shaping the "new" Jewish national identity. The former intended to erase the history of the Jewish people in the Diaspora by associating the Zionist movement with *dor ha'midbar* (the generation of the desert), namely, the children of the Exodus generation, who were born in freedom and conquered the promised land. The latter sought to disclaim the history of the Palestinian presence in the land, depicting the Zionists as the redeemers of the land, *dor rishon l'geula* (the first generation of redemption).

As I see it, the programmatic negation of the histories of the Diaspora and Palestine fulfilled a vital psychological function: the narratives of negation complemented each other, lending support to Zionist youths' rejection of the Jewish life in exile and their emigration to Palestine. The notion of the "empty land" awaiting revival was of crucial importance in partially alleviating the painful and guilt-provoking severance of close family ties and the ideological rejection of national history, lifestyle, and the religious heritage of the Diaspora. An acknowledgment that the land was owned and populated by others would have undermined the rationale for *she'lilat ha'golah;* it would have classified the Zionist settlement in Palestine as equivalent to yet another Diaspora, that is, yet another Jewish community under foreign domination. Furthermore, the admission that the land was cultivated by others would have invalidated the poetic notion of rescuing the motherland from its two-thousand-year-old devastation. Such an acknowledgment could not have sustained the identification of the Zionist pioneers with the biblical Jewish heroic warriors and rulers.

The mottoes of negation underscored the centrality of the revolutionary national transformation to the Zionist platform. To paraphrase Theodor Herzl's novel *Altneuland,* the "transformed" Jew will live in his sovereign state, speaking in an old-new voice of independence, a voice which reverberates with Jewish heroism and freedom in antiquity. Ironically, the mention of Herzl and his vision of the "new" Jew calls attention to the fact that the identification with heroic biblical figures to the exclusion of the histories of the Diaspora and Arab Palestine was not the ultimate Zionist goal. It is true that the Zionist ideology propagated both economic and cultural exclusion of the Palestinian inhabitants of the land; it is also true that the movement vehemently denounced the Diaspora, including its languages, cultural orientation, and religious practices, as well as its history of powerlessness and persecution of the Jews. At the same time, the allusion to Herzl's utopian novel reminds us to what extent the imitation of the West was the objective of Zionist national identity. The politics of discommunication needs to be considered in the context of the overriding Zionist telos of a Jewish state in a dialogic relation with the West. The powerful desire to establish an independent, secular nation-state motivated the Zionist rejection of the culture of the Jewish Diaspora; the adherence to Western culture precluded association with the local Palestinian culture. In a very real sense the Zionists were leaving Europe inspired by Herzl's vision of a model Western state that would disseminate European civilization in the East. In this sense, the Zionists' identification with biblical heroes can be seen as a metaphorical representation of the desire to become as free and powerful as the Europeans.

Paradoxically, the Zionists sought to imitate the Europeans, whose relentless and—as they well realized—incurable anti-Semitism they were fleeing. This illogicality sheds light on the complex psychological underpinnings of the seemingly straightforward idea of the Jewish state as a solution to the "Jewish problem." The desire to establish a state modeled upon the image of the West and the wish to refashion the Jew in the person of the enlightened European reveal a deeply embedded dependency on the West. By assuming the role of the colonists—some might say colonizers—in Palestine, the Zionists perpetuated the ambivalence of the Jews as a colonized minority in Europe. As they saw it, the desire to become a self-liberated Jew in the motherland could only be realized with the approval of the enlightened Western nations. Europe's recognition and acceptance of the Zionist concept was therefore indispensable in forging a new Jewish identity.

The connection between Jewish Zionist identity and European recognition recalls Hegel's famous discussion of the master and the slave, which opens with the dictum, "Self-consciousness exists in and for itself when, and by the fact that, it so exists for another; that is, it exists only in being acknowledged."[9] Hegel's postulation highlights the crucial importance of recognition in the process of identity construction: we attain self-consciousness only when our being is acknowledged by others. In view of the indispensability of recognition to the sense of self, I would argue that the selection of the individuals or groups whose recognition one seeks is an important indicator of the nature of interaction between the parties. In other words, the agency to which we attribute the power to grant us the sense of self provides an insight into the way in which we perceive ourselves with respect to the other. In light of this realization, the Zionist striving for Western recognition signals a pervasive sense of inferiority vis-à-vis Europe. For the "new" Jew to gain a sense of self-worth, acknowledgment of the former masters must be secured. Furthermore, the desire to gain recognition from this particular agency accounts for the negation of others. The single-minded progression toward becoming like an enlightened nation does not leave room for alternative routes of identity building. Perceived as obstacles to the telos of European recognition, affinities to both Diaspora and Palestinian histories had to be obliterated.

In light of the overriding need for European acknowledgment, literature that focused on the ideologically decreed denial of others posited a problem for mainstream Zionism. The texts, both Jewish and Arab, tell the story of suffering and victimization of the defeated Palestinian population. In one sense, therefore, the story restores the visibility of the Arab in the "empty" land and calls into question the unequivocal Zionist claim to the land. In another sense, by contrast, the story of the suffering that the triumphant Jews inflicted on the defenseless, defeated Arab population invokes the history of Jewish persecution and victimization in the Diaspora. Against the doctrine of exclusion, the literary representations reassert in the Israeli consciousness the denied histories of the Palestinian Arab and the Diaspora Jew. At the same time, the repercussions of this disclosure affect Israel's Western self-identification. The brutalities committed against the Palestinian population under occupation and the legal discrimination against the Arabs in the State of Israel clash with the European culture of the Enlightenment and its ideals of liberalism, humanism, and equality. The story of dispossession and oppression of a helpless minority hinders Israel's teleological progression toward recognition as an enlightened and liberal nation.

It is therefore not surprising that the Zionist cultural establishment was unwilling to heed the voices of dissension and chose to ignore their moral signification. This evasive attitude attests to the extent of anxiety that the dissenting message has evoked, anxiety reflected in the tactic of interpretation. In general, the critics and the reviewers of this literature adopted patterns of interpretive co-optation that allowed them to include the texts in the Israeli literary canon. The strategy of canonization fulfilled two interrelated goals: it not only neutralized the dissident aspect in the text but also permitted Israel to claim an affinity to the European liberal tradition. Thus, the critical reception of these works saw the Arab in the story as a universal symbol of suffering, while the story itself was perceived as a representation of the human condition at large. In light of this approach, the works reflected either the existentialist weltanschauung—in terms of its despair over the collapse of the liberal-humanist values in the postwar, postmodern world—or the Enlightenment and its hopeful conviction that humanism and liberal ideals would prevail. The strategy of canonical co-optation perpetuated the ideological exclusion of unwanted histories and, at the same time, promoted the telos of European recognition. By situating the fiction, both Jewish and Arab, in the tradition of European writing, the Zionist cultural establishment reaffirmed its European affiliation.

The critical reception of the dissenting literatures demonstrates the extent of threat that they presented to the doctrine of the "new" Jew. The seriousness of this literary deviation from the collective mindset is reflected in the fervor with which the establishment critics strove to abstract the controversial message. The critical response invokes the questions of the power of literature vis-à-vis culture that I raised at the outset. At this point it is possible to rephrase the questions in a more specific way: Does this literature signal the potential to unsettle the practices of separation and imitation that continue to dominate Israel's culture and politics? If so, where does this potential lie and what new perspectives does it offer? Is there a possibility of change? Naturally, it is impossible to answer these questions in a definitive manner.

It is my belief that literature affects human consciousness and effects changes in social practices, yet its impact is imperceptible, often delayed, and hard to measure. In the particular case of Israeli Arab and Jewish fictions, the texts before us delve into narratives that have been intentionally elided from collective memory. Counteracting the politics of suppression, they bring to the fore moral issues that were downplayed or simply dismissed for the sake of cultural identification with the West. Ironically, the literary illumination of the denied history of the land and of the unacknowledged oppression of the Arab evokes a critical response whose tactics of abstraction and co-optation point in the direction where potential change may lie.

In the preceding discussion I have identified the inherent ambivalence in Zionist identity. Despite its declaration of liberation from the subjection of the Diaspora, to a considerable extent the Zionist project still feels the need to establish its credibility with the West. Following Hegel's dictum of the role of the acknowledgment by another in one's self-conscious existence, I suggested that the selection of the recognition giver offers an important indication of the self-perception of the recognition seeker. As the tactics of the critical evasion show, the "new" Jewish national identity continues to seek validation in recognition by the West. The proclivity of the critics to subscribe to Western literary and philosophical trends permits one to infer that that the anxiety-provoking aspect of this literature lies in a search for recognition *other than that of the West*. In other words, the insistence to anchor the texts in the universalizing modes of Western thought indicates that the center of defiance lies in the selection of the recognition giver that the recognition seeker has made.

Indeed, the dissenting story in the texts before us demonstrates the twofold quest for a recognition giver. At one level the narrative that reaffirms the history of the Arab calls for its recognition by the majority Hebrew readership. In confronting the mainstream with the story of the victims of the 1948 war, that is, the defeat of the Arabs and its tragic aftermath for the Palestinian population, each literature collapses the collectively accepted doctrine of denial. The Jewish texts acknowledge the Palestinian life in the land and its history, which were cut short by the Israeli victory; the Arab texts bring to the fore the brutality of dispossession and exile that ended the national history of the Palestinians. While each springs from a different sociopolitical context, both literatures converge in the twofold desire to rewrite the history of Israeli victory and to confront the readership of victors with a re-presentation of this history. By exposing the untold story of the victim vis-à-vis the triumphal story of the victor, the dissenting texts disrupt the mainstream national narrative. At this level the dissenting tale of the defeated unsettles the dominant, one-sided, single-minded consensus; it forces the readership to engage in self-reflection, which impels the recognition not only of the defeated other but also of its own acts of injustice.

It is important to note that both fictions search for recognition in a story whose historical evidence paradoxically lies in the tragedy of its violent effacement. Ironically, the doctrine of the "empty land" materialized, in a large measure, in the 1948 war, which resulted in the demolition of hundreds of Arab villages and the exile or escape of the majority of the Palestinian people. This realization leads to the next level in the search for recognition. Here the text does not seek the reader but rather exposes the reader to a quest for recognition that takes place within the fictional boundaries of the story. A comparative reading of the fiction reveals that the 1948 defeat and destruction of Arab life in the land ensued in a postwar trauma for both victors and vanquished. While the outcome of the war resulted in political, legal, and social inequalities between Jews and Arabs, the war also created traumatic and pressing psychological and ethical situations for both parties. As was already mentioned, the haunting consciousness of the brutalities committed against the Arab population confronted the Jewish protagonist with the moral issue of his Zionist identification, whereas the same consciousness of the defeat and the dispersion of the Palestinian people confronted the Arab protagonist with the moral implications of his self-identification as a citizen of the Zionist state. For each the possibility of release from the trauma lay in an act of confession that would involve shame, regret, guilt, and tormenting memories. In this sense, the search for recognition takes the form of the search for a confessor.

The protagonist's selection of the listener/confessor demonstrates an ineluctable interdependence of Arab and Jewish protagonists: each party's designated listener is the other. In other words, each protagonist assumes the double role of both recognition seeker and recognition giver. Whereas the vanquished must tell the story of his humiliation and misery to the victor, the conqueror must confess his torment as oppressor to the oppressed. The past cannot be undone, but it may be revisited on the plane of discourse. The hope of redemption is therefore predicated upon reaching an understanding *with* and *of* the adversary. As my reading demonstrates, there is no "happy ending"; the promise of a recognition is rarely, if ever, fully realized. It is, however, the overwhelming desire for the opponent to both tell his story and hear the story of the other that intimates, however tenuously, the potential for a future dialogue.

The search of Jews and Arabs for each other's recognition is marked by dissent because it undermines the sociopolitical order of inequality between the victorious Jewish majority and the defeated Arab minority. The possibility of dialogic interaction between victors and victims, which signifies a relationship of equals, unsettles the normative understanding of victory and defeat. Instead of separating the parties, the political and military conflict has created a mutual need for recognition. It is this potential for reciprocal recognition that represents the threat of the literature of dissent to the establishment. The indispensability of the Jew and the Arab to each other transforms the identity construct of the "new" Jew. The interaction between Jews and Arabs defies the Zionist concept of national identity based on separation from the Arab and imitation of the enlightened European. Instead, literatures of dissent suggest a concept of identity grounded in the acknowledgment of an ineluctable and irreversible interpenetration of the Jewish and Arab selves at profound psychological and ethical levels.

The question of the impact of literature on culture still awaits an answer. In view of the continuing "bonding" of Arabs and Jews in violence and enmity, the literary solution of bonding in reciprocal recognition appears unrealistic, if not unreal. Yet the motif in both literatures that insists upon connectedness rather than disruption reflects a tortuous and convoluted quest for mutual recognition. As an alternative to hatred and despair, the acknowledgment of this quest in the world outside the text may yet prove redeeming.

It may be helpful to explain the rationale behind the selection of texts and the construction of this study. The first part of this study examines the inception of the dominant separatist orientation and the failure of those opposed to the politics of separation toward the Arab inhabitants of the land. Many Israeli Jewish writers focus on the dominant ideology of exclusion of the Arabs from mainstream Israeli society. My choice of texts by S. Yizhar, A. B. Yehoshua, Amos Oz, and David Grossman was based, first and foremost, on thematic consideration and on the outstanding artistic quality of their writings. Interrelated and no less important in the selection process was the prominent position of these writers in the Israeli cultural establishment.

As I demonstrate in the second part, these writers have become an integral part of the Israeli literary canon. Leading literary critics— Gershon Shaked being the most prominent—interpreted their writings in the spirit of Western existentialism, thus adjusting them to the Israeli's mainstream literary corpus. In this sense, Shaked and the critics that followed him not only complied but also colluded with the separatist mainstays of the Zionist ideology. The literary establishment demonstrated an approach of ideological appropriation to Israeli Arab writings similar to that which it employed in the case of Israeli Jewish literature. The critics neutralized the Israeli Arab dissent by treating the literary texts as expressions of Western humanism. By incorporating the Arab texts into the Israeli literary canon, the establishment was able to preserve the Zionist ideological tenets of exclusion and separation.

The third part of this study demonstrates how literatures are capable of breaking through ideologically imposed perceptions of reality. My comparative interpretation is based on the supposition that the juxtaposition of Israeli Jewish and Israeli Arab texts will illuminate aspects of meaning obfuscated by the conformist, programmatic interpretive reading. Indeed, a comparative approach to these texts leads to the conclusion that, in contrast to the dominant ideology of separation, the stories reveal an inextricable bonding between Israeli Jews and Israeli Arabs.

In terms of Israeli Arab literature, the selection of texts was much more limited than in the case of Israeli Jewish fiction. The fiction of Atallah Mansour, Emile Habiby, and Anton Shammas practically constitutes the corpus of Israeli Arab literature in Hebrew.[10] It is fortunate that the outstanding artistic quality of their writing permitted a fruitful and enriching comparative study of both literatures. Since I do not read Arabic, I had to rely on Shammas's excellent translations of Habiby's works. It is important to note that Shammas's translations were done with Habiby's full approval and cooperation. I strongly believe that even though working with translations is not the best option, the opportunity to present a critical appreciation of Habiby's work to the general public outweighs the drawbacks of translation.

In terms of availability, all the Israeli Jewish texts except for Yizhar's "Hirbet Hizah" are available in English translations; the same holds true for the Israeli Arab texts, with the exception of Habiby's *Ikhtayyeh* and *Saraya, Daughter of the Ghoul*. Synopses of these literary works first appear in the second part of this study and are amplified in the third part. Citations of the texts in English follow the official English translations except where my own translations are indicated. My analysis is based on the Hebrew text.

PART 1

Zionism and the Discourses of Negation
Is Post-Zionism Really "Post"?

We shall pronounce here the bitter and terrible truth—that our leaders . . . have not paid appropriate attention to the great value of neighborly relations. . . . Beginning with Herzl and his idea of political Zionism, the Zionist propaganda in all countries and in all languages has described the land . . . as a desert, an abandoned and empty land where nobody lives . . . a virgin land. . . . Based on this presumption the Zionists have set out to settle in the land, taking care of everything except the one thing that they seem to have forgotten, namely, the people [the Arabs] who inhabit this land. . . .

I cannot endure those who prefer Zionism to Judaism in contrast to us, [who] link Judaism with nationalism . . . and don't believe in nationalism solely for its own sake. Time has proven that those Zionists who maintain their Jewish identity have remained loyal to the national idea, and, on the contrary, those Zionists who have monopolized nationalism for their personal benefit and distanced themselves from Judaism ended up abandoning the national idea as well . . . because nationalism without Jewish tradition is rooted in self-interest and has no real existence.

Yosef Eliahu Chelouche (a prominent founder of Tel Aviv)

Introduction

Toward Rediscovery of the Present in the Past

To a remarkable extent, the "bitter and terrible truth[s]" that Yosef Eliahu Chelouche directs at the Zionist project sound very much like the "truths" of the contemporary critical revision of the Zionist project; the objectives of Chelouche's disapproval seem to anticipate the Zionist discourses of negation that many years later became the targets of the so-called post-Zionist critical trend. I examine these discourses at length in subsequent chapters. Here I briefly wish to introduce the Zionist twofold concept of negation that elicited Chelouche's passionate objections. The first is the Zionist refusal to acknowledge the existence of the Arab population in the land, an ideological position encapsulated in the catchphrase "the empty land"; the second is the Zionist denial of the Jewish heritage and tradition, a credo encapsulated in the catchphrase "the negation of the Diaspora."

Chelouche's disapproval, expressed in the first decades of the twentieth century, shows how early critical views of the Zionist ideology were articulated. This realization helps to dispel the notion of the "post-Zionist" critique of Zionism as a new historical development in the history of Zionism. At the same time, early criticism of Zionism by dedicated builders of the land, such as Chelouche, calls into question the seemingly antithetical positions of establishment Zionists and post-Zionists. Is it possible that perceptive and ardent

Zionists, such as Chelouche, could intuitively foresee the end (the "post") of viable Zionist ideology embedded in the very politics of the Yishuv? Is it possible that today's critical voices, bolstered by academic research and scholarly evidence, largely reconfirm the failings that others, such as Chelouche, observed when Zionism was in the making?

Chelouche, a prominent member of the pre-Zionist Yishuv, was passionately engaged in establishing the Jewish community in Eretz Israel; he was especially proud of being one of the founders of Tel Aviv. Born in 1870 in Palestine, Chelouche truly believed in Jewish renewal in the land and considered himself a Jewish nationalist.[1] A deeply religious Jew dedicated to building the Jewish homeland, he lived and worked closely with Arabs—both Muslims and Christians—before the advent of Zionism. It is therefore in light of his particular life experience that one should understand the criticism of the Zionist enterprise as expressed in his memoirs. Chelouche deplored the Zionist disregard of the Arab population, an attitude that destroyed the peaceful relations he himself had cultivated. At the same time, he claimed that the Zionist rejection of Jewish tradition and observance deprived Zionist nationalism of its roots and therefore rendered it meaningless.

As I will show, this early criticism echoed even earlier voices belonging to such prominent Zionists as Ahad Ha'Am (1856–1927) and Martin Buber (1878–1965). The consciousness of these voices of criticism puts into question today's vehement rejection of the post-Zionist revisionist approach to Zionism by establishment Zionists. Today's criticism of the Zionist doctrine calling for separation from the Arab population and a rejection of the Jewish heritage is not new; in effect, it can be traced to the very inception of the movement. One could argue that in a very real sense post-Zionists differ from people like Chelouche not so much in terms of what they say but rather in how the former substantiate their ideas through academic formal methods. The dividing lines between establishment Zionists and post-Zionists may not be as clear-cut as the opponents of the post-Zionist critique assume.

It may prove useful to examine briefly the establishment Zionist and post-Zionist evaluations of the Zionist project taking place now, half a century after the establishment of the Zionist state and over a century since the inception of the movement. In a fairly recent essay Adi Ophir, a philosopher and a prominent post-Zionist, has claimed that post-Zionist academics do what any researcher is supposed to do, namely, distance themselves from the object of research and look at it from a different perspective. In terms of their scholarship, they reexamine the existing ideological concepts, "calling in question the polarized, teleological Zionist narrative, which constructs a monolithic, immutable Jewish identity and confronts it with [a] no less monolithic and immutable identity of the non-Jewish world." Ophir claims that the novelty of this research lies mainly in the fact that "for the first time Zionist criticism has been presented in a pseudo-scientific jargon and gained recognition by the academic community."[2]

Here one should note that the increased stature of Zionism as a scholarly field is to be attributed to new resources of which the post-Zionist academics—or, as they are called, the "new historians" and the "critical sociologists"—could avail themselves of recently. Specifically, they could reassess the Yishuv and the Zionist state in light of documents in Israeli and Western archives dealing with Palestine/Israel, which opened in the late 1970s. From among the plethora of revisionist studies—the so-called post-Zionist publications—two pioneering studies dealing with discourses of negation stand out. Tom Segev's book *The Seventh Million,* which discusses the Zionist exploitation of the tragedy of the Holocaust, initiated a reexamination of the politics based on the doctrine of Diaspora negation. Benny Morris's study *The Birth of the Palestinian Refugee Problem* brought to light the expulsion of the Palestinians in the 1948 war, thus exposing a history informed by the negation of the Arab in the land.[3]

Needless to say, the establishment Zionists have not remained silent in the face of these damning findings.[4] In fact, the term "post-Zionism" often signifies the derogatory, if not hateful, attitude of establishment Zionists toward revisionist scholars. As Adi Ophir notes, the epithet "post-Zionist" has become "an abbreviated curse" of the opponent who is a cynical and self-hating relativist.[5] Indeed, some prominent academics even see the revision of Zionism as anti-Zionism and, consequently, a betrayal of the Zionist idea and—even more seriously—of the Jewish state. They judge the revisionists as, at best, a group of misguided individuals.[6]

The intensity of this ideological conflict reached new heights during the celebrations of Israel's fiftieth anniversary in the Israeli media. The controversy was by no means overlooked in foreign coverage of the event.[7] Domestically, a documentary viewed on Israeli television that depicted the expulsion of Palestinians at the time of the 1948 war resulted in a vociferous denunciation of the post-Zionists by the conservative wing of Israeli society. It is worth noting that the anger was directed almost exclusively at Israeli Jewish reappraisal of Zionism, although harsh criticism of Israel's discrimination against Israeli Arabs had been raised for years by Arab political figures, such as Emile Habiby, a longtime communist Knesset member. It was the serious attention that Israeli Jewish scholars, categorized as post-Zionists, finally paid to the Palestinian refugee problem and to the grievances of the Israeli Arabs that evoked the antagonistic responses of the establishment Zionists.

The accusation that the revision of the Zionist enterprise threatens to destroy the Zionist state is largely exaggerated. However painful the new historical findings might be, the general tenor of this post-Zionist orientation is unlikely to result in any damage to Zionist achievements.[8] The intention that prevails is not to dismiss and destroy but rather to gain a more balanced perspective of the past and thus rethink, mend, and correct the present.[9] To repeat, post-Zionist studies of the Zionist project strive to establish scholarly grounds for a more objective and historically more accurate discussion of Zionism. They focus on a number of topics: Israeli wars and the Palestinian refugee problem; Israel's relationship with the Diaspora and its attitude to the Holocaust; its treatment of Israeli Arabs and Palestinians in the occupied territories; and the discriminatory politics of the Israeli mainstream toward those on the fringes, such as Mizrahi Jews and women.

While the post-Zionist probing of the Zionist project and its ideological grounding may seem too radical and intense to old-time Zionists, a closer look reveals that quite often it does not differ dramatically from the criticism by those who see themselves as loyal adherents to the Zionist idea.[10] The similarities prove that the definition of anti-Zionism is quite arbitrary; it extends from those few who negate the Zionist idea of the Jewish state altogether to those who support the state but look critically at its history.[11]

Eliezer Schweid, an eminent Israeli philosopher and an establishment Zionist, professes to have no tolerance for the post-Zionist critique. Schweid strongly maintains that "like American 'post-modernism,' which it imitates, ideological 'post-Zionism' leads 'beyond' the social, cultural and political accomplishments of Zionism. . . . [It] exemplifies alienation by its very being."[12] Even though Schweid rejects post-Zionism because of its denial of Zionist "accomplishments," he does not credit Zionism with these accomplishments either. While he acknowledges the *political* success of the Zionist movement, he expresses a very negative opinion about the *social* and *cultural* failures of the Zionist movement and urges it to "engage in self-criticism, to rethink and to redefine its goals."[13]

Among the main issues that Schweid thinks need to be addressed is the failure of the Jewish state to become the spiritual and cultural center of the Jewish world. Clearly, Schweid claims, this failure is the result of Zionist detachment from Judaism and its cultural heritage. Interestingly, Schweid's argument is closer to post-Zionist thought when he calls into question the "Canaanite-Israeli" identity, that is, the construct of the "new Hebrew."[14]

The enormous significance of the "new Hebrew" concept in the formation of Israeli society will be discussed at a later point. Here one should mention that the notion signified a Zionist pioneering Jew who has completely severed ties with his or her Jewish heritage. According to the Zionist-Canaanite project, the new Hebrews will reenact the history of the biblical Hebrews in their heroic self-liberation from the Diaspora, the return to the land, and its redemption.

Schweid certainly does not approve of the idea of the new Hebrew, which alienated the Israelis from their historical roots. Even more interesting is his acknowledgment that "the problem [of national identity] raised by 'post-Zionism' is deeply embedded in the Zionist movement itself, in the consciousness and meaning that it [Zionism] has in the recent period assigned to the function of the Zionist idea in the life of its followers."[15] Schweid claims that, having achieved the political goal of a sovereign state, Zionism equated Jewish identity with Zionist Israeli identity and thus severed the Israeli Jew from his or her national history and culture.

Schweid presents an ambitious plan for the reconstruction of the broken ties between Israel and the Diaspora. "The role of Zionism in the next generation," Schweid postulates, "is to become the framework for the cultural revival of the [Jewish] people."[16] In fact, Schweid's plan favors the dismantling of one of the fundamental Zionist ideals of a new Jew as the antithesis of the Jew in the Diaspora. As I demonstrate, the rejection of the Diaspora and the creation of the new Hebrew constitute an indelible and incontrovertible ground rule of the Zionist plan. From this perspective, Schweid's demand to reacknowledge cultural and national ties with the Diaspora contradicts at the most profound level the notion of the Zionist movement as a new chapter in the history of the Jewish people.[17] I wish to reemphasize that Zionist indoctrination of contempt for the Diaspora and adoption of an attitude of superiority toward the Diaspora Jews was and still is officially sanctioned.[18] In this sense, it is hard not to notice that the radicalness of Schweid's demand to reconsider the Zionist credo of the new Hebrew echoes the post-Zionist desire to reexamine critically the most fundamental tenets of the Zionist project.

It is, of course, impossible to deny that the post-Zionists and the establishment Zionists approach the dominant ideology from a different ideological and philosophical standpoint. While the former wish to reform the Zionist idea in the spirit of pluralism and recognition of the other, the latter—as exemplified by Schweid—turn to conservatism, ethnic particularism, and national religious tradition. Nonetheless, Schweid's argument demonstrates that even those who profess loyalty to the Zionist tenets have profound reservations about its fundamental premises.

The controversy between establishment Zionists and post-Zionists dramatically highlights the constitutive problems of the Zionist project. The consciousness of these problems, however, did not emerge with the post-Zionists; rather, it has existed since the inception of the national movement. Besides Chelouche, I would mention Yitzhak Epstein, an ardent Zionist and a prominent Hebrew educator. Epstein presented his ideas concerning the Arab population in his 1907 article "She'elah ne'elamah" [The hidden question] in *Hashiloah*, an Odessa-based Hebrew monthly issued under Hayyim Nahman Bialik's editorship. Epstein's words recall an essay Ahad Ha'Am wrote upon his return from a journey to Eretz Israel in 1889. Epstein claimed: "When we come to our homeland, we must uproot all thoughts of conquest or expropriation. Our motto must be: Live and let live! Let us not cause harm to any nation, and certainly not to a numerous people, whose enmity is very dangerous." Anticipating Buber, Epstein argued, "We must enter into a covenant with the Arabs which will be productive to both sides and to humanity as a whole. We will certainly agree to this covenant, but it also requires the agreement of the other side; and that we shall gain it gradually through practical deeds which are of benefit to the land, to us and to the Arabs."[19]

The preceding discussion has attempted to demonstrate the inaccuracy—and perhaps a certain degree of superfluity—in the distinctions between Zionists and post-Zionists. In light of intense critical tradition within the Zionist movement, the above categorization seems rather redundant. As will become apparent in the next chapter, the flaws of exclusion in Zionist thought, whether with respect to Arabs or the Jewish tradition were noted before the official founding of the Zionist movement in Basel, Switzerland, in 1897. The two prominent Zionist intellectuals who engaged in a lifelong struggle against the tenets of exclusion were Ahad Ha'Am and Martin Buber. Though unheeded in their time, these thinkers anticipated and warned against political, cultural, and social repercussions of the Zionist position, encapsulated in the slogans "negation of the Diaspora" and the "empty land." Against the single-minded orientation of Theodor Herzl's (1860–1904) political Zionism, Ahad Ha'Am defied the Zionist rejection of the Diaspora. He insisted that the Jewish settlement in Eretz Israel should become a cultural and spiritual center for the Jewish people at large. Buber saw the settlement in Eretz Israel as the Jewish mission to the world. He insisted that this mission should be implemented through cooperation and dialogic interaction with the Palestinian Arab population.

My discussion of Ahad Ha'Am's and Buber's positions has a twofold purpose. On the one hand, the analysis of their criticism of the Zionist separatist discourse both in relation to the Diaspora and to Arabs in the land provides a historical perspective on the dissenting post-Zionist trend prevalent today. On the other hand, a study of the objections of these important Zionist thinkers to Zionist politics of separation (the subject of chapter 1) will illuminate the reasons and circumstances that engendered the separatist weltanschauung (chapter 2). What are the cultural phenomena, the psychological inhibitions, and the political considerations that inform and nurture the Zionist ideology of separation and exclusion? Before tackling this question, I wish to exmine Ahad Ha'Am's and Buber's Zionist visions and their (pre/post?) Zionist critical views of Jewish settlement in Eretz Israel.

1

Zionist Voices of Dissent

Ahad Ha'Am and Martin Buber

Against a Jewish State Like All States

The determination with which both Ahad Ha'Am and Martin Buber disapproved of political Zionism would most likely have earned them vehement denunciations from the establishment Zionists of today.[1] In its own time the dominance of political Zionism effectively silenced dissenting voices. Although it is true that neither Ahad Ha'Am nor Buber could be completely ignored in the Zionist arena due to their intellectual stature, their position that the Zionist project of Jewish return to the land should by no means imitate Western colonialist nation-states hardly left a mark on the Zionist platform, while their opposition to the Zionist emphasis on utilitarian political interests went largely unnoticed. Nonetheless both intellectuals persisted in their unpopular positions despite personal grief and disenchantment. Based on the conviction that human beings have some degree of control over their fates and therefore must assume responsibility for charting their historical destinies, both Ahad Ha'Am and Buber continued to speak and write of their vision of Zionism as a source of spiritual renewal for the Jewish people rather than a means to achieve Jewish political sovereignty.

It is impossible to gauge the effect of their foresight had they been accorded a measure of attention when the Yishuv in Eretz Israel was in its initial, pioneering stages. Prominent Zionist scholars reject the "what would have happened if" question, claiming that speculations about hypothetical historical developments cannot replace the facts

27

that actually occurred.[2] However, in view of today's intensifying debate over the character of the Zionist Jewish state and its position vis-à-vis Israeli Arabs as well as the Palestinians under Israeli occupation, this question has assumed increasing relevance. The two thinkers remind us that there were voices that opposed the Zionist politics of denial and negation of others and their histories. Indeed, their perspectives have increasingly been recognized in scholarly and popular debates on Zionism.[3]

In an important 1897 essay entitled "The Jewish State and the Jewish Problem," written in response to the First Zionist Congress, Ahad Ha'Am denounced the spiritual destitution of the Zionist political platform. As he foresaw it, the desire for political sovereignty would lead to excessive materialism, which would preclude national unity and its safeguards of Jewish moral tradition and historical memory: "A political ideal which is not grounded in our national culture is apt to seduce us from loyalty to our own inner spirit and to beget in us a tendency to find the path of glory in the attainment of *material power* and *political dominion,* thus breaking the thread that unites us with the past and undermining our historical foundation."[4]

Fifty years later (June 1947), before the decisive partition plan vote in November,[5] Buber spoke about the Palestinian problem on Dutch radio. Buber claimed that excessive materialistic considerations motivated the drive for political power and prevented Jewish settlers from establishing relationships of trust and cooperation with the Palestinian people. He observed that "the society of men, infected by the *domination of the political element,* seeks to achieve *more than what it truly needs.*" In Palestine, Buber claimed, "there is no doubt that the possibilities for cooperation, flowing from the two peoples' common origin and shared task, could have overcome all . . . obstacles—were it not for the intervention of the political element . . . [that] has interfered to an ever-increasing extent with the creation of . . . mutual trust."[6]

Both thinkers characterize Zionist political ambitions as the wish to possess more in order to control and subjugate those who have less. According to them, the desire for economic gain is integral to a system of governance predicated upon enslavement and exploitation of the weak. At the same time it is important to keep in mind that both Ahad Ha'Am and Buber fully subscribed to the Zionist idea of an independent, persecution-free, full Jewish life in the ancestral land. For neither, however, did homeland signify political sovereignty. On the contrary, the Yishuv in Eretz Israel should have become the source of spiritual and cultural revival of the Jewish people. They saw the Jewish settlement in Palestine as a unique opportunity to create a model of governance *other* than that of a nation-state; they talked about creating a community that would be a truly enlightening example to the world. The conventional political construct of a nation-state ruled out the danger of moral degeneration. Both ardent Zionists dedicated to the ideal of a Jewish homeland in Eretz Israel, Ahad Ha'am and Buber feared that by becoming like all the other nations and states, the Jewish people would forfeit their particular historical destiny as "light to the nations."[7]

Ahad Ha'Am and Berdyczewski: The Struggle for Jewish Revival

Ahad Ha'Am predicted that Jewish sovereignty would engender just another "puny State . . . tossed about like a ball between its powerful neighbors."[8] Instead of focusing on political goals, the Zionists in Palestine should cultivate the uniqueness of Jewish ethics. The Jewish people, Ahad Ha'Am argued, "does not need an independent state, but only . . . a good-sized settlement of Jews [that] will become . . . the center of the nation, wherein its spirit will find pure expression and develop in all its aspects to the highest degree of perfection. . . . [F]rom this center, the spirit of Judaism will radiate . . . to all the communities of the Diaspora, to inspire them with new life and to preserve the over-all unity of our people."[9]

In contrast to the Zionist concept of severance from exilic Judaism, Ahad Ha'Am did not perceive the Zionist enterprise in Palestine as antithetical to the Diaspora. Indeed, in his 1909 essay "The Negation of the Diaspora" he reiterated that "since dispersion must remain a permanent feature in our life . . . [Jewish] national life must be strengthened."[10] Ahad Ha'Am envisioned a strong, spiritually nurturing connection between the Disaspora and Eretz Israel. He claimed that the Jewish center in the homeland would reinvigorate Jewish cultural and ethical values everywhere. I have already discussed how today's Israeli thinkers grapple with the deep ideological and cultural divide separating Israeli Jews and Diaspora Jewry. In view of the disconnection between Israel and the Diaspora, Ahad Ha'Am's desire to create an organic link between Eretz Israel and the Jewish world reflects a remarkably prescient diagnosis of the future problem.

The Zionists' deprecatory dismissal of the Diaspora stood in diametrical opposition to Ahad Ha'Am's vision of Jewish national unity. In particular, it was the concept of the "Hebrew Jew"—often referred to as the "new Jew" or the "new Hebrew"—that triggered Ahad Ha'Am's most passionate denunciation. This concept was propagated by Tseirim (the Young Ones), a group of Zionist intellectuals headed by its founder, Micha Josef Berdyczewski (1865–1921), a *maskil* (an educated and emancipated Jew), a writer, and an essayist. Berdyczewski intended to free the Jew from the spiritual, psychological, and economic depletion of the Diaspora, in particular from the stifling burden of rabbinic Judaism. I shall return to Tseirim and the part it played in the formation of the "Canaanite-Israeli" identity, which Schweid unequivocally denounced. Here it is important to establish Berdyczewski's impact on the Zionist movement as embodied in the idea of the "Hebrew Jew."

Berdyczewski blamed the fossilized existence of the Jews on their passive submission to the authority of the rabbis; he promulgated the notion of a new type of Jew, the "Hebrew Jew," completely liberated from Judaism. Even though Ahad Ha'Am also wanted to free the Jew from rabbinic rule, he strongly opposed Berdyczewski by propagating a revival of Jewish culture that would reform the old tradition by synthesizing it with modernity and secular ethics. Menachem Brinker, a noted scholar of Israeli literature and culture, has summed up the difference between the two: "Ahad Ha'Am identified the Jewish problem as the bifurcation and disintegration of Jewish culture in the present, while Berdyczewski identified the problem as excessive uniformity of Jewish culture."[11] In other words, Ahad Ha'Am saw the Jewish people in a state of strife and disunity, vacillating between the deadening Diaspora existence and the assimilationist impact of modernity. By contrast, Berdyczewski saw the danger in the unanimity of the Jewish conformist deference to rabbinic rule.

In truth, Berdyczewski was tragically torn between his desire for the outside world of universal values of humanism and aesthetics and his personal world of Judaism and its religious tradition.[12] That is why he did not believe in a political solution to the Jewish predicament. According to Berdyczewski, the political solution may dry some of the "tears" that have torn the Jewish soul asunder, but it will never heal the "tear" that pierced its heart (qera sh'ba'lev).

Understandably, the Zionist movement preferred to identify with the Berdyczewski who rebelled against the ghetto, the rabbis, and Jewish religious tradition. As scholars of Berdyczewski's oeuvre point out, his writings provided the Zionist movement—especially Ben-Gurion and his Labor Zionist party—with an intellectual validation of the rejection of the Diaspora and its religious heritage. "It is not difficult to understand," maintains Avner Holtzman, an eminent scholar of Hebrew literature and the editor of Berdyczewski's papers, "why Berdyczewski's ideas were so much more exciting for young Zionists in Eastern Europe, and why Ben-Gurion and his friends later confirmed that they found Berdyczewski's ideas more attractive than those of Ahad Ha'Am." Holtzman goes on to claim that Berdyczewski's negation of the Diaspora reaffirmed the Zionist desire to create a productive, secular, national life in Eretz Israel far removed from the misery of the Diaspora. This was a principle antithetical to the desire to perpetuate Jewish lifelessness that Berdyczewski imputed to Ahad Ha'Am.[13] As the Zionists saw it, Berdyczewski proclaimed the end of the history of suffering and demanded the cultivation of the "liveliness of life [*haim he'haim*]." Ben-Gurion and his fellow Zionist pioneers chose to emulate the recalcitrant aspect of Berdyczewski's weltanschauung, whereby he maintained that the time had come for the Jews to replace the "book [*sefer*]" with the "sword [*sayif*]."[14]

Indeed, the *halutsim* (Zionist pioneers) must have been on Berdyczewski's mind when he wrote: "[W]e feel the need for a 'transformation of the center' in the roots of our soul from Judaism to Jews, from immaterial Jews[15] to Hebrew Jews."[16] He claimed that "by making this essential and substantial change, we shall leave our narrow world for a world that binds together humanistic and national freedom."[17] Berdyczewski's redefinition of the Jew as a humanistic nationalist was perfectly attuned to the negative attitude of the secular Zionists toward the Diaspora and Jewish tradition.

It was, however, Berdyczewski's redefinition of the Jew in terms of superior physical attributes—based upon Nietzsche's *Übermensch*—that fueled Ahad Ha'Am's most determined protest. Indeed, Berdyczewski seemed to model his Hebrew Jew on Nietzsche's principle of the "transvaluation of values,"[18] which glorified the individual's will to power and attributed the highest possible merit to physical strength and beauty.[19] In an essay ironically titled "The Transvaluation of Values" (1898) Ahad Ha'Am argued, against Berdyczewski, that Jewish renewal certainly does not lie in an identification with the physical qualities of Nietzsche's Arian superman or, as he called it, the "fair beast."[20] The Jew will stand proud because he has regained control over his destiny by submitting "to the yoke of most exacting and arduous obligations." The willingness to recognize these obligations embedded in the Jewish tradition will lead to the restoration of the true spirit of Israel. Such restoration can be accomplished only in the ancestral land, where, "independent of the opinion or the will of others," the Jewish people will find a basis for "developing its genius for morality, and fulfilling its 'mission' as the Supernation" of "living the highest type of moral life," which will eventually fulfill the prophecy of Israel as "light to the nations."[21]

Ahad Ha'Am's essay, which denounced the Jewish search for a model of the "fair beast" in Nietzsche, is essential to any discussion of Zionist suppression of Diaspora history. Ahad Ha'Am was, of course, aware of the fact that for the secular Zionist pioneers Diaspora life represented nothing but rabbinic despotism. Thus, he feared the attractiveness of Berdyczewski's rebellious irreverence, which presented the danger of an even deeper national disunity. Even though he himself found the "ghettoized" life in the Diaspora detrimental to the Jewish people, he engaged in a fierce intellectual struggle against the perception of Jewish history through the eyes of the Tseirim.

Ahad Ha'Am feared Zionist secular nationalism, which he considered empty of Jewish content. He saw the Zionist disengagement from the Jewish world of the Diaspora as a threat to Jewish national identity. Seeking compromise, Ahad Ha'Am strove to infuse into Berdyczewski's model of "humanistic national freedom" the content of Jewish ethics. "The whole object of my argument," he claimed, "has been to show that there is no incompatibility between the need for a national revival and the 'moral' theory of Judaism."[22] What Ahad Ha'Am wanted was a new national identity steeped not in religious observance but in the ethics of Judaism.

It is possible to argue that in place of Berdyczewski's "Hebrew Jew" Ahad Ha'Am promulgated his own particular idea of a "new" Jew. Indeed, he claimed that the objective of the Jewish settlement in Palestine was to create a type of Jewish person different from the Diaspora Jew. This "new" Jew, however, would not be a Nietzschean "physical" superman. Ahad Ha'Am's "new" Jews would infuse their exilic, lifeless existence with renewed energy and the spirit of Jewish ethics. These Jews would reaffirm the chosenness of the Jewish nation by settling in Eretz Israel, where they would remodel and reform their lives in the spirit of Jewish morality and justice.

The Vision of Zionist Failure

Ahad Ha'Am knew very well that he was engaging in an uphill struggle. Even before he became involved in a fierce polemical battle with Berdyczewski, he personally witnessed the moral decline of the colonies in Palestine. On his journeys to Palestine in 1891 and 1893, Ahad Ha'Am saw how far the colonies had strayed from the restoration of the Jewish "genius for morality" in Eretz Israel. He had an opportunity to observe the shocking tendency of the Jewish settlers to forsake all moral considerations in their ruthless pursuit of profit and domination. In fact, Ahad Ha'Am was dismayed at the settlers' corruption, inefficiency, and mismanagement of resources. Even more distressing was the immoral conduct of the settlers. In his essay "Truth from Eretz Israel," which he wrote in the wake of his first visit, Ahad Ha'Am drew a scathingly critical portrait of the Jewish community that offered a remarkably insightful and prescient perspective on the Jewish treatment of the Arab inhabitants of the land:

There is certainly one thing we could have learned from our *past and present* history: how careful we must be not to arouse the anger of other people against ourselves by reprehensible conduct. How much more, then, should we be careful, in our conduct toward a foreign people among whom we live once again, to walk together in love and respect, and needless to say in justice and righteousness. And what do our brethren in Eretz Israel do? . . . They were slaves in their land of exile, and they suddenly find themselves with unlimited freedom. . . . . This sudden change has engendered in them an impulse to despotism, as always happens when "a slave becomes a king," and behold they walk with the Arabs in hostility and cruelty, unjustly encroaching upon them, shamefully beating them for no good reason, and even bragging about what they do, and there is no one to stand in the breach and call a halt to this dangerous and despicable impulse. To be sure our people are correct in saying that the Arab respects only those who demonstrate strength and courage, but this is relevant only when he feels that his rival is acting justly; it is not the case if there is reason to think his rival's actions are oppressive and unjust. Then, even if he restrains himself and remains silent forever, the rage will remain in his heart and he is unrivaled in "taking vengeance and bearing the grudge."[23]

This short passage presents quite a unique late-nineteenth-century portrait of the dynamics of colonization. Here Ahad Ha'Am did not hesitate to pass moral judgment on his own people, whom he saw as ethically blind oppressors of a destitute population. One need only recall the description of colonialist practices as a "mission civilisatrice" on the part of the imperialist nations toward the "uncivilized Orient" to appreciate the humanistic relevance of this passage.

Besides the universal humanist concern expressed in the essay, Ahad Ha'Am was relating to the particular historical situation of Hovevei Tsion (Lovers of Zion), the first wave of Jewish immigrants to Palestine (1881). From this perspective one realizes the accuracy of his foresight with regard to the future of the Zionist settlement in Palestine. It is hard to disregard the prescience of his indication of the colonists' brutal domination of the native population as the origin of the future Jewish-Arab conflict. One notes his unflinching, honest identification of the Jews as the instigators of this conflict. As Ahad Ha'Am saw it, the land was not "empty"; it was populated with native people who needed to be treated with respect and fairness.

This text demonstrates Ahad Ha'Am's personal integrity. Indeed, his indignant response to the Jewish oppression of the Arabs in Palestine presents him as the "new" Jew that he envisioned. "The Truth from Eretz Israel" does not simply offer a trenchant criticism of the settlers, nor is it merely a moral sermon calling upon them to mend their ways. Ahad Ha'am faced the situation, evaluated it in an unbiased manner, and then confronted his readers with an image they

preferred not to see. Thus, he actualized the non-negotiable obligation of the "new" Jew, who must uphold the ideals of morality and
justice. Both the title and the content of the essay indicate that, like
the prophets he emulated, Ahad Ha'Am did not shirk his moral obligation to stand up for justice, no matter how painful for either the
writer or the reader.

In the introduction to his translation of "The Truth from Eretz
Israel," Alan Dowty remarks that "diaries and letters of the first *aliya*
pioneers pay surprisingly little attention to the surrounding Arab
population . . . , and when the Arabs appear on these pages it is
usually as a nuisance."[24] In light of this observation, Ahad Ha'Am's
essay delivers an unwanted truth and shatters illusions. His description of the Arab dispels the myth of the "empty land" and, with it,
the exclusivity of the Jewish claim to it. Furthermore, his critical opinion of Jewish behavior undermines the self-perception of the settlers
as liberated, new Jews. In denouncing the brutality of the settlers by
comparing them to "a slave who becomes a king," Ahad Ha'Am indicts them for their viciousness and inhumanity. By depicting them
as cruel slave masters, he dispels yet another myth, that of the settlers
as Hebrew Jews—perhaps even Jewish supermen—dedicated to Jewish ethics of morality and justice. In writing "The Truth from Eretz
Israel," Ahad Ha'Am in a sense engages in a prophetic battle of justice. Eschewing compromises and tactical considerations, he raises his
voice in defense of the powerless and the oppressed even if it means
branding his own people as oppressors.

Ahad Ha'Am's lucid analysis of the situation in Palestine reveals
a psychological connection between the idea of the Hebrew Jew and
the abusive treatment of the native Arab population. In terms of its
effect, the doctrine of the "negation of the Diaspora" allows for the
rationalization of contempt for the Arab in the land. The disavowal
of the history of Jewish suffering brought forth the glorification of
physical prowess, the preference of the "sword" over the "book," to
recall Berdyczewski. Such a "transvaluation of values" allowed the
Jewish settlers to see the Arabs, who were poor and weak and, therefore, inferior, as merely "a nuisance" not worthy of their attention.
The insignificance of the Arab validated the contention of the "empty
land," and their "invisibility" permitted the transformation of the
Jews into ruthless, oppressing colonizers.

It is not difficult to imagine that the visit to the Jewish settlements must have dealt a terrible blow to the idea of Eretz Israel as the center of Jewish cultural, ethical, and spiritual revival. Instead of the rebirth of the Jewish people as a model for the world at large, Ahad Ha'Am was dismayed to see the degree of moral corruption of the Hebrew Jews as evidenced by their unconscionable acts of brutality and injustice. In their dishonorable and unjust actions he discerned ominous signs of irreparable damage. Over a hundred years ago Ahad Ha'Am observed the moral transgressions committed by his people and foresaw how the hatred growing out of the oppression, injustice, and humiliation of the inhabitants of the land would eventually turn Jews and Arabs into bitter adversaries.

Buber's *Grosszionismus* and the Failure of Vision

Almost thirty years later (1918) Buber corroborated Ahad Ha'Am's pessimistic view of the future of the Yishuv when he wrote to Hugo Bergman: "We must face the fact that most leading Zionists (and probably also most of those who are led) today are thoroughly unrestrained nationalists (following the European example), imperialists, even unconscious mercantilists and idolaters of success. They speak about rebirth and mean enterprise. If we do not succeed in erecting an authoritative [Zionist] opposition, the soul of the movement will be corrupted, perhaps forever."[25] Indeed, to the end of his life Buber opposed vigorously and with utmost dedication excessive nationalism, materialism, and desire for power. As was noted, he knew that he had failed to reverse the vitiating flow, but today's revision of Zionist politics reconfirms to a remarkable degree Buber's premonition about the direction the Yishuv was taking.

Buber, who followed in Ahad Ha'Am's footsteps, emphasized the spiritual needs of the Jewish people. He was aware of the need for a safe haven for Jews in Eretz Israel and expressed this conviction in his famous letter to Gandhi.[26] At the same time, the model Buber had in mind was a community in Eretz Israel that would serve as a spiritual and ethical center for the Jewish people and for humanity at large. For Buber *Grosszionismus*, or greater Zionism, which was animated by moral forces and not by political interests, took precedence over the objective of Jewish political sovereignty, which he considered *Kleinzionismus,* or petty, small-minded Zionism, which was capable of producing no more than another small state, a Jewish Albania.[27]

Like Ahad Ha'Am, Buber believed that a model other than that of a nation-state was necessary for the peculiar character of the Jewish people and their particular historical destiny. Ahad Ha'Am wished to create in Eretz Israel a community of cultural and spiritual Zionism to be emulated by the Jewish world at large. Buber developed this model further in the spirit of political ethics. He perceived the life of the Jewish nation in Eretz Israel "not as an end in itself" but only a "part in the building of a greater structure."[28] To be "like unto all the nations" is egotistic and shortsighted because it "[affirms] itself in the face of the world without affirming the world's reciprocal power."[29] The destiny of the Jewish nation cannot be achieved in the restrictive self-enclosure of a nation-state but rather in opening itself up to the world in a dialogic interaction. Without conceding its peculiarity, the Jewish nation must gain recognition through reciprocal relations with the world.

Buber's concept of national mission, which superseded that of the nation-state, was by no means wishful theorizing but rather a pragmatic attempt to resolve the issue of Jewish settlement in Palestine. The recognition of the Jewish nation in the world and the materialization of the Jews' unique destiny must take place in the concrete reality of the Yishuv. As Buber saw it, the fulfillment of the Jewish mission to the world was predicated upon the establishment of a collaborative modus vivendi with the Arab population in Palestine.[30] The actualization of this goal lay in the creation of a binational state.

For decades, Buber worked indefatigably and against immense odds towards this goal. In 1925, he participated together with Arthur Ruppin and Gershom Scholem in founding Brith Shalom, a movement which promoted a binational state. In 1942 he was, together with Judah Magnes, Robert Weltsch, Ernst Akivah Simon, a founding member of the Ihud association, which promoted reconciliation and political program for a binational state. In 1949, the Ihud party founded a new Hebrew journal, *Ner (Light): Bi-weekly for Political and Social Problems and for Arab-Jewish Rapprochement.* The mission of the journal, which also had an Arabic edition, was to watch and warn against possible transgressions of justice in the newly born state.[31] With the birth of the Jewish state, Buber realized that the idea of a binational state would not materialize. Nonetheless, he never gave up the struggle for a just treatment of the Arab minority. To the end of his life Buber publicly addressed the issues of Arab refugees, Arab equal rights, and the confiscation of Arab lands.[32]

As was already mentioned, the impact of Buber and his friends on the political arena was negligible, and the solution of a binational state was never seriously considered in mainstream Zionism.[33] Indeed, Buber's concept of a binational state seemed at the time—and today perhaps more than ever—a utopian project. Neither Jews nor Palestinians supported Brith Shalom, which promoted sharing political powers between the two peoples regardless of the size of the population. The Jews resented the idea of reneging on the goal of creating a Jewish majority in Palestine. The Arabs resisted the idea of giving up their majority rights.[34] Yet Buber's totally accepting and supportive response to the establishment of the Jewish state in 1948 demonstrated that for him the idea of the binational state was not a sine qua non but rather a type of compromise that would have let the Jews achieve national independence without having to participate in the establishment of a politically sovereign nation-state.[35]

Buber's significance lies not in the futility of his plan of a binational state but rather in his unflinching insistence on Jewish-Arab collaborative existence.[36] What conviction—one obviously stronger than the frustration and disappointment—sustained Buber's determination to bring about a rapprochement between the two peoples? How can one explain his decades-long tenacity and advocacy of a Jewish-Arab dialogue? As the tragic ongoing conflict between the two peoples seems to indicate quite clearly, Buber must have understood the urgent need for a change in the ideologically acceptable practice of exploitation, humiliation, and oppression of the Arabs. While Ahad Ha'Am before him foresaw the enmity between the two populations, Buber was actually witnessing the materialization of the conflict. The foreboding reality of an irrevocable entrenchment in mutual hatred sustained Buber's work toward establishing mutual respect through dialogue.

Obviously, Buber could not accede to the propaganda of the "empty land." Nor would he accept the doctrine of the "historical right" to the land. Such a right, he claimed, was nonexistent in view of the long history of conquests to which Palestine was subjected. As Buber saw it, the right of the Jewish people to the land was predicated upon their ancient mission to the world, a destiny they could fulfill only in Eretz Israel. Yet despite or, rather, because of this special destiny, the problem of the Palestinian Arab ownership of the land could not be ignored. The Jews could not disregard the fact that "Palestine already had another population, which feels and sees this land to be its homeland."[37] Buber claimed that "no contradiction [of this mission] would be greater . . . than for us to build a true communal life . . . while . . . excluding the other inhabitants of the country from participation."[38] He knew that the universalist mission, which must acknowledge the Arab in the land, conflicted drastically with the Jewish national interest of establishing a homeland in Palestine. Unlike the Zionist mainstream leaders, who preferred to evade the issue either by propagating the notion of the "empty land," placing the blame for the Palestinian plight on the Arab states, or insisting on the Jews' "historical right" to the land, Buber openly recognized the problem.

The post-Zionist revision of the Zionist project has vindicated Buber not so much because some of the post-Zionists have raised the option of a binational state; rather his foresight has been validated by the need to reevaluate the fundamentals of Zionism. The appearance of the "new historians" and of "critical sociologists," and the phenomenon of dissenting literatures reaffirmed what Buber had known all along. He was profoundly convinced that the moral problem of the dispossession of the Arab inhabitants of the land would not disappear from the collective psyche. Indeed, as the present study of the literature will show, neither the demonization of the Arab, nor the manipulation of the Jewish history of victimization, nor the multiple military victories over the neighboring Arab states liberated the society of the "new" Jews from the haunting sense of moral failure. The denial of committed injustice has resulted in increased violence, which decreases the chance for a dialogue. From this perspective, the ongoing and exacerbating conflict between Jews and

Palestinians validates Buber's assessment that the Zionist ideological and political doctrine of the "invisibility" of the Arab has precluded any rapprochement between the warring sides.

Two cultural events held on the occasion of the fiftieth anniversary of the State of Israel demonstrate the accuracy of Buber's vision. In an exhibition entitled "To the East: Orientalism in the Arts in Israel" held at the Israel Museum in Jerusalem, visual confessions of acts of injustice and of haunting guilt were displayed in exhibits that included paintings, sculptures, and plastic representations of Palestinian victimization, eviction, destruction of villages—all created by Israeli Jewish artists. Significantly, since Palestinian artists refused to participate, the possibility of a dialogue did not materialize. In his introduction to the handsome catalogue, curator Yigal Zalmona claims that the goal of the exhibition is to represent the changes in Israel's perception of the East. Summing up these changes, he admits that "until the thirties, Zionists saw in the East an object of longing and desire, a source of power, an opportunity of redemption. At the same time, however, they [saw the East] from the position of Western arrogance, in an atmosphere of fear and suspicion, which also made them see the East as a threat."[39]

The other event—or, rather, indicative reaction to the events— was the uproar caused by a television screening of the Israeli documentary *Tekumah* [Revival], especially created for the anniversary. One segment in particular showed the exile of the Palestinian population in 1948. "The anger at *'T'kumah,'*" wrote Aryeh Caspi in the daily *Ha'Aretz*, "is because we don't want to know and we can't bear the sense of guilt. The establishment of the State of Israel was justice for the Jews, but it was accompanied by a terrible injustice to the Palestinians."[40]

The responses to these cultural events—the enraged Israeli reaction to the film and the conspicuous absence of Palestinian art at the exhibition—corroborate Buber's predictions: whereas the guilt on the Israeli side has become too intense to be confronted and admitted, the rage and hatred on the Palestinian side has become too powerful to permit any kind of dialogue. Buber's preoccupation with the problem of Jewish self-deception was clearly communicated in the 1929 speech he delivered two months after the fearful riots that the Arabs waged against the Yishuv. Though conscious of the general repudia-

tion of his view, Buber reaffirmed Arab rights and urged reconciliation even at a time of a violent discord.[41] While conceding that "there
can be no life without injustice," he exhorted Jews to admit the injustice committed against the Arabs when the Jews "[are] coming into
the country in increasing numbers, year by year, taking it away from
[them]."[42]

To minimize the unavoidable injustice resulting from the Jewish
settlement in Palestine, Buber proposed the principle of "Hebrew humanism." This concept of biblical *humanitas* enjoins the necessary
protection of self-interests while consciously striving toward the possibly highest degree of moral behavior.[43] In practical terms this meant
seeking a genuine rapprochement with the Arabs. Buber warned the
Yishuv against living "alongside [*neben*]" the Arabs and urged it to
settle "together with [*mit*]" the Arabs.[44] Being together, as Buber affirmed in *The Knowledge of Man,* signifies "turning to the other in
a face-to-face situation." The sense of togetherness indicates "confirmation and acceptance" of the other as a partner in a "genuine
dialogue."[45] It is noteworthy that Baruch Kimmerling, a prominent
"critical sociologist," used a similar vocabulary to evaluate the Zionist refusal to seek coexistence with the Arabs. According to Kimmerling, the "*asymmetry of side-by-side-existence* [with the Arabs]
not only institutionalized the conflict and the 'existential anxiety'
of the Jews; it reconfirmed the goal of constant Jewish territorial
expansion."[46]

For Buber the face-to-face dialogic relationship was an indispensable condition for the successful establishment of the Jewish homeland in Palestine. However, the situation was not balanced because
the participants represented different realities. Buber turned the Zionist conviction of Jewish Western superiority over the "uncivilized"
native population on its head: "They, not we have something which
can be called a Palestinian style; the huts of the village *fellahin* [peas-
ants] have grown out of this earth, while the houses of Tel Aviv were
built on its back."[47] Since the Jews wished to settle in Palestine and
envisioned the Jewish national future there, it was up to them to "get
to know [the] reality" of their partners by means of a dialogue. As
Buber saw it, the dialogue depended on the Jews developing greater
attentiveness to the environment they were entering. They needed to
learn about Islam and establish contacts with its religious authorities;

they also needed to study the Arabic language and engage in genuine social interaction with the Arabs. Buber urged "a cultural accommodation with Arabism as a whole, cultural exchange in educational institutions, exchange of cultural values and achievements, real cooperation."[48]

In 1921 Buber still hoped that through the socialist underpinnings of the Zionist movement "the solidarity of true common interests" between the Jews and the Arabs would develop.[49] But almost twenty years later (1939) he recognized the failure of collaborative relationships with the Arabs, which he attributed to Zionist identification with a Western imperialist orientation. In a sense, the presentiment he expressed in his 1918 letter to Hugo Bergman had materialized.

As I hope to demonstrate, Western influences played an enormously important role in shaping the culture of the Zionist enterprise. Specifically, I argue that to a remarkable extent adherence to the West informed the Zionist discourses of separation from the inhabitants of the land and negation of the Jewish past. In this sense Buber's early criticism of the Zionist identification with Western imperialist weltanschauung is highly relevant to my analysis of the inception of Zionism and its Western context. To appreciate more fully Buber's prescient understanding of Zionist adherence to Western imperialism and its repercussions, it is important to consider briefly the emphasis on this particular issue in today's post-Zionist revision of the Zionist project. The following overview of post-Zionist research in the areas of colonization, economics, and politics demonstrates the extent to which the revisionist approach corroborates the fears of Western imperialist influence of such early Zionists as Ahad Ha'Am, Buber, Chelouche, Epstein, among others.

Between Myth and Fact: How to Read the Zionist Story

Gershon Shafir, a pioneering "critical sociologist," provides a new approach to the Zionist story of settlement. He refutes the standard notion of the uniqueness of the Zionist settlement enterprise. By examining the return to the land as a colonial settlement comparable to other colonial settlements, Shafir situates the Zionist project in an illuminating context. As the comparative framework shows, in many respects the Zionist settlement shared similarities with other colonial systems, especially that of a "pure settlement colony," characterized as a homogeneous system of labor carried out solely by colonizing settlers. Such a system typifies the colonizing process in North America and Australia. The ideal of the *haluts,* the pioneering "new" Hebrew Jew, returning to redeem the "empty land" ruled out the use of local labor. In this sense the Zionist settlement reveals traits similar to these "pure settlement colonies," where the labor was the domain solely of white European immigrants.[50]

The ideological exclusion of the Palestinian workers invalidates the common argument that the universalist-socialist orientation of the Zionist movement prevented typical colonialist iniquities. Shafir clearly demonstrates that from the 1930s onward the Histadrut (the labor union) systematically and relentlessly strove to establish a self-sufficient, separatist Jewish market. The latter was based exclusively on Jewish labor. The propagandist catchphrase "avodah ivrit" (Hebrew work), a euphemism for exclusively Jewish labor, signified an ideologically propagated exclusion of the Palestinian workforce from Jewish agricultural and industrial markets. "Economic bifurcation," Shafir claims, "was a goal for which the Jewish labor movement struggled in Palestine."[51]

A personal recollection corroborates Shafir's scholarly findings of the politics of economic separatism. In his psychoanalytical study of Zionism, Jay Gonen remembers the propagandist campaign of the 1940s whose slogan was "totseret ha'aretz" (produce of the land). This campaign insisted upon the purchase of agricultural and industrial goods produced exclusively by Jews. Collective pressure eventually forced Gonen's mother to discontinue buying eggs from the Arab who used to deliver them every Friday. As he recalls, she was reluctant to dismiss him after many years of reliable service, but in the end she had to give in: "Mother had to stand with her tribe or people. . . . [The Arab] left and we never saw him again."[52] In this case the psychological tactic of group pressure was applied to achieve the ideological goal of separation. The elimination of the Arab from the Jewish market was by no means theoretical. The actual disappearance of the Arab egg seller from the Jewish settlement demonstrates the policy of pure settlement colonization. The Zionist discourses of negation exemplified by the physical exclusion of the Arab in the Jewish community made him "invisible," thus reinforcing the illusion of the "empty" land.

The policy of exclusion of the native Arab peoples was exacerbated after the establishment of the state. In her study Susan Slymovics focuses on the post-1948 period, specifically on the transformation of the Arab village of Ein Houd into the Hebrew-named Jewish artists' village of Ein Hod. Slymovics presents Ein Hod as a representative example of the destruction of hundreds of Arab villages and the eviction of their Arab inhabitants. The defeated Arabs disappeared from the Jewish field of vision. As such, according to Slymovics, Israel remains "a colonial settler-state, however unique its genesis and strategic location."[53]

To complete this admittedly sketchy review of post-Zionist findings, it is important to mention the Yishuv's Western self-identification at the time of the British Mandate. In her study, tellingly entitled *The Roots of Separatism in Palestine: British Economic Policy, 1920–1929*, Barbara J. Smith draws attention to the Yishuv's special relationship with British rule until the Arab riots of 1929. The British looked favorably upon Jews because of their European origins. Their stature was enhanced thanks to economic support resulting from the Diaspora, as well as the political support of the British government as evinced in the Balfour Declaration for a Jewish national home in Palestine. The British were inclined to be partial toward the Jews at the expense of the Arab "natives." Smith claims that the British "created a suitable environment" for the growth of a Jewish modern capitalist industrial sector "which was programmed to cater largely to the tastes of Western immigrants."[54] The preferential treatment of the Yishuv by the Mandatory rule not only helped the Yishuv to build a Jewish economy but also strengthened the Zionist separatist policy vis-à-vis the Arabs.

Buber and Said: An Unlikely Meeting of Minds?

As these contemporary studies of Zionism prove, Buber was correct in concluding that the Zionists were establishing an exclusionary, Western-oriented political system. Instead of embracing their new surroundings in the spirit of inclusion, the Jews were pursuing a model of Western colonialist governance involving domination over an "invisible" native people. Buber insisted that the Jewish settlers were reenacting "the colonial politics of the states of modern Europe."[55] Their colonialist orientation was setting them further apart from the social environment in which they sought refuge and renewal. The latter, as Buber saw it, was predicated upon devising an "*independent policy* [and] *new political forms*" intended to promote "cooperation between people."[56]

As Buber saw it, the Zionist adherence to the Western system of imperialism reflected an attitude that completely distorted the Jewish historical mission. Buber was deeply disappointed in what he perceived as Zionist "dependent policy" and its adoption of "old political forms." He expressed his sentiments in a response to the White Paper of May 1939 published by the League for Jewish-Arab Rapprochement in August of that year: "Our error lay in acting within the scheme of western colonial policies, which has only two parties, the one engaged in colonization and the other that suffers it. We acted within that scheme for our own purposes, which were so different that we were necessarily coopted on one side, that of the *ruler,* and *we gave ourselves over entirely to its rule.* The result is that we received *the stamp of the agent of imperialism,* although its cause is not at all linked internally to our own."[57]

The long history of anti-Israeli Arab propaganda proved Buber correct. As a result of its affiliation with the West, Zionism gained the image of a colonialist-imperialist movement.[58] This political stance, which set the Zionist community apart from the other societies of the region, fortified the opposition to Jewish settlement in the Middle East. Indeed, by siding with the West the Zionists played into the hands of the most radical critics of the Jewish state, who saw the Zionist movement as a partner of the British, French, and later U.S. imperialist powers. Maxime Rodison, among others, condemns "the creation of the State of Israel on Palestinian soil [as] the culmination of a process that fits perfectly into the great European-American movement of expansion in the nineteenth and twentieth centuries whose aim was to settle new inhabitants among other peoples or to dominate them economically and politically."[59]

A more nuanced perception of the Yishuv's imperialist orientation emerges in Edward Said's critical discussion of Zionist colonialism. Said does not deny the roots of Zionism in the tragic history
of Jews in Europe. A student of Western intellectual thought, Said
admits that "unlike most other Arab intellectuals . . . I can understand the intertwined terror and the exultation out of which Zionism has been nourished, and I think I can at least grasp the meaning of Israel for Jews."[60] Nonetheless, Said's understanding of the
historical roots of Zionism does not modify his negative perception of
the Yishuv and its colonialist practices. Said advances the argument
that it was the Zionists' "uncompromisingly exclusionary, discriminatory, colonialist praxis" that engendered visceral animosity between the Yishuv—and, later, the State of Israel—and the Palestinian
Arabs.

Said's identification of the roots of the conflict in Zionist exclusionary practices recalls Buber's tireless exhortations to enter dialogic
relationships with the Arabs. Ironically, Said seems to reiterate Buber's condemnation of the Zionist exclusion of the Arabs as immoral
arrogance, unjustified feelings of superiority, and myopic self-deception. The uproar against the portrayal of Palestinian expulsion in the
1948 war, as depicted in the documentary *T'kumah*, clearly demonstrates that the denial of this historical reality persists in Israeli society
at large. This disingenuous attitude reaffirms Said's observation that
a "not sizeable segment of the Israeli population has as yet been able
to confront the terrible social and political injustice done to the native
Palestinian."[61]

Said's position does not appear far from that of Buber and Ahad
Ha'Am when he claims that "ideas expressed to Arabs [communi-
cated] *only* a rejection of Arabs." Clearly, the Jewish discourse of
the "empty land" could not have contributed to creating a positive
Arab attitude toward the Yishuv. The latter's refusal to acknowledge
the Palestinian inhabitants and its efforts to distance itself from them
caused the Arabs to perceive Zionism as a power that *only* mis-
treated them, never benefiting them in any way. Said joins Buber
when he blames Zionist separatism for thwarting all chances for a
dialogue: "The consequences of the bifurcation in the Zionist program for Palestine have been immense, especially for Arabs who have

tried seriously to deal with Israel."[62] Thus, the Palestinian intellectual validates the Jewish philosopher's worst fears of a complete break in communication between the two nations. Not unlike Buber, Said claims that the roots of the mutual animosity lie in the Jewish adherence to the dominant Western culture. He maintains that, like the Western colonizing powers, Zionism viewed all non-Europeans as "inferior, marginal, and irrelevant." In Palestine Zionism became "*the agent* [of] an essentially discriminatory and powerful [Western] culture."[63]

One should recall that Buber also deplored the "stamp of the agent of imperialism" that determined the identity of the Zionist Yishuv. Nonetheless, it is in the varying significations of "agent" that the different visions of Zionism emerge. From Said's point of view the Zionist is an "agent" of imperialism in the sense of being a *representative* of the imperialist system; for Buber the Zionist is an "agent" in the sense of being the *servant* of an imperialist power.

As Said sees it, the Zionist movement did not differ from other colonizing powers. Like them, it subscribed to the theory of the racial, cultural, and social superiority of Europeans over non-Europeans. Furthermore, like all imperialist powers whose racial attitudes allowed them to see the subjugated territory as uninhabited, the Zionists, in Said's view, "accepted the generic racial concepts of European culture." These concepts allowed them to view Palestine "as an empty territory paradoxically 'filled' with ignoble . . . backward people, over which [they] *ought* to be dominant."[64] Although he professes to understand the Jewish history of religious and racial persecutions in Europe, Said appears convinced that once they ceased to be *victims* the Jews became willing and ready bearers of the imperialist banner—and in their role of imperialists have become *victimizers* of others. The Zionist settlement became a member of the imperialist club, acting upon the colonialist racial orientation that it had integrated in the "host" countries in the Diaspora.

As Buber saw it—and here is where he differs from Said—the Zionist movement is not an imperialist power but rather a servant, an "agent . . . under the rule" of the imperialist power. Against Said, who claims that the Zionists have already *realized* their nationalist dream by becoming a Western colonialist nation, Buber—and, to a large extent, Ahad Ha'Am—saw in the Zionist colonialist attitudes the *unrealized* desire to become *like* other Western nations (which also happened to be imperialist at the time).

Recall Ahad Ha'Am's reaction of dismay at the brutal treatment of Arab peasants by Jewish settlers in the 1890s. Ahad Ha'Am did not see the settlers as liberated people but rather as individuals compulsively repeating the patterns of cruelty that they themselves experienced. As he saw it, the "reprehensible conduct" of the Jews toward the Palestinians emerged from their inability to be free. Like the Hebrew slave who left Egypt, the Zionist colonialists were unable to liberate themselves from the psychological effects of their enslavement; the sudden sense of power made them behave like the proverbial "slave who becomes a king."[65] Pretending to have become an independent agent, the "new" Jew remained trapped in his slave mentality. While no longer oppressed, his cruel behavior toward those whom he oppressed reenacted the behavior of his oppressors.

Ahad Ha'Am's use of the biblical proverb "slave who becomes a king" encapsulates the psychology of the liberated slave. As such, it invokes Hegel's famous concept of lord and bondsman. To better understand the sources of the Jewish-Palestinian conflict, it is necessary briefly to consider Hegel's notion of recognition between the dominator and the dominated. According to Hegel, recognition is indispensable to the self-consciousness of the individual; without the recognition of the other, that is, without seeing the reflection of myself in other, I cannot attain the consciousness of my self. In the lord-bondsman relation, however, there is a basic inequality between the parties, "one being only *recognized,* the other only *recognizing.*"[66] The bondsman is the recognizing party who yearns to be recognized yet cannot obtain the lord's recognition upon which his sense of self depends.

When applied to the Zionist situation, Hegel's reasoning implies a twofold problem of recognition. As oppressors, the Zionist settlers deprived the Palestinian population of recognition. In this sense, the concept of the "empty land," which makes the Palestinians "invisible," denies recognition to the other, a situation that, according to Hegel, voids the dominated of the sense of self. At the same time, as oppressors in Palestine, the Jewish settlers imitate their European oppressors; the desire to become like them indicates *their* yearning to be recognized and, consequently, *their* entrapment in their old role of slave. The imitation of the colonizing patterns of the West vis-à-vis the Arab reflects the unfulfilled desire of the Zionist movement to be recognized by the Western nations as their equal. I shall return to Hegel's notion of lord-bondsman interdependency in the examination of the texts in part 3.

The view of the Yishuv through the Hegelian perspective sheds light on Buber's notion of Zionism as the "agent of imperialism." In contrast to Said, who sees the Zionist project as an *agency,* part and parcel of the imperialist system, for Buber the Zionist project communicates the continual Jewish dependence on European nations. Buber's position further underscores his insistence on the dialogic engagement with the Arab inhabitants of the land. In a general sense, the dialogue would signify spiritual and ethical renewal on a global scale through reciprocal relations with the world. In a more particular sense, it would also liberate the Zionist Jews in Palestine from their dependency on Europe. In the language of the proverb, in a face-to-face dialogue there will be neither kings nor slaves, for the parties will enter a reciprocal relationship: each party will give recognition *to* the other *and* will receive recognition *by* the other.

Buber, of course, was too pragmatic to advocate the Yishuv's severance from the West. He acknowledged that the West—especially as represented by the League of Nations—was instrumental in facilitating the immigration of Jews to Palestine, and he knew that the West's political recognition was crucial to the Yishuv's survival.[67] At the same time, he rejected an exclusive alliance with the West that the Zionists practiced in Palestine. The Zionist determination to identify with the imperialist powers created an exclusionary discourse. This discourse eliminated or, rather, was intended to eliminate from Zionist consciousness not only the presence of the "primitive" Arab but also the presence of the "obscurantist" Jew in the Diaspora shtetl. At the same time, identification with the West communicated an unwillingness—perhaps even an inability—to engage in creating new, liberating forms of national identity. Even though geographically distant from Europe, the Zionists' attitude toward the Arab population attested to their entrapment in the mentality of the Diaspora Jew, a mentality they despised. The perspective of the early Zionists—with Ahad Ha'Am and Buber as precursors of today's revisionist or post-Zionist trend—leads to the realization that an unresolved emotional dependency on the past situation of subjugation and oppression lies at the very foundation of the movement that professed to have created a "new" Jew. This realization necessitates an investigation of the Zionists' compulsive bonding with the West through an examination of the roots and the role these bonds played in the creation of a new Jewish history that Zionism professed.

2

The Zionists

Colonized Colonizers

The Revolutionary Mimics

The Zionist movement declared that upon returning to the motherland Jews would undergo a transformation from a subjugated minority in anti-Semitic Europe to an independent nation possessing its
own territory. The Zionists saw themselves as true revolutionaries,
"new" Jews composing a new chapter—indeed, a new book—in the
history of the Jewish people. As we have already seen, this new Zionist history recognized neither those Jews who lived apart from the
land nor those Palestinian Arabs who lived within the land but obviously were not Jews. As "new" Jews, the *halutsim* felt they were ush-
ering in a new, unprecedented era of what Ben-Gurion and others
termed the "Jewish revolution."[1]

The Jewish revolution claimed its legitimacy in the ancient Jewish
commonwealth. As late as 1937, when the intensity of Arab nationalism manifested itself in riots against Jews, Ben-Gurion was adamant
about the indisputable Jewish claim to the land: "We are here in our
own right to solve the Jewish problem. . . . It is not to give the Jews
equal rights in Palestine. It is to change their position as a people.
There is no other race and nation as a whole which regards this country as their only homeland." While at this point in history the Arab
inhabitants of the land could hardly be ignored, they did not figure
in Ben-Gurion's project of national restoration. With sweeping rhetoric he affirmed the exclusivity of the Zionist undertaking: "As a child
cannot be bought of another woman, a mother must give birth to

51

her child, so the [Jewish] people itself must give birth to, must create by its own effort, by its own work, its country, its homeland."[2]

It is not difficult to detect the fear of history behind Ben-Gurion's uncompromising, non-negotiable claim to the land. As he saw it, the solution presented by Palestine could not, under any circumstances, turn into yet another historical defeat in the Jewish struggle for equality. Like his contemporaries, Ben-Gurion witnessed the miserable failure of the emancipation of Jews in Europe. According to Ben-Gurion, the principal objective of Zionism must be "making the Jewish people masters of their own destiny as any other free independent people." The settlement in the ancient homeland could not be another land of dispersion, where Jews would again be forced to vie for equal rights. Ben-Gurion was determined to rule out such an option: "We do not intend to create in Palestine the same intolerable position for the Jews as in all other countries. . . . [We are here] to remove a grievance, a historical grievance of the Jewish people against the whole Christian world."[3]

Irrefutable in view of the unhappy history of the Jews in Europe, the argument of grievance against the Christian world nonetheless seems puzzling, especially in terms of the Zionists' assiduous adherence to Europe. Rather than seeking allies who had no part in the history of anti-Semitism in Europe, the "Jewish revolution" sought to tie its destiny to Europe. It would have been plausible for the revolutionary proponents of Jewish liberation and national renewal to treat Europe with reservations and to invest energy and effort in the quest for meaningful relations with the world of the Middle East. Yet, in contrast to Buber, Magnes, and other members of Brith Shalom and Ihud who struggled for a rapprochement with the Arabs, Ben-Gurion sought protection from Britain. In 1937 Ben-Gurion did not even consider—at least not publicly—the plan of the Jewish national home as a state. Rather, as he stated, "We should like this country to be attached to a greater unit, a unit that is called the British Commonwealth of Nations . . . and we should only be glad if in the future, when the Jewish National Home is fully established . . . it should be a member of . . . the British Commonwealth of Nations."[4]

Indeed, as Buber's observations and the research of post-Zionist scholars have shown, from the very beginning the Zionist movement identified itself with the imperialist West. Although it is true that a few years later Ben-Gurion—who, in the meantime, had turned into a devotee of *mamlakhtiyut* (statehood)—was to become the founder of the Jewish state, even then his need for an alliance with the West did not change. One must not forget his struggle against the British Mandate prior to the establishment of the state. Once the state was established, the desire for an alliance with the West remained dominant. In his essay on Ben-Gurion and the Diaspora, Ze'ev Tsahor notes that in the wake of the Holocaust Ben-Gurion was even more determined to tie the destiny of the Jewish state to the great powers. Tsahor maintains that Ben-Gurion's "anxiety of the Holocaust" motivated him "to align Israel with the British-French plot to capture the Suez Canal in 1956"; the same fear caused his withdrawal from Sinai a few months later.[5]

Ben-Gurion's pre-Holocaust plan to join the British Commonwealth demonstrates the extent of the Zionist desire to remain within the orbit of the West. In the post-Holocaust era, the desire had not abated, as demonstrated by the Sinai Campaign. It is true that the Zionists' defiant claim that "ha'olam khulo negdeinu" (the entire world is against us) is as viable today as it was in the time of Ben-Gurion. It is also true that the Zionists' political leadership continued to cultivate connections with Europe. Ben-Gurion's reestablishment of relations with post-Holocaust Germany and his acceptance of reparations can be seen as evidence of the depth of these connections.

Homi Bhabha's discussion of "the ambivalence of colonial mimicry" may help illuminate the origins of the Zionist attachment to Europe. "Colonial mimicry," as Bhabha tells us, originates in the colonizer's permitting the colonized to become "the same but not quite."[6] In other words, the colonizer turns the colonized into a likeness of himself or herself by promoting an integration that will never be actualized. Bhabha's approach complements the major thesis in Albert Memmi's classic study *The Colonizer and the Colonized* (1957), which examines the psychological motivation of the colonized. Memmi shows how the Jews, as a colonized minority, fell into the trap of psychological self-colonization in their efforts to become "the same" as the colonizer.[7]

For both Bhabha and Memmi colonization does not amount solely to territorial occupation and economic exploitation of the native population. Both critics see colonization in terms of its psychological impact on both colonized mimic and mimicked colonizers. The colonized fail to transcend the act of mimicry and never attain a true state of liberation; they remain trapped in the role of mimics. At the same time, their mimicry confronts the colonizers with the vitiating consequences of colonialist oppression. In the distorted reality of the act of mimicry the colonizers see the corrupting effects of the oppression of the other. Mimicked by the colonized, the Enlightenment values parody the "'normalized' knowledges and disciplinary powers" of the authorities. "Mimicry," Bhabha claims, "is at once resemblance and menace."[8]

Bhabha's perspective draws attention to the complexity of the identity transformation from Diaspora Jews into Zionists. In terms of the particular colonization of European Jews, unlike native populations, whose colonization follows the conquest of their territories, European Jewry was a colonized nation within the metropolises of Europe. For centuries Jews represented the only colonized non-Christian minority ruled by the native Christian majority.[9] For example, unlike such colonized nations as the African countries, which, upon winning their independence in the 1950s and the 1960s, saw the imperial powers leave, in order to obtain national independence the Zionists needed to emigrate from Europe to a land they claimed was historically their own.

Why would European Jews opt for the difficult step of emigration from their place of birth to pursue the Zionist ideal? It has already been mentioned that the inception of the Jewish national movement resulted, to a large extent, from the failure of emancipation. Let us briefly consider the anatomy of this failure. Following Bhabha's concept of colonization, it is possible to claim that the Enlightenment transformed the Jews from a physically, politically, and culturally segregated ghetto population into the "mimic people" of Europe. While the *maskilim*, the enlightened Jews, wished to integrate fully into European society, the uncertainty of European acceptance remained a perennial source of frustration.

At one end of the spectrum were those Jews who espoused the ideal of humanistic universalism. These individuals strongly identified with the concept of *Bildung*, which held that ethical and aesthetic self-cultivation would result in a bias-free society. According to this concept, everybody has the potential for moral, spiritual, and cultural self-improvement, so the *maskilim* thought it possible to work their way into the enlightened society.[10] At the other end of the spectrum were Jews who tried to set themselves free of Judaism altogether. These individuals adopted an approach that Sandor Gilman has termed Jewish anti-Semitism or Jewish self-hatred.[11] They internalized anti-Semitic stereotypes and often considered conversion as a venue to erase the Jewish stigma and become "true" Europeans.[12] This paradigm highlights the component of mimicry. Some *maskilim* chose to mimic the liberal humanists, while others mimicked the racists and the bigots. Even though their orientations differed, both types reflected a desire to enter the mainstream of the Enlightenment and become indistinguishable from the Europeans. In this sense their mimicking represents the rejection of that aspect of Jewish life that did not identify with the Enlightenment, that is, the traditional, religiously observant Jewish way of life.

The hope to gain acceptance in Christian society was dashed time and again as a result of the exacerbating anti-Semitic climate. The Damascus affair in 1840, the pogroms of 1881 in Russia, the Dreyfus trial in 1894–95, and the Kishinev pogrom in 1903 were among the landmarks that demonstrated the persistence of violent anti-Semitism. These events signaled the diminishing influence of the universalist ideals of the Enlightenment, instead marking the intensification of nationalistic particularism. The emerging definition of nations as ethnic groups excluded the Jewish "mimics," whether they believed in *Bildung* or identified with anti-Semitic slogans.

The Enlightenment did not fulfill its promise of social equality, which would have erased religious and ethnic differences. The failure of the emancipation became the catalyst for the rise of Jewish nationalism.[13] The socialist Jewish workers' organization Bund, founded in 1897, promoted the struggle for Jewish national and cultural autonomy in the Diaspora.[14] In contrast, the platform of the Zionist national movement, launched under the leadership of Herzl that same year at the First Zionist Congress in Basel, proposed the establishment of the Jewish state in Palestine.

Herzl's political Zionism promised liberation of the Jews from European anti-Semitic oppression in a state *like* Western European states yet geographically *distant from* Europe. This plan naively assumed that the "transfer" (I use this charged term advisedly)[15] of the Jews to their own state would ensure liberation from emotional inhibitions created by/in the European exile. In fact, the implementation of Herzl's deceptively simple idea initiated a remarkably complex, highly controversial, extremely violent history of Jewish national liberation in Palestine, which was later to become the State of Israel. Thinkers such as Ahad Ha'Am and Buber disagreed with Herzl's idea of national liberation, claiming that geographical distance from Europe would not guarantee true liberation of "ruach ha'am" [the spirit of the people]. Indeed, the story of the Zionist settlement in Palestine points to a paradoxical situation of a colonizer seized in self-identification as a colonized.

On the one hand, the founding fathers became de facto colonialists, expanding their territory,[16] building settler-colonies, and studiously ignoring the presence of the native people. They perceived themselves as the rightful masters of the land, the descendants of Joshua, the kings of Judah, and the Maccabees. This self-image of empowerment was to a large extent defined by the rejection of the Diaspora past or, as Zeev Sternhell, a noted scholar of Zionism, terms it, practically visceral "hatred of the Diaspora."[17] On the other hand, the Zionists continued to play the part of the colonized vis-à-vis Europe. Persisting in the role of the mimic, they aspired to be accepted into the family of Western nations. Characteristic of all oppressed minorities who feel the need to excel in order to enter the dominant mainstream, the Zionists' need to prove their worth, or *Bildung*, escalated. To ingratiate themselves with Europe, the Zionists proposed to surpass it by creating an exemplary Western nation-state. In an ironic elaboration on Bhabha's notion of the colonized mimic as "almost the same, but not quite," the Jewish state, as its founders envisioned it, was meant to be *like* Western European states yet *even more* accomplished.

This ambitious, somewhat hubristic utopian aspiration was clearly articulated by Herzl, who declared, "Yes, we are strong enough to form a State, and, indeed, a model State."[18] The utopian aspiration was adapted by some socialist Zionists, who wished to create a model socialist state. Resorting to powerful Christian rhetoric, in 1898 Nachman Syrkin claimed that the Jewish state would be "the first to realize the socialist vision. . . . Israel's tragic history has resulted in a high mission. He will redeem the world which has crucified him."[19] Almost fifty years later (1944) Ben-Gurion concurred with Syrkin, though not in Christian metaphors, when he predicted that the Jewish revolution "will some day serve as a model for the workers' movement of the world."[20] This is a distorted perception of a socialist enterprise. How could a socialist model state coexist with an ideology that championed Jewish labor at the expense of Arab workers? This vision of a model state is clearly irreconcilable with the ideology of the "empty land," a deliberate exclusion of Arabs in the land.

There were, of course, the unheeded voices of opposition, such as Brith Shalom and, later, Ihud, which opposed the discrepancies between the universalist declarations and discriminatory practices of the Zionist mainstream. Yet, the discourse of Brith Shalom and Ihud, which supported a binational democratic state, joined the other silenced discourses, namely, the Arab in the land and the Diaspora Jew. The elimination of all opposing views exposes the dogmatic nature of the Zionist revolution.

With the expansion of the Yishuv, the predilection toward separatism was gaining power. David Vital's remarks concerning the detrimental effects of the Zionist negation of the Diaspora are worth quoting: "[It was] the arch-thesis that *Galut* was commensurate neither with national survival nor with individual dignity that finally and definitively set the Zionists apart from every other significant movement in contemporary Jewry."[21] This observation points to the radicalism with which Zionism effectively suppressed every alternative discourse. It is my supposition that the reasons for the politics of the exclusion *of* the other and the separation *from* the other should be sought in the "unfinished business" of the Jew as colonized European mimic. The unresolved tension between, on the one hand, the unshakable conviction of the superiority of the West and, on the other, the desire to replicate and even supersede this superiority points up the need to eliminate—or at least neutralize—all differing views and opinions. In order to prove this supposition, I must examine the inception of the movement as represented by the life, ideas, and weltanschauung of its founder, Theodor Herzl.

Herzl's Utopia: A Jewish West in the East

The Zionist need to imitate and even outdo Europe is particularly ironic in view of the circumstances that engendered the movement. Zionism was born out of the realization that, as Herzl himself put it, "[Jewish] equality before the law, granted by the statute, has become practically a dead letter."[22] Max Nordau reinforced Herzl's observations in his opening speech at the First Zionist Congress when he talked about the Western Jew, who "regarded emancipation as real liberation, and hastened to draw final conclusions from it. But the nations of the world made him realize that he erred in being so thoughtlessly logical."[23]

To validate—perhaps even justify—his attraction to the Western world despite its ongoing politics of discrimination against the Jews, Herzl resorted to argumentation so spurious and self-contradictory that one doubts whether he believed it himself. To reassure Europe that the departure of the Jews was not subversive in any way, he claimed that Jewish emigration from Europe would benefit the former host countries because "there will be an inner migration of Christian citizens into the position evacuated by Jews." Furthermore, he claimed that the departure of the Jews would finally create the conditions whereby Europe could actualize the ideals of the Enlightenment. The relocation of the Jews would strengthen the European world, which, as Herzl put it at the conclusion of *The Jewish State,* "will be freed by our liberty, enriched by our wealth, magnified by our greatness."[24]

Could it be that Herzl was unaware of the irony of his rhetoric? To persuade the Europeans of his good intentions, he presented himself and the prospective Zionists as deferential mimics of Europe. Unwittingly his mimicry confronted the Europeans with the deceit and hypocrisy of the practices of the Enlightenment. In this sense Herzl's argument illustrates Bhabha's notion of mimicry, which ineluctably informs the relationships of the colonizer and the colonized. The removal of Jews from Europe so that the Europeans could practice the values of toleration, equality, and human fellowship mocked these ideals and, in fact, rendered them meaningless. Paradoxically, in urging Jewish emigration to Palestine, Herzl was mimicking the anti-Semitic cries for the "transfer" of the Jews, which, as he admits, he himself heard "clearly enunciated in that classic Berlin phrase: '*Juden Raus*' [Jews Out]."[25]

Perhaps even more paradoxical was the mimicry component in Herzl's enticement to the prospective Jewish emigrants to leave. As he presented it, the attraction of the emigration lay in the replication of the Western lifestyle in Palestine. It is interesting to note Herzl's use of biblical imagery to depict the "Europeanization" of Palestine: "When we journey out of Egypt again, we shall not leave the fleshpots behind. Every man will find his [European] customs again in the local groups, but they will be better, more beautiful, and more agreeable than before."[26] This complete distortion of the signification of the Egyptian "fleshpots" underscores the degree of Zionist mimicry of the European Diaspora. The biblical Exodus gave birth to the Hebrew nation through a painful severance from the "fleshpots," or comforts, of Egypt. Herzl redefined the liberation of the Jews as cultivation of the European "Egypt" and its comforts. The Zionist "revolution"—*pace* Herzl—would signify an elevated European lifestyle in Palestine that was free of anti-Semitism.

Indeed, Herzl's utopian novel *Altneuland* [Old-New Land] centers on the idea of the Jewish Europeanization of Palestine. Written in 1902, this utopian novel was, to a large extent, an elaboration of the blueprint of the Jewish state outlined in *Der Judenstaat*, only this time as a fictional narrative. In its emphasis on the imitation the West, *Old-New Land* is a fictional representation of a dream come true: the Jews finally become "true" Europeans. The novel, in the form of a bildungsroman, tells how, thanks to the mentorship of the European aristocrat Kingscourt, Friedrich Loewenberg, an effeminate, depressed, weak Jew, grows into a strong, handsome, and resourceful young man.[27] As Jacques Kornberg observes, "In *Old-New Land,* Herzl foresaw Zionism's contribution to the consummation of European emancipation. . . . [A]ntisemitism had been eliminated, European assimilation was no longer an act of subservience, disloyalty, or cowardice."[28] Indeed, the novel progresses toward a peculiar twofold utopia. On the one hand, it presents an idealized vision of Europe free of Jews and therefore freed of anti-Semitism; on the other, it offers an idealized portrait of these same Jews, who have become Europeans in Palestine.

The two utopian desires materialize in the novel's denouement. Upon arriving in Palestine, Kingscourt confirms Loewenberg's successful *Bildung*: "Young fellow," the European aristocrat tells the Jew, "you talk like a man of my own heart." It is interesting to note that Kingscourt makes this declaration of friendship in the context of a humorous exchange about Jewish greed. The enlightened European aristocrat's liberation from anti-Semitic prejudice emerges in his general statement about the vitiating power of money: "I have always said that money is a fine and useful thing. It's man who has spoilt it."[29] At the same time, Kingscourt's pronouncement that Loewenberg is a man "of my own heart" marks the Jew's acceptance into the world of enlightened Europe of which he is a representative. Indeed, as the novel shows time and again, Loewenberg has come to personify the ideal of *Bildung;* he is now a resourceful and decisive young man, ready to raise a family of his own and contribute to society.

Daniel Boyarin sees this kind of Jewish "normalization" as "a parodic imitation of colonialism . . . [of] 'effeminate' Jews disguised as 'men.' "[30] If Boyarin's contention is true, then the Jewish colonists in the novel—and most probably their author—fail to discern the irony of their situation. They perceive themselves as empowered missionaries who faithfully serve the Western ideal of human progress. "Civilization is all," proudly declares one of the characters. "We Jews brought civilization to the country." Consequently, the "native" population enthusiastically endorses the colonizing/civilizing mission of the Jews. The representative Arab character in the novel affirms that "Jewish immigration was a blessing for all of us," mainly because it improved the Arab economic situation. According to Herzl's vision, the Arab, converted to the "religion" of Western progress, has adjusted effortlessly into a Europeanized Palestine governed by Europeanized Jews. Indeed, the novel concludes in the manner of a manifesto of Western Christian humanism, sounding a note of a "new and happier form of human society" that entered the land with the arrival of the enlightened Jews. The unanimous chorus acknowledges the blessings of "the united nation, the new technology, knowledge, willpower, the forces of nature, tolerance, self-assurance, love and suffering, and God."[31]

Yosef Haim Brenner and the Impossibility of Self-Liberation

Herzl's vision of Westernized Palestine continues to be highly valued even today, especially by establishment Zionists. In his introduction to Herzl's diaries, Shlomo Avineri, an eminent Israeli political scientist, writes in praise of Herzl's vision of the state. Avineri approvingly reaffirms Herzl's affinity with Western modernity, maintaining that the perspective in the novel is "lucid, rational, well reasoned, and founded upon the achievements of modern science and modern social thought."[32] Avineri seems to suggest that *Old-New Land* represents a wholesale transplantation of modernity to the Jewish state. In contrast, my reading of the text suggests that Herzl's idea of the Jewish state as a paragon of modernity and progress necessitates a certain amount of identity manipulation. The infusion of Western ideas in Palestine was predicated upon the transformation of the Jew into an enlightened European Christian, which, in turn, was predicated upon the transformation of the Palestinian Arab into an enlightened European-like Jew. This clearly reveals the implausibility—indeed, the impossibility—of Herzl's vision of the Jewish state. In this replica of a Western state, the Jews were required to forget their history of persecutions in the Diaspora and the Arabs had to forget their own history in the land.

To demonstrate the extent of Herzl's lack of understanding of the concrete signification of his idea of the Jewish state, it is illuminating to examine a short narrative of a settler's life by the Hebrew writer Yosef Haim Brenner, who immigrated to Palestine in 1909 and was killed by Arab rioters in 1921. A few weeks before his tragic death, he wrote a short—most probably autobiographical—account simply entitled "M'pinqas" [From a notebook]. Brenner's last piece of writing offers a poignantly critical commentary on the ideological foundations of the Zionist project. It is, in a sense, a testimonial whose unsparingly ironic critical tone illuminates the myopia and self-deception of Herzl's project. Furthermore, the poignant observations of the *haluts* belies the discourses of negation of both the Arab and the Diaspora Jew engendered in Herzl's vision.

The piece consists of a first-person narrative. As the narrator wanders through a citrus grove, a thought crosses his mind that the orchard belongs to the Arabs, who are "the sons of the land." Subsequently he passes four Arab men: the *effendi* (the landlord), two elderly neighbors, and a young man of twenty. They do not respond to the narrator's greeting and look at him with open hostility—or at least that is how he interprets it. The narrator reacts silently but with extreme bitterness; in his heart he denounces the Arabs and promises himself not to "ever wish them peace and well-being," even though they may be "of the blood of the remnant of Israel."[33] (He is referring to the romantic and, at the time, widely accepted speculation that the Arab peasants were, in fact, the descendants of the ancient Hebrews and Canaanites and consequently related by blood to the Jewish people).[34]

Even though he is aware that the Arabs detest his presence, the narrator is determined that he "must pass by them, whether they like it or not." Fully aware of being unwelcome, he claims the right to walk through the grove owned by "the sons of the land." He tells himself that the Arabs' behavior is more hateful than that of eastern European anti-Semites, labeling the unfriendly Arabs "Poles of the East."[35] The narrator sees the reality of the Jewish immigrant in Palestine as a reenactment of the Jewish situation in the Diaspora. He feels that he is being treated by the native Arabs with the same hostility and contempt he experienced from the anti-Semitic population in Europe. Accordingly, his response to the Arabs is the same as it would have been in Europe; once again feeling powerless and humiliated, he curses the Arabs in his heart as he used to curse the Poles.

The narrator's feelings of humiliation and helplessness dissipate a moment later when he is greeted as *Hawaja* (master) by a young Arab boy of thirteen or fourteen. The narrator is unable to communicate with the boy since, as he regretfully admits, "I did not teach myself to speak Arabic."[36] He somehow understands the boy's miserable situation; he is an orphan exploited by the *effendi*. The narrator tries to communicate to the boy that he has not been paid fairly. The boy, however, understands otherwise and tries to justify his earnings. For the second time the narrator feels guilty for not having taught himself Arabic.

By now the narrator's previous feelings of enraged helplessness have disappeared. The new situation has transformed him from an estranged, humiliated Jew into a respected confessor and counselor.

Facing the boy, who treats him with a degree of deference reserved for elders, the narrator becomes conscious of his elevated social status vis-à-vis the unenlightened Arabs. He eventually comes to the realization that, "whether [the Arab boy is] close or not in terms of blood," this "working orphan," is his "young brother." This insight leads the narrator to an understanding of his obligation toward the boy: "I have a responsibility toward you to open your eyes, give you a taste of human relations!" The narrator knows that in the future "we [the Yishuv] shall be involved in politics, despite ourselves, out of desperation, for lack of choice." However, he also knows that politics, especially the socialist revolution, is not important. What is important is "the communion of souls with no ulterior motive . . . with no goal . . . with no intention, except that of a brother, friend and companion."[37]

Seeing the narrator preoccupied with his thoughts, the boy bids him goodbye. The narrator notices that the boy is proud of having engaged in a conversation with a grown man and having spoken to him in a mature fashion just like an older person. "My peace unto you," he answers the boy's words of farewell while noting that "my heart warmed to him and to myself."[38] Then he resumes his wandering along the dusty paths of the grove.

Brenner's last piece of writing—especially its emphasis on the brotherly relations between Jews and Arabs—attracted a fair amount of critical attention.[39] Edna Amir Coffin sees the story in terms of Brenner's socialist ideas, maintaining that Brenner, "like many other socialist ideologists, preferred to believe that class bonds could bridge the gap" of national concerns.[40] Warren Bargad interprets the story as a reflection on the universality of human suffering, albeit with a socialist slant. He emphasizes the narrator's identification with the boy, who is "a symbol of all downtrodden peoples. . . . Identification . . . is the issue; Arab and Jew are united, in Brenner's egalitarian vision, by common human needs and goals."[41] In a more insightful reading Ariel Hirschfeld sees the piece as an honest self-analysis of an immigrant Jew in Eretz Israel confronting the "sons of the land" to whom the latter belongs. Rather than stressing the text's socialist message, Hirschfeld explores the moral dimension of the story, identifying it as an attempt to establish meaningful relationships between individuals, specifically, a dialogic relationship between Arabs and

Jews. Referring to the narrator's reservations about Zionist socialist politics, Hirschfeld argues that the Jewish engagement "out of desperation" in political revolutions is "the absolute opposite to [Brenner's] intentions." According to Hirschfeld, Brenner's "perspective [is] far wider than that entailed in the political dialogue." This critic detects a "tragic irony" in Brenner's vision, because the dialogue that Brenner has in mind is "rare and distant."[42] Hirschfeld concludes his interpretation by turning to the present-day politics of discommunication as evidence that attempts at a meaningful dialogue, as Brenner understood it, have irrevocably failed.

In contrast to Hirschfeld, I wish to argue that the foreshadowed failure of dialogue in Brenner's narrative, far from reflecting merely an out-of-control political situation, represents further complexity. I suggest that the reason for the failure to communicate lies in the narrator's narcissistic need for recognition and in his passive self-centeredness, qualities that preclude both an understanding of self and of others.

Even though the narrator professes to be deeply affected by the boy's plight, his sympathy does not lead to any effort to improve the boy's lot. Even though he blames himself for his inability to speak Arabic, there is no indication that he will attempt to master the language. Furthermore, the narrator's comprehension of his responsibility to give the boy, his "young brother," "a taste of human relations" leads to no concrete action on his part. On the contrary, the story ends when, content and satisfied, the narrator passively watches his "young brother" go back to his miserable existence. He clearly understands as little about human relations as before.

The issue of the boy's welfare does not move the narrator to social action. Rather than involving himself with the socially deprived "young brother," he is preoccupied with compensating for his hurt pride. One recalls that his first encounter with the Arabs left him seething with impotent rage. Even though it would have made more sense to attribute the hostility of the Arabs to their anxiety about the intentions of the stranger in their midst, the insulted *haluts* had chosen to associate the incident with his past victimization in Europe. His narcissism comes to the fore when, rather than focusing on the problem of his presence for "the sons of the land," the narrator, full of self-pity, sees "the sons of the land" as reincarnations of his Polish persecutors and himself as their victim. While the hostile behavior of the Arabs belies their "invisibility" in the "empty land," the hostile response of the narrator implants, so to speak, the "negated Diaspora" in the land. It is therefore possible to understand how, by contrast, the admiration by the Arab boy makes up for the narrator's bruised ego. The deference of the young boy reaffirms the narrator's superior position as a "civilized" European. The narrator's self-laudatory reading of the boy's mind signals the desire to be recognized and respected. The Jew, who had felt humiliated just a moment earlier, now imagines himself in the role of an enlightened mentor to the "backward" native.

Buber, one recalls, urged the Zionist pioneers to become students of Arab culture and language in the hope that the Jews would be able to engage in meaningful and friendly relationships with the inhabitants of the land. In Brenner's text, however, the Arabs do not appear as counterparts to the Jew; rather, seen entirely from the Jew's perspective, they serve as mirrors to a Jewish split identity. In the first encounter Brenner's narrator identifies the Arabs with European anti-Semites, which makes him decide to "pass by them, whether they like it or not." He thus intuitively reenters his "old" self of the victimized Diaspora Jew. In the second encounter the boy causes the narrator to cast off the role of the Diaspora Jew and assume the role of a "new," liberated European Jew. In this role he feels competent to act as an authority and mentor in a world whose language he does not know and whose customs he does not understand. It is ironic that he projects upon the new and unknown reality of Palestine the value system of enlightened Europe. The attitude in the second episode can be seen as a reaction to the humiliation experienced in the first. The sense of potency in the meeting with the young boy compensates for the previous self-perception as a helpless victim. The Zionist's ambivalent self-identification as both self-pitying victim and enlightened benefactor signals a psychological stasis that contradicts the portrayal of the *haluts* as a dynamic, progressive, and enterprising "new" Jew.

Identical sentences frame the text. The story begins with the narrator recalling how, all alone, "in darkness I was wandering in the dusty path of the grove." It concludes with the narrator saying how, alone once again, "I continued my wandering in the darkness." Note the recurring motifs of darkness and solitude, as well as the use of the root "*ta'a*," which designates both "wandering" and "getting lost / losing one's way." The circular movement of the story, which ends as it began, indicates an absence of progress; the ending of aimless and lonely wandering or erring exposes the illusory nature of the narrator's narcissistic contentment, induced by the boy's deferential attitude.

The circular movement of the text precludes a decisive conclusion, resolution, or even an indication of a teleological direction. It reflects the failure of the "wandering," "lost," Zionists, such as Brenner's narrator, engaged in a futile search for a way out of the Diaspora past toward national rebirth as an independent Jewish nation among the Arab "sons of the land." Is it possible to claim that unresolved psychological issues have forestalled the break with the past and precluded the start of a new beginning? Freud's concept of transference may help to elucidate the problem.[43] According to Freud, the therapy progresses from repetition to remembering through the stage of transference. "[T]he repetition," Freud says, "is the transference of the forgotten past . . . to all the other aspects of the current situation." The patient "lives it [the past experience] through" his transference "as something real and actual," until he is capable of remembering it rather than repeating it. Remembering amounts to "translating [the experience] back again into terms of the past." The key to the transformation of repetition into memory lies in overcoming resistance to such a transformation.[44] In the final stage of a successful therapy, transference is no longer necessary because the vicious cycle of repetition has stopped. Now the experience becomes a memory of an event in the patient's past.

In Brenner's narrative the past experience of anti-Semitic victimization enters the stage of transference in the first episode. In his response to Arab hostility, the narrator projects his past fears of persecution onto the reality of Palestine. Had he understood his reaction as transference, the narrator would have gained a clearer perception of himself and others under the current circumstances. Such a perception might have allowed him to understand the hostility of the Arabs as a response to the threatening intrusion of the *Yahud* (the Jew). In this way he would have attained a better understanding of "the sons of the land" and their perception of the Jew. Second, an understanding of the Arabs' motivation would have enabled him to escape the cycles of transference and to restore the Diaspora past to memory. In other words, a deeper self-understanding might have made him realize that the situation in Palestine is not comparable to the anti-Semitic victimization of the Jews in Poland; rather, it presents a different problem elicited by different historical circumstances.

Indeed, the meeting with the Arab boy demonstrates the narrator's desire to escape the transference of the fearful Jewish past to Palestine. But then he falls into yet another transference, namely, that of the mimcry *maskilim* practiced in Europe. Thus, for a brief moment Brenner's narrator is able to assume the identity of an enlightened European Jew who bears the message of Western civilization and its socialist ideas to the "natives." His resumption of aimless wandering and its circular trajectory signals the incapacity of the *haluts* to liberate himself from the past. The compulsive transference of the roles of Jewish victim and European mimic indicates the inability to adjust to the reality of the "Old-New Land" of Palestine.

I wish to return briefly to Herzl's vision in *Old-New Land*. The failure of Brenner's narrator to establish meaningful relationships with either the *effendi* or with the latter's young serf demonstrates the extent of Herzl's misunderstanding of the true meaning of his project. I have already noted the transformation of the young Loewenberg from a weak Diaspora Jew to an enlightened western European. Under the tutelage of Kingscourt, the enlightened European aristocrat, Loewenberg developed into an individual capable of bringing prosperity and progress to the Arab population in the Jewish state in Palestine. To quote Avineri again, this state is "lucid, rational, well thought out, and founded upon the achievements of modern science and modern social thought." The irony of Brenner's short narrative, which most probably documents his own experience as a Jewish settler in Palestine, dispels the myth of Herzl's vision of the Jewish state. Perceptively, Brenner's story identifies the utopian, unrealistic dimension of the Zionist vision of Jewish liberation in the unresolved problem, the "unfinished business" of mimicry that the Zionists brought from the Diaspora to the "empty land" of the future state. As Brenner's vision in this ironically prophetic narrative reveals, the failure of the Zionist project lies in its inability to attain a true liberation of its inner self from the past.

The Canaanites, the *Muskeljuden,* and the Strategies of Negation

As an insightful representation of the Zionists' psychological dependence on the past, Brenner's "M'pinqas" is of particular interest
in view of the writer's lifelong vehement disavowal of Jewish life in
the Diaspora. Poignantly, this last piece of writing presents more than
just the Zionist failure to rewrite the history of the Jewish people. If,
as is generally believed, the narrative is autobiographical, then
"M'pinqas" also represents Brenner's failure to rewrite his personal
history as a Zionist.

Brenner belonged to the aforementioned Tseirim, a group of
young Jewish intellectuals who passionately rejected the Diaspora.
Brenner's contempt for Jewish life in the Diaspora was inordinate.
Even Berdyczewski, the leader of the group, who urged Jews to take
up their swords and reject the book, was appalled by Brenner's attitude. After a meeting with Brenner, Berdyczewski wrote: "This man
is no longer a Jew in his heart since he curses Judaism, as he sees its
ending and perhaps even wants it [to end]."[45] Indeed, in his 1914
essay "Self-Criticism" Brenner unequivocally announced the disintegration of the Jewish nation: "We have no inheritance. Each generation gives nothing of its own to its successor. And whatever is trans-
mitted—the rabbinical literature—were better never handed down
to us. . . . [T]here are masses of Jews who live biologically, like ants,
but a living Jewish people in any sociological sense . . . such a people
hardly exists any longer." To save ourselves, he declared, "we need
our own environment" in which "our character must be radically
changed."[46]

Ironically, "M'pinqas," Brenner's last statement, indicates that
"our own environment" in Palestine did not produce a transformed
or "radically changed" Jewish character. Such a radical transformation of character would have required a redefinition of the Jewish
self in the new environment. Instead, as "M'pinqas" shows, the transference of centuries-old Jewish fears from Europe to Palestine, and
further, in the reenactment of colonial mimicry disguised in discourses of negation and denial. In other words, instead of—to recall
Freud—recognizing the repetitive patterns of Diaspora behavior, a
recognition that would have transform repetition into remembrance,

the Tseirim opted for a vehement and unequivocal denial of the rabbinic tradition and the history of suffering in exile.

The Tseirim were succeeded by the Canaanite movement, which
represented the most aggressive and most extreme degree of negation of the Diaspora. The movement was established by the poet
Yonathan Ratosh in the 1940s, years after Tseirim, which was
active in the first decades of the twentieth century. Nonetheless, without Berdyczewski, Brenner, and other promulgators of the Hebrew Jew, concludes Yaacov Shavit, "Canaanism could never have
seen the [light of] day." The Canaanite platform defied Judaism,
promising to create "a Middle East of a new type . . . a *Hebrew*
Middle East."[47]

Even though the Canaanite movement never gained any political
power, its ideology informed the Israeli consciousness in profound
ways. The continuing impact of this movement has not been lost on
today's Zionist scholars. Recall Schweid's critique of the "Canaanite-
Israeli," namely, of those Israelis who continue to deny their ties with
the culture and the heritage of the Diaspora. In his seminal study
James Diamond confirms the persisting influence of the movement.
Diamond claims that the Canaanite weltanschauung still exists, presenting "an implicit challenge within the Israeli body politic."[48]

The Canaanite doctrine took the Zionist negation of the Diaspora
ad absurdum. The extremism of the Canaanites was most evident in
their attacks on Diaspora Jewry even at the time of the Holocaust.[49]
Their platform proposed to replace the Jewish tradition with pan-
Hebraism, which would impose Hebrew culture on the Middle East
region. I would argue that the Canaanite movement conflated the
two Zionist discourses of negation, negating the histories of both the
Diaspora Jew and the Palestinian Arab. This platform not only severed all connection with European Jewry but also propagated the
erasure of Palestinian national identity. The Canaanite platform
urged nothing less than a military enforcement of Hebrew government and culture over the region. According to the Canaanites, Shavit
writes, "the role of Hebrew nationalism is to liberate the 'natural'
nations of the Middle East . . . from the yoke of pan-Arabism and
to create a new Hebrew covenant of nations and reinstate the ancient
Hebrew glory."[50]

The implementation of the big plan of pan-Hebraism was to be preceded by the rebirth of the Hebrew nation on the territory of greater Palestine.[51] The Canaanite concept of Hebrew domination amounted to the elimination of the Arab cultural presence. According to the Canaanite plan, the Arab inhabitants would be incorporated into the Yishuv through "a uniform educational and cultural system which would establish a standard national [Hebrew] identity."[52] Indeed, the final point in the 1951 Canaanite twenty-four-point program promoted "a stimulation of the culture of the homeland based on the *national Hebrew revival,* drawing on the values intrinsic to this land, and *transmitting* them to *all its inhabitants.*"[53] The transmission of these values to the Arabs would not be difficult, as Ratosh envisioned it, due to an obvious "[modern] national, cultural superiority of the *Yishuv* over the 'medieval,' 'lower' culture of the Arab population."[54]

It seems that the immense impact of the Canaanite ideology on the Zionist/Israeli psyche lies in its conflation of the negation of the Diaspora and the exclusion of the Arab. In the words of Shimoni, in their "monumentally fallacious notion of the inherently Hebrew character of the territory,"[55] the Canaanites reinforced and, to a large extent, finalized the Zionist doctrine of separatism. The Canaanite emphasis on Hebrew culture and language vehemently negated the Diaspora cultures and languages and, at the same time, was bent on discarding the culture and language of the native Palestinian. The Canaanite insistence on a "uniform educational and cultural system" based on the Hebrew model made the exclusion of the Arabs total.

Indeed, the Canaanite program is recognizable in the uniform educational Hebrew system imposed on Israeli Arabs with the establishment of the State of Israel. Israeli educational hegemony dispossessed the Arabs of their cultural and linguistic heritage; at the same time, however, it did not erase the inferior situation of the Israeli Arab in the State of Israel. In short, for Israeli Arabs Hebrew education by no means signified entrance into the mainstream Israeli Jewish society. Ironically, the domination of Hebrew language, culture, and education produced a situation of colonial mimicry that, to recall Bhabha, effectively divested the Arabs of their cultural distinctness and at the same time distanced them from the dominant mainstream. As Hebrew-speaking, culturally colonized, second-class citizens,[56] Israeli

Arabs have remained on the threshold, suspended between cultures and national identities.

The use of the educational system to turn Israeli Arabs into mimics of the Israeli Jewish mainstream leads back to the concept of a "mission civilisatrice." This "mission" of the French and British colonialists promoted the Western culture and language dissemination to the colonized native populations. By transforming the natives into "almost but not quite" Europeans, the "civilizing" process effectively erased the cultural identity of the natives. Recall Buber's exhortations to the Yishuv about the importance of the study of the Arab culture and the Arabic language. It is hard to disregard the contrast between Buber's recognition of the importance of the Arab cultural environment and the Zionist-Canaanite imposition of Hebrew culture on its Arab population. This discrepancy leads to the ironic realization that despite protestations of the moral and just foundations of the Zionist state and the equality of all its citizens, according to Israel's declaration of independence the treatment of its Arab citizens was modeled upon the colonialist practices of the West.

The influence of the West also emerges in the Zionist insistence on the exclusivity of Hebrew culture and language. The emphasis on original language and unique culture as integral national components was typical of western European national movements. As Michael Berkowitz has noted, early Zionist promoters of Hebrew culture reiterated Herder's and Schlegel's declarations about the importance of cultivating the "speech of the fathers" and the right of a people to develop "a literature unique to itself." This recourse to European thinkers placed the Zionist concern for Hebrew *Kultur* "within the realm of [European] progress and modernity."[57] Thus, the propagation of Hebrew culture as a unique and central component of the national identity of the Jewish state reaffirmed the prominence of European philosophical and social trends in Zionist thought.

To become a nation like all nations, the hegemony of the Hebrew culture needed to prevail over other potentially contesting cultures. We have observed how the imposition of Hebrew education abrogated Arab culture and language in the territory of the state. At the same time, the absolute domination of the Hebrew language in its secular Zionist context reinforced the barriers separating the Yishuv from the Diaspora. One need only recall the manifest contempt for

Yiddish culture, or the deliberately cultivated ignorance of Jewish religious customs and rituals. Israel's disdainful attitude toward the cultural and scholarly heritage of the Diaspora is common knowledge. The disparaging image of the parasitic, helpless, and *effeminate* Diaspora Jew was propagated to promote the productive, self-sufficient, and *manly* Hebrew Jew in Palestine. Zeev Jabotinsky summed up such propagandistic practices with brutal, anti-Semitic bluntness: "Because the *Yid* is ugly and sickly, and lacks decorum, we shall endow the ideal image of the Hebrew with masculine beauty. The *Yid* is downtrodden upon and easily frightened and, therefore, the Hebrew ought to be proud and independent."[58]

An early example of Zionist efforts to create a physically strong Jew was Max Nordau's idea of the *Muskeljude,* the Jew characterized by might rather than learning. Nordau promoted the Bar Khohba Jewish gymnastics club. He glorified the Bar Khohba's revolt of 135 B.C.E. as a historical model for Jewish prowess and heroism.[59] As Yael Zerubavel has shown, the Zionists' manipulation of historical events, such as the Bar Khohba revolt, was intended to create models of Jewish military strength and national pride. Zerubavel demonstrates that the myth of the heroic Jewish struggle for independence was meant to ground the Zionist call for the transformation of the Jew in the ancient tradition of Jewish heroism.[60] In reality, the harking back to antiquity implied the desire to become "physical," like the Europeans. According to Berkowitz, "The Jewish gymnastic movement borrowed extensively from its German and Slavic national counterparts."[61] The image of the *Muskeljude* was intended, first and foremost, to counteract the image of the *Mauschel,* the negative stereotype of the contemptible European Jew. In classic anti-Semitic language Herzl described him as "a distortion of the human character, unspeakably mean and repellent . . . impudent and arrogant . . . [who] pursues his own dirty business . . . [and] squeals whenever he becomes frightened."[62]

As the Zionist movement had claimed since its inception, the transformation of the *Mauschel* into a *Muskeljude* was possible only in the context of Jewish sovereignty in Eretz Israel. The reterritorialization of the Jewish nation in its *Altneuland* was the sine qua non of the Zionist vision of the "new" Jew and the reborn Jewish nation. National rebirth was predicated upon the restoration of the desolate motherland. Organic ties with the land needed to be reestablished. Once direct contact with the land was achieved, it would transform the weak and despised Diaspora Jew into a "new" Jew in the image of the heroic ancient Hebrews.

The ineluctable interdependence between the revival of the land and the rebirth of the nation confronted the individual Zionist with a problem of immense magnitude. The uncompromising demand of re-territorialization was of biblical proportions. Like Abraham, the Zionist was required to forsake family, tradition, and place of birth and journey to a "forsaken" desert land. The departure for Eretz Israel signified multiple—physical, moral, and emotional—aspects of abandonment. How could the guilt of abandonment of parental home for a completely unknown place be transformed into virtue? How could an unfamiliar land be transformed into a homeland? In the next chapter I focus on the discourses of negation as strategies for such a transformation and demonstrate how the negation of others was indispensable to the Zionist dream of a return to the land and national restoration, and how, ironically, this very politics of negation sabotaged the dream.

3

The Land as Homeland?

Is it possible that although the expectations of physical return and of political sovereignty have been fulfilled, the dream of transforming the land into a homeland has not been actualized? Is it possible that the repossession and revival of the land has failed to create an organic tie with the place? Do feelings of alienation and hostility, such as those Brenner depicts in "M'pinqas," persist despite Zionist efforts to create the consciousness of "being-in-place"?

"About the Place," a thought-provoking essay by Zali Gurevitch and Gideon Aran, argues for impossibility of a spiritual connection with the land. Despite the expectation that dwelling in the land and its cultivation would lead to "a new Jewish totality," this goal has remained elusive. The authors of the essay maintain that "an essential estrangement from the place did not disappear with the return to Zion." They reach the conclusion that the metaphysical quality of the "place" precludes a total physical and spiritual repossession of the ancient land.[1] These writers ground the notion of being-out-of-place, even when physically in-place, in the inherent motif of exile in Jewish historical narrative from its biblical inception.

Other studies of the question of land as homeland do not resort to metaphysics, focusing instead on the psychological and ideological issues of emigration and immigration. For example, Hannah Naveh claims that the Zionist idea of return called on the immigrants to fulfill a mission of "monumental proportions." The mission of starting their history anew in Palestine entailed "the negation of the old home in the Diaspora, which, as they predicted, was doomed to destruction." The project was conceived by young people who wished

74

to reinvent themselves as "new" Hebrews and urged complete severance from their parental home. Naveh claims that there was a degree
of "mental" infancy, a certain "blindness" in this belief that "it was
enough to want to turn over a new leaf for a new leaf to actually
turn over." Drawing upon Brenner's lucid representations of the experiences of Zionist *halutsim* in Palestine, Naveh maintains that
while the immigrants/pioneers wished to start anew, they could not
possibly get rid of the psychological baggage of the past that curtailed
their ability to build a new life in the New World.[2]

Naveh advances the psychological impossibility of the erasure of
one's personal and national past in the reality of a new place. Looking
at the Zionist experience in Palestine from a different perspective,
Amnon Raz-Krakotzkin attributes the estrangement from the land to
ideological flaws. He links the claim of the "empty land" to the desire
of the Zionists to reject the Diaspora and to identify with ancient
Hebrews. As Raz-Krakotzkin sees it, the ancient Hebrews, the indigenous peoples of the past, apparently presented the ideal model for
the Zionist "new" Jews, who aspired to refashion themselves as the
native people of the land. Since the ancient Hebrews no longer exist,
in order to become natives the Jews had to model themselves upon
the Arabs, the existing indigenous peoples. As such, the Arab "represented a competition to the new Jew." Raz-Krakotzkin observes that
the Zionist pioneers developed a twofold attitude toward the Arab.
In their desire to "appropriate the myth" of nativism, they cultivated
the ideal image of the "native" Arab. At the same time, they separated
themselves from the "real" Arab in order to cultivate the myth of the
"empty land."[3] The Arabs were like the ancient Hebrews and therefore had to be idealized; however, the fact of their being like the ancient Hebrews subverted the Zionists' exclusivity as the descendants
of the ancient Hebrews, which explains why the Arab presence had
to be denied. Raz-Krakotzkin maintains that the negation of the Diaspora and the myth of the "empty land" reflected the intention of the
Zionists to turn the land into their exclusive and only homeland.

While the argument that views the Zionist desire for exclusive
possession of the land is certainly true, the complex attitude toward
the Arabs that Raz-Krakotzkin attributes to the "new" Jew seems
implausible. The incongruity of this argument is especially apparent
in light of the history of the Zionist/Canaanite attitude toward the

Arabs. Even though the Zionist pioneers portrayed themselves as sons and daughters returning to the ancient motherland, could the native Arab become a serious, bona fide model of identification for the newly arrived Europeans? It is true that some of the early Yishuv writers—notably Moshe Smilanski, Yehuda Burla, and Yitzhak Shami—extolled the dashing and fearless Arab horsemen.[4] This naive enthusiasm, however, raises the question as to whether the romantic perception of the native Arab as a "noble savage" was, in a large measure, an imitation of the genre of European colonialist literature populated with idealized, unsophisticated, "close to nature" natives. Did the romantic representation of the Arab carry more weight for the Zionist settlers than, say, the romantic myth of the Indian warriors for the American pioneering settlers? Such romanticized or, rather, sentimentalized images seem to partake of adolescent fantasies. Considering the extent of the Zionist desire to become like all (Western) nations, it seems quite unlikely that the Arab inhabitants of the land could serve as a model for the European Zionist colonist who came to repossess the land.

Indeed, my previous discussion of early Zionist and contemporary post-Zionist thinkers leads to a well-founded conclusion that the predominant model for the "new" Jew was the enlightened European nationalist. Though the ideal of the "new" Jew often assumed the guise of the ancient heroic Hebrew, the national revival that this "new" Jew/ancient Hebrew was supposed to engender was deeply steeped in Western nationalism. According to Herzl's vision, one will recall, the liberated, "new" Jew will build an exemplary replica of a Western nation-state in the land of Palestine. As my discussion of Zionist politics and culture attempted to show, the success of a modern Zionist nation-state was predicated on the dual negation of the Diaspora Jew and the Arab in the land. From this point of view, the silencing of the voices of Jewish Diaspora history and the inhabitant of the land were ideological strategies to establish a direct, organic contact with the land of the biblical Hebrew ancestors. The ongoing Israeli-Palestinian conflict over the land, which turned it into a place of perennial war, demonstrates that the ideal of the *Old-New Land* as homeland has failed to materialize. This realization leads to a number of questions: Why, despite the legendary self-sacrifice of the *halut-*

sim, does the sense of estrangement and alienation in the land persist? Why, despite repeated attempts to assert a mythical right to the land, does the sense of ownership remain elusive? Why has the land not become a homeland, as the early Zionists had dreamed?

A partial answer to these questions lies in Naveh's argument that it is impossible to erase the past; the scars and the damages of violent anti-Semitism, of the humiliating and constricting rabbinic rule, of centuries-long political impotence could not be discarded with the undertaking of the pioneering mission in the land. Naveh's argument leads us to the psychological aspect of the Zionist pioneering enterprise, namely that of the attention to the emotional consequences of the unequivocal and incontrovertible decision to reject the parental home. On an ideological level, the Zionist sons and daughters must have felt justified in leaving behind them the miserable situation of domination, suffering, and powerlessness. On a personal level, however, the departure must have created painful feelings of guilt and betrayal.

The discrepancy between the ideological and the personal highlights the difficulty in transforming the land into a homeland. The decision to leave the family home for Palestine must have been reached at an enormous emotional cost. To comprehend the traumatic aspect of this decision, one needs to empathize with the traumatic experience of the departure. The departure for Palestine signified leaving behind one's birthplace, way of life and, above all, close relatives, who were never safe from persecution and almost always destitute. The hate of the despotic rabbis, the ossified life of the shtetl, and even the liberation from anti-Semitic humiliation and persecution could hardly alleviate the pain of abandoning loved ones or, perhaps worse, the anticipation of their disappointment, anger, and condemnation. Recall that immigration to Palestine was considered an irreversible decision, that is, a definitive departure from the parental home. The Jews who were immigrating to America at the time of the first *aliyot* (immigrations) to Eretz Israel could console themselves and their relatives with the promise that they would "make it" and bring the family to the New World. In contrast, the *halutsim*—who upheld the socialist ideal by pledging to build kibbutzim in the desert of Palestine—could hardly entertain the hope of family reunification.

Thus, while the rejection of the parental home affirmed ideological convictions, the emotional longings for home must have been quite unbearable.

The extent of the trauma can be gauged in some of the seemingly purely ideological Zionist vocabulary. On one level these expressions sound like slogans and catchphrases championing biblical facets of the Zionist project. On another level they reflect the need to compensate for the loss of a parental home. Thus, the *haluts* was charged with the obligation of the *aliya* (ascension) rather than *hagira* (immigration) to Eretz Israel in order to engage in "g'ulat ha'aretz" (redemption/rescuing of the land). The desolate and abandoned "ima adama" (motherland) has waited for millennia for her children to return and engage in "khibush ha'adama" (the conquest or repossession of the land). This metaphoric vocabulary indicates that the land has assumed the two-tiered role of the mother, who needs to be rescued and restored from desolation, and the virgin-bride, who waits to be impregnated. It follows that the *haluts* has assumed the double role of son and husband, in other words, of both cultivator and guardian of the land. The Oedipal undertones of communion with the land present the latter as an object of desire and, at the same time, invest it with the qualities of family and home. Equally significant are the religious undertones of "avodat ha'adama," an expression that signifies both cultivation and worship of the land. This combination defined a new faith that bespoke mystical oneness with the land.[5] The religious tradition of the Diaspora was replaced with the sacred service of the land, one that the *haluts*, a dutiful son and a devoted lover, was obligated to perform.

The Zionist yearning for oneness with the land adds yet another dimension to the "empty land" discourse. As a replacement for the parental home in Europe, the motherland whose children have returned from exile can no longer recognize the Arabs, the native "sons of the land." The suppression of the Arab presence in the "empty" land, which had been waiting to be rescued by the "new" Hebrews, was a necessary a rationalization to explain the rejection of family and place of birth. The new home/land replaced the old home, while its "emptiness" and destitution supplied the sense of mission, which compensated for the betrayal and alleviated the longings. At the same time, the elimination of the "backward" Arab as a potential—Buber would say natural—partner in the modern development of the land was necessary to legitimize the Zionist claim to an equal standing among the European nations. As things turned out, however, the two-fold suppression—that of the parental home in the Diaspora and that of the Palestinian home in the land—ironically defeated the Zionist ideal of land-as-homeland. The politics of separatism entrapped the "new" Hebrews not only in endless political and military struggle but also in the psychological entanglement of ambivalence and self-doubt kept alive by the haunting voices of the suppressed discourses.

The suppressed or, rather, negated realities intervened in the Zionist relationship with the land and prevented a complete repossession. The denied voices come back in the literature of the land; they arise not only in stories of the "returning sons" but also in stories of the "sons of the land." The exploration of the land as a locus of suppression, fear, and guilt has become a prominent theme in Israeli Jewish and Israeli Arab literature. Both literatures have produced works of dissension that denounce the Zionist discourses of negation. The subsequent discussion in this volume focuses on fictions of both Jews and Arabs who restore and reaffirm the Arab presence or "visibility" in the land. My analysis of these literatures will demonstrate the inextricable bonding of Jews and Arabs in the land and the extent to which this bonding has shaped each other's identity.

This goal hardly meets the ideological objectives of the mainstream Zionist establishment, which continues to cultivate the discourses of negation. Hence, in order to appreciate the obstacles that both Jewish and Arab literary voices of dissent encounter in their search for rapprochement one first needs to investigate the attempts on the part of the establishment to silence these voices. The second part of this study examines the tactics the Zionist ideology of culture has employed to neutralize the literary voices of dissent by incorporating them into an Israeli Western weltanschauung.

PART 2

Dissenting Literatures and the Literary Canon

The dominant discourse produces an audience, context, and text in which the reigning political framework appears as "normality" itself: any other socio-political nuances of a text are rendered either imperceptible . . . or impossible to take seriously.

James H. Kavanagh, "Ideology"

In order to understand the historical circumstances determining the constitution of the literary canon . . . we must understand that the history of literature is not only a question of *what* we read but of *who* reads and *who* writes, and *in what circumstances;* it is also the question of what kinds . . . of texts are written, and for what audiences.

John Guillory, "Canon"

Introduction

Modern Hebrew Literature and Its Ideological Boundaries

In his discussion of the "cultural controversy" among the various Zionist camps on the threshold of the twentieth century, Avner Holtzman identifies three projections of Jewish culture in the future Jewish state. First was "cultural Zionism," whose most prominent leaders were Ahad Ha'Am and Berdyczewski. The considerable differences between them notwithstanding, both thinkers envisioned the Jewish settlement in Eretz Israel as the center of secular Hebrew national culture along the lines that the Jewish *maskilim* had developed in eastern Europe. Second was "political Zionism," which, as represented by Herzl, saw the cultural character of the future state as a reflection of western European culture. Third was "religious Zionism," which viewed the Jewish state as the complete fulfillment of the Torah commandments.

The debates among the camps—and especially within that of "cultural Zionism"—were for the most part fruitless because, as Holtzman tells us, the real problem lay in the "the absence of a body of literary texts . . . which would concretely shape the identity of the secular Hebrew culture." The controversy was resolved with the sudden efflorescence of Hebrew literature in Europe in the first decades of the twentieth century. Having produced such literary giants as Hayyim Nahman Bialik, Shaul Tchernichovski, and Yosef Chaim Brenner, this literature defined the nature of Hebrew culture as a combination of the national and the universal. Composed in Hebrew, it did not, according to Holtzman, "limit itself to the national issues and Jewish suffering, but opened itself to the beautiful and to the humane in the world at large," thus adopting the universalist values of an enlightened society. Holtzman concludes his essay with the realization that "this modern, profound, and rich literature constituted for both its writers and its readers the focus of secular Hebrew identity and laid the foundations for the future development of secular Hebrew culture."[1]

The emphasis on the modern and secular foundations of Hebrew literature illuminates the centrality of the European heritage in Israeli culture. In its secularization of the Hebrew language and its separation from rabbinic literature, the new literature followed the European weltanschauung and its modernist artistic trends. While the Hebrew language identified this literature as national, the central themes of individuality, alienation, and the modern world highlighted the impact of European culture and its humanistic universalist attitudes.

The nationalist Western orientation of Hebrew literature did not change when the center of Hebrew culture was transferred from Europe to Palestine. The culture of the Yishuv, and later of the state, has continued to define itself in terms of humanistic universalist values. At the same time, the growing cultural establishment maintained the exclusionary nationalist boundaries that promoted the Yishuv's ideology of separation. That is to say, by defining itself in terms of the West, Hebrew culture severed ties with its Jewish Diaspora heritage in Europe and dismissed the Arab tradition in the land.

Thus, Hebrew culture has shaped writers and readers, who have produced and received literature in a manner compatible with the Zionist telos to become like a Western nation. Perhaps most important, as the epigraphs to this chapter remind us, the self-definition of the Zionists as a European nation has determined the parameters of cultural "normality." These parameters determined the "constitution of the literary canon," which condoned either ignoring or appropriating and, in this sense, neutralizing anything that might disrupt the prevailing political norms of identification and conduct.

A specific example of contemporary literary production and its reception provides a convenient starting point for an exploration of the parameters of the Hebrew literary canon. In his volume of collected lectures A. B. Yehoshua makes an impassioned plea for moral literature. The book, significantly titled *The Terrible Power of a Minor Guilt,* urges fellow writers to "make an effort to represent and incorporate in our stories not only that which moves us and makes us marvel but also that which we consider good and bad." Yehoshua believes that literature plays an important role in society because it is "relevant to the moral conflicts among people" and "a source of spiritual authority."[2] According to Yehoshua, to engage in moral issues is incumbent upon the responsible writer.

Significant in this respect is the reaction of Ran Edelist, a reviewer of Yehoshua's book, who shifts from seemingly effusive praise of Yehoshua's exhortation as "perhaps the most moving appeal since Emile Zola entreated his friends to stand by Dreyfus" to a complete reversal:

It is completely beyond my comprehension how Yehoshua, a respected writer, is capable of conducting a learned discussion on the moral role of literature in a state in which there exist two official concepts of justice and discriminatory attitudes dividing Jews and Arabs. Since the establishment of the state, literature has had a great deal to say about this matter and has expressed itself quite clearly. Yet all this has not stopped Israeli society from sinking into the morass of the Israeli-Arab conflict. It is true that literature contributed, if only partially, to the *trahison des clercs,* and this fact accurately reveals the terrible power of the great body of Hebrew literature when compared with that of a small stone thrown by a Palestinian boy.[3]

This is a harsh criticism of the collusion of Israeli literature or, rather, of its writers in upholding the double standard of discriminatory politics of the state. The indictment of the Israeli writers' failure to act effectively in the name of justice, which the reviewer sees as a "trahison des clercs,"[4] illuminates the multiple layers of irony in his reference to Zola, which exposes the superficiality of the Israeli writers' identification with European values of equality, justice, and humanism. The weakness of their moral conviction sharply contrasts with that of the author of *J'accuse,* who enlisted literature and intellectuals in the struggle for an unjustly incriminated, victimized individual. This historical model exposes the hypocrisy of Yehoshua's call for a moralistic orientation in Israeli literature. More important, the reference to Zola also draws attention to the impotence of Israeli intellectuals vis-à-vis Israel's political establishment. Unlike Zola, who successfully challenged legal and social injustice in France, Israeli writers can claim no victories with regard to the consistent discrimination against its Arab citizens or the oppression of the Palestinians under Israeli occupation.

Zola's defense of Dreyfus, which became a cause célèbre and changed the history of France, had a major impact on the history of the Jews. In the background of this pivotal historical event looms the figure of another, lesser writer who, as a result of the Dreyfus trial (according to the widely accepted though anecdotal evidence) experienced an epiphany in terms of the Zionist solution to the Jewish problem.[5] I am, of course, referring to Herzl, author of *Der Judenstaat* and *Altneuland* and visionary of the Jewish state. Herzl's obsessive and total dedication to the Zionist idea, his determination to end Jewish oppression, and his ability to galvanize the Jewish people are common knowledge.

Mention should be made here of Max Likin's essay on Zola and Herzl. While these two historical figures differed on many counts, they shared a common belief in the ideals of equality and justice as well as a willingness to sacrifice their lives for these ideals. As Likin explains, "Both practiced a potent combination of *Gesinnungsethik* [ethic of conviction] and *Verantwortungsethik* [ethic of responsibility]. Both were obsessive in their conviction in the principle of Law . . . regardless of personal consequences."[6] The portrayal of Zola and Herzl as totally committed to the struggle against injustice and discrimination underscores the irony of Zionism's vacuous identification with the great humanistic values of the Enlightenment while at the same time practicing oppression. This irony is further enhanced by the fact that the Jewish state, which transgresses the values it claims to represent, was established thanks largely to unyielding and uncompromising defenders of human rights, such as a Zola and a Herzl.

Why has the moral protest of Israeli writers been ineffective vis-à-vis the ideological position of the state? As the epigraph by Kavanagh tells us, when a literary representation deviates from the "normal," it is either rendered "imperceptible" or "impossible to take seriously." The diffusion of dissension is activated through the institution of canonical reception. As we shall see, the canonical reception of Hebrew culture tends to neutralize the subversive literary writings under the rubric of Western modern and postmodern universalist trends. Furthermore, quite often the authors themselves, comfortably ensconced in their canonical status, blur the rebellious message of their art in their journalistic pronouncements and public appearances.

In the third part of this study I will demonstrate how, once liberated from the parameters of the canonical interpretation, the texts refuse to collude with the "reigning political framework," to recall Kavanagh, instead presenting a vision that opposes the ideological consensus. In the forthcoming discussion I demonstrate how the reading of the fiction of dissent through the prism of the reigning ideological framework co-opts it into the canon. I focus on the Jewish writers A. B. Yehoshua, Amos Oz, and David Grossman and on Israeli Arab writers Atallah Mansour, Emile Habiby, and Anton Shammas (who translated Habiby's fiction from the Arabic into the Hebrew), all of whom published their work in Hebrew. The discussion of Israeli Jewish literature suggests that the powerlessness of this literature derives not solely from the critical neutralization of the message in the text. The reasons for the ineffectiveness of the message should also be sought in the writers' "trahison des clercs," that is, in their collusion with the neutralizing, conformist tendencies of canonization. I next examine the challenges that face the cultural establishment as a result of the emergence of an Israeli-Arab fiction of dissent. This is followed by an investigation of the interpretive strategies involved in the integration of the Arab story into the canon of Hebrew literature.

4

Israeli Jewish Fiction of Dissent, Its Writers, and the Canon

Literature and Ideology: A Symbiotic Relationship

The lack of influence of Hebrew literature on the political scene can be ascribed neither to its lack of attention to the Israeli-Palestinian conflict nor to an absence of critical interest. In fact, numerous critical studies of the representation of the Arab in Hebrew literature have been published,[1] placing the potentially explosive works into the national literary canon. Here I have chosen to focus on a few such works: Amos Oz's tales "The Nomad and the Viper" (1964) and My Michael (1972), A. B. Yehoshua's "Facing the Forests" (1968) and The Lover (1978), and David Grossman's novel The Smile of the Lamb (1983). These works have gained critical recognition as landmarks in the history of Israeli fiction.[2]

These texts—which are deeply concerned with the history of the Palestinian Arabs, especially their defeat, dispossession, and unjust treatment—criticize harshly the discriminatory politics of the state. They denounce the notion of the "empty land" and the "invisibility" of the Arab; they reject the slogans "purity of weapons" of the Israeli army and of "humanitarian occupation"; and they disclose the brutal reality of Israeli victories. Furthermore, these works of fiction attempt to discredit the Zionist ethos, which is intent on demonizing the Arabs as implacable enemies of Israel and of the Jewish people generally. The writers undermine the negative view of the Arab and dispel the myth of the humane Jewish fighter.

As was mentioned earlier, a close comparative study of the Jewish and Arab texts in order to release them from their canonical interpretations occupies the third part of this study.[3] Here I wish to elucidate the strategies behind the canonical reception of Jewish Israeli fiction that demonstrates quite a radical attitude of dissent. Yehoshua's celebrated story "Facing the Forests" restores the Arab history in the land to the consciousness of the unsuspecting Israeli protagonist. The latter literally resurrects the history of the Arab defeat when he inadvertently discovers the ruins of an Arab village destroyed in the 1948 war, which remained concealed under a young, recently planted Israeli forest. In Yehoshua's famous novel *The Lover,* Naim, a young Arab boy, enters Israeli society and exposes its moral disintegration. By contrast, his growing indispensability to the Israeli Jewish family highlights the "absent presence" of the Arab laborers, who work for Jewish employers but otherwise remain invisible. Even though the novel ends in a renewed separation between the Jew and the Arab, it seems that the short experience of togetherness allowed each to gain an understanding of the vulnerability of the other. Oz's well-known story "Nomad and Viper" contains a trenchant criticism of Israeli society as represented by a kibbutz community in its encounter with a Bedouin tribe. The story reveals how the Israelis project their unresolved problem of insecurity upon the Arabs. One of the themes dwells on the sexual attraction of a female kibbutz member for an Arab. The fear and desire evoked by the strangers prove to be so threatening to the kibbutz that all appearances of civilization collapse, turning the kibbutz members into a horde of brutal victimizers. In Oz's famous novel *My Michael,* Hannah, the protagonist, dreams about her childhood Arab friends, who disappeared in the refugee camps during the 1948 war. Her explicitly sexual, sadomasochistic dreams and fantasies demonstrate the haunting psychological impact of the suppressed memory of the Arab upon the Israeli subconscious. Her husband and son, whose lives evolve "normally"—that is, in conformity with the Zionist ethos of the "new" Jew—remain completely unaware of the madness that looms under the surface of normalcy. *The Smile of the Lamb,* the novel that catapulted Grossman into the limelight of the Israeli cultural mainstream, deals with the occupied territories, showing how the moral corruption of Israel's ruthless domination destroyed every possibility of closeness between

Jews and Arabs. The theme of dispossession and humiliation of the Palestinian Arabs belies the official image of Israel's humanistic occupation. It is a story of betrayal and defeat of the values of humanism and empathy as represented by the protagonist, Uri.

Despite its bitterly critical attitude toward Israel's victimization and oppression of the Arab, this fiction entered the canon of Israeli literature. Moreover, despite the radicalness of their deviation from the then accepted ideological line, these works launched the three writers into Israel's cultural center and made them famous both within Israel and abroad. In Israel the work of Yehoshua, Oz, and Grossman was widely publicized and anthologized; their fiction was adapted into plays, films, and television dramas; and their new works invariably made the best-seller lists. Furthermore, despite their moral condemnation of Israel's military and political practices, these writings became an integral part of Hebrew literature curricula in high schools and in academia. The three writers also attained international fame. While Israeli literature in general remains confined to an Israeli Hebrew-reading audience, practically all fiction and collections of essays by Yehoshua, Oz, and Grossman have been translated into English as well as many other languages. Their work has been critically acclaimed all over the world, especially in Europe and the United States. Besides garnering numerous national and international honors and prizes, two of these writers (Yehoshua and Oz) received Israel's most prestigious award, the Israel Prize for literature. Grossman is undoubtedly a prospective recipient of the award.[4]

The canonical status of this literature raises questions not only because of its antagonistic position toward the dominant ideology. Canonization of dissidents is, after all, quite a common phenomenon; one need only recall such famous examples as Salman Rushdie, Aleksandr Solzhenitsyn, and Milan Kundera, who defied the ideologies of their countries. Their courageous dissension turned them into standard bearers of freedom, elevated them to the status of celebrities, and canonized their writings in the free world, *away from* their countries of origin, which repudiated them. One need only to remember the death sentence meted out to Rushdie by Moslem orthodoxy. In contrast, Yehoshua, Oz, and Grossman have gained canonical legitimacy *from* the cultural establishment that was founded upon the ideological orientation they defied.

The canonical acceptance of dissent draws attention to the indelible interrelationship of the artists, their art, and the ideology in the reality of the Zionist state. The cultural mainstream's response reflects the impossibility of distinguishing between the Hebrew work of fiction, however dissenting it may be, and the Zionist idea from which this fiction has emerged. This interconnection has been determined by the Zionist revival of the Hebrew language, or, more precisely, by the Zionist ethos of the Hebrew cultural revival. In other words, by virtue of writing in Hebrew, the Israeli Jewish writer has been indelibly shaped by the dominant ideology. As was previously mentioned, the idea of secular Hebrew culture has become one of the imperatives of the "Jewish revolution," with the revival of the Hebrew language its centerpiece, a sine qua non to the Jewish national revival in Eretz Israel.[5] In his discussion of the ideological cornerstones of the Zionist enterprise, the historian Yosef Gorni reaffirms the notion of "the renaissance of the Hebrew language and culture as the precondition both for the national revival of the people in its historical land and as a means to create a common denominator for the Jewish dispersion that will return to the land in the future."[6]

The emergence of Israeli Jewish literature therefore attests to the success of the "Jewish revolution"; the literature affirms the birth of Israeli culture. At the same time, the claim that Israeli literature owes its language and subject matter to the Zionist project of national revival is by no means hyperbole. Thematically this literature, written exclusively in Hebrew, predominantly focuses on the reality of the Zionist state. In this sense Zionist ideology and Hebrew literature are symbiotically interconnected.[7] The literary representations of the Arab in the above-mentioned texts highlight the ironic and quite paradoxical aspect of this indelible connection. Although by virtue of its dissent the fiction defies the Zionist ideology of exclusion— achieved, to a large extent, by the emergence of Hebrew culture in Eretz Israel—the Zionist mainstream endorses this dissenting fiction, sanctioning it by endowing it with canonical status. Why would the establishment claim canonical status for a literature so critical of the Zionist revolution? How does the establishment justify the canonical status of this fiction?

To pursue and explore these questions, a starting point would be Fredric Jameson's comment that "we never really confront a text

immediately, in all its freshness as a thing-in-itself." The reception
of the text is informed by "inherited interpretive traditions" that
allow the critics to rewrite the text "in terms of a particular interpretive master code" to which they subscribe. The identification of the
master code leads to the study of "metacommentary," that is, an examination of the underlying codes that inform the interpretation itself. This focus on the codes of interpretation discloses the "political
unconscious" imposed on the text by "sedimented layers of previous
interpretations."[8] In Jameson's view, the meaning of the text arises,
so to speak, from under its interpretations, which are informed by
deeply integrated traditions and tendencies. This premise leads to an
exploration of the interpretive "master code" that enabled the Zionist cultural establishment to canonize these dissenting texts.

To understand the canonical status of a body of fiction that denounces the Zionist politics of exclusion, dispossession, and victimization of the Arab population, it might be helpful to look for a comparable example of canonized dissenting fiction. The canonical status
conferred upon the novels of J. M. Coetzee, the celebrated white
South African writer who wrote against the ideology and practice of
apartheid, provides an edifying example. In his discussion of Coetzee's privileged mainstream status, Derek Attridge lists the literary
properties of the text that facilitate canonical acceptance. Attridge
identifies intertextual references to masterpieces, a meticulous literary
style that parallels that of great works of literature, and universal
thematic interest as factors that appeal to a general readership. These
factors outweigh the dissenting component by claiming that the text's
aesthetic and narrative pedigree belongs in the tradition of canonical
masterworks. As great works of literary art, Coetzee's novels "appear
to locate themselves in an established literary culture." The association with the majority culture fulfills the requirements of the canon
because the latter is "complicit with a mode of literature—and of
criticism—that dehistoricizes and dematerializes the acts of writing
and reading while promoting a myth of transcendent human truths
and values."[9] Attridge seems to discern the "master code" of canonizing interpretation in the tendency of the critical establishment to universalize literary texts by taking them out of their historical context.
In other words, the code of canonizing interpretation lies in investi-
gating the text as a representation of general and ahistorical issues

rather than as a representation of issues particular to a specific historical situation. As we shall see, this observation is quite illuminating in terms of the reception of Israeli fiction of dissent.

Attridge recognizes that besides text-based reasons for canonical reception there exist "factors external to the writing [that] also bear on the question of canonization." What facilitates the acceptance of this subversive literature by the establishment is the fact that "as a white male Coetzee has a degree of privileged access to most canons."[10] Stated differently, the canonical reception of the South African writer is largely determined by his social status. The racial superiority that the writer shares with the establishment—as well as his gender—motivates the critical interpretation that defuses his dissident, anti-apartheid message and keeps the dissenter within the communal fold.

Although the nature of Israeli literary dissidence is different from the South African case,[11] Attridge's identification of the external social factors involved in the process of canonization points to an important similarity. Coetzee's superior status as a facilitator of his canonization parallels the Israeli writers' social standing as a factor in the process of their reception. It seems reasonable to suggest that in the case of Israeli literature of dissent, the common ethnic roots and ideological premises that the writers share with the establishment facilitated, to a considerable extent, their canonical acceptance; the same factors of ethnic and ideological commonality explain the writers' acquiescence to the canonical reading of their works. Thus, in both cases of critics and writers, the ethnic, that is, Jewish singularity of Israeli Hebrew literature born in the Zionist state, has elicited a response, grounded in "tribal" solidarity that predetermined the reading of the text. The critics read the dissenting authors, first and foremost, as individuals who share with them the identity of Israeli Jewish Zionists.[12] As we shall see, this "master code" of collective identity also impelled the writers-especially in terms of their political pronouncements—to seek strategies that would mitigate the radically critical exposure of Israeli politics in their literary writings.

The notion of mitigation is crucial since, if taken literally, the dissent in this fiction presents a serious threat to Zionist national identity. As I have shown, the national identity of the "new" Jew was largely shaped by the perception of the land as "empty" and by the radical severance from the Diaspora past. The notion of the "empty land" was central to the Zionist project of building a state like all other Western states; an acknowledgment of the presence of the Arabs and their culture would have identified the Yishuv with the Orient rather than with the West. At the same time, the myth of the land waiting to be rescued after two thousand years of desolation provided the rationalization for the ruthless repudiation of the parental home in the Diaspora as well as the rejection of a two-thousand-year-old heritage.

The literature of dissent infuses the visibility of the Arab into the Israeli consciousness and exposes not only the deceit of the "empty land" but also the injustice committed to perpetuate this deceit. In this sense, this literature undermines the Zionist revolution, which affirmed its raison d'être in the politics of separatism and exclusion, that is, away from both the European Diaspora and the Palestinian Arab culture. At the same time, by claiming the visibility, and therefore the inclusion, of the Arab, this literature—a product of the Zionist revolution founded upon the tenet of exclusion—undermines its own raison d'être. Ironically, in order to preserve the Zionist idea, which upholds the viability of Israeli literature, the dissenting story must be "rescued" from itself, that is, from its self-destructive propensities.

In large measure the Israeli codes of canonizing interpretation illustrate the factors listed by Attridge in connection with the canonization of Coetzee, especially those of dehistorization and universalization of dissension. In general, the Israeli establishment critics interpreted the dissenting text as a metonymic representation of an idea or a situation that transcends the particular Israeli circumstances. Thus, the land, as depicted in the texts, is perceived as a representation of an abstract, unidentifiable locale rather than a particular geographic locus, while the representations of Israeli reality are seen as explorations of the universal human condition in the spirit of Western philosophical trends. The dissension from the Zionist ideology is attributed to the writer's subscription to the pessimism of a Western weltanschauung, which focuses on the moral collapse of the modern (and postmodern) postwar world.

The following "metacommentary" on the tactics of canonization discerns a two-tiered interpretive code. In one sense, in order to protect the myth of the "empty land" and the discriminatory practices that it implies, the code dislocates the specificity of place to the unspecified spaces of humanism at large. In another sense, the interpretation of the narrative as an expression of universal angst dehistoricizes the suffering of the Arab, thereby turning him into a symbol of eternal Jewish-like victimhood.

The Reception of Dissent and the Unconscious Politics of the Canon

In a review entitled "Portrait of a Historian of Literature as a Creator of Reality" Ziva Shamir, a professor of Hebrew literature, pays tribute to Gershon Shaked, an eminent scholar of Hebrew literature, for his "monumental accomplishment" as *the* historian of Hebrew literature. In the final volume of Shaked's massive project most of the writers discussed belong to the "new wave," a term that the critic clearly "borrowed" from the *nouvelle vague* of the French cinema in the 1960s. The "new wave" writers, among them Yehoshua and Oz, started writing in the 1960s and 1970s under the influence of French existentialism. Shamir notes that Shaked was "the first to receive their writing, illuminate their work through (always constructive!) interpretation, *shape public opinion,* and spread their fame beyond their immediate, local circle." She goes on to affirm that Shaked's criticism "followed the output of these writers, opened doors for their writing *out of a sense of identification,* and to a considerable extent helped to *create the reality described in the novel.*"[13]

This exuberant unreserved, and uncritical profile of Shaked presents him as an establishment literary critic. One might say that Shamir's portrait of Shaked is that of a literary historian who so to speak "established the literary establishment" in that he single-handedly shaped the canonical parameters of Israeli literature. In the case of "new wave" writers in particular, Shaked's accomplishment, according to Shamir, lies in his harmonious collaboration, "*out of a sense of identification,*" with the writer, with the text, and—most significantly for the present discussion of the canon—with the audience. The notion of "identification" signals both solidarity with and approval of communal uniformity. The "sense of identification" requires that the critic "*shape public opinion*" by approximating the perspective in the text to the reader's ideological outlook. This function of the critic as the creator of the canon establishes *him or her* as a canonical fixture in the field of Hebrew letters. In his canonical capacity, Shaked becomes a metaphoric father figure who *"created the reality described in the novel."* The implication is that, in terms of its meaning and message, the novel was, in a sense, begotten by the critic's interpretation. The critic molded—perhaps even *created*—the world of the novel in a form acceptable to the communal ideological outlook; through his interpretation he established the canonical position of the "new wave" fiction. Through his ideological perception, which reflects the consensus, Shaked reaffirmed and consolidated the orientation of mainstream cultural reality.

A consideration of Shaked's codes of interpretation elucidates canonization as defusion of literary dissension. Yehoshua and Oz are probably the best-known writers of the "new wave." According to Shaked, Grossman, who began publishing in the early 1980s, continues the tradition as a "legitimate heir" to the "new wave." Shaked postulates that the writers of the "new wave" (especially Yehoshua and Oz) "saw themselves as prophets to the House of Israel in their fiction as well as in their extraliterary activities."[14] The critic, however, does not seem to concur with what he sees as the writers' claim to prophetic vision. Rather, the rhetoric of Shaked's interpretation implies a sense of threat that needs to be defused. He unhappily acknowledges that, like Yehoshua in "Facing the Forests," Oz in *My Michael* "does not take for granted the fundamental values of the 'Zionist platform' and doubts their indestructibility." Shaked's desire to rationalize and deflect the transgression of the writers can be detected in the images he uses to depict their "bizarre attraction to the foreign force which preys on the 'citadels of culture.'"[15]

Shaked nonetheless resolutely avoids an acknowledgment of the writers' dissension from the Zionist idea. He hastens to reassure the reader that it is not the Zionist enterprise that is under attack in the "new wave" literature: "I emphatically repeat: The roots of the problem are not in the [Zionist] subject matter but rather in the world picture . . . that projects its values on the [Zionist] reality that represents it."[16] As Shaked sees it, Zionist reality has been used as an allegorical representation of the general sense of uncertainty, anxiety, and doubt about modern life. Serving as the "material" for this pessimistic orientation, Zionist existence has been painted in dark, bleak colors. Shaked seems to attribute this literary ideologically unsettling weltanschauung mainly to the weltschmerz of the writers.

While the universal issues of present-day reality of the world at large seem to provide one avenue to evade the specific politicohistorical questions that this fiction raises, the psychological argument is another way to avoid the deviations from the common ideological path. Shaked classifies *My Michael* as a "psychological" rather than a "social" novel. While he concedes that the Arab twins in the protagonist's dreams are portrayed as terrorist fighters, he sees them as no more than a figment of a neurotic woman's imagination.[17] It is interesting to note in passing that a similar universalizing view of the representation of the Arab is in Menahem Perry, who sees the treatment of the Arab in the literature of the 1960s as "a *metaphor* of his [the Jewish character's] unconscious" and the treatment of the conflict as "a psychological one [that] leads to its 'universalization.'"[18]

Sometimes it seems as if Shaked's evasive psychologizing has reached a dead end and can no longer effectively fend off the specific moral issues of oppression and victimization. At such moments one hopes that the critic will finally confront the problem of dissenting literature and its impact on the establishment. Occasionally Shaked seems about to do so, only to evade the inescapable conclusion at a crucial moment. Thus, he admits that in "Facing the Forests" and in *The Lover* Yehoshua goes as far as questioning the "legitimacy of Zionist existence." In "Facing the Forests," Shaked tells us, "the poignant question is who has the right to this land?"[19] Having identified the explosive message in the story, however, Shaked resorts to the argument of the aesthetic, claiming that "a story is not merely a political experience; it is first and foremost a story, and its fictional quality is certainly more important than all its political and nonpolitical messages."[20]

In view of the centrality of the "empty land" in the Zionist project, it is not difficult to see the rationale for Shaked's evasive rhetoric. An inquiry into the right to the land would have called into question the ideological "master code" of the Jewish unequivocal right to the land. Such an inquiry would also have submitted for investigation the recurring motif of the paralyzing effect of the repressed trauma of victory on the Israeli protagonist, which is central to my discussion of dissent in Israeli Jewish fiction in the third part of this study. Instead, the ineffectuality of the "new" Jew in the "new wave" literature is ascribed to the universal sense of *malaise*.

In order to sidestep these risky investigative paths, Shaked offers a sweeping universalization of the issue by contending that "Yehoshua does not deal with real connections between Jews and Arabs but rather with a fundamental myth that explains, in a paradoxical manner, the Jewish existence in the land."[21] It is, however, Shaked's rationalization for the victimization of the Arabs that seems most paradoxical, if not downright cynical. His interpretation draws upon an identification of Arabs and Jews in that it erases the distinctions between oppressors and oppressed, characterizing both as victims of history. This reading of the texts leads the critic to the conclusion that "the Jews, who, from being the persecuted turned into persecutors, have been persecuted by their [guilt] complex, while the persecuted Arab has turned into a Jew in his actions and his mentality. . . . The position of the Arab as a minority among the Jews transformed the Arab stranger into the likeness of a Jew, but the Jew has not disappeared. . . . Both Jews and Arabs are persecuted—and history is the persecutor."[22]

As Shaked sees it, the Arab is "guilty" of having turned the Jews into the victims of their guilt vis-à-vis the Arab, whereas the identity of the oppressed turns the Arab into yet another victimized Jew. In essence, Shaked would like us to believe that the suffering of both sides was predetermined by history, and that history is therefore to be blamed for the injustice that has been committed. This disingenuous argument illustrates the lengths to which the establishment critic may go to defuse the antiestablishment message in the text. The fallacy that erases the distinction between victim and victimizer eliminates the issue of blame and facilitates the abstraction of dissent. The interpretation of the works of fiction thus creates a fictional narrative of its own, or, to recall Shamir, "creates the reality in the novel." As presented by the establishment critic, this reality in the novel neutralizes Israel's moral responsibility toward the defeated Arab population, thus perpetuating the myth of the "empty land," which is now justified under the rubric of the universal myth. In his monumental history of Hebrew literature, Shaked ushered the writer, the critic, and the reader into the equanimity of the canon.

Other Israeli scholars followed in Shaked's footsteps. A case in point is the interpretive perspective of Nurith Gertz, a noted scholar of Israeli literature. Having by and large adopted Shaked's historical periodization of Israeli literature,[23] Gertz agrees that the literature of the 1960s and the 1970s was mainly the product of left-wing writers, such as Yehoshua and Oz. As she sees it, "from French literature, from Kafka's works, and from Sartre" the Israeli writers adopted the specific perspective of death, war, social alienation, and estrangement from nature. Existentialist motifs echo in Israel's growing sense of doom, induced by the constant threat of war and further exacerbated by the "haunting memories of the Holocaust." According to Gertz, the fear of entrapment in "a strange land, surrounded by enemies, a land which is ready to expel us" created an apocalyptic literature focused on war and death.[24] From the perspective of existential doom, Israel is metonymous for the general *malaise* of the modern world. The prevalent motifs of anticipated disaster as redemption from the meaningless existence of the modern man in both Yehoshua and Oz reflect the trend of the absurd in Western literature and drama.

How does Gertz interpret the representations of the Arab in these existentialist works of alienation and despair? As she sees it, modernist Israeli writers as a rule lack the ability to represent the Arab as a *bona fide* character, that is, a fully-fledged, believable figure. Rather, the literary representations of the Arab served a different purpose, mainly as refractions of Israeli Jewish psyche. In this literature, as Gertz sees it, the positive representations of the Arab signified the "metaphor of the freedom and of the organic connections with the land that the Jew had been dreaming about," whereas negative characterizations of the Arab figure should be seen as "projections of the suppressed instincts of aggression and destruction of the Jew."[25] In this respect Gertz seems to concur with Shaked, who sees representations of the Arab in terms of the Jewish character's psychological problems; one recalls how he views the Arab twins in *My Michael* as figments of Hannah's psychotic imagination. In a similar way, Gertz sees the characters of the Arabs as refractions of Israeli Jewish existential ambivalence in terms of their hopes, fears, and anxieties.

According to Gertz, the postmodern era has not produced believable Arab characters either; an authentic Arab protagonist has yet to emerge. At the same time, postmodern writing is determined to dismantle both Arab and Jewish identities. Gertz identifies such a tendency in Grossman's novel *The Smile of the Lamb*. Here the writer "dissolves completely both Jewish and Arab qualities and demolishes the categories that characterize both societies." The novel opens itself up "to a rich pluralism of creeds and perceptions, and thus presents a position different from that which has excluded the foreign and the other from the Jewish collective." Nevertheless, the erasure of differences has not empowered the literature as a political message. On the contrary the critic claims that, "this openness dissolves all creeds and perspectives and calls into question the positions of the novel itself."[26] According to Gertz's reading, Grossman's novel neutralizes and relativizes itself by deconstructing all viewpoints, including its own.

Despite the similarities these two critics share, it is interesting to note the differing "codes" (to recall Jameson) that inform their interpretive readings. Where Shaked discerns a threat to Zionist domination, Gertz seems to dismiss the possibility of political subversion. For instance, Shaked's evasion of the explosive issue of the claim to the land implies the critic's anxious awareness of the subversive potential of this literature. Thus, Shaked adopts the code of the universal meaning of literature to evade the question of the right to the land that repeatedly arises in this literature. By contrast, Gertz sees the failure to create plausible Arab characters as a sign that the writers themselves wish to evade the political issues that underscore Israeli injustice toward the Arabs. Gertz seems quite certain that the writers' deep identification with Western trends invests their writing with very little subversive power. It is possible to argue that, according to Gertz, Israeli literature does not present any danger to the Zionist idea since it *depoliticizes itself*, either through adherence to Western existentialism or through its adoption of a Western postmodern orientation. By contrast, Shaked's interpretation "creates a reality" that *depoliticizes the message* of this literature, which seems to threaten the fundamental Zionist tenet of the right to the land. While their interpretive approaches differ, they coalesce in the "metacommentary" of the intention to neutralize or dismiss the dissent.

In different ways both critics shy away from an interpretation that would recognize an attitude of dissent, thereby challenging the Zionist claim to the land. That is why the critical approach that

evades the issue of dissent by canonizing the work not only neutralizes the potentially dangerous message but turns the writers into cultural icons of the ideologically conformist mainstream. With its dissent abstracted, this literature ironically bears testimony to Israel's
democracy and freedom of speech, thus claiming its place among
Western literatures.

Turning to the writers themselves, one notes their acceptance of
the canonical position. As Attridge tells us, "every writer who desires
to be read . . . has to seek admittance to the canon. . . . Awareness
of this necessity, conscious or not, governs the act of writing. . . .
[T]he same imperative drives our self-presentations and representations; unless we are read, we are nothing."[27] As the large number of
their nonfictional publications shows, Yehoshua, Oz, and Grossman
wish to be read not only as fiction writers but also as intellectuals
engaged in current public affairs and political matters. All three make
frequent public appearances and often have their essays and articles
published in newspapers and magazines. As the succeeding discussion
demonstrates, it is especially in their journalistic commentaries, essays, and other nonfictional writings where the collusion of the dissenting writers with the canonizing establishment becomes quite obvious. Ironically, their identity as "new" Jews, products of the Zionist
project, allows the writers to define themselves as left-wing dissenters
and, at the same time, remain Zionists in good standing.

The Liberal Left-wing Zionist as a Canonical Writer

The preceding discussion of canonical reception raises the question of the political intention of the writers. Are they in agreement
with the depoliticizing interpretation of their literary work? Do they
accept their canonical stature, which neutralizes their dissenting message? As I have already noted, it would appear that none of the writers have objected to this type of reception, which not only ensures
them publicity and a comfortable lifestyle[28] but also identifies them
as left-wing liberal Zionists.[29]

The identification of the writers as left-wing Zionists presents a
difficulty. The conflation of "left-wing" and "Zionists" is intended
to reconcile contradictory ideological positions. It indicates, on the
one hand, a left-wing subscription to the universal values of equality,

justice, and freedom and, on the other, adherence to the Zionist ideology, which, as I explained in the first part of this study, has violated these values in the name of national interests. One sees how the definition prescribes a precarious balance between human rights and national needs. Yehoshua, Oz, and Grossman, among others, have attempted to fulfill both roles, namely, defenders of human rights and loyal Zionists. They have established themselves as left-wing proponents of the resolution of the Israeli-Palestinian conflict. They tirelessly speak about the Palestinian right of self-determination in a Palestinian state. At the same time, they have invariably affirmed Israel's right to exist and expressed the absolute need for the Palestinian people to acknowledge this right. This evenhanded approach has allowed the writers to be identified as liberal left-wing advocates of the oppressed as well as Zionists committed to the existence of the Jewish state.

In their nonfictional pronouncements these writers have made a considerable effort to maintain this balance. In 1987 Grossman published a journalistic report entitled *The Yellow Wind on the West Bank*. As the author states in his introduction, his purpose is to strengthen Israel's spirit in order "to bring the occupation to an end and arrive at what seems to me to be the only possible solution—a Palestinian state alongside Israel." At the same time, the author insists that "the Palestinians also need maturity and strong leadership to enable them to face up to things as they are and understand that a realistic settlement requires compromise and the surrender of absolutist aspirations."[30]

Oz's well-known motto "the clash of right and right" aptly communicates the intention of the left-wing writers to remain unbiased. In general, Oz claims that each side in the Israeli-Palestinian conflict has an equally strong case. Nonetheless, in "A Letter to a Palestinian Friend," published in a major Israeli daily in 1996, Oz presents a more complex view of the evolving situation. At first he seems quite objective when he tells his "Palestinian friend" that "the core of the Oslo accord is simple and clear: We will cease ruling and oppressing you, and you will recognize Israel and stop killing us." Then he tips the scales by claiming that the implementation of the agreement has been unilateral: "So far, Israel has removed its rule of oppression from over eighty-five percent of the residents of the occupied territories, whereas you have not stopped killing us." In view of the well-known fact that both sides violated the agreement, Oz's argument seems spurious and disingenuous. In a further indictment of what he perceives as asymmetrical relations, Oz poses a series of rhetorical questions that communicate Israel's undeniable moral superiority over its Palestinian adversaries: "Where is your peace movement? Where are your spiritual leaders and the forgers of public opinion? Where are your teachers of religion and poets? Where is your denunciation of the murderers and their supporters? Where is the Palestinian Israel Kings Square of 'Peace Now'?"[31]

Yehoshua sees the establishment of the Palestinian state as only a matter of time—practically a fait accompli—but only based on certain conditions. In an article written on the occasion of the fiftieth anniversary of the state, he claimed that "we [Israel] should demand that the Palestinians apply a similar law [the Law of Return] to their state when it is established," and thus resolve the refugee problem. The Palestinian state "would be responsible for resolving the problem of the Palestinian people on its own, within its own territory." In fact, Yehoshua claimed that the Palestinian state should copy the Jewish state. As Yehoshua sees it, the Israeli model will resolve not only the problem of Palestinian refugees of 1948 but also the national predicament of the Israeli Arab minority. Israeli Arabs will be given "cultural autonomy" in the State of Israel, but their national needs will be satisfied in the context of the Palestinian state. According to Yehoshua, "the *correct balance* could [then] be struck between the rights of the Arab minority and Israel's identity as a Jewish nation-state."[32]

These examples present a profile of the writers' ideological identifications. Despite obvious correspondences among the three—especially in terms of their public image as left-wing intellectuals—a closer look reveals a wide spectrum of ideological positions. While Grossman emphasizes the suffering of the oppressed, Yehoshua focuses on Israel's national interests. The "*correct balance* of rights," as Yehoshua sees it, has different connotations than the balance grounded in moral actions urged by Grossman. Grossman is deeply indebted to the existentialist ethics of accountability.[33] Despite its author's attempts to remain impartial and hopeful, *The Yellow Wind* presents a pessimistic view of human nature. Grossman concludes his travelogue in the West Bank with a reference to Camus's concept of moral acts as an indicator of humaneness. Feeling implicated in im-moral acts of occupation, Grossman wonders precisely "how many times during the last twenty years I had been worthy of being called human and how many people among the millions participating in this drama are worthy of it."[34] An adherent of the existentialist code of ethics, Grossman feels guilty for not fulfilling his moral responsibil-ities toward the wronged Arab. In contrast to Grossman, who blames himself for compromising his humanity in the situation of oppres-sion, Oz proclaims his faith in the ideals of humanism and finds the opponent guilty in not living up to these ideals. As we have seen in the above-quoted letter, Oz blames the Palestinians for enmity to-ward the peace-loving Jews, a situation that precludes friendship and reconciliation. Whereas the Israelis have practiced honesty and justice in the interest of peace, the Palestinians have failed to understand the notion of moral obligation.

Though their assessments of the situation differ, both Grossman and Oz posit the code of ethics and justice as the cornerstone of future relations between Israelis and Palestinians. Both writers see the solu-tion to the conflict in terms of a political separation of the two nations and in coexistence based on mutual respect and recognition of human and national rights. It is quite obvious that both Grossman and Oz realize that the solution of the conflict is possible only through a rec-onciliation of the ideals of universal humanism with Israel's particu-lar national interests.

Yehoshua's vision of the Palestinian state as a national home for Israeli Arab citizens presents a different position. His plan downplays the importance of impartial moral values while promoting the na-tional interests of the Jewish state. One should note in passing that Yehoshua's "plan" for Israeli Arabs reconfirms Edelist's critical re-view of Yehoshua's study *The Terrible Power of a Minor Guilt,* where, as I have already noted, the writer admonishes his fellow writ-ers to promote moral values in their writings. Yehoshua's "trahison des clercs" emerges even more prominently in his disingenuous claim that Israel's existence was legitimized by the U.N. Charter on the premise that it would become a political haven for all Jews. In reality, the charter was emphatic that the partition plan was *by no means* intended as a home for all Jews. The charter clearly stated that under no circumstances would the Jewish settlement in Palestine become the place for all Jews in dispersion, nor would it become the solution for the Jewish refugee problem as a result of the war.[35] In light of his misreading of the charter, the correspondence that Yehoshua draws between the Jewish state as a solution to all Jews and the Palestinian state as a solution to all Palestinians is fallacious.

An even more serious problem arises from the designation of the Palestinian state as the locus of Israeli Arab national identification. Such a designation clearly intends to void the citizenship of the Israeli Arab of its political and cultural content. In this sense Yehoshua's plan raises questions as to the writer's true motivation in supporting the Palestinian state. Is it really the compensation for the suffering that Israel caused to the Palestinian people that he has at heart? If followed consistently, Yehoshua's vision for the Palestinian state would allow Israel to maintain the politics of Israeli Arab invisibility and segregation, which, in turn, would ensure the monolithic Jewish national identity of Israel. The voice of the Arab national minority would be silenced, whereas the "cultural autonomy" of the Arab minority would bar the Israeli Arabs from participation in Hebrew culture. It is clear that Yehoshua's vision of the future does not see Arab citizens as equal partners/citizens in the State of Israel.

It is, I believe, only fair to note that, contrary to Yehoshua's attempts to actualize the old Zionist dream of the "empty land," another voice of a different tenor and intentions also exists. In his second journalistic account, which focuses on the Israeli Arabs, Grossman engages in a courageous act of soul-searching: "How could I not have ever exposed myself, until now, to the tangle of emotions and anguish of the Arab who wishes to be part of the Israeli reality yet finds himself endlessly rejected, suspected, detested?" Grossman admits that his Zionist upbringing, which "abstracted" the Arab, occluded the possibility of an honest and sincere encounter. Grossman wishes to rid himself of misconceptions and stereotypes and promote Jewish-Arab togetherness in Israel "in the framework of a single general civil identity."[36]

Grossman's indication of the Israeli Arabs' desire to live in Israel is reaffirmed by their clearly expressed reluctance to see their future in the Palestinian state. In fact, while not rejecting their ties with the Palestinian people, Israeli Arabs have been increasingly vocal about equal participation in Israel's state affairs.[37] A case in point is Oz's

1983 interview with Atallah Najar, an Israeli Arab intellectual, a graduate of the Hebrew University, and a senior reporter at an Arab newspaper. In response to the question as to whether he would move to a Palestinian state, Najar answered decisively, "No way. I am an Israeli. It's a matter of a sense of identity. Even though I am discriminated against in Israel, a third-class citizen, I consider myself absolutely Israeli, and I will remain Israeli." He went on to explain that his sense of Israeli identity stemmed from "education, experience, friendships with Jews [and] from [my] attachment to the Israeli life style." Najar responded to the hypothetical question as to whether he would prefer serving as the Israeli ambassador to Palestine or as the Palestinian ambassador to Israel, "I'm an Israeli, can't help it . . . I'd choose to be the Israeli ambassador."[38]

Najar's response is by no means an isolated voice of Israeli Arab identification with Israel. The same attitude has been expressed in more recent interviews. For instance, Muhammad Ali Taha, an Israeli Arab educator and writer, defines his sense of belonging in the same way: "Even if there is a Palestinian state I will stay here. This is my home. . . . I have something that belongs to the Galilee, to Haifa more than Gaza."[39] Salem Jubran, a graduate of Haifa University and a codirector of the Center for Arabic Studies at the Givat Haviva Institute, declares, "I am influenced by [Israeli culture] and I influence it. I am an Israeli citizen. I am a Palestinian Arab, but I am an Israeli citizen for good or bad." Jubran leaves no doubt that "if an Arab state is to be established, I will live in my homeland and on my land. . . . I am in love with this land, with the scenery of the Galilee."[40]

It is doubtful whether the declarations of affinity with Israeli culture would be welcomed by Yehoshua, who sees an enormous threat in the Israeli Arabs' contributions to Israel's culture. In a revealing interview with Bernard Horn, Yehoshua openly expresses his anxiety about the fact that "for the first time in Jewish history, a minority is penetrating deep into our culture." He observes that Israeli Arabs undertake the study of "Bible and Hebrew language and Hebrew literature, and they are starting to reveal our secrets." In particular, Yehoshua finds it "very embarrassing" that they speak "really perfect Hebrew."[41] Note once again the contrast between Yehoshua and Grossman. In *Sleeping on a Wire* Grossman observes with great satisfaction the fact that "the everyday conversation of Palestinian Israelis sparkles with expressions from the Bible and the Talmud, from Bialik and Rabbi Yehuda Halevy and Agnon." Consistent with his liberal, humanistic orientation of pluralistic inclusion, Grossman applauds the Arab minority's proficiency in Hebrew and notes approvingly the fact that "the Arabs and Jews in Israel have a common language, with all it implies,"[42] Whereas Grossman is impressed by the Arab immersion in Hebrew culture, Yehoshua feels threatened by this trend toward integration, especially by the Arabs' knowledge of Hebrew.

More recently Yehoshua must once again have felt threatened and embarrassed, this time by the publication of Ibrahim Taha's Hebrew study *The Smile of an Opsimistic Lover,* a literary interpretation of Israeli and Palestinian novels. The back cover states that Ibrahim Taha lectures at the University of Haifa and that "he is considered a prominent literary critic among those who emerged from the Arab minority in Israel."[43] Incidentally, Taha's title conflates the titles of both Jewish and Arab novels: Grossman's *Smile of the Lamb,* Habiby's *Pessoptimist,* and Yehoshua's *Lover.*

It is therefore somewhat ironic—and perhaps disappointing—that Taha's interpretation is strictly confined to the aesthetic properties of the Hebrew and Palestinian texts. This is particularly puzzling in view of the fact that Taha analyses the literary strategies in the texts in terms of reception. His discussion of reception ignores the reader's response to the political aspect of the texts. Yet Taha studiously avoids the discussion of this literature's central theme of relationships between Arabs and Jews. In fact, he avoids the political and ethical aspects of this theme altogether, an omission that, recalling Jameson, reveals the "master code" of the suppressed minority voice.

Thus, in the particular case of Yehoshua's novel *The Lover* Taha reaches the conclusion that the indeterminacy of the text creates "a bizarre textual reality which does not conform adequately and convincingly to the extra-textual reality." Yet he never specifies the non-conformity to which he refers. Instead, he claims that the literary strategies and the allegorical ambivalence of the novel both delight readers and invite them to construct their own meaning of the text. It is thus of interest to note Taha's own construction of meaning with regard to Naim, the young Arab protagonist in Yehoshua's novel. The characterization of the young Arab boy reflects the disorientation of the Israeli Arab, who moves between the worlds of the Jewish city and his Arab village and becomes extremely ambivalent about his identity. In a statement that sums up his very brief discussion of this ambivalence, Taha notes the failed attempt of Adam, the Israeli Jewish protagonist, to resolve Naim's identity split. "Such an attempt," Taha tells us, "must fail, because it intentionally disregards the fact that contradictions and paradoxes are part of life and that sometimes we have to accept them and live with them."[44] Significantly, in terms of the "master code" of suppression that supports this interpretation, the unavoidable "contradictions" and "paradoxes" of life (whose life?) remain unspecified.

In my previous discussion of Shaked and Gertz I concluded that the critics neutralized the dissension in the text. They depoliticized the text by displacing it in the universalist context of Western cultural trends. The purpose of this tactic was, of course, political: the strategy is aimed at maintaining the Zionist ideology as well as the canonical position of the writer. Taha's interpretation effects an even more comprehensive abstraction of the political issue, an abstraction that is, of course, equally political. The view that life consists of compromises and requires acceptance of the inevitable translates the political language of the text into the universal language of folk wisdom. Like Shaked, who, according to Shamir, created a "reality in the novel," Taha also undertakes the creation of a reality in the novels he examines, one that erases all political significations and thus abstracts both Arab and Jewish characters.

Interestingly, it is Yehoshua himself who returns to *The Lover* in order to repoliticize it, that is, to reposition it in the context of Israeli binational reality. In the same interview with Horn—in which he complains about Arab intellectuals penetrating the Jewish sanctum sanctorum of Hebrew language and literature—Yehoshua speaks about his inauthentic characterization of Naim. He confesses that he "believed then that [I] could really describe an Arab from inside." At the time the character of a young Arab boy with "some love of Hebrew literature" seemed to meet the conditions necessary to represent "in a realistic way" the character of an Israeli Arab. Now he realizes that this was not sufficient. "If you would ask me to describe an Arab today, I would not be able to do it anymore."[45] There is hardly any need to dwell on Yehoshua's obviously condescending

characterization of an Arab as an individual with "some love of Hebrew literature." Of more importance are the reasons that prompted
the Israeli Jewish writer to concede artistic failure. Why would Yehoshua, despite the highly canonical status of *The Lover* and the continuing popularity of the novel, arrive at the conclusion that the veri-
similitude of his narrative is flawed? Furthermore, why, in view of
his desire to exclude Arabs from Israeli Jewish life, should he be concerned about his characterization of the Arab?

Yehoshua's comment is by no means a regretful confession of his
artistic limitations, nor does it emerge from a sudden change of heart
about the immorality of the Zionist treatment of the Arab minority.
It is, rather, an acknowledgment of his irritation and annoyance
sparked by the challenging novel *Arabesques,* by Anton Shammas,[46]
who is an Israeli Arab Christian. Although I will shortly discuss the
reception of Shammas's novel, here it is important to note that this
fictional autobiography of an Israeli Arab, written in exquisite Hebrew, confirmed to Yehoshua his inability to create a plausible Arab
figure. This cultural phenomenon of an Arab producing outstanding
Hebrew fiction illustrates Yehoshua's concern about the Arabs unsettling the hegemony of Israeli Jewish culture. Indeed, the Hebrew of
Shammas's novel put an end to the Jewish writers' exclusive right to
the language, while the content of the novel ended the monopoly of
the Jews over representations of the Arab in Israeli literature. "As
Shammas's novel makes it clear," Yehoshua admits, "they [the Ar-
abs] are becoming so special, so complicated, so unique in their existence that I would not be able to speak in [*sic*] behalf of them as I
did in *The Lover.*"[47]

Such a condescending acknowledgment by the left-wing writer of
the growing sophistication of the Arabs attests not only to Yehoshua's bias but to his lack of sensitivity and knowledge of the subject.
Ironically, the emergence of a Palestinian story in Hebrew creates a
cultural affinity with the Israeli Arab, one that the Jew can barely
endure. As we have seen, it is the idea of separation from the Arab
minority and its culture that informs Yehoshua's vision of Israel's
future. Yet despite Yehoshua's proposed segregation of the two national groups, his perception of the Arab novel as a political event
and his acknowledgment of its literary excellence attest to his recognition of a cultural transformation in progress. Biased and reluctant as

it is, Yehoshua's observation of the developing Arab Hebrew culture amounts to an acknowledgment of the Arab's "threatening" presence in the Israeli cultural environment. However grudging, the recognition of the Arab novel by a canonical—perhaps even canonized—Israeli Jewish writer signifies the acceptance of the Arab and his fiction by the dominant culture and its canons.

The emergence of the Arab Israeli *Hebrew* writer confronts the Zionist cultural establishment with the ambivalence of its self-definition. One need only recall Holtzman's characterization of early Hebrew literature, which laid the foundation for the state's Hebrew culture, as a body of writing that liberated itself from the religious constraints of Diaspora Judaism and its rabbinic literature, defined itself in terms of secular nationalism, and by and large adopted the modernist—and, later, postmodernist—perspectives of Western culture. In its self-identification as a secular Hebrew nation reborn in the image of Western modernity, the Zionist mainstream culture could not envision the emergence of the phenomenon of Arab literature *in Hebrew*. Thus, the mainstream Jewish Israeli culture has been faced with the unsettling impact of this literature not just on its exclusionary ideological orientation; the emergence of the Arab perspective threatened to shed a critical light upon the Zionist self-image.

Resentfully, yet quite accurately, Yehoshua identifies the source of Zionist discomfort—perhaps even anxiety—with regard to Israeli Arab Hebrew writing: "They [the Arabs] even try to strike us with the [Hebrew] language. They . . . use [our] sources to teach us some lessons from our legacy [in order] to show us how wrong we are and how we are betraying our own past and our own spiritual values by doing to them what we are doing."[48] The combination of guilt and indignation apparent in Yehoshua's tone indicates the moral challenge of Israeli Arab Hebrew writing. The implications of the Arab story, which undermines the Zionist moral self-image, present the establishment with a particular problem of reception. In the next chapter I demonstrate that reception of this critical representation of Zionist hegemony is possible thanks to interpretive neutralization, which defuses dissent and facilitates the incorporation of Arab literature into the Hebrew canon.

5

Israeli Arab Fiction and the Mainstream

Dissent and Strategies of Canonization

The Challenge of Hebrew and the Issue of Translation

The phenomenon of Israeli Arab writers and their dissenting fiction[1] presents the establishment with a specific issue of reception. In this case canonical appropriation or co-optation cannot, of course, root itself in a Jewish/Zionist brotherhood, as was the case with left-wing Zionist writers. Instead of Israeli Jewish texts that protest the oppression of the Arabs, the cultural establishment is presented with texts authored by the victims of this oppression. The works of these writers—Atallah Mansour, Emile Habiby, and Anton Shammas—are quite unsparing in their negative representations of Israeli domination. As we shall see, they denounce Zionism as an ideology of colonialist dispossession, charge Israel with bias and discrimination against its Arab minority, and expose the brutality of the conquest and the occupation.

Narrated by victims, the exposure of the ruthless underside of the Zionist project is difficult to accept. At the same time, the decision of the Arab to write in Hebrew, the language of the hegemony, denies the possibility of evasion. Ineluctably, the Hebrew text confronts the Israeli mainstream with a twofold challenge. First, its subject matter presents the Jewish majority with the Arab minority's perception of the moral failings of the Zionist project. Second, its Hebrew language dismantles the Zionist exclusionary claim to Hebrew culture. Yet, as

111

this chapter demonstrates, neither the minority's testimony of oppression nor its claim to Hebrew culture precluded the incorporation of this small but significant body of fiction into the Israeli literary canon. At this point one should note that despite the extent of criticism of the Zionist state in their writings, the three writers have for many years been highly respected and well known in mainstream cultural circles.

Atallah Mansour is the author of the first Hebrew novel written by an Arab. *In a New Light* (1966) was favorably received and was soon translated into the English. Mansour has worked for many years at *Ha'Aretz,* the most respected Israeli newspaper, where he writes mainly on Arab issues in Israel. Anton Shammas, who now lives in the United States, worked as a journalist for prominent Israeli newspapers and literary magazines. He is a published poet both in Hebrew and Arabic, but it was the publication of *Arabesques,* his first novel, in 1986 that gained him instant fame in Israel. Shammas gained international recognition when, once his novel had been translated into English in 1988, it appeared among the best books of the year in the *New York Times Book Review.* Emile Habiby, an eminent politician and man of letters, has authored short stories and three novels. Originally published in Arabic, the novels—*The Secret Life of Saeed the Pessoptimist* (1974), *Ikhtayyeh* (1985) and *Saraya, Daughter of the Ghoul* (1991)—were translated into Hebrew by Shammas, who was Habiby's very close friend.

Habiby, who died in 1996, was a well-known, highly controversial political figure in both Arab and Jewish milieus. He was a founding member of the Israeli Communist party, a long-time Communist Knesset member, and editor-in-chief of *Al-Ittihad,* Israel's leading Arab Communist weekly. Habiby wrote in Arabic, and his first novel, *The Pessoptimist,* made him famous throughout the Arab world. In 1990 in Cairo he was awarded the State of Palestine Certificate of Merit and the Medal of Jerusalem for Culture, Literature, and Art by Yassir Arafat, then chairman of the PLO. Two years later in Jerusalem, at an Independence Day celebration, he received the Israel Prize for literature from the Israeli minister of education and Israel's prime minister. The awarding of Israel's highest prize is incontrovertible evidence of Habiby's canonical status on the Israeli cultural scene, even though there were many Israelis and Arabs who opposed his nomination. Habiby's acceptance of the Israel Prize gained him an almost unanimous condemnation from Arab intellectuals,[2] quite vehement criticism from Israeli Arab intellectuals,[3] and, on a more limited but no less hostile scale, a dramatic protest from Israeli right-wing politicians.[4]

These responses demonstrate the extent to which Habiby's official acceptance in mainstream Israeli culture was politicized in both Arab and Israeli spheres. The following anecdote further elucidates the political significance of Habiby's achievement in the context of Israel's relations with the Arab minority. When asked about the Israel Prize award, Habiby related that his literary career started as a response to the denigrating comment made by Yig'al Alon, the then minister of education in the Israeli cabinet: "Had there been a Palestinian people, it surely would have had a literary legacy." It was at this moment that, as Habiby used to admit in his interviews with Israeli journalists, "I became determined to create in this country a Palestinian literature that would outlive both me and him."[5] Though Alon retracted his comment, his unfortunate *lapsus linguae* in effect characterized the official negation of the Palestinian national identity prevalent in the history of the state in the years preceding the first intifada, or Palestinian uprising. The most notorious was the dismissive remark by Israeli Prime Minister Golda Meir: "There was no such thing as Palestinians. . . . They did not exist."[6]

In view of such public statements that recognized Palestinian Arabs neither as a culture nor as a nation, Habiby's prize reflected a drastic shift in Israel's perception of the Israeli Arab. The prize signified official recognition of a member of Israel's Arab minority as an Israeli writer, a symbolic event that placed Israeli Arabs on Israel's cultural map. Nonetheless, the tenor of Habiby's recollection of the encounter with Alon and his frequent retelling of the event shows that he neither forgot nor forgave the insulting comment. At the same time, his desire to affirm the cultural identity of the Palestinian people did not abate.

In one way, Habiby's claim to have created Palestinian literature sounds like an unfounded—perhaps even arrogant—hyperbolic remark. As has been documented in two fairly recent studies,[7] Palestinian literature existed in Israel before Habiby embarked on his magnificent multivolume storytelling effort. From another perspective, however, Habiby's argument sounds quite plausible. Considering the extent of defiance directed against Israel's hegemony in Habiby's fiction, one must admit that the writer and his work created a new challenge for Israeli literary reception. It is true that Mansour had already confronted the Israeli establishment with a Hebrew novel in 1966. However, the art and scope of Habiby's oeuvre, as well as its timing—it appeared after the 1967 Six-Day War and extended beyond the first intifada in the late 1980s—have challenged Israel's cultural self-definition in a fundamental way.

Habiby's determination to create Arabic-written Palestinian literature in Israel and then deliberately have it translated into the language of the Zionist oppressor leaves no doubt about his cultural and national self-identification as an Israeli Arab. The highly critical oeuvre in Hebrew clearly targets an Israeli Jewish readership. In this sense, the political signification of Habiby's literary work reflects a demand for the recognition *and* acceptance—no matter how critical—of the Arab minority on the Israeli Jewish cultural scene.

Habiby's search for self-affirmation as an Israeli Arab is puzzling. Why would he insist on claiming his place in Israeli society, especially in view of the quite predictable opposition to his perception on the Israeli scene? Why would he engage in a search for Israeli recognition that, when finally granted, would affect his reputation in the Arab world and cause him the emotional pain and distress of denunciation and repudiation by close friends and associates?

The interesting example of the African writer Ngũgĩ wa Thiong'o, who translated his own work from the African language Gĩkũyũ into English may offer an insight into Habiby's case. Here is how this Kenyan writer, who customarily writes in English, explains his decision to write his book in his native tribal language: "In choosing to write in Gĩkũyũ, I was doing something abnormal." Kenyan writers write in English, and the decision to write "in the language that the people use" was a symbolic political act of anti-imperialist struggle.[8] The novel *Devil on the Cross*, whose central character is a woman, focuses on the twofold struggle against the patriarchal structures of Africa and neocolonialist exploitation. In its original language the novel challenged Western domination, its aesthetic, and—as the choice of the language demonstrates—Western politics of the canon.

In another surprising symbolic gesture, Ngũgĩ translated the novel into English.[9]

In his fine discussion of the significance of Ngũgĩ's translation, Patrick McGee affirms that the translation "epitomized . . . the politically self-conscious relation of African writing to the hegemonic culture in Europe. . . . [It showed] that cultural, linguistic hegemony is never total—that it has the principle of reversibility inscribed in it." In other words, what the writer's translation amounts to is an act of resistance to the colonization of the native culture through the use of the imperial language. The translated text is intended for the English-speaking reader; however, the information provided on the title page—"Translated from the Gĩkũyũ by the author"[10]—communicates the author's affirmation of his native tongue as his primary language, a decision that challenges the domination of a Western Eurocentric aesthetic.

Ngũgĩ's twofold defiance of the dominant system lies in the political aspect of the decision to write *one* of his books in his *native* tongue and subsequently to *translate* the book into English as a political act. In contrast, Habiby, who *always* wrote in his *native* tongue, defied the dominant Israeli mainstream through the political act of *translating* his oeuvre into Hebrew. While their approaches differ, each of these writers' translations contends against forms of cultural colonization. Ngũgĩ 's translation resists the colonialist ideology of the "mission civilisatrice" geared to "primitive" societies. It opposes the British intention to divest the colonized populations of their indigenous identity by reshaping the community in the image of the West. In contrast, as we have seen, the Zionist ideology constructed the invisibility of the Israeli Arab minority by means of political, economic, and cultural exclusion. As the imperial language, English was the instrument of appropriation and acculturation of the colonized nations. As the language of Jewish national revival, Hebrew became an ideological barrier that separated and segregated Israeli Jews from both the Arab and the Diaspora Jew.[11]

Thus, the defiance of each of the two writers addresses different ideological targets. Ngũgĩ's original text in his native tongue represents a symbolic act of liberation of his ethnic tradition from the dominant culture of the West, while the translated story communicates the possibility of "de-acculturation" of the native heritage. Ngũgĩ's translation posits the text as any other translation for the benefit of a readership that cannot read the original. In this sense his translation into English affirms the original culture that the colonizers wished to replace with their own. In contrast, Habiby's translation represents a symbolic act of reaffirmation of the Palestinian culture that the exclusionary Zionist weltanschauung wished to ignore. In its Hebrew translation the story claims the recognition of Arab presence, tradition, and history. Indeed, in his response to those Arabs critical of his acceptance of the Israel Prize, Habiby claims that the awarding of the prize made Israel realize that "it cannot be rid of us" and that the presence of Arabs is "a *fait accompli.*"[12]

The translations by the two writers therefore respond to different forms of cultural colonization. Of course, the ideological concept behind the "mission civilisatrice" of the European colonial system differs from the Zionist doctrine of the "empty land." Nevertheless, the choice by both writers to translate their works into the language of the hegemony represents a desire for recognition of the story by the dominant power. By translating his work, the writer engages the dominant culture in his tale of oppression. Whether to disentangle themselves from the colonizing influence or to gain access to the hegemony, both writers wish their story to reach those who attempted to erase it.

The insistence that the story of the dominated be included in the dominant consciousness—even if this involves switching from the native language to the language of the dominator—indicates that the precolonial situation cannot be restored for either the colonized or the colonizer. While the colonizer may wish to ignore or suppress the story of the colonized, the story liberates itself from the imposed silence in the dominant language, as evinced by both Ngũgĩ and Habiby. The emergence of the story proves that the process of colonization has bound the dominating and the dominated in a common fate and has affected them both.

In my earlier discussion of Israeli Jewish writers I noted the extreme reluctance to recognize the story of the victim. In particular, Yehoshua's plan to preclude Israeli Arab participation in Israel's mainstream culture demonstrates the dominator's fear of Arab "visibility." Surprisingly, a voice urging rapprochement and interaction between Jews and Arabs belongs to an avowed critic of Zionism. A prominent Palestinian poet, Mahmoud Darwish has certainly been no proponent of Israel. Nonetheless, in an interview with an Israeli journalist, Darwish, who was born in pre-state Palestine and who received his formative education in Israel, confirmed the impossibility of the disengagement between the two peoples: "The Israelis are not the same as they were when they came, and the Palestinians are not the same people either. Each dwells inside the other. . . . The other is a responsibility and a test. . . . Will the third emerge out of the two? This is the test."[13]

Ostensibly, the Israeli Arab story in Hebrew seems to be staging a situation conducive to the creation of the "third." It therefore seems reasonable to expect that the Arab story addressed to the Israeli public would, despite its critical tone, be told in a conciliatory manner. Such an approach would have created a more positive attitude toward the plight of the Israeli Arab minority. A nonconfrontational story might have led to a revision of the history of the victor, which would recognize the history of the victim. A revision of the past might have engendered a new history of mutual recognition.

This apparently rational and optimistic scenario is far from reflecting the Israeli Arab fiction. The story that this fiction tells represents anything but a reconciliation with the dominating majority. Recall Yehoshua's indignation at the Arabs, who "show us how wrong we are and how we are betraying our own past and our own spiritual values by doing to them what we are doing." Indeed, the degree of defiance and condemnation in the narratives of the Arab writers seems to call into question the possibility of creating a "third." The following recapitulation of the narratives will demonstrate the extent to which the stories must remain unpalatable to the Zionist reader. As we shall see, these narratives communicate virulent criticism of the state and represent a vituperative and unsparing indictment of its policies of degradation and exploitation of the Israeli Arab minority. They also openly mourn the defeat, dispossession, and exile of the Palestinian people. In this sense the Israeli Arab fiction invariably speaks with the acute bitterness of unrelieved pain, incontrovertible loss, and unforgivable degradation. Before considering the strategies of the canonical reception of this fiction, I first wish to look more closely at the challenges with which the Arab narratives confronted the establishment.

The Challenge of the Victim's Story

Mansour's early novel *In a New Light* takes aim at the institution of the kibbutz, the quintessential representation of the Zionist socialist ideal. By exposing the hypocrisy of the kibbutz members, Mansour's story destabilizes the moral foundations of the Zionist movement. Not unlike the young forest in Yehoshua's story, the kibbutz is founded on the ruins of an Arab village destroyed in the 1948 war. The kibbutz members unconscionably exploit and manipulate the destitute Arabs, who live on the outskirts of the land they had previously owned. Mansour's protagonist, Yossi, is an Arab orphan who witnessed the murder of his father. Traumatized, Yossi has erased his Arab identity and wishes to make the kibbutz his home. He also engages in a love affair with a kibbutz member. The socialist, egalitarian ideology of the kibbutz is severely tested when it is revealed that Yossi is an Arab. For political reasons—the elections are close and the kibbutz does not want to tarnish its socialist image by a public scandal—the kibbutz members eventually endorse Yossi's application for membership on condition that his national identity be conveniently ignored. Ironically, the disaffected Yossi begins to see the world "in a new light."

In Habiby's novels the Israelis fare even worse. In fact, in their conversations with Habiby some interviewers observed that his fiction had conspicuously failed to attribute any redeeming features either to the State of Israel or its Jewish citizens.[14] While the journalists never obtained a satisfactory explanation from the author, a look at Habiby's plots seems to confirm their observations. There simply are no "good" Israeli Jews in Habiby's novels, whereas blatantly cruel, stupid, and prejudiced Jewish characters appear by the dozen in each novel. Though critical of his Palestinian characters as well, Habiby accords sympathy only to the Arabs, never to Israeli Jews.

In *The Pessoptimist* the protagonist, Saeed, an Israeli Arab who has "sold out" as an informer, has an opportunity to view the Israeli Secret Service from the inside. His vituperative satirical representation of the arrogant, corrupt, and brutal agents and their horrible treatment of the Arab population often verges on the grotesque. In its relentless victimization of Israeli Arabs the Israeli Secret Service becomes a metonymic representation of the State of Israel. For instance, in one of the episodes the "big man," as Saeed calls the secret service agent, instructs Saeed about the rules of behavior in the Shatta prison where he is about to "plant" Saeed as an informer. "While he was going through these lessons," Saeed comments, "I became ever more certain that what is required of us inside prison is no different from what is required of us on the outside."[15] A central metaphor in the novel involves the protagonist sitting naked on a stake, unable to descend. Israeli Arabs, discriminated against by the Israeli oppressor and separated from their fellow Palestinians in exile, find themselves in the impossible situation of "suspension." Another prominent metaphor involves undersea and subterranean caves, which ironically represent the only place where the Israeli Arab can "breathe." These symbolic images of the "dead-end" situation of the Arab under Israeli rule determine the tenor of the novel.

In the novel *Ikhtayyeh*, especially in the first part ("Notebook"), the emphasis is on the flawed Israeli justice system. The setting of Haifa and its history as a predominantly Arab city before 1948 is essential to the depiction of the abuse of the Arabs, now a minority population. The novel opens with an episode involving an enormous traffic jam. The police investigation of the incident exposes an exorbitant, almost parodic degree of prejudice and discrimination against the Arabs. The episode serves as a powerful metaphor of Arab freedom lost under the Israeli regime. The narrator offers a description of his own "jammed" existence. In an imaginary sequence he is harassed by a grotesque army of midgets, who block the path of his car and will not let him proceed. "Sometimes," he says, "they are a few dozen of little Ben-Gurions that all look the same, and occasionally a great number of little Dayans that all look the same. . . . [S]hould they prevail and overpower my car, I would stop and fall asleep waiting for them to go away and let me be."[16] The other "Notebooks" focus on memories of childhood and on longing for a tradition that was tragically severed with the loss of the land. The recurring image of the vanished girl, the love of his youth, whose name, Ikhtayyeh, means sin, is a metaphoric representation of the motherland as well as a reminder of the sin of those who have abandoned her. The motif of a betrayed lover signals the sense of guilt of the Israeli Arabs, who submitted themselves to Israeli domination.

The novel *Saraya* represents the least satirical and most poignant indictment of Israel as a military power. It condemns Israel's fascination with war and the atrocities the state committed against the Arabs. The story opens in the summer of the 1983 war in Lebanon. The narrator arrives at the realization that for Israelis each war has its particular moment of glory and joy in victory, but when the sounds of war reach him, they are "like voices that arise from an untrodden forest on a moonless night, or like a hiss of terrified ghosts escaping into the forest." This chilling realization leads him to the understanding that all the stories he told after 1948 have, in fact, been attempts to decode the sounds of each war, for these sounds vary from one war to another. This insight into his own writing occurred when he heard a "radio reporter . . . claim that the thunder of Israeli cannons and the moans of the wounded Arabs sounded like a 'magnificent symphony.' "[17] This lyrical novel is also a recollection of his lost, magical childhood and his former love for Carmel and Haifa. The stories, partly true and partly imagined, reemerge from the past. These are lamentations of the irrecoverable loss of the Palestinian life as a result of the Israeli conquest. A prominent motif deals with severed family ties. Even though the refugees in Lebanon were finally allowed to visit family members in Israel, the severance was too traumatic and the separation too long for the uprooted existences to come together. The most traumatic event is the departure of the narrator's mother, who prefers to be with her family in exile rather than with her son, who has become a Communist politician. In a very real sense the novel is the narrator's poignant elegy for a world that was brutally and unaccountably taken away from him.

Shammas's *Arabesques* is an audacious text both in terms of form and content. While the form presents a sophisticated confluence of genres, the content presents the Israeli reader with a complex political challenge. The narrative weaves together two stories. "The Tale" is a recollection of family history in terms of its myths, legends, a magical childhood, and the beloved family home. It is also the story of the powerlessness of the defeated community and the emerging consciousness that "the tale . . . does not have sufficient power to restore the earth pulled from under our feet."[18] This power dissipated with the defeat of 1948. The other story, "The Teller," focuses on the existential predicament of an Israeli Arab intellectual in the State of Israel. In this tale the narrator describes the humiliation of the Arab as a second-class citizen, as represented by the patronizing view of the Arab in Israeli literature by writers such as A. B. Yehoshua (thinly disguised in the novel as Yehoshua Bar-On). He despairs over the loneliness and alienation of the Arab in the hostile Israeli environment and deplores the Israeli Arab's uprootedness from his native culture and tradition. The interweaving stories in *Arabesques* center on the two most serious transgressions of Israel's exclusionary politics and *mores*. The first is the narrator's love affair with Shlomith, an Israeli Jewish woman, the wife of an army officer. Even though the love affair has ended, the narrator's longings for his lost Israeli lover permeate his narrative. The second represents the narrator's obsessive search for his older cousin, Michael Abyad. Abyad, the narrator's alter-ego, model, and mentor, is also a member of an anti-Israeli terrorist organization. The search for Michael and the eventual meeting with a Palestinian cousin in Iowa constitute subversive acts against the state. Both clandestine connections—the Israeli lover and the terrorist cousin—signal the impossible situation of the Israeli Arab suspended between two worlds, that of the Israeli mainstream and that of the Palestinian freedom fighters. The impossibility of belonging to either endows the tale with an unbearable sense of displacement and alienation.

The taboos of ethnic purity and state security that Shammas's narrator so openly addresses and transgresses represent the complexity of the issues that the Arab minority faces in the Jewish state. The narrative of victimization and oppression in Arab Israeli fiction defies the ideological mainstays of the Zionist enterprise, such as the separatist tenet of the "empty land," and denounces the moral standing of the Zionist movement. These difficult issues faced by the Israeli Jewish readership lead back to the question of reception. As was previously mentioned, despite their explosive content, which repudiates the dominant ideology and the policies of the state, the texts and their writers were recognized by Israel's mainstream culture. Having demonstrated the prominence of Mansour, Habiby, and Shammas as well-established journalists, poets, and nationally and internationally known writers, I wish to examine the strategies of critical reception, or "master codes," that facilitated the incorporation of their dissenting texts into the Hebrew literary canon.

Arab Fiction and Israeli Culture: The Codes of Reception

This brief preamble is intended to highlight the problematic position of Israeli Arab fiction. In the case of Jewish dissenting fiction, the critical establishment attributed the deviation from Zionist norms to Western trends of existentialism and postmodernism. The literary representations of Arab suffering by Jewish writers were abstracted as metaphors of the existentialist struggle against an incomprehensible human fate, the futile search for the meaning of life, and universal victimhood and displacement. Because their faith in the Zionist writers' loyalty to the Zionist idea was unshaken, Zionist critics could afford to be permissive and tolerant toward the defiant "new wave" writers. From their position as staunch Zionists with Western proclivities, the critics looked with benevolence—even pride—upon the misguided "prophets to the House of Israel," clearly affected by the zeitgeist of postwar left-wing existentialist Paris. With their representations of *angst* and *malaise,* the "new wave" Israeli writers were entering the mainstream Western culture.

These interpretive "master codes," grounded in ethnic and ideological kinship with the writers, could not be applied to Israeli Arab fiction. However, since the latter was written in Hebrew, it could not be ignored either. But, then, neither could the establishment ignore the radicalness of this literature's indictment of the state, its ideology, and its policies. Since the Arab perspective dispelled such fundamentals as the invisibility of the Arabs and the humanistic idealism of the Zionist movement, a different critical strategy was needed to neutralize the disruptive Arab narratives.

I wish to argue that in order to keep the Zionist political and moral image intact, the literary establishment reversed its interpretive "master codes." Rather than attributing Western liberal perspectives *to* the texts, as they did in the case of Israeli Jewish fiction, the critics looked at the Israeli Arab fiction *from* the perspective of Western liberal humanism. That is to say, when faced with the Arab story, the critical establishment changed from the national Zionist position to a humanistic-liberal orientation. The approach of enlightened tolerance, which validates all stories in the name of democratic liberties, legitimized the story of the Arab. Through the lens of humanistic universality the establishment could abstract the bluntness of Arab antiestablishment dissent and incorporate it into the canon.

Jacques Derrida's comment on the disempowerment of literature in Western democracies helps to elucidate the interpretive code that made the acceptance of Arab fiction of dissent possible. According to Derrida, "The critico-political function of literature, in the West, remains very ambiguous. The freedom to say everything is a very powerful *political weapon,* but one which might immediately *let itself be neutralized as a fiction.* This revolutionary power can become very conservative."[19] Derrida suggests that the "freedom to say everything" with impunity ironically divests free speech of its political power—or even of its factuality—turning everything said into the subjective and, therefore, fictional. If, in the name of freedom of speech, anything can be said and everything is acceptable, it is impossible to discern fact from fiction. Everything can therefore be labeled as "a fiction," that is, an imaginative, subjective representation of a particular situation. In this sense, the freedom to say anything gives license to fictionalize everything. Fictionalization disconnects political or historical events from their concrete time and place because it infuses them with the sense of fictionality. In this way the prism of fictionality relieves the reader of the responsibility of shaping opinion with regard to the moral transgressions represented in the text.

Consequently, Western liberalism allows one not only to say everything but also to accept everything with equanimity. Thus, canonization of a dissenting story, on the one hand, reaffirms the democratic value of reception and, on the other hand, neutralizes the particular reality of the story. Acting as the vehicle of equality and freedom of speech, reception silences the dissenting outlook of the story. Since every story is given the same measure of trust and recognition, nothing is true or false anymore. In this sense the story of the Arab is recognized as any other story would be. Considered one of many other possible representations of history, the Arab story of victimization and injustice can be accorded recognition that, paradoxically, will neutralize and silence the protest of its dissent.

A brief note about Shammas that appeared in the main evening newspaper aptly illustrates the process of neutralization. The congratulatory note mentions the inclusion of Shammas's work among the best books of the year in the *New York Times* and claims it as a credit to "Hebrew Israeli literature." The note goes on to say that "everybody knows that Shammas, a native of Fassuta, is a Christian Arab—his novel, *Arabesques,* is most clearly autobiographical. He also has annoyed many people with his [political] opinions as to what [kind of state] Israel should become." The unidentified author admonishes the reader that "this [Shammas's controversial opinion] does not detract from the fact that *Arabesques* is written in Hebrew and therefore Anton Shammas is a limb of limbs of Israel [*ever m'evrei*], and therefore an integral part of Hebrew literature created in the State of Israel."[20]

Let us look at this journalistic note in terms of the rhetorical strategies employed to appropriate the novel and include it in the corpus of Hebrew literature despite the controversy it caused in Israel. With disarming openness the reporter acknowledges the origins of the writer and his unpopular political views. At the same time, the anticipation of opposition in "this does not detract" and the affirmation "limb of limbs" (a very powerful Hebrew metaphor that denotes an extraordinary degree of filiation) are clearly intended to outweigh the national and political differences, which might place Shammas outside the normative profile of an Israeli Hebrew writer. The semantics of the text are intended to show the openness and tolerance of the Israeli establishment. While it recognizes Shammas's ethnic origin and his dissident ideas, the establishment claims his work for the Israeli canon. The inclusion downplays and thus neutralizes the writer's critical ideas concerning the state and its ideology. After all, the system that recognized the Arab writer who has defied it so harshly cannot be totally evil.

M.D.'s circular argumentation downplays Shammas's political antagonism, contending that Shammas belongs to the Israeli fold. Other reviews of the novel follow the same path; practically all dismiss the political message on aesthetic grounds. Claiming to be unbiased and impartial readers, the critics tend to dismiss the politically problematic parts of *Arabesques*—especially those that appear in episodes of "The Teller"—as writing of inferior artistic quality. Like M.D., critic and reviewer Yael Lotan argues that *Arabesques* is "an organic Hebrew Israeli novel." She extols the beauty of "The Tale," comparing the narrative of the family saga to that of Marcel Proust. Ironically, even though she maintains that nobody "should be telling the writer how to tell his story," she unwittingly goes on to postulate that segments of "The Teller" should have been left out since they "do not connect organically with the other parts of the story." The ultimate attempt to neutralize the novel's political, historical, and geographical signification emerges in Lotan's conclusion, in which she admonishes the readers to "see the book *as it is—as if* they were reading, for instance, a South American novel."[21]

Similarly, an evenhanded position emerges in the interpretation of Heda Boshas, a respected book reviewer. Boshas favorably compares "The Tale" to the magic of Fellini's films. Though she is receptive to Shammas's political views, Boshas finds that the "conceptual world of the novel is not political but rather literary-poetic." She minimizes the politically dissenting sections, claiming that although they are "brilliant pieces of journalism," they are "simplistically symbolic, lacking the magical fireflies of the other chapters."[22]

It is of interest to note that both critics seek legitimation for their enthusiastic praise for Shammas's nonpolitical writing by invoking canonical Western artists, such as Proust and Fellini. In fact, Dan Laor finds Shammas's association with Proust the main—perhaps the only—redeeming feature in the novel. "The failure of Shammas's *Arabesques*," he writes, "consists first and foremost in the writer's lack of determination [and] consistency to write a novel that would focus exclusively on . . . his Galilean childhood village, Fassuta." According to Laor, Shammas can be compared favorably to Proust in his childhood recollections, yet he has failed to explore fully the force of memory, the wellspring of the novel. This failure is due to the unnecessary focus on political issues. Like the other critics, Laor is critical of "The Teller" episodes, which, according to him, clearly detract from the artistic value of the novel. "For whom and why is all this needed?" he asks rhetorically with reference to "The Teller." Laor then elaborates: "Why would Shammas decide to give his readers his 'Diary' at this particular time and confess . . . at length to his identity crisis . . .

which he attributes to his being 'an Arab poet from Israel' who writes in Hebrew and tries to establish himself in Hebrew literature?"[23] Beneath Laor's concern for the artistic coherence of the novel one notices the critic's ambivalence—verging on resentment—at Shammas's self-exposure as an alienated Arab in mainstream Israeli society. His opinion that the confession of the identity crisis is superfluous is revealing. It shows the depth of Laor's anxiety about the subversive use of Hebrew by an Arab writer who "tries to establish" the story of his alienation in mainstream Hebrew literature.

Yael Feldman's critical article seems to display a similar anxiety by literally distancing Shammas's story from the reality of Israel and locating it in the reality of the Arab world. Feldman claims that the main interest of the novel's subversive aspect is not the oppression of the Arabs in the Jewish state but rather the persecution of Christian Arabs, the inhabitants of Shammas's native village, by Muslim Arabs at the time of the great Arab revolt in 1936–39. Feldman argues that Shammas would never have dared to write it in Arabic, but he "has dared here, in Hebrew, . . . to force open a memory, in a minor key, the memory of the Arab Christian minority, by tracing its roots to an internal Arab conflict."[24] In Feldman's view, for Shammas the Hebrew language has become the language of liberation that set free the forbidden story of an internal Arab conflict. Feldman attributes the raison d'être of the choice of the Hebrew to the secrecy of the religious conflict between Arab Christians and Moslems in nineteenth- and twentieth-century Palestine. I would argue that, while interesting, this reading places in relief a secondary theme in *Arabesques* and thus downplays its main thematic concern, namely, that of the history of Arab defeat in 1948 and the post-defeat estrangement of the Arab minority in the Israeli mainstream.

Not all critics are prepared to either evade the political issue or disguise it under aesthetic considerations. In an ambitious essay Hannan Hever tackles the subversive meaning of the novel by resorting to Gilles Deleuze and Félix Guattari's theory of minor literature. In Hever's opinion, Shammas enters the exclusive domain of the Hebrew culture and destabilizes the existing status quo of Jewish domination and Arab submission. Hever contends that "as an Arab writer, breaking into the linguistic and literary citadel of the Israeli Jews, Shammas calls into question their claim to exclusive possession of the language of traditional Zionism." Divesting the language of its past tradition and exclusivity, Shammas seems to be working toward "a truly democratic society." Advancing the liberal notion of progress toward fellowship of human beings, Hever sees Shammas's appropriation of the language as "a utopian unification of the language of Arabs and Jews . . . capable of bringing about a better future."[25] At the same time, however, Hever is quite conscious of the fact that the utopian notion of Israeli Arabs and Jews coming together through language would signify transgression of accepted boundaries. He admits that the possibility of such a drastic change "makes it difficult for Israeli Jews to identify easily with him or adopt him as one of their own."[26]

The extent of the difficulty Shammas's text represents for Israeli Jews emerges in the review of *Arabesques* by Dan Miron, an eminent scholar of Hebrew literature. In contrast to Hever, Miron blames the novel for having failed to present a universal, humanistic vision of harmony and empathy. Shammas, Miron tells us, "failed to turn the remembered experiences into a kernel of a more general and unified outlook." The roots of the writer's failure lie in his "emotional, cultural, and literary problems, which have not been resolved." This psychological predicament leads the writer to adopt a destructive attitude that lacks empathy for both his family and his readers. As this critic sees it, Shammas "consistently destroys the personalities of his people" in order to demonstrate "his superiority over the poor and naive relatives that he has left behind in the village." Miron claims that this negative attitude toward his own people "purposely and maliciously prevents his readers, the Jews who destroyed the tranquility of the village, from enjoying the story." In a revealing comment Miron complains that Shammas boasts about his "too perfect, too smoothed out Hebrew, not without the intention to 'provoke,' because he wishes to show off to his Israeli Jewish counterparts his so much greater mastery of their Hebrew language." In conclusion, Miron postulates that the writer "stumbles and falls [because] he has not yet digested and internalized his several years' long bitterness, nor has he as yet liberated himself from the spiritual barrenness of [the Israeli Arab minority, which feels] displaced and alienated."[27]

It is, of course, doubly ironic that Miron's rancorous appraisal of Shammas as a mean-spirited writer identifies the essence of the novel and, at the same time, reveals the Israeli bias more clearly than any of the other critics. The novel *is* indeed about the undigested bitterness of life-long humiliation, alienation, and displacement. Moreover, it *is* an audacious attempt by an Israeli Arab intellectual to adopt the Hebrew language in order to gain recognition in the dominant cultural milieu. But the derogatory tenor of Miron's astute observations reveals the "master codes" of his interpretation. One observes here a liberal, humanistic position that seeks its own reflection in the work. Whereas other critics feel that the universalist motif in the family saga portions of *Arabesques* outweighs the political and moral issues in the novel, Miron refuses to evade the political issue. Rather than dismissing the politically disagreeable parts as aesthetically wanting, Miron dismisses the novel altogether for its lack of a tolerant, benevolent, and dispassionate view of humanity. He predicates *his* acceptance of the story upon a liberal message of reconciliation, one that would have neutralized the story of alienation with a note of hope.

The interpretive reading of shared humanistic liberal values between critic and writer emerges prominently in critical interpretations of Habiby's work. The critics acknowledge the aesthetic value of Habiby's writing and go to extremes to "humanize" his merciless, bitterly satirical representations of the state. Habiby emerges in these critical readings as an old, wise man who looks with benevolent impartiality upon the folly of human beings, be it Jews or Arabs. By emphasizing correspondences with literary masterpieces of humanistic satire, such as Voltaire's *Candide* and Jaroslav Hašek's *Good Soldier Schweik*, critics universalize his message, thereby blunting the sharpness of Habiby's defiance of the present-day situation.

Thus, Sasson Somekh, an eminent scholar of Arab literature, emphasizes Habiby's Voltairesque characteristics and contends that Habiby has also "shaped a new Arab literary style . . . in which the elements of the old tradition figure prominently . . . but that also draws upon modern European and American literature." Somekh downplays the political theme, arguing that "the best quality [of *The Pessoptimist*] lies in Habiby's literary strategies, so that the book is funny and irresistible and the 'message' gets through the back door."[28] Immanuel Sivan, a noted scholar and expert on the Middle East, praises Habiby's Arabic. As Sivan sees it, through his incomparable mastery of the language Habiby "softened, distilled and refined the description of Arab life in Israel under military rule." Sivan notes that "even more stunning is his avoidance of the linguistic ideological trap of the Communist *Al-Ittihad,* which Habiby edited."[29] While several scholars praise Habiby's use of genre and language as well as his avoidance of politics, Shulamith Hareven, a well-known writer and essayist, extols the "still small voice" of irony, compassion, and humor that distinguishes Habiby's rich literary work from arid political writing. Hareven sees Habiby's works as completely immersed in the humanistic tradition. She claims that "in Habiby's writing a human being is precisely that, a human being, rather than a symbol or a message, and the ability to contain the human being in the human framework is the indubitable sign of a humanistic writer."[30]

Hannan Hever has noticed the tendency of left-wing Israeli critics to "legitimate Habiby by concealing the political character of his writing." In his reading Hever presents Habiby's universalism as a strategy that the writer employs to enter the Israeli canon. As he did with Shammas, Hever examines Habiby from the perspective of Deleuze and Guattari's critical apparatus, namely, he uses their model of minority literature, which, they insist, invades and subverts the majority culture. Hever claims that Habiby conceals his controversial political message under the guise of a humanist. The critic surmises that the "thematic patterns" of "self-criticism" and the importance of women in Habiby's fiction appeal to the left-wing reader's ideological horizon because they follow the "general humanistic norms, which are typically Western and universalist." He maintains that the universalist norms are further emphasized by Habiby's criticism of the Arab League, which balances the criticism directed at the Jewish state. In Hever's view, the subversive allusions in Habiby's fiction are meant to "undermine the universal narrative." The writer's dissenting orientation shuns prominence, preferring to communicate its message stealthily in the form of "fragmented and incomplete" narrative pieces and insights.[31]

I wish to suggest that Hever's sophisticated interpretation—which tries to present Habiby as a writer who disguises his subversive interests under a humanistic guise in order to enter the canon—is a misreading of the Israeli Arab writer. Ironically, Hever's reading discloses the critic's "master code" of Western humanism. The example of the balance that Habiby strikes between his criticism of the State of Israel and of the Arab League is indicative of Hever's need to see Habiby as a humanistic author. It is impossible not to notice the extent to which the few instances of general criticism directed at the Arab League in Habiby's writing are outweighed by his relentless and vituperative condemnation of Israel. It is hardly possible even to suppose that any Israeli Jew who was raised to believe in the Israeli army's "purity of arms," that is, the humanitarian attitude of the Israeli military toward the Arab civilian population, could accept Habiby's denunciations of the Israeli army's politics of victimization as "typically universalist."

The following episode from *Pessoptimist* illustrates Habiby's utterly undisguised condemnation of the Israeli state. The governor of the Israeli Secret Police found in the field "a peasant [Palestinian] woman . . . in her lap a child, his eyes wide in terror." When she hesitated to answer his questions about her whereabouts, the governor "pointed his gun straight to the child's head and screamed, 'Reply, or I'll empty it into him!'" When she confessed that she was going back to her village of Berwah, the governor yelled, "Didn't we warn you that anyone returning there will be killed? . . . Go anywhere you like to the east. And if I ever see you again on this road I'll show you no mercy." The woman and the child turn east and Saeed, who narrates the story, observes the "amazing phenomenon" that "the farther the woman and the child went from where we were . . . the taller they grew . . . [until] they had become bigger than the plain of Acre itself. The governor still stood there. . . . Finally he asked in amazement: 'Will they never disappear?'" Saeed then transcends the boundaries of fiction and makes the historically plausible observation that the child might have been the poet Mahmoud Darwish, a native of Berwah. To prove his conjecture Saeed quotes from one of Darwish's poems written fifteen years later: "I laud the executioner, victor over a dark-eyed maiden; Hurrah for the vanquisher of villages, hurrah for the butcher of infants."[32]

I feel that the Berwah episode exposes the implausibility of a type of critical reception that attempts to read Habiby's message in light of universal humanism. It would be hard to categorize this episode under the general rubric of war atrocities. It would be equally hard

to fictionalize the Berwah episode in accordance with Derrida's notion of fictionalized factuality, namely, that fiction and factuality are,
in effect, indistinguishable. The humanistic generalization as well as
the confluence of fact and fiction are belied by the historical accuracy
of the event. The location is real and the event of the expulsion of
the Palestinian peasants is factual. There is, of course, the moment
that mythologizes the undiminished stature of the victims. But the
text reaches beyond this poetic moment to document the historical,
factual existence of the exiles. The reference to Mahmoud Darwish,
a real person and a bona fide exile, and the inclusion of his poetic
commemoration of the event point to Saeed's efforts to authenticate
his testimony. The concreteness of this horrific victimization of a
mother and child leaves no room for the attenuating humanistic-
universalist guises that Hever seems to impose on Habiby's invective.
As I see it, the story is unequivocally contemptuous of the barbarity
of the oppression; it is also unrestrained in its derisive depiction of
the oppressor.

The positive reception of such extremely negative representations
of Arab Israeli reality puzzled Arab writers. Indeed, in his autobiography Mansour writes that at the time he found the favorable reception
of his novel *In a New Light* quite disturbing. He recalls that after the
publication of the novel, the prestigious newspaper *Ma'ariv* publicly
invited him to join the Hebrew Writers Association. The writer recalls
that he found it hard to believe that "no one had taken offense at
my attack on Israeli society [in the novel]." He asks himself, "What
had made my reviewers actually welcome my criticisms?" Mansour
speculates that the novelty of a Hebrew novel by an Arab and the
"more relaxed climate of 1966" might have contributed to the positive reception. Most important, he also feels that "the novel was han-
dled by the regular book reviewers, who were mostly liberal intellectuals with a guilty conscience."[33]

Indeed, a perusal of the reviews of Mansour's novel reveals a positive reception. In general, the Israeli Arab writer is identified as a
moralist who confronts Israeli society with its failings. The reviewers
treat the novel as a humanistic text that passes an objective judgment on Israeli Jewish society, exposing the transgressions of the universal ideals of morality and justice. The oppression of the Arab is

interpreted as a representative example of the general failure of Israel's socialist foundations. In concurrence with this code of interpretation, Mansour is presented as the prescient other, the outsider, who
holds up the mirror of truth to a society that has strayed from its
ideals.

For instance, Yona Bahir agrees with Mansour's derogatory representation of the Jewish majority as "characterized by chauvinism,
arrogance and the practically automatic assumption that the Arab is
a stranger and an enemy." According to this reviewer, Mansour
"should have aimed his arrows at more significant targets [than the
kibbutz] that demonstrate the inequality between the two peoples,
such as the existence of an Arab ghetto in a democratic, peace-loving
country as ours."[34] According to Ora Ardon, the novel proves that
"the revolution of concepts and sentiments that the [Zionist] founders dreamed did not materialize." Ardon draws attention to Israel's
ethical and ideological failure, which Mansour exposes when he
"judges the Israeli society according to its own values. . . . In contrast
with what we would have expected, it is not the relationships between
Jews and Arabs that preoccupy the author . . . but rather the attitude
of the Jewish community toward its own ideals."[35] Iza Perlis reinforces the image of Mansour as a moral guide who carries a message
of peace and harmony. She asks her readers to follow the example
of Mansour, whom she quotes saying: "As an Arab writer who writes
in Hebrew, who lives in Arab society and writes for the Jewish community, conditions compel me to act as a bridge between the two
nations. . . . I feel that to annoy readers means, in many cases, to
prompt them to think. If I have managed to do so, my purpose has
been accomplished." Perlis responds to Mansour with a concluding
self-critical comment: "These courageous words will teach us not to
hide behind 'objective reality.' . . . We could have prevented much
suffering and insult, bitterness and disappointment, had we been able
to see both ourselves and the other in 'a new light.' "[36]

6

The Canon and the "True Heart of Europe"

In retrospect, it is possible to argue that the critical response to Mansour's first novel in Hebrew by an Israeli Arab presaged the subsequent critical reception of Israeli Arab fiction. The type of reception that claims the Arab texts for the canon consistently refuses to grapple with the failures of morality and justice at the very core of the Zionist idea, which this literature denounces. Rather, as the Israeli establishment critics prefer to see it, this literature denounces the failure to live up to the ideals of Western humanistic liberalism that Zionism represents. In this sense, paradoxically, the Arab writer becomes a social critic and a moralist who confronts the "new" Jews with their inability to implement their mission of bringing "light to the nations" or, in other words, to become the paragons of progress, justice, and humanism in the "old-new land," as Herzl envisioned it.

In the critical appreciations of his work, Mansour, the first Arab Hebrew writer, emerges as the defender of Zionism and its socialist ideals of equality for all. This view of the Arab writer as a moralist was reinforced a few years later with regard to Habiby. Through a complex and painful process of reception—recall the negative responses to his Israel Prize—Habiby emerged as a wizened old man who, in the tradition of Western humanistic satire, regards with equanimity the "human folly" of both Arabs and Jews. In a similar way, adherence to the ideals of universal humanism determined the readings of Shammas's *Arabesques*. Whether accepting or condemning, the "master codes" behind the critical appraisal of Shammas's novel drew upon the norms of Western cultural canons and the moral values of enlightened humanism.

Humanistic norms determine the reception of Jewish literary dissent as well. Here the flawed conduct of Zionist society is seen in terms of the moral collapse of postwar Western society; the moral transgressions of Israeli society are the metonymical representations of the world's failure to live up to the values of liberal humanism and the ideals of enlightened progress. Whether moralistic and positive, as in the reception of Arab fiction, or pessimistic and despairing, as in the reception of Jewish fiction, the canonical readings of both literatures are informed by a Western humanistic discourse. Underlying the humanistic discourse is the "master code" reflecting the desire to maintain the separation between Jews and Arabs or, so to speak, to dismiss the presence of the Arab in the Zionist project. The recourse to humanism allows certain critics to perpetuate the "invisibility" of the defeated minority by highlighting the universal, humanistic position of its writers. The strategies of canonization in relation to both national literatures that I have outlined are intended to neutralize and consequently silence the voices that, in both literatures, denounce Israel's practices of inequality and oppression.

The aim of the third part of this study is to liberate the silenced voices of dissent. My discussion shows how, when released from the ideological ties of canonization, the dissenting Jewish and Arab fictions reveal indelible interconnections between Arabs and Jews. In this sense the texts on both sides of the political divide defy the doctrine of separatism anchored in the Zionist fascination with the West.

To conclude my discussion of the canonical binds of separatism and begin my analysis of bonding between Arabs and Jews, I wish briefly to mention Shammas's remarkably insightful essay "Kitsch 22," where he discusses the cultural relations between the Jewish majority and the Arab minority in Israel. Shammas begins by identifying Israel's compulsive attraction to Western culture. Quoting Milan Kundera's perception of Israel as "the true heart of Europe, a strange heart which lies far from the body," Shammas locates the obsession with Europe at the very inception of the Zionist movement. It started with Herzl, Nordau, and Jabotinsky, all of whom stressed the Zionist mission to bring European civilization to Asia. As Shammas reminds us, Herzl hoped that Zionism would "fulfill the role of cultural vanguard facing the barbarians, "whereas Jabotinsky hoped that the movement would "carry the moral boundary of Europe as far as the Euphrates."[1] As Shammas sees it, the Zionists viewed themselves as the emissaries of the enlightened West in the "backward" East and rejected the possibility of integration into the region.

In the first part of this study I demonstrated how the Zionists' adherence to the West shaped the doctrines of the "negation of the Diaspora" and of the "empty land." In this second part I have examined the implementations of the Zionist politics of negation and separation in the cultural domain of the literary canon. Recall Yehoshua's view of the Palestinian state as a way to keep the two cultures, Jewish and Arab, apart. Indeed, in his essay Shammas mentions the brutally insensitive comment made by Yehoshua, a fellow writer, whom he used to consider a close friend. He recalls how "a certain Hebrew writer . . . recently urged me to take my belongings and move one hundred meters to the east, to the Palestinian state-to-come, if I wish to fulfill my whole national identity." To this unconscionable breach of trust Shammas responds with a remarkable insight: "But he [Yehoshua] does not realize that his left hand is already part of my Israeli being, just as at least one finger of his right hand is one of mine."[2] Shammas's image communicates the irrevocable bonding of Israeli Arabs and Israeli Jews, while also acknowledging the difficulty in recognizing and accepting this bond. This twofold insight illuminates our journey into the two fictions of dissent as an arena of a complex and as yet unfinished process involving the recognition of the other as an integral part of one's identity.

PART 3
Discourses of Bonding

Peace is a dialogue between two stories, none of which should be imposed on either party. My country has two names: Palestine and Israel, and my dream is to build one shared history on the same land.

Mahmoud Darwish, "Palestine: The Imaginary and the Real"

Introduction

Toward a Redefinition of History

> Only that historian will have the gift of fanning the spark of hope in the past who is firmly convinced that *even the dead* will not be safe from the enemy if he wins. . . . Whoever has emerged victorious participates to this day in the triumphal procession in which the present rulers step over those who are lying prostrate. . . . There is no document of civilization which is not at the same time a document of barbarism. . . . A historical materialist therefore dissociates himself from it as far as possible. He regards it as his task to brush history against the grain.
> —*Walter Benjamin, "Theses on the Philosophy of History"*

In the first two parts of this study I examined the canonical fabric of liberalism, humanism, and enlightenment that makes the Zionist project look like a "document of civilization" or, rather, an offshoot of the Western Enlightenment. This ideologically informed critical approach successfully appropriated the texts of dissent into the Zionist-Western fold. Identified as part of the canon, the dissent in the texts functions as a corrective to the deviations from the universalist, liberal foundations of Zionism. In other words, it is not the ideological creed that this literature disavows but rather the failure of the "new" Jews to live up to this creed.

It is my contention that when they are stripped of their canonical codification, both the Jewish and Arab texts reveal a stratum of defiance directed at the core of the Zionist concept. More specifically, they undermine the concept of the "new" Jew, which was largely the product of the dogmas of the "empty land" and the "negation of the Diaspora." As I claimed in the first part, the ethos of the "emptiness" and the devastation of the land had to be constructed to justify the deliberate, ideologically rationalized rejection of the Diaspora home. The need to overcome the pain of self-incurred orphanhood explains the metaphoric perception of the land as "mother" and "bride" alongside the concept of the land as a wilderness that needs to be "conquered" and restored to its former biblical glory.

From this perspective, the presence of the Arab represented a threat to the Zionist idea of return. The recognition of an inhabited land would have invalidated the Zionist rationale for rejecting the Diaspora, which entailed the difficult act of leaving the parental home. The myth of the land as a wasteland waiting to be redeemed was necessary in order to suppress the guilt of betrayal of the closest family, especially in view of the worsening situation is Europe, eventually culminating in the tragedy of the Holocaust. In this sense the abstraction of the Arab in the canonical scheme communicates the desire to evade a reality that threatens the psychological and ethical mainstays of the Zionist enterprise.

In the following discussion I will demonstrate how, once liberated from these ideologically imposed restraints, the texts lend themselves to psychological and ethical insights that defy the canonizing discourse. Once one gains the ability to hear their voice of dissent, according to Benjamin, they will communicate "the retroactive force [that] . . . constantly [calls] in question every victory, past and present, of the rulers."[1] The stories that "brush history against the grain" defy the triumphalist narrative of the victors. They act against the narrative of the "new" Jew, whose triumphalism denounced the Jewish life in the Diaspora and, at the same time, effaced the history of the Palestinian inhabitant of the land. The story of the despoliation of the Palestinian disrupts the narrative of Israel's victory. In this sense it illustrates Benjamin's view of the history of the victim, which disrupts the present with the story of the past.

The voices that emerge from the stories tell us that the reconstitution of the vanquished past is not the exclusive domain of the victims. The representations of dissent examined here are not confined to those of the defeated minority of Israeli Arab writers that challenge the story of the victor; the voices of dissent also emerge from the victorious camp of Israeli Jews. The phenomenon of a double opposition to the dominant history presents an asymmetrical configuration that arises from the margins as well as from the midst of the ruling majority. A brief digression involving South African white literature of dissent, that is, the literature of dissent of South African caucasians, sheds light upon the phenomenon of oppositional literature. In a thought-provoking article Neil Lazarus discusses the dissident literature of the mainstream writers at the time of apartheid. Lazarus claims that the factor "that renders [the work of these authors] oppositional . . . [is] the manner in which this work enters into history— or, more precisely, refuses to be encoded seamlessly into history. In other words, the work refuses to be incorporated into a history defined by Walter Benjamin in his 'Theses on the Philosophy of History,' as the relentlessly totalitarian and reductive discourse of the oppressor."[2] Lazarus's observation draws attention to the fact that the literature of dissent by Caucasian writers antagonizes the political system of oppression of which it is an integral part.

I do not propose to draw parallels between South African and Israeli literatures. Nor do I wish to compare the treatment as traitors and outcasts accorded the Caucasian South African dissenting writers with the Israeli left-wing writers' risk-free and privileged social status, which I discussed in the second part of this study.[3] I would, however, like to draw attention to the mainstream reaction to the writings, which have, in the words of the epigraph, brushed history or, rather, the dominant ideology against the grain in both situations. Lazarus describes "the enormous gulf" between the perceptions of the dissenting writers and the "inflexibility and oneiric conformism of predominant white opinion."[4] As he points out, to maintain its "white opinion," the establishment may either appropriate, denounce, or simply ignore those who wage war against injustice

I have already observed how, to maintain the ideological consensus, the Israeli cultural establishment universalized and consequently neutralized the dissent of the Israeli Jewish writers. The universalist approach conferred a privileged position on the dissident writers, thus enhancing the enlightened and liberal reputation of the Israeli cultural establishment. From this perspective the Arab character became the emblem of either universal victimhood and suffering or, conversely, of existential fear of the Jewish protagonist. One should note, however, that some of the critical responses to the Arab charac-ter in Israeli fiction were not quite as liberal and universalist. For instance, right-wing critic Mordechai Shalev accused Yehoshua of us-ing the Arab in his story "Facing the Forests" as a camouflage for a message that amounted to the betrayal of the Zionist founding fathers and therefore to the disintegration of the Zionist ideal. Specifically, Shalev sees Yehoshua's approach in terms of Oedipal rebellion of sons against fathers. The story represents the failure of the fathers' generation to transmit the ideal to the next generation, where the Arab serves to disguise the struggle between the founders and their successors.[5] Thus, while some critics disarmed the texts by appropri-ating them through universalization, others attacked them for un-dermining the Zionist hegemony as established by the founders. Both critical approaches seem intent on displacing the figure of the Arab, thereby dismissing the prominent psychological and ethical issues that consistently emerge in the fictional representations of Jewish-Arab encounters.

Whatever direction they take, these critics maintain a steadfast consensus regarding the continuing "invisibility" of the Arab. Over the years the attitude favoring the dismissal of the Arab has by no means become the domain of the past. Indeed, Azmi Bishara, an Is-raeli Arab Knesset member, philosopher, and scholar, has reaffirmed the deliberate erasure of the Arab from the consciousness of the Is-raeli Jew. In his editor's introduction to a volume poignantly entitled *Between "I" and "We": The Construction of Identities and Israeli Identity,* Bishara claims that "the place of the other, that is, the Pales-tinian Arab, is a question that, like a ghost, refuses to disappear. The presence of the Arab has left its traces on each and every component of Israeli [Jewish] identity that negated it, denied it, and made its memory disappear in both language and culture."[6] An article in the *Jerusalem Report,* a Jewish publication that promotes an objective stance with respect to the Middle East, concurs with Bishara's obser-vations, claiming that "fifty years of overwhelmingly good citizenship didn't bring them [Israeli Arabs] full integration into the Jewish state." It also points out that the latest "annual report on the equality and integration of the Arab citizens paints a bleak picture."[7] It is important to note that the tragic incident resulting from the intifada Al-Aqsa, where thirteen Israeli Arabs were killed by Israeli police, unfortunately proved the above perceptions correct.[8]

In contrast to the seemingly complete disconnectedness between Israeli Jews and Israeli Arabs, the Israeli Jewish texts discussed here trace an inexorable trajectory of rapprochement. To use Bishara's terms, these writings invoke the "ghosts" that lead them to the Arab history in the land. In this context it is important to stress that the need to acknowledge the "ghosts" opposed to the prevailing ideology of separation arises from writers who were born in Eretz Israel, who have been firm believers in Zionism, and who owe their identity as Israeli Hebrew writers to the Zionist ideal of national and linguistic revival.

The identity and the system of beliefs into which these writers were born accentuate the complexity of their criticism of the Zionist project. Their re-presentation of the suppressed memory of Arab dispossession and victimization contradicts the general consensus on national memorialization. To determine the extent to which these literary works run counter to the mainstream, one can turn to Maurice Halbwachs's view on the formation of social beliefs. Halbwachs maintains that "society admits all ideas [and traditions], provided . . . that they have a place in its thought and that they still interest present-day people who understand them." Furthermore, he postulates that "only those recollections subsist that . . . society, working within its present-day frameworks, can reconstruct."[9] In view of my previous discussion of the Zionists—the "new" Jews who claimed they were restoring the pre-exilic, biblical history of Jewish sovereignty and who, in fact, desired to create a Western state in Palestine—it is quite evident that the Israeli Jewish majority had no interest in cultivating the history of the Palestinian Arab. As I have shown in my discussion of post-Zionist tendencies in the first part of this study, despite the critical voices that have arisen, recollections of Israeli society for the most part still center on the Yishuv creating a haven for persecuted Diaspora Jews (mainly Holocaust survivors), the *halutsim* "conquering" the land, and young, fearless fighters sacrificing their lives first to establish and then to protect the Jewish state. The Israelis still glorify the Zionist pioneers who single-handedly "made the desert bloom," "conquered the empty land," and through their toil and blood managed to reconstruct the ideal ancient Israel. Such still vibrant collective memories leave no room for the history of the Palestinian Arabs in the land.

These generally accepted and proudly shared national memories seem not only to follow Halbwachs's concept of collective memory but also to concur with Benjamin's claim that victorious history eliminates those memories that do not enhance the victorious narrative of self-glorification. I have already mentioned Yael Zerubavel's insightful analysis of the construction and impact of national myths. Her discussion of the defense of Masada, the Bar Kokba revolt, and the Battle of Tel Hai provides three fascinating case studies of the ways in which the Zionist collective memory was shaped. Zerubavel's study demonstrates the programmatic insistence and dogmatic zeal with which the indelible connections with antiquity were propagated in everyday Israeli life.[10]

This insistence on the Zionists' direct link to antiquity explains the need to neutralize a literature that, in the words of Lazarus, refused "to be encoded seamlessly" into the one-sided history of victory. At the same time, the myth of the "empty land"—which connected the Zionists with the ancient Hebrews and upon which the Israeli Jewish writers were raised—elucidates the problematic issues of the literary representations of the Arab story. Recall Gertz's observation of the absence of plausible Arab characters in Israeli literature and Yehoshua's admission of failure to create an authentic Arab character in *The Lover*. The failure to translate the plight of the Arab into the language of art attests to the powerful domination of the Zionist victory, which erected solid barriers between victor and victim, an observation that illustrates Benjamin's notion of the erasure of the memory of the defeated. The forgotten story of the Arabs in the land and their tale of defeat, discrimination, and oppression needed to be assembled from fragmented memories, traces of recollections, and ghostly voices from the past.

Why, then, would mainstream writers engage in the socially and emotionally risky task of telling a story so completely opposed to the Zionist tenet of the "empty" land? As I demonstrated in the second part, in terms of social impact the writers' dissenting position hardly makes a dent in the dominant ideological mind-set. In fact, the dissenting writers pay the price of canonical appropriation by becoming the showcase for Israel's enlightenment and tolerance. The emotional repercussions of the dissenting position are more complex. By immersing themselves in the story of the Arab, Jewish writers must engage in an ethically risky self-scrutiny that threatens their national identity. Their self-image as oppressors is likely to undermine their own faith in an ideology that gave them the freedom to create Israel's national literature in Hebrew—Israel's national language. Consequently, as I also previously demonstrated, the writers' compliance with the establishment's neutralization of their dissenting message signals the reluctance of these members of the ideologically unified collective to consciously and fully recognize the triumphalist elimination of the memory of the other. At the same time, as their texts attest, despite their self-identification as Zionists, the Jewish writers are ineluctably driven to explore the "invisible" presence of the Arabs as well as the effaced Arab history in the land.

The contradiction between ideological and ethical positions raises the question of the impulse to create stories whose truth is difficult to acknowledge under the Zionist state. What emotional need motivated the mainstream Jewish writer to rediscover the suppressed story of the Arab? The question suggests a perspective quite different from that of Benjamin's "triumphal procession in which the present rulers step over those who are lying prostrate," which he promoted in his "Theses on the Philosophy of History."[11] I take recourse to the archetypal "crise de conscience" of the victors in Freud's *Totem and Taboo*. Before addressing Freud's position, it is important to note that Benjamin was writing in 1940, faced with the reality of Nazi rule. The question of conscience seemed to have disappeared in light of the horror of tyranny. His observation of the situation was reflected in his Marxist-cum-theological view of history, namely, that redemption was possible only when the defeated became conscious of their misery and exposed—through the story of their suffering—the triumphalism of the oppressors. As Benjamin's tragic suicide suggests, he did not consider such a moment to be in sight. In contrast, Freud wrote *Totem and Taboo* in 1913, when the world was still at peace and a preoccupation with emotions and ethics seemed to fit the zeitgeist.

Freud saw victory as psychologically transforming, an event bound to undermine the victor and to affect the course of social

history. Paradoxically, the act of violence that brings victory dimin-
ishes the expected gains because it engenders unexpected feelings of
guilt and remorse. Freud grounded his theory in the archetypal
murder of the father, the dominating ruler of the tribe. As a result
of the elimination of the father, the sons became the heirs and masters
they had wished to be, but in view of its psychological consequences,
they soon learned that their triumph assumed an altogether unexpected meaning. Most significantly, they discovered the hitherto unacknowledged love and compassion for the hated opponent *after* his
elimination.

Recall Benjamin's position that with victory *"even the dead,"*
namely, the ancestral history of the defeated community, will be
erased from public consciousness. In contrast, Freud claims that the
victim of the murder will remain in the consciousness of the murderers forever: the *"dead father became stronger than the living one had
been."*[12] As Freud sees it, the committed violence paradoxically engenders *post factum* "deferred obedience,"[13] which changes the victors' self-image as well as the image of the physically eliminated other.
The contrition of the winners not only warrants the remembrance of
the victim but also brings to the fore the concept of social ethics.

The differences between the two thinkers notwithstanding, both
Benjamin and Freud consider victory as an initiation of a dialectics
that antagonizes the victors' triumphalism. As Benjamin sees it, victory creates a social class of *victims* that eventually implants the suppressed story of their victimization in the victor's consciousness. According to Freud, the triumph imbues the psyche of the *victors* with
the suffering they inflicted. It is the guilt and contrition over the crime
committed against another that engenders a new consciousness. As
Mikkel Borch-Jacobsen states, this consciousness places "an ethical
respect before it is a political submission, respect for others before
being political submission to oneself."[14] In other words, guilt and
contrition produce an ethics of respect that places the others above
political loyalties and even one's narcissistic desires.

The dilemma of the "new" Jew as a victor whose sense of guilt
conflicted with the politics of triumphalism was first articulated in
S. Yizhar's controversial story "Hirbet Hizah," published in 1949.[15]
The story describes acts of brutality committed by an Israeli platoon
against harmless inhabitants of an Arab village during the 1948 war,

the demolition of the village, and especially the expulsion of the villagers. As Gila Ramraz-Rauch observes, the story raised responses that "concern ideology rather than aesthetics," since its theme, namely, the "maltreatment of Arabs vis-à-vis Israeli conscience"[16] was difficult for the Israeli readership to accept. Indeed, the choice of Yizhar's "Hirbet Hizah" as the starting point of this discussion gains validation in view of the half-century-long controversy surrounding the story, which shows no sign of abating. In her survey of the reception of Yizhar's story—which has found its way into high school literature curricula and whose cinematic version was shown on Israeli national television—Israeli historian Anita Shapira concludes that despite the continuous presence of the story on the public scene, "on a more subliminal level . . . collective memory did not 'assimilate' the messages conveyed by 'Hirbet Hizah,'" whose "unpleasant memory continues to linger."[17] In support of Shapira's conclusion, while staying in Israel I watched a televised debate among prominent Israeli scholars and intellectuals in which a brief episode of the cinematic version of "Hirbet Hizah" was shown in connection with the discussion of conscientious objectors.

Perhaps the most dramatic illustration of the indelible mark that "Hirbet Hizah" has left on the Israeli consciousness occurred during an interview with Yizhar. When asked about the role of the writer as "the conscience of the nation," Yizhar observed, "First of all, there must be a need for such a thing at a time of sudden distortion of values. The need to find a different voice. You do not believe politicians; you do not believe public speakers. You are waiting for somebody to speak out. Writers are people who speak out. In language, in words. Occasionally a thing happens, like Zola's '*J'accuse.*' A great number of those writers who changed things raised their voices against wrongdoing. . . . It [the change] is impossible to predict; is something like mutation. Perhaps this is the key word. A writer is a mutation."[18] Note the recurrent reference to Zola as the writer who changed the course of moral history. As I stated in the second part of this study, Zola was mentioned in the trenchant critique of Yehoshua's affirmation of moral responsibility of Israeli writers. The Israeli writer's call for morality was denounced as hypocritical in a country whose intellectuals betrayed the moral cause by colluding with the ideological zeitgeist that justifies occupation and discriminates against Arab citizens. Yizhar's claim, however, cannot be dismissed as disingenuous. The obvious differences between Zola and Yizhar notwithstanding, the reception of Yizhar's "Hirbet Hizah" represents a rare example of a Zolaesque literary work whose accusation has penetrated the public consciousness.

As the ongoing debate over "Hirbet Hizah" proves, the voice that the story raised against wrongdoing produced a "mutation" in the Israeli mind. In particular, one scene in the closing section of the story continues to disturb the public. When the narrator shows concern about the ruthlessness of the conquest—specifically about the forced expulsion of the villagers of Hirbet Hizah—a soldier named Moishe impresses upon him a vision of the future: "To Hirbet, what's-its-name, immigrants will be coming. Are you listening? And they'll take this land and they'll till it and everything here will be fine."[19] The process of obliterating the memory of the defeated has already started with the conqueror's dismissive reference to the village's name. The past will disappear with the displacement of the Arab village by a flourishing and productive Israeli Jewish settlement. It is important to note that Moishe's optimistic visualization of the future is contingent upon erasure of more than one refugee story: the immigrants will be able to make the village flourish only after renouncing their own story. By replacing the Arab villagers with the turned-into-*halutsim* Diaspora Jews, the Zionist project will consolidate its main tenets, namely, the "empty land" and the "negation of the Diaspora."

In response to this projection of a future devoid of history, the narrator foresees the life of the Diaspora Jews, who will be transformed into "new" Jews haunted by the memory of past injustice: "But these people who come to live in this village—will not the walls cry out in their ears? Will not those sights, those cries which were uttered and those which were not uttered . . . [will not] the submissiveness of the weak and their strength—that they are unable to do anything, these mute weaklings—will they not make the air alive with shadows, voices and hidden looks?"[20] While Moishe recites the Zionist truisms with the arrogant confidence of the victor, the narrator hears voices that foretell the moral failure of the Zionist enterprise. The ghostlike memories of the vanquished will defy the notion of the "empty land" and thus defeat the ideal of the "new" Jew grounded in the "negation of the Diaspora."

How do these antithetical perspectives in "Hirbet Hizah" connect with—perhaps even engender—the psychological-ethical issues raised in the writings of the Jewish and Arab authors discussed in this study? Specifically, how accurately had Yizhar, the grand old man of Israeli literature, presaged the complex relationships of victors and victims as they reemerged a few decades later in both Israeli Jewish and Arab fictional writing?

To appreciate Yizhar's foresight, one must consider it in light of the accepted periodization of Israeli Jewish literature. I have already discussed Shaked's identification of the "new wave" literature produced by the so-called Statehood generation, that is, writers active from the 1960s to the 1980s who were deeply influenced by the existentialist wave of postwar Europe. What preceded the "new wave" was the so-called Palmach generation,[21] a group of Israeli-born "new Jews" who fought in the War of Independence. The native tongue of the writers of the Palmach generation was Hebrew, and they were adamantly creating a new Hebrew culture. As Shaked postulates, the literature of this period was shaped by the value system of the Zionist Youth Movement. Its members were young Zionists of a socialist persuasion who believed in both military and agricultural conquest of the land.[22]

This categorization defines the distinctness of the literatures of the Statehood and Palmach generations. The self-assurance of the heroic, idealistic, and moral protagonist of the Palmach generation, a figure who represented noble communal norms and collectively shared values, underwent a transformation in the Statehood period to become a figure characterized by self-doubt, indifference, and a pervasive sense of alienation. In contrast to the typical member of the Palmach collective, who was guided by the unequivocal certainties of the Zionist ideology, the individual of the Statehood generation has struggled with an existentialist malaise. The heroic, single-minded Israeli-born Sabras were succeeded by disaffected, socially estranged, and introspective protagonists in the writings of Yehoshua, Oz, and Grossman, among others.[23]

Against Shaked's periodization, I propose that "Hirbet Hizah" cuts through the Palmach and Statehood categorizations and does not resort to the universalist lenses of postwar Western philosophical trends.[24] My reading focuses on the concrete historical occurrences that it depicts. From this perspective, the universal value of the story should be sought on two factual levels: first, in the specific atrocities committed by Israeli Jewish soldiers against Palestinian Arabs in the village; and, second, in the oppositional reaction of one of the soldiers and his determination to tell the story.

The emphasis on the brutality of the conquest and the response of opposition to this brutality thwarts the intention to abstract or neutralize the dissent in the story. The stress on the concrete acts of violence and the rejection of violence highlights the conflict between the "will to power" and the "will to ethics" that was observed in my earlier discussion of Benjamin and Freud. The clash between these two "wills" underlies and shapes the particular situation of the conquest of the Arab village in the 1948 war. For the collective of victorious soldiers, the brutal subjection of the defeated population writes the narrative of their triumph. For the narrator, who is emotionally unable to remain indifferent to the plight of the defeated, the experience turns into a *via dolorosa* of moral reckoning. Whereas for the majority the victory justifies the narrative of brutality and injustice, for the narrator the eruption of triumphalist brutality raises serious questions about the Zionist cause.

In "Hirbet Hizah" neither the military unit as a collective nor the individual who tells the story fulfills the norms of the Palmach generation. In other words, neither the arrogant and cruel conduct of the group nor the misery, self-recriminations, and helplessness of the narrator match the representation of the heroic, idealistic, and moral protagonist of this type of literature. They certainly do not correspond to the protagonists in Moshe Shamir's prototypical Palmach novels. Nothing could be further from the portrayal of the narrator and his comrades in "Hirbet Hizah" than, for instance, the portrayal of Elik in Shamir's *With His Own Hands: Stories of Elik,* who "was born of the sea," that is, liberated from the burden of history of the Diaspora to become a fearless fighter for the land, or of Uri in *He Walked in the Fields,*[25] a representative of the courageous, pragmatic, and straightforward Zionist youth ready to give his life for the land.[26]

Against these representations of the unshakable faith in and commitment to the Zionist claim to the land, "Hirbet Hizah" dramatizes the narrator's contravening response. The polarized responses of the soldiers and the narrator range from deeply empathic sorrow to cruel indifference, thus ineluctably dividing the winning camp. The split within the ideologically molded collective is marked by the trauma of the collapsed ideal. The victory has given birth to a consciousness that, on the one hand, feels an obligation to the discourse of the triumphalist ideology and, on the other hand, experiences a compelling sense of responsibility toward the vanquished. I wish to argue that in Yizhar's story the breakup of the unified front of winners signals the inception of the incontrovertible bonding between victors and vanquished. The story is seminal because it established the patterns governing the difficult, tortuous, complex, yet indelible relationships between Jews and Arabs. These patterns were further developed in both Jewish and Arab fiction that was published in the wake of Yizhar's story. In the following chapters I investigate the evolution of these difficult relationships. The readings focus on the unfolding consciousness of the inextricable bonding between Jews and Arabs.

Chapter 7 examines the traumatic impact of Israeli-Arab wars on both victors and victims. While the Jewish narrator-victor in "Hirbet Hizah" dissents from the triumphalist collective, the Arab narrator-victim in *The Pessoptimist* reacts against the reality of defeat. The confessional genres of the narratives signal the quests of both victors and victims for posttraumatic self-reaffirmation. Both narratives emphasize the risk of alienation, madness, and death in the reencounter with the traumatic past. Chapter 8 focuses on the evolution of the dialogue between Jew and Arab as it emerges in A. B. Yehoshua's "Facing the Forests" and Atallah Mansour's *In a New Light*. The overriding need of the political adversaries to seek some sort of resolution in the acts of telling and listening creates relationships of emotional interdependence. The disclosure, confrontation, and acknowledgment *to each other* of the tragic past of the adversaries not only validates the victim but also frees the victor from the traumatic effects of victory. In chapter 9 I single out Amos Oz's "Nomad and Viper" as the point where the path toward rapprochement reaches a dead end and there is a complete breakdown in communication. This is the moment where violence seems to be the only way for victor and victim to connect. The story points up the dangers of the unexamined collective psyche of Israeli society with regard to the Arab, a psychological mind-set whose gravitation toward barbarism forebodes the end of Israel as a civilized society. My readings of Oz's *My Michael* and of Habiby's *Saraya, Daughter of the Ghoul* in chapter 10 stress the need for introspection and self-examination before contacts between the camps may be resumed. While the post-victory / post-defeat world incessantly moves forward toward political achievements and self-actualization, the haunting narratives that mourn the war casualties refuse to comply with the ideological injunction to forget the past. The incompatibility and contradistinctions between the public / future-oriented and the private / past-oriented spheres indicate that conscious accountability for the history of triumph and defeat is necessary before a meaningful trajectory toward the future may be constructed. Chapter 11 focuses on David Grossman's novel *The Smile of the Lamb* and Anton Shammas's *Arabesques*. Here I explore how the paternal stories of love weave inextricable ties between Jews and Arabs. The permutations of these oral legacies, which transcend the boundaries of ethnic traditions and national histories, reaffirm a difficult yet inescapable bonding of the two nations. The acknowledgment of this bonding is predicated upon a weltanschauung that demonstrates an awareness and understanding of the relativity and mutability of human connections. The ability to acknowledge the inexorable interdependence that has shaped—and continues to shape—the identities of both Jews and Arabs carries the promise of a meaningful interaction.

7

The Traumas of Victory
and Defeat

S. Yizhar's "Hirbet Hizah" and
Emile Habiby's *Pessoptimist*

The Confession of the Powerless Victor

In his discussion of the autobiographical genre, John Freccero postulates that "every narrative of the self is the story of a conversion [that] implies the death of the self as character and the resurrection of the self as author."[1] From this point of view, autobiographical writing signals a twofold transmutation. The emergence of an autobiography implies a fundamental change in the worldview of the subject, one that empowers the subject with self-consciousness, which prompts the emergence of the story.

Freccero's concept of the autobiographical genre as psychological rebirth draws attention to the factual component in the fiction of "Hirbet Hizah." Years after the story was published, Yizhar, who fought in the War of Independence, reaffirmed its autobiographical component, admitting that witnessing events like those depicted in "Hirbet Hirzah" as a soldier determined his "birth" as a writer. Yizhar confided, "one or two events concerning injustice toward the Arabs, which I witnessed at the end of the war, created an explosion in my life, which made me a writer. . . . It was that *trauma* of that *personal fall from innocence* that led me to write my stories [when]

153

certain axioms in my life crumbled [such as] the belief that there are
certain things that Jews just don't do."[2]

Yizhar's disclosure illustrates Freccero's view of the autobiographical genre as a story of conversion. The first-person narrative
in "Hirbet Hizah" presents a hardly disguised fictional representation
of an emotionally and ideologically shattering upheaval in the writer's life. The traumatic realization of the "barbaric" underside of the
Zionist enterprise results in Yizhar's transformation into the author
of his own story, who relates his traumatic fall from innocence.

To better understand the conversion of the narrator of "Hirbet
Hizah" from character to author, it is important briefly to consider
the signification of a traumatic experience. Freud defined trauma as
"any excitations from the outside which are powerful enough to
break through the protective shield" and warned that "an external
trauma is bound to provoke a disturbance on a large scale in the
functioning of the organism's energy and to set in motion every possible defense measure."[3] Because of the immediate mobilization of the
defense mechanism, trauma communicates itself in aftermath manifestations, or, in psychological terms, through posttraumatic syndromes. Freud also revealed that "the traumatic neuroses demonstrate very clearly that a fixation to the moment of the traumatic
occurrence lies at their root." The victims of trauma reproduce the
situation in their dreams, "as though [they] had not yet been able
to deal adequately with the situation."[4] Cathy Caruth elaborates on
Freud's definition, emphasizing "the surprising *literality* and nonsym-
bolic nature of traumatic dreams and flashbacks." She claims that
the enigmatic core of trauma lies in "incompletion in knowing . . .
an overwhelming occurrence that then remains, in its insistent return,
absolutely *true* to the event."[5]

Indeed, Yizhar's narrative seems to corroborate the above concep-
tualizations of the traumatic event. His narrator begins the story by
admitting that "though all this happened a long time ago, it would
not let me be," and he declares that it was the persistently returning
memory of the event that initiated his writing. Yet it is not only the
past that torments him; the present is also affected by the recurring
memory. What he sees around him is "this large community of liars—
marked by ignorance, self-serving indifference, or just shameless
selfishness." He finds that these liars "betray the truth with the facile

shrewdness of an old sinner." The narrator then admits that even though he wished to be like everybody else and for a long time tried to banish such heretical thoughts, he can no longer hold his peace, feeling compelled to break his silence and write down his tale.[6]

This "community of liars" refers to the group of people who in his pretraumatic life the narrator considered his closest friends—brothers united by common beliefs, morals, and values. It is important to keep in mind the consciousness of "brotherhood" that characterized the weltanschauung of the fighting Israelis. Today comrades-in-arms of the Palmach generation are still glorified for their unwavering, brotherly loyalty to each other. The narrator's derogatory view of his fellow fighters—a society to whom he had pledged his loyalty before the incident in the village took place—indicates a dramatic "conversion," in the words of Freccero. The change is so extreme that, in an attempt to gain a measure of comprehension of self and others, he needs to reconstruct the transforming incident. He admits that he is engaging in a search for understanding that has eluded him thus far: "I can no longer straddle the fence, and even though *I have not yet found the way out,* I believe that, rather than keep silent, I had better start telling the tale" (HH 43).

The narrator's sense of desperation arises from the collapse of his ideological modus vivendi: the hitherto indubitable ethical norms of the Zionist project proved deceitful. But it is also his own gullibility that evokes his rage; his naivet made him trust a "community of liars." Indeed, Yizhar's narrator's disillusionment illustrates Ronnie Janoff-Bulman's postulation that the traumatic event manifests itself in "a profound impact on fundamental assumptions about the world. . . . Core assumptions are shattered by the traumatic experience."[7]

What is the nature of the experience that transformed the narrator from a trusting and cooperative friend and comrade-in-arms into a suspicious and embittered individual, estranged from his social circle? Robert Jay Lifton's claim that trauma must involve a "contact with death in some bodily or psychic fashion"[8] directs our attention to the psychological nature of the narrator's trauma. Under no circumstance was either the narrator or his fellow soldiers in any danger in the village. Rather, the narrator's traumatic experience is of a symbolic nature; it is the death, the disintegration of his idealistic beliefs, or, as Yizhar himself calls it, "the fall from innocence." The latter, which shattered the narrator's "core assumptions" about the world, was not the result of an unmediated experience but rather the vicarious experience of seeing others in a life-threatening situation. The trauma is exacerbated by the fact that the suffering of the innocent victims was inflicted with terrible cruelty by his comrades-in-arms. It is the *victims'* expropriation and expulsion under the threat of death that led to the transformation of the *victor*.

A closer look at the situation reveals that the brutal eviction of the villagers effected identity transformation among all the parties involved. The conquest produced a drastic "conversion" of the vanquished Arab villagers, the Jewish conquerors, and the dissenting narrator. I have already established the fact that the narrator's inability to accept the unjustified cruelty of the conquest and its moral transgressions led to his conversion from an idealistic Zionist into a disaffected and disillusioned individual. It is important to note that the vanquished also undergo a transformation from established villagers into dispossessed exiles. Ruthlessly uprooted, the villagers are transformed into an anonymous, unidentifiable mass. Consequently, the transformation of the Arabs from villagers to refugees affects the identity of their conquerors. The Israelis, who were raised on the Zionist socialist ideals of freedom and equality, have become brutal oppressors. In particular, the narrator finds it painfully ironic that the "new" Jews who claim to have made a fresh start by moving away from the Diaspora have turned into victimizers and "expellers" of the weak. He is dismayed at his friends' lack of moral concern, their total oblivion of Diaspora history and the persecutions of the Jews, which should have made them sensitive to the suffering of others. "What measure of indifference have we got," he laments, "as if we have never done anything else but expropriate and exile" (HH 111). As I have already mentioned, the irony of the situation lies precisely in the ideological injunction to "negate the Diaspora," that is, to forget the hundreds of years of exile. It is the erasure of the expulsions that allows the Jewish conquerors to become a nation of evictors and expropriators.

On one level, then, "Hirbet Hizah" can indeed be viewed as a manifesto of humanistic universal values. Like the proverbial lonely voice of the "prophets to the House of Israel," the narrator indicts the ruthless victors and expresses compassion for the victims. The interpretation that views the story as a general condemnation of moral transgression canonizes it as a literary defense of humanism and in this way neutralizes its dissent from a specific political-social situation. Indeed, one reading of Yizhar's story reiterates the strategy of neutralization I discussed in connection with the "new wave" writers. "It is not the Arab that interests Yizhar," this critic argues, "but the ideal of a free humanistic man. . . . The Arab is only a test case for the conflict between a humanistic system of values and a military one."[9] It is true that the opening apologia for writing the story stresses the compelling moral, humanistic obligation to confront the community. After having deferred for a long time, and "despite the fact that no resolution has been found," the narrator tells us that the trauma continues to haunt him and thus "instead of keeping quiet, I had better start telling the story" (HH 43).

On a deeper level, however, the story asks us to—perhaps even demands that we—pay attention to the narrator's double voice. Underlying the pronouncements of humanism and justice is the tone of dejection of an excluded mainstream member. The narrator's desire to impress his truth upon "the community of liars" conflicts with his need to come to terms with his own alienation from his community, which has now become the target of his indictment. Thus, the story itself discloses a more complex rationale for telling. I have already mentioned how the narrator's obstructionist attitude has dissolved the seamless uniformity of the fighting group, setting him apart from his fellow soldiers. The estrangement is signaled, first of all, by the absence of the narrator's name. It is important to note that his comrades never address him by name, even when responding to his misgivings. The anonymity of the narrator marks his position as a pariah. Indeed, the narrator's objections to the enforced expulsion of the villagers evokes growing impatience and anger from his comrades, who end up ignoring his complaints. Eventually the narrator comprehends his helplessness: "Everything in me cried out. Colonizers, it cried. Lies, it cried. Hirbet Hizah is not ours. . . . *I knew I would not cry out.* Why in the devil's name was I the only one to get excited? *What sort of useless stuff was I made of?* . . . To whom could I speak and be listened to? They would only laugh at me. . . . I knew one thing . . . that it was impossible for me to come to terms with anything so long as the tears were springing from the eyes of a sobbing child."[10]

While the narrator finds it impossible to assume the role of the conqueror, he also finds it impossible to disregard the hard implications of *his* position. It is not only his friends' contemptuous attitude that silences him. It is also his contemptuous self-perception as "useless stuff." A product of the formative ideology of the "new" Jew and the Palmach generation, he perceives his sensitivity toward the suffering other as a sign of weakness of character. Thus, from his perspective this weakness, which emasculates him, not only deprives him of the respect of others but also erodes his self-respect.

This realization leads me to conclude that the nonconformist attitude of the narrator has reduced him to the ranks of the defeated. Interesting similarities can be noted between the narrator and the Arab villagers. Like the nameless Arab villagers who dare to step forward and plead for mercy, the narrator, who pleads for the victims, remains nameless. Like the desperate victims of expulsion, whose cries fall on deaf ears, the narrator realizes the futility of his intercession and grows silent. Even though he at first insists that speaking the truth about the affliction caused by the conquest is the right thing to do, he also acknowledges his own weakness and the uselessness of his dissent. Yizhar's narrator's intimidation demonstrates the disempowering effect of Zionist triumphalism not only on the defeated Arabs but also on the objecting Jews. I therefore wish to argue that what impels Yizhar's narrator to write his story is not just the iniquity he witnesses but, to a large degree, the shame of his impotence. Seen from this perspective, "Hirbet Hizah" is not only the objector's indignant *indictment* of the conquest and expulsion; it is also the objector's shameful *confession* of his weakness vis-à-vis the establishment.

Who were the intended readers of Yizhar's narrator's indictment-cum-confession? As the 1949 publication date indicates, these were first and foremost his Palmach friends and other "new" Jews in the newly created state; in other words, a collective shaped by Zionist ideology. The narrator thus addresses an audience that is by no means ready for his criticism and complaints. As already mentioned, the story caused an immense uproar and mixed reviews from establishment critics, some of whom were extremely accusatory and bitter.[11] In a social atmosphere hardly well disposed toward dissenters, the writer's self-exposure to this particular audience raises a question. Why would Yizhar, only thinly disguised as his autobiographical narrator, insist on exhibiting his impotence to the "community of liars" once again risking the pain of contempt and ostracism that he had already experienced at the time of the events narrated in the story?

I will leave this question unanswered for the moment in order to compare it with an even more perplexing case of a similar self-exposure to a hostile audience. I am referring to Emile Habiby's novel *The Pessoptimist,* first published in Arabic in 1974 and subsequently translated into Hebrew by Anton Shammas and published in 1984. Not as openly autobiographical as Yizhar's "Hirbert Hizah," *The Pessoptimist* is nonetheless based on the author's life story. Though Habiby never disclosed the details about his so-called escape affair, it is known that he crossed the Lebanese border in the spring of 1948 after Haifa had fallen to the Israeli forces. Presumably Habiby was among the group of Arab Communists who were allowed to return to Israel in the summer of 1948. As Yaira Genosar tells us, "the affair of Habiby's return to Israel was alluded to in his fascinating story *The Secret Life of Saeed, the Pessoptimist.*"[12]

At the very least, the opening of the story of the protagonist-narrator Saeed is similar to that of his author. Saeed fled Haifa in the 1948 war, in the wake of which he chose to return. Upon his return, he turned informer for the Israeli Secret Service. *The Pessoptimist* is a picaresque novel that draws upon Voltaire's *Candide* in order to expose the naiveté of an enlightened weltanschauung in the face of the Israeli-Palestinian conflict. We have seen how the canonical critical reception understood Habiby's subscription to Voltairesque satire as an expression of his benevolent humanism. A closer reading of *The Pessoptimist,* however, will show that the satirical representation of Israeli Arab life, especially in the chapter entitled "The Amazing Similarity between Candide and Saeed," draws upon the picaresque misfortunes of Candide in order to provide a context for the tragedies that befell the Palestinian people. Unlike *Candide,* the novel does not end with the famous directive "chacun doit cultiver son jardin." Habiby's tale of his ill-fated narrator invalidates the notion that remaining aloof from the world guarantees a secure existence. The stability implied in Candide's eventual withdrawal from public affairs to the private sphere is an implausible solution for Saeed, whose overpowering fear and weakness of character hold him hostage in the enemy world while condemning him to an existence of unrelieved alienation.

In a sense, *The Pessoptimist* takes up where the story line of "Hirbert Hizah" left off. Yizhar's story concludes on a note of resignation and despair. As his narrator envisages the future, the new reality of the conquest will take over, the cries of the victims will be silenced, and the affliction of the exiled will be forgotten because, as the narrator foresees it, "silence would soon descend upon the final scene . . . [and it] would blanket everything and no man would disturb the tranquility." What follows is a biblical reference to God meting out justice to Sodom and Gomorrah, "God would come down to the valley to see if the deeds that were done matched the cries,"[13] which demonstrates the extent of the narrator's hopelessness regarding the injustice and inhumanity of his own community. In Yizhar's view, the possibility of redemption has been deferred indefinitely to Judgment Day. Habiby's novel, however, defies Yizhar's pessimistic conclusion. While justice is by no means redressed in *The Pessoptimist*, the story of Saeed, the dispossessed Arab refugee who returns to the homeland he has lost and decides to write about his experience of victimization, breaks the silence that has suppressed the cries of the victims in "Hirbet Hizah."

The intended readers of the Hebrew translation of *The Pessoptimist* are, of course, the Israeli victors, who, to resort to Benjamin's theory of history, have erased from memory the barbaric subtext of their victory. The twenty-year narrative of *The Pessoptimist* spans the interwar period of Israel's subjugation of its Arab minority. The story, which starts with the war of 1948 and ends after the war of 1967, records Israel's ruthless treatment of Palestinian Arabs both inside and outside the "green line." Temporarily disrupting the fictional make-believe, Saeed quotes a 1950 article in the *Jerusalem Post* that argues that since the Arabs were defeated, "they have no right to complain when they are asked to pay the price for the defeat which they have suffered."[14] In the aftermath of the 1967 war, Israel's policy in the occupied territories also exacted the price of defeat. As Saeed ironically notes, under the "most compassionate [occupation] known on earth ever since Paradise was liberated from its occupation by Adam and Eve" (P 124–25), the price of defeat has been imprisonment, exile, and demolition of Arab homes.

While both "Hirbet Hizah" and *The Pessoptimist* in its Hebrew translation address the readership of the conquering rulers, the Arab story presents a more complex case. After all, Yizhar's identity as a *tsabar* (a native of Palestine/Israel), his Jewish ethnicity, native fluency in Hebrew, military service, and Zionist orientation assured him of a forgiving albeit often begrudging and bitter reception. In contrast, Habiby's decision to have *The Pessoptimist* translated from the Arabic—his mother tongue and the language of his ethnic community—into Hebrew indicates a deliberately targeted hostile Israeli Jewish audience. Certainly this audience does not promise to be as forgiving to the Arab writer, as it was to Yizhar, one of its own. The Hebrew translations of his two subsequent novels, *Ikhatayyeh* and *Saraya, Daughter of the Ghoul,* reaffirm Habiby's conscious desire to address this adversarial readership through his oeuvre.

At the most obvious level, the translation of Israeli Arab literature into Hebrew signifies a subversive political act. To use James C. Scott's terminology, the translation makes the "hidden transcripts" public. The latter are practices of resistance by the subjugated that contravene the dogmatic unanimity of the "public transcripts" imposed by the dominant group. Therefore hidden transcripts are "kept offstage and unavowed" by the oppressed.[15] In this sense Habiby's fiction in Arabic can be seen as hidden transcripts since, even though Arabic is the second official language of the State of Israel, it has remained a foreign, practically unknown language to the majority of the Israeli Jewish population. The publication in Hebrew is, in this sense, an act of open dissension because it reveals a hitherto hidden transcript to the ruling Israeli mainstream. The translation becomes a subversive act of penetration into the dominating hegemony.

In view of its confessional genre, however, the text implies that political subversion may not be the only reason why the Israeli Arab has chosen to expose his story to an Israeli readership. While it indicts Israel's cruelty and injustice, the confessional aspect of the text highlights the confessor's moral dilemma. The question concerning the rationale for the self-exposure of the confessor to unfriendly—even antagonistic—readers that arose in Yizhar's story and that I have left unanswered is even more compelling in Habiby's case.

Why confess weakness to Israeli dominators whose animosity toward the Arabs has not by any means diminished? Why risk a hostile reaction to self-representation that might deepen the negative stereotypes of the Arab minority in Israeli society? One must conclude that the consciousness of the oppressors, ruthless and insensitive as they may be, is indispensable to the act of confession. Paradoxically, in both narratives the confession of impotence and moral failing intended for the oppressor indicates a movement toward self-liberation not only from the trauma of defeat but also from the trauma of victory. This perception leads to the understanding that empowerment lies in the acknowledgment and confession of cowardice and powerlessness even—or, perhaps, especially—by those who dared to expose the weaknesses and failings of the victim. The following analysis of the texts shows how in each of the narratives the narrator's exposure of his weakness to the oppressor converts the ostracized/enslaved, the so-called objectified character, into an authorial subject.

Writing the Trauma of Defeat

Robert Jay Lifton has observed that "extreme trauma creates a second self." The traumatized self is "a form of doubling" that contains "elements that are at odds in the two selves, including ethical contradictions." Recovery cannot occur until "that traumatized self is reintegrated."[16] Lifton's observation draws attention to the ethical implications of trauma. A traumatic experience not only shatters the victim's core assumptions about the external world but also splits the inner moral core of the traumatized individual. Trauma affects the individual's sense of moral responsibility toward oneself and others. Lifton seems to suggest that liberation from posttraumatic "doubling" is predicated upon the restoration of moral integrity.

Lifton's insight helps to elucidate Habiby's narrator's moral crisis, engendered by the trauma of his war experience. The split of Saeed's moral self occurred at a moment of extreme danger. In effect, it is possible to claim that his "second self" was born out of a close physical confrontation with death. In the course of the 1948 war Saeed's family was ambushed while escaping from the attacking Israeli army, with Saeed's father killed beside him. Saeed was saved thanks to a strange coincidence. As he recalls it, "I was born again thanks to an ass. . . . I escaped [death] because a stray donkey came into the line of fire and they shot it, so it died in place of me" (*P* 6). While one donkey rescued him from the Israelis, another donkey replaced him under their rule. Saeed decides to return to his homeland, now officially the State of Israel. Riding a donkey, he arrives at the headquarters of the military governor, where he assumes a new identity as an informer for the Israeli Secret Service (*P* 11). Henceforth he will lead a secret life that, he hopes, will allow him to remain safe in his conquered homeland under the protection of the victorious Israelis.

Needless to say, Saeed's postwar "second self" as an agent of the Israeli conqueror is at odds with his "original self" as a member of the Palestinian community, which de facto no longer exists due to the split effected by the defeat. Haunting memories constantly disrupt his secret life as a collaborator. Eventually the relentless consciousness of the lost world he betrayed infiltrates Saeed's other secret life. The latter emerges from the ineluctable need to restore the past. The desire translates into an incessant search for two irretrievable losses. He searches for the treasure hidden in an undersea cave by the fathers of the defeated generation and for Yuaad, the woman he loved in his prewar life and whose whereabouts as a refugee in one of the camps are unknown.

The undersea treasure is a metaphor for lost independence, national pride, and tradition. The search for the treasure gives Saeed the illusion of a national sense of belonging, thus alleviating the ethical predicament incurred by his double life as an informer. "When I realized that through this treasure I had become one of you [members of the split Palestinian community]," says Saeed, "a great burden was lifted from my mind" (*P* 89). Sharing the longing for the prewar life of independence reconnects him with his people and eases his pangs of conscience. As long as the search for the past remains a "hidden transcript," that is, a clandestine act of resistance, Saeed can lead his double life relatively safely. For a while he is capable of maintaining a precarious balance between his two secret selves.

This balance collapses when the memory of his love becomes a reality. Upon meeting the "second Yuaad," as he calls the daughter of his first love (whose name was also Yuaad), Saeed's desire to go back in time is so powerful that he feels he can undo history: "I felt like a bridegroom on his wedding night. I simply tossed those twenty lost years in the garbage can in the courtyard and flew up those stairs as if on wings, inspired by the presence of Yuaad" (*P* 150). Instantly the illusion—or, rather, the delusion—is shattered. Like her mother years earlier, Yuaad is taken away from Saeed by Israeli soldiers, to be deported to the occupied territories. When Yuaad the daughter asks Saeed whether he had kissed her mother before she was taken away from him, he answers, "No, they [the soldiers] were standing between us." "In that case you have missed the second kiss too," the daughter tells him, and for a second time Saeed must let his beloved go (*P* 156). At this moment Saeed realizes that his transformation into an obsequious subordinate to his Israeli masters, which has forced him to adopt the role of an imposter vis-à-vis his people, has irreversibly changed the course of his life.

History cannot be undone. Prewar relationships cannot be repossessed. Love belongs to a different era, which has disappeared with the defeat. The Israeli soldiers wedged between the lovers are a concrete reminder of the history that irreversibly split the Palestinian people. The domination of the Israeli conquerors in Arab life is a reality that can neither be ignored nor forgotten. As the episode of the "second Yuaad" demonstrates, the prewar past is impossible to reconstruct. Ironically, Saeed's "second birth" placed him in an impossible situation of complete alienation from his people as well as from his occupier. As an Israeli Arab his ties with the Palestinian people in exile have been severed. As a secret agent for the Israeli authorities he became estranged from the Israeli Arab community. As a defeated minority member and a secret agent he became a twofold outsider. Consequently he finds himself in a "no-man's land," distant from his own people and "invisible" to his dominators.

As a metaphor of his situation, Saeed's recurring nightmare of being suspended on a stake attests to the extent of his uprootedness and alienation. In the dream he shares both the stake and the situation of suspension with his Israeli masters, but the parties cannot see each other. And even though his Arab friends, his wife, and his lovers urge him to climb down from the stake, Saeed can neither join them "in the streets" nor will he go with them to the "exile's grave" (*P* 158–59). Traumatically divided by the "ethical contradiction" of loyalty to his people and collaboration with the enemy, Saeed remains "suspended" in total isolation, unable to communicate, immobilized by fear.

Nothing short of a miracle can free Saeed from his emotional paralysis, the result of this ethical conundrum. Indeed, fantastic extraterrestrial creatures or "masters," as he calls them, liberate him from his torment. The deus ex machina appearance of the masters, however, does not indicate a miraculous restitution of the pretraumatic, prewar life. Saeed's outer-space mentors rescue him from suspension on the stake, only to demand that he revisit his terrible experience of alienation by an act of writing. In other words, they tell him to write his life story. Complying with their demand, Saeed writes his confession in a series of letters. Thus, the intended Israeli readers of *The Pessoptimist* in its Hebrew translation are the recipients of the letters that Saeed sent to an unnamed gentleman, pleading with him to get his "weird" story out to the world (*P* 3). This story is a fictional epistolary autobiography that, as its full title indicates, tells the Israeli reader about *The Secret Life of Saeed, the Pessoptimist.*

The "secret life" of the protagonist's servitude, betrayal, and dissimulation leads back to the previously posed question. Why would an Israeli Arab writer expose such an ethically problematic representation of an Israeli Arab character to the world at large—and to the Israeli world in particular? Does the confession not reconfirm the stereotypical, negative opinion of the Arab as devious and cowardly?

To elucidate the desire to publicize such self-damaging truth in hostile circles, I return to Freccero's observation that "every narrative of the self is a story of a conversion" that proclaims the "death of the self as character and the resurrection of the self as author." In this connection one should recall the double-sided narrative in "Hirbet Hizah." At the same time as he raises his voice against the moral disintegration of the Zionist ideal, Yizhar' narrator-author also paints his own self-critical picture. He has mustered the courage to reveal his passivity, powerlessness, and even his self-pity. Is it possible to discern a similarly double-sided narrative in *The Pessoptimist*? Indeed a parallel construct emerges in Habiby's story. On the one hand we hear the voice of Saeed, the Candidesque, resilient *ingénu* who rebounds from any misfortune, while, on the other hand, we hear Saeed's critical self-scrutiny. The tale of Saeed's often comical adventures in the wake of his "donkey rebirth" evolves alongside a pathetic confession-lamentation over the irretrievable past and the ordeal of the double "second life."

Thus, time and again Saeed returns to the traumatic event of the defeat that robbed him of his national history and identity. I have already mentioned the trauma victim who, as Caruth in her introduction points out, can see only the "literal nature" of the event and is therefore bound to return, in his memory, to the event as it was. I have also mentioned Freud's postulation that the traumatized individual is fixated on the event itself and becomes hostage to the previously experienced fear, which he or she relives with every recollection. In this sense the search for meaning indicates a progression toward a larger perspective that would liberate the individual from painful repetitions of the particular event.

What is this larger perspective and how can it be attained? According to Walter A. Davis, it is a "movement toward active reversal." Such a reversal occurs when, "through the breaking down of defenses and the opening of oneself to anxiety, one 'repeats' one's conflicts in a new way." Davis suggests that active reversal aims neither at closure nor recovery but rather at introspection in light of the traumatic experience. The reversal is active because it requires a conscious shift of self-perception. Since the process is bound to expose new aspects of the self to the examining consciousness, it requires "working up the courage to go after what one has been after all along."[17]

What was this knowledge of self that Saeed lacked the courage to pursue all along? His conclusion in the episode of his "donkey rebirth" seems to offer a clue. Here is how Saeed sums up the traumatic episode of the rebirth: "My subsequent life in Israel, then, was really a gift from that unfortunate beast. What *value,* then, . . . should we assign to this life of mine?" (*P* 6; emphasis added). The subsequent episode, in a way, answers Saeed's question. By "selling out" as an informer he communicates a sense of lost self-value, of complete unworthiness. The initial fearful confrontation with death *devalued* Saeed's life, transforming him into a self-effacing, cowardly, servile subordinate of the enemy. In light of Davis's suggestion, in Saeed's case an "active reversal" would therefore require a courageous confession of his deliberate self-denigration prompted by a fear of death.

The emotional dynamic of Saeed's self-devaluation before his Israeli masters out of fear of death echoes Hegel's famous discussion of the bondsman's subjection to the lord. Hegel claims that servitude "contain[s] within itself this truth of pure negativity" since in his relationship with the lord "the whole being [of the bondsman] has been seized with dread; for [his being] experienced the fear of death, the absolute Lord . . . [and] in that experience everything solid and stable has been shaken to its foundations." The fear of death that paralyzes the bondsman effectively pronounces his "pure negativity," that is, his death as a human subject.[18] The threat of death represented by the lord reifies the bondsman; it divests him of self-consciousness and free will, transforming him into a tool dedicated to his master's desires.

The relation that Hegel affirms between the fear of death and servitude provides an insight into Saeed's trauma. His submission to the Israeli conquerors is rooted in an encounter with death that eliminated his sense of self-worth. The experience of having become an object of a sniper's target effaced him as a subject. This brief moment of indiscriminate violence and his accidental rescue erased the difference between a human being and an ass. Desperately seeking release from the paralyzing dread of death, Saeed turns into a mindless, dutiful, unself-conscious servant of those who have the power to kill him. Ironically, along with his life as "a gift from that unfortunate beast" Saeed seems to have inherited some asslike qualities. Like his donkey-savior's "thoughtless" straying into the line of fire, time and again Saeed foolishly strays into dangerous situations as he misinterprets circumstances, misjudges people, and gets "shot."

A case in point is Saeed's quite comical yet telling blunder at the time of the Six-Day War. Unable to distinguish between "those [Arabs] defeated in this [1967] war with those defeated by the Treaty of Rhodes," Saeed decides that "it would be safe to regard [himself] as one of those 'defeated'" (*P* 120). Thus, to be on the safe side Saeed places a white flag of capitulation on the roof of his home in Haifa. This action indicates to his Israeli masters that in 1967—almost twenty years after the city fell to the Israeli forces—Saeed still considers Haifa an Arab city at war rather than an integral part of the Jewish state. Consequently, they call him "an ass" and punish him with "double" invisibility (*P* 122), not only locking him up but also making him the prison's secret agent.

Ironically, the Israeli masters have inadvertently identified Saeed's problem correctly. His historical confusion indicates that he has remained trapped in the trauma of war, which ended with the Arab defeat and the destruction of his people. Even though Saeed's "second" self as a collaborator was born of his desire to protect himself at all costs, the arbitrariness of his existence continues to haunt him. The 1967 Arab defeat evokes the anxiety of the initial trauma in 1948. In his so-called surrender of Haifa, Saeed's misplaced complicity demonstrates the extent to which the initial trauma undermined his self-confidence and his sense of security. From this perspective it is possible to understand why, despite constant physical abuse and moral degradation, Saeed's second self grows increasingly "mulish," stubbornly and abjectly clinging to his oppressors.

Eventually the emerging consciousness of his misery prevails. I have already referred to Saeed's meeting with Yuaad and the realization that he can no longer pretend that the past can be restored. Ironically, the dream of the stake awakens him to the horrific reality of his alienation. In a sense the dream marks the end of the life story of Saeed, the servile, self-devalued character, and begins the narrative of Saeed, the self-evaluating author. Saeed's call for rescue, which brings forth his extraterrestrial mentors, indicates the emergence of the hitherto suppressed emotions and initiates the restoration of his subjectivity. The cry for help demonstrates that the self-negation as a "bondsman" has become more terrifying than death. The threat of the self being reduced to an invisible object estranged from humanity has proved even more anxiety- provoking than the trauma of the accidental rescue.

Hegel predicates conscious existence upon human interaction. In his "Notion of Recognition" he proposes that one gains and maintains self-consciousness only through intersubjective recognition: "Self-consciousness exists only in being acknowledged."[19] Through the recognition of oneself as subject for another and the recognition of another as subject, one obtains the necessary distance from oneself to gain self-consciousness. The interaction as equals between both parties does not exist in the case of servitude, whose premise of inequality precludes the recognition of the subjugated. Since recognition by another is the foundation of one's self-consciousness, its absence will affect one's sense of worth. As Davis concludes, "Wanting and being denied minimal recognition, that of the victim, the slave's desire undergoes a radical transformation into what Hegel terms *desire restrained and checked*. Through that experience, a new kind of suffering is born: self-contempt."[20]

Indeed, Saeed's introspection is bitterly ironic and derogatory. The critical dream of the stake taught him that instead of the hoped-for safety and protection against unforeseen perils, his life as a secret agent has produced frightful uprootedness and disorientation. Thus, he discovers that by assuming the silent, docile, unthinking existence of an "ass," he has compromised his integrity by giving up solidarity with his people. Having attained this realization, Saeed understands, with obvious self-contempt, his situation of being "restrained and checked," like a meowing cat. With remarkable openness he embarks on an "active reversal" that results in an unsparing self-evaluation: "I lived in the outside world . . . for twenty years, unable to breathe. . . . But I did not die. . . . I was a prisoner unable to escape. But I did remain unchained. How often I yelled . . . 'Please, everyone! I groan at the burden of the great secret I bear on my shoulders.' . . . But all that came from beneath my moustache was a meowing sound, like that of a cat. Eventually I came to believe in the transmigration of souls. . . . That's how I've been for twenty years, meowing and whimpering so much that this idea of transmigration has become a reality in my mind" (*P* 76).

The end of Saeed's servitude manifests itself in his growing capacity for critical self-revision, which he feels compelled to write down in order to share with others. He defies the fear that imprisoned him in the silence of servitude by disclosing in his letters the dishonorable secret that has weighed him down all these years. Although his extra-terrestrial mentors—the inner voices of "active reversal"—mercilessly inform him that he has adopted literature to "clothe the shame of [his] impotence with a paper wisdom" because he "lack[s] power for anything more" (*P* 77), they nonetheless command Saeed to write. They recognize that nowadays the "paper wisdom" of confession signifies courage, since writing about the shame of powerlessness attests to the capability of self-evaluation from authorial distance. The articulation of a twenty-year-long frustration involving "meowing and whimpering" marks a progression toward self-consciousness.

As I previously indicated, Yizhar's story and Habiby's novel in its Hebrew translation addressed a Hebrew readership. To avoid confusion, I wish to reiterate that the literary representations of Israeli society in these works are meant to confront the Israeli readership with its own scathingly critical image, especially the denunciation of its oppression of the Arab. It is therefore not unreasonable to conjecture that an ending with some redeeming qualities for the Israelis might have appeased the reader and ensured a more positive reception of the texts. It would also be quite reasonable to expect that a hope-filled closure might have incurred a measure of recognition for the defeated and the ostracized. As I demonstrated in the second part of this study, the difficult messages were neutralized through the politics of canonization. Here, in attempting to free these fictions from their canonical interpretations, I note the absence of an optimistic closure. On the contrary, each story ends on a note of deep disillusion, whereby each narrative depicts its failure to reach—let alone affect—the intended audience. To put it even more plainly, both narrators admit that their intention to disseminate the story they have struggled so hard to tell has not materialized.

Thus, the anonymity of Yizhar's narrator reemphasizes his continuing estrangement. The final scene of "blanketing" silence that descends on the tragedy of expulsion highlights the impossibility of redemption. Hopelessness is also clearly communicated in Habiby's novel. While Yizhar's narrator *remains* anonymous throughout the story, Saeed *becomes* anonymous once he has sent off the letters containing the story. Significantly, the novel concludes with Saeed's disappearance without a trace. Nobody is able to locate his name in the register of the mental hospital in Acre where he allegedly spent the last months of his life (*P* 162). The association of Saeed's disappearance with madness and presumed death highlights an unbridgeable gap between the life story of an Israeli Arab and the intended recipients of his letters, namely, a Jewish Israeli readership. While his missives in Hebrew translation have reached the reader, the Israeli Arab author of this sarcastic depiction of the Zionist state, who has rejected the role of a servile "ass," has no place in Israeli society. In this sense a parallel situation seals the fate of Yizhar's dissenting narrator, who remains an outcast on the Israeli social landscape.

No change in attitude of the Israeli mainstream toward Arabs is registered in either story. In terms of the previously discussed significations of victory by Freud and Benjamin, both texts seem to corroborate Benjamin's view of the victors, whose history consistently erases the history of the victims. This intransigence is hardly surprising. The dominators in both texts are uniformly cruel, arrogant, despotic, and completely lacking empathy, let alone "guilt and remorse," emotions that Freud saw emerging in the aftermath of the destruction of the opponent.

The realization of the consistently negative portrayal of the victor points to a complex, seemingly self-contradictory configuration of victim-victor relations in both narratives. On one level the victims' growing capacity for introspection marks a movement toward self-liberation that conspicuously contrasts with the rigid position of the victors. The narrators' autobiographical stories demonstrate progress toward what Davis calls an "active reversal," that is, a new self-understanding in the wake of his traumatic experience. As the narrator's transformation proceeds, the victors remain caught up in the obtuseness of their triumphalism.

On another level, however, the configuration of the relationships demonstrates that the differentiation between victim and victor is not as clear-cut as we would expect. The issue of the readership, which I have emphasized all along, leads to the realization that the victims' progress toward liberation from trauma cannot take place separated from the ruling mainstream. Despite the fact that, to recall Hegel, the "lord" does not recognize the "bondsman," the presence of the oppressor is indispensable to the emerging self-consciousness of the oppressed. Thus, even though stereotypical, one-dimensional, and thoroughly negative, the victor plays an essential part in the victim's self-liberation from emotional captivity.

What is the part that the dominator plays in these fictions? The confessional genre of the stories points to the importance of the oppressor in the act of telling. Even though unresponsive and hostile, the Israeli readership becomes, by virtue of the story's confessional genre and its Hebrew translation, the recipient of the confession. The confessing character speaks against history as written by the triumphant victor, a history that has silenced him and rendered him helpless. From this perspective, potency is regained not only through the denunciation of the oppressor but even more so through a courageous admission of the lack of courage to oppose oppression. Since this audacious confession seems to have no effect on the dominator, it appears purposeless. I wish to suggest that, paradoxically, it is the seeming futility of the confession that determines its meaningfulness. The narrator's written confession amounts to an act of self-reaffirmation as a free individual. The written testimony attests to the conversion of the character into author; it therefore constitutes a demand for recognition that, as both narratives show, is bound to be denied. It is precisely the risk of demanding recognition despite the certainty of failure that signifies liberation. As Davis tells us, "One of the things that makes us subjects is that we can stake our lives and lose ourselves irretrievably. . . . The *will* to do so is the act that makes one master—master over oneself."[21] It is not so much the teller's desire to reform the oppressor as his desire to reaffirm his subjectivity through *telling* that motivates the confessional narratives of "Hirbet Hizah" and *The Pessoptimist*.

8

Bonds of Confession

A. B. Yehoshua's "Facing the Forests" and Atallah Mansour's *In a New Light*

The Importance of Telling and Listening

In the previous chapter I focused on the striking absence of inter-action between the victors and the defeated in Yizhar's "Hirbet Hi-zah" and Habiby's *Pessoptimist*. As represented in these stories, the Zionist mainstream, locked in its doctrine of exclusion, remained oblivious to the stories of its oppressive rule that the narrators strove to tell. While the telling performs an important role in the narrators' progress toward self-liberation, the *written* confessions highlight the complete solitude of each narrator, who fails to find a listener even in his own community. This chapter explores the moment when the stories of Jews and Arabs can no longer evade each other. In their representation of the complex inseparability of the opponents, A. B. Yehoshua's novella "Facing the Forests" (1963) and Atallah Man-sour's novel *In a New Light* (1966) break down the barriers between victors and victims. The overpowering need to have the adversary listen to the confession both reveals and articulates the indelible bonds between Jews and Arabs. Even if fleeting, this moment of shar-ing provides a consciousness of connectedness and ties that can no longer be denied.

The stories take place in the aftermath of the 1948 war in the first decade of the state. Yehoshua's "Facing the Forests," a third-person stream-of-consciousness narrative, tells the story of an Israeli Jew, an "eternal" history student. Engaged as a fire watcher in a newly planted forest, the student encounters his helper, an Israeli Arab, a former Palestinian villager. A peculiar relationship develops between them. Seemingly by coincidence, the fire watcher discovers the ruins of the Arab's village under the trees. The village was ruthlessly destroyed and its inhabitants killed in the 1948 war. With the Jew's tacit consent, the Arab burns down the forest, exposing the ruins of his destroyed village. The fire watcher implicates the Arab, who is arrested.

Atallah Mansour's *In a New Light* is a fictional autobiography/ confession of Yossi, an Arab who "passes" as a Jew. Yossi's parents were murdered by unidentified British, Arab, or Jewish killers. Yossi believes in the socialist ideal, as implemented in the Zionist kibbutz movement. In an effort to become a kibbutz member, he renounces his Arab identity, national roots, and ethnic heritage. When the question of Yossi's Arab identity eventually arises, the kibbutz confronts the issue of whether to accept an Arab as a full member of the community. The membership is approved on condition that Yossi's Arab identity remain undisclosed.

Both texts position the Jewish and the Arab characters in situations of proximity, where they are no longer separated by geographical distance, political/military hostilities, or emotional obtuseness. Ironically, it is the failure of the nameless Israeli Jew in Yehoshua's story to adapt to the postwar zeitgeist of Israeli society that places him in the prewar domain of the nameless Arab, literally on top of the Arab's destroyed village. In Mansour's novel Yossi's inability to identify with the defeated Arab community drives him to the kibbutz, which was literally built on the ruins of an Arab village. In either story the protagonist's quest for self-redefinition vis-à-vis the adversary and his story does not conclude with a definitive resolution of his identity crisis. The stories end on an inconclusive and perhaps even pessimistic note, underscoring the immense difficulties that characterize relationships between Jews and Arabs. Nonetheless, the quite dramatic encounters in the stories demonstrate that, when only for a brief moment the boundaries between the two peoples are removed, the definitions of victor and victim shift and lose their commonly accepted significations.

My discussion of "Hirbet Hizah" and *The Pessoptimist* has shown Israel's triumphalist attitude toward the Arab population; the steadfast belief in the supreme righteousness of the cause allowed the Palmach generation to remain impervious to the rare voices of opposition—even those of Jewish objectors, let alone those of the defeated Arab minority. To return briefly to Benjamin, Israeli Jews were capable of writing their history of triumph while remaining oblivious of the subtext of suffering they inflicted on the defeated. While the myths of the "empty land" and the "new" Jew reconstruct the glorious history of the powerful ancient Hebrews and thus dissociate Israeli Jews from the powerless Diaspora, they also suppress the ugly underside of their story of victory. In the texts I discuss in this chapter, the suppressed story returns, reverberating with undeniable and inescapable evidence of committed injustice. While the suppressed story fails to penetrate and transform the consciousness of the Israeli public sphere, it initiates personal relationships between victor and victim. Even though limited and transient, this connection marks a significant change from the narratives of "Hirbet Hizah" and *The Pessoptimist*, where the confessions of the protagonists-narrators fell on deaf ears. In "Facing the Forests" and *In a New Light*, each story reaches the opponent, thus transforming the enemy into a confessor.

To appreciate the implications of this transformation, the psychological dynamics of the confession needs to be explored briefly. The phenomenon of telling indicates a delayed impact of trauma, which, when it finally arises in the protagonist's consciousness, manifests itself in the need to share the fearful story of irretrievable loss. Freud claims that the consciousness of the loss can be repossessed by "developing the anxiety whose omission was the cause of the traumatic neurosis." That is, the individual must reconstruct the event in order to reexperience the emotions blocked at the time of its occurrence and in this way attain a measure of relief from "traumatic neurosis."[1] For the reconstruction to be effective, it must be articulated. The necessity to articulate indicates that liberation from posttraumatic fear and anxiety requires that the recollection be communicated to a responding other. Recall, in passing, that the confessions in "Hirbet Hizah" and *The Pessoptimist* did not affect the intended confessor (the Israeli public), leaving the narrators-confessors in the twilight zone of estrangement, madness, and presumably death. Relief from traumatic syndromes is predicated on telling as well as listening, As students of trauma unanimously agree, the role of the listener, whether in the formal setting of analysis or in an informal interaction, is crucial to the resolution of the posttraumatic syndrome.

Eric Santner, for instance, maintains that the anxiety blocked at the moment of trauma can be recuperated in the presence of an "empathic analyst, who co-constitute[s] the space in which loss may come to be symbolically and affectively mastered."[2] In his discussion of the trauma of Holocaust survivors, Dominick LaCapra suggests that "the interviewer and the analyst" should present themselves "through a labor of listening and attending that exposes the self to empathetic understanding and hence to at least muted trauma."[3] Caruth assigns to "the therapeutic listener . . . the challenge . . . *how to listen to* [*the victim's*] *departure*" from the site of the traumatic event.[4] Lifton identifies himself as an empathic listener; although an outsider to the traumatic event, he tries "to take in their stories [of trauma survivors], and to form imagery in [his] own mind about what they're saying."[5]

This virtually uniform approach to trauma therapy calls attention to the listener-teller relationships in the narratives. I have already established the fact that the war constituted a traumatic experience for both the winner and the loser. If so, then liberation from the trauma of war signifies for each of the parties a difficult and painful process of telling and listening. Since the themes of "Facing the Forests" and *In a New Light* focus on the indelible interaction between Israeli Jews and Israeli Arabs, the search for relief from traumatic memories impels the Jewish and Arab characters to share their stories *with each other*.

The question that arises at this point concerns the relationships between winners and losers. Why would the victors and the defeated wish to tell each other about their traumas? Why would they expect empathic understanding, so indispensable to the healing process, in a listener who belongs to the enemy camp? I shall argue that the psychoanalytical concept of transference elucidates the relatedness between the parties, which explains the ineluctable need for interaction between winners and losers.

The fear and anxiety of the posttraumatic syndrome engenders unwillingness and fear to relive the trauma as well as the desire to share the story with the listener. The latter is invested with both positive and negative attributes that determine the degree of the teller's resistance to tell the story. As Freud claimed, " 'positive transference,' " characterized by "sympathy, friendship, trust," is instrumental in helping patients overcome resistance and tell their stories. Consequently, Freud has argued that "an attitude of affectionate and devoted attachment [to the physician] can surmount any difficulty in confession; *in analogous situations in real life* we say: 'I don't feel ashamed with you; I can tell you everything.' "[6] It is important to emphasize that Freud predicated the readiness of the teller to speak upon the readiness of the empathic listener to listen.

Acknowledging his indebtedness to Freud, Jacques Lacan has described the dynamics of transference in terms of the "subject supposed to know [sujet supposé savoir]." Lacan claims that the consciousness of a listener who is supposed to know how to solve the problem is essential to the process of transference: "As soon as the subject who is supposed to know exists somewhere . . . there is transference." In other words, for transference to take place, the analysand must attribute to the analyst some vital knowledge that in reality the analyst does not possess. Like Freud, who discerned situations of transference in therapy as well as in "analogous situations in real life," Lacan identified "the subject supposed to know" as an "individual, *whether or not an analyst.*"[7] Both thinkers recognize that the dynamics of transference exists in everyday interactions among people and not only in the specific context of therapy.

The prevalence of transference in everyday telling-listening situations illuminates the dual telling-listening interaction between the Jewish and Arab characters in these two texts. The stories present us with a complex configuration of double roles, whereby each character is the teller of his own story as well as the listener to the story of the other. In a way similar to that in which the patient sees the therapist as the "subject who is supposed to know" how to resolve the problem, each character, in his capacity as a teller, sees in the other the hope of liberation from the delayed posttraumatic effects. Conversely, as a listener each character is considered instrumental in healing traumatic injuries.

As I will show in the following discussion of "Facing the Forests" and *In a New Light,* the particular configuration of the Jewish victorious majority and the Arab defeated minority has created a particular expectation of each side from the other. As a teller, the defeated Arab expects the Jew to enable him to restore his self-respect and dignity, whereas by telling his story the victorious Jew hopes to attain his moral rehabilitation from committed atrocities through the Arab. Arabs and Jews alternately become the object of each other's desire; they are possessors of the coveted means to reconstitute that which the other has lost and is compelled to retrieve at any cost. Note that the interchangeability of the roles refutes the canonical interpretation of the auxiliary role of the Arab as a symbolic representation of the Jewish existentialist angst. In contrast to the approach that hopes to neutralize the signification of the Arab presence, I intend to show that the alternating roles of each character point to the mutual recognition of Jews and Arabs, and that the mutual recognition presupposes equal status for both parties.

The perspective of the double transference sheds light on the relations between Arab and Jewish characters in Yehoshua's and Mansour's fiction. While in "Hirbet Hizah" and *The Pessoptimist* the traumatic story of the victim was aimed at *self*-recognition, in "Facing the Forests" and *In a New Light* one notes a desire to regain the sense of self through *mutual* recognition. As we shall see, the transferential interaction is complex and does not necessarily guarantee a hopeful closure. Indeed, these texts portray not only the complexity but also the evanescence of such a meeting between adversaries. While a permanent resolution seems out of reach, the reading of the texts in terms of transferential interaction communicates a concrete possibility of rapprochement.

The Power of Destroyed History

In the closing pages of "Facing the Forests" the forest burns down. Both the nameless, taciturn Israeli Jew, referred to as "the fire watcher" (*ha-tsofe*), and the nameless, mute Israeli Arab, referred to as "the Arab" (*ha'aravi*) undergo an intense police interrogation. At the same time as the police officers are questioning the fire watcher, "inside the building they are conducting a simultaneous interrogation of the Arab, in Arabic eked out with gestures. Only the questions are audible." A few hours later, discomfort and exhaustion break the fire watcher's resolve and he "is prepared to suggest the Arab as a possible clue." The Arab is immediately "bundled in a police car." Even though he is being arrested and his distraught young daughter "clings to him desperately . . . there is a gratified expression in his eyes now, a sense of achievement." At that moment the fire watcher "suddenly . . . walks over to the forest manager and boldly demands a solution for the child." The forest manager, a staunch, old-line Zionist, stares at the fire watcher "with vacant eyes as though he, too, has lost the words, as though he understood nothing." The fire watcher "repeats his demand in a loud voice." Enraged by the fire watcher's demand, the old forest manager "attacks him with shriveled fists, hits out at him."[8]

The episode engages the three parties—the Arab, the Jew, and the forest manager—in incongruous, somewhat absurd behavior. The Arab, who is being taken into custody, projects a sense of triumphant self-fulfillment. The fire watcher, who betrayed the Arab, turns into an outspoken advocate for the daughter's welfare. The previously arrogant, self-confident forest manager succumbs to impotent rage, losing control over his speech and actions; he, who has been zealously fulfilling the Zionist ideal of the revival of the land, and who has boasted of having "harnessed" nature to "our [Zionist] enterprise" (FF 103) of forest planting, is witnessing his raison d'être literally go up in smoke. The fire watcher's bold request on behalf of the child and his careless attitude toward the forest (he coolly and cynically expresses his certainty that the forest was insured) trigger the old man's wrath. He indignantly blames the intellectual with "the dim glasses," the "one with his books" (FF 116) for having brought on the disaster. Significantly, the manager directs his aggression at the Jew rather than the Arab. Recall the soldiers in "Hirbet Hizah," whose firm adherence to the Zionist claim to the land allowed them to disregard not only the Arab victims but also their dissenting comrade. In the postwar reality of "Facing the Forests," the despairing forest manager sees in the hapless scholar the cause of the disaster. The destruction of the forest symbolizes the collapse of Zionist idealism. A Jew who dares to express an opinion that does not conform to the Zionist cause of reviving the land is a dissenter and therefore the real enemy.

Ironically, it was the manager's impatience with the previous fire watchers—"the diverse social cases, the invalids, the cripples, the cranks" (FF 87)—that prompted him to employ the bookish student as a fire watcher. At the time the manager could not have guessed that the scholarly applicant was more of a misfit than those he rejected. The truth is that this "eternal" student turned out to be an unfortunate "social case" in his own circle of friends, considered a "lost case" among his former fellow students. He remains unmotivated by the professional and economic success of his friends, who "may be seen carrying bulging briefcases, on their way to work every morning" (FF 85). In the expedient environment of dedicated functionaries and ambitious academics, the student's interminably carefree, goal-free, lethargic lifestyle is perceived as an intolerable aberration.

The extent to which the student's indolence has alarmed and threatened his friends manifests itself in their determination to change him. Drawing upon their organizational skills, they efficiently set out to reform him. In no time they find him a position as a fire watcher, personally pack his books in a suitcase, and even decide on the topic for the research he will be conducting in the woods. Scholarly research of the Crusades is bound to turn him into a respectable, socially adjusted historian. The reintegration of the student into the establishment is predicated upon his academic achievement in his forest exile. The scholarly "conquest" of the Holy Land will liberate him from inertia, somnolence, and aimless drifting.

At first the student truly feels that study of the Crusades might be the right path back to society. The mystery of the Latin quotations seems to hold the promise of making him an active and alert participant in the world. Thus, "he feels certain that there is some dark issue buried within the subject . . . [and] it will be just out of this drowsiness that envelopes his mind like a permanent cloud that the matter will be revealed to him" (FF 93). For a brief moment, therefore, the history of the Crusades has become the locus of transference, an object of desire that holds the key to his social redemption. He feels that the secret knowledge contained in these books provides a new scientific understanding of a distant event, one that will restore him to the mainstream. Indeed, the directive from his friends that he "ought to bring some startling scientific theory [about the Crusades] back from the forests" (FF 89) reinforces the notion that the discovery of this secret knowledge lies in a rational, methodical interpretation of a historical event.

The spell of a scientific discovery, however, is soon broken. By the time his mistress—the wife of a friend back in the city—comes to visit him several weeks later, both the objective and the method of his study of the Crusades has shifted. To her mocking inquiries about the new ideas for his "brilliant research" among the trees he responds: "Novel ideas? . . . Maybe, though not what they [the friends] imagine . . . not exactly scientific. . . . Rather, human" (FF 107).

Instead of the scientific approach to the history of the Crusades, the student has discovered the human idea that underlies history. He discovers the human aspect of history when, undisciplined as always, he procrastinates, allowing himself to be distracted from the abstract hard road of the scientific method to marginal matters in the texts. Thus he pores over illustrations of "monks, cardinals; a few blurred kings, thin knights, tiny villainous Jews," as well as the "prefaces, various acknowledgments, publication data" (FF 93) that he finds in the books. These findings expose the human subtext of the abstract treatise as well as the personal aspect of the book itself. The illustrations that accompany the Latin documents render concrete the people whose religious fanaticism, hatred of the Jews, and violent instincts resulted in the creation of a casus belli that sent them on the disastrous adventure of the Crusades. The seemingly irrelevant acknowledgments and dates of publication are evidence of humanity's continuing search for knowledge; they also attest to the personal imprint of those who preceded and inspired the search.

Thus, as objects of desire the books do indeed reveal a secret knowledge, albeit not, as expected, in the sphere of scientific theory. Rather, they reveal to the student a hitherto unrecognized knowledge of himself. Instead of converting into a conforming *social* being, he discovers that he has become an empathic *human* being. This newly discovered aspect of his personality is literally tested by fire. When the burning forest threatens the observation post, the fire watcher knows that "he ought to take his two suitcases and disappear. But he only takes the child. . . . He seizes the trembling child by the hand, goes down and begins his retreat. . . . He arrives at the yellow waste, the wadi, his dream. . . . He sits the barefoot girl on the ground, slumps beside her. His exhaustion erupts within him and covers them both" (FF 112–13).

One of two suitcases is full of books on the Crusades. In the other are his city clothes. The contents of the suitcases that he leaves to burn hold the ticket, so to speak, of the student's return to the conformist task-and-achievement community back in the city. The decision to save the girl rather than his belongings signifies the failure of the watcher's reintegration into the mainstream. At the same time, however, the decision to protect the girl, which demonstrates his capacity to act out of a concern for another, signals a hitherto unsuspected inner strength. Subsequently this new sense of empowerment manifests itself in the *bold* and *loud* demand to find a solution for the Arab girl. As we have seen, he repeatedly and provocatively addresses this demand to the distraught forest manager. This behavior reflects the student's complete indifference to the manager's personal agony over the collapse of the Zionist enterprise of afforestation of the "empty land," and it doesn't reveal any concern about the forest.

This boldly expressed obstreperousness draws attention to yet another, more significant, aspect of the student's transformation. As the narrative repeatedly insists, the student has somehow lost the ability to express himself. "Words," we are told in the very beginning, "weary him. . . . He plainly needs to renew his acquaintance with words. . . . Even with himself he hardly manages to exchange a word" (FF 85, 86, 93). He hesitates, mumbles, and stutters, revealing his uncertainty, social maladjustment, and sense of misplacement. Thus, the unusual eloquence of his outburst to the forest manager is the only other instance of the student's eloquent and lucid articulation. The first clearly enunciated expression of his thoughts occurs in a climactic encounter with the Arab.

With his contract as fire watcher ending, the student fears that "he [the Arab] too [like the books] will fail to convey anything and it will all remain dark." Afraid that the Arab will not communicate some crucial knowledge in his possession, the Jew initiates the interaction by telling the Arab the story of the Crusades. The Jew is cogent and articulate as he talks "quietly, reasonably, in a positively didactic manner." He tells the Arab about "the fervor, about the cruelty, about the Jews committing suicide, about the Children's Crusade; things he has picked from the books, the unfounded theories he has framed himself." As he talks, his voice grows "warm, alive with imagination." The Arab, who knows no Hebrew, at first listens to the "alien words as one absorbing melody"; then, his "tension [mounting]," he "is filled with hate" (FF 110).

The student's narration of the Crusades is followed by the Arab's narration. The Arab, whose "tongue was cut out during the war" (FF 92), communicates with hurried, confused gestures and with a "squirming severed tongue." The student deduces from the Arab's contorted body language "that this is his house and that there used to be a village here as well and that they had simply hidden it all, buried in the big forest. . . . Apparently his wives have been murdered here as well." Despite the fact that he clearly understands the Arab's story, the student assumes a noncommittal attitude, telling himself that this is "a dark affair, no doubt" and "moves away, pretending not to understand." The Arab nonetheless continues to pursue him; he seems to believe that "only he, the fire watcher, can understand him" (FF 110–11). The protagonists exchange stories in languages incomprehensible to one another. While the Arab does not understand Hebrew, the comprehension of his pantomime depends a lot upon the Jew's imagination. In each case comprehension is not predicated upon verbal communication. Rather, to a large extent communication between the characters arises through intuitive and associative inferences.

While the juxtaposed stories reveal disparities both in content and form, their reception demonstrates the uniformity of mutual rejection. The student delivers a didactic lecture based on "unfounded theories" about the cruelty and suffering of the Jews at the time of the Crusades. The Arab reciprocates with a factual story of destruction in a passionate, frenzied "pantomime" (FF 110). The factuality of the story imprinted in the Arab's muteness underscores the fictional aspect of the Crusades story as authored by the Jew. Whereas the dramatic testimony of the witness/victim reenacts the trauma of the destruction on the site of the destroyed village, the story of the Crusades evolves in the student's imagination. It is interesting to note the unanimity of the negative reception of the stories. The Arab is filled with hate at the Crusades story, whereas the Jew tries to distance himself from evidence of the Israeli conquest, murder, and destruction of Arab lives and culture.

One aspect in particular of the psychoanalytical concept of transference[9] helps to explain these negative responses. Each protagonist-as-listener is "supposed to know," to possess a secret knowledge that he is supposed to impart to the teller and thus resolve the latter's problem. Neither seems to have gained this secret knowledge from the other, and their reactions communicate each protagonist's disappointment in this respect. Yet the question of the mutual desire for each other's knowledge persists. Why would the adversaries wish to obtain knowledge from the other? What is each of them "supposed to know"? Do they really "know" how to redeem each other from posttraumatic anxieties? I here wish to suggest that the key to understanding the knowledge each of the characters seeks in the other may be found in two preceding episodes. I shall call the first "The Whispered Name" and the second "The Map."

From the hikers in the forest, who appear to him "like a procession of Crusaders" (FF 100), the student learns about the destroyed Arab village underneath the forest. Observe, in passing, the dual historical irony in this comparison of the Israeli hikers to Crusaders. The Crusaders were the persecutors of Jews; they were also the conquerors of the Holy Land. In a further ironic twist, these Israelis who look like Crusaders impart knowledge that affects the student in a most dramatic way. This information brings home to him the reality of the war and the destruction that it caused, an awareness that, as we shall see, alerts the student to his responsibility as a member of society.

It is not simply that until his meeting with the Israeli "Crusaders" the student had not known about the war and the destruction it produced. Rather, it is the suppression of an empathic understanding of the terrible effects of war that now produces a delayed traumatic effect. The realization of actually being on the site of the destruction shakes the student out of his lethargic state of mind. The depth of the shock is evinced in the episode I have called "The Whispered Name," where, in the middle of the night, the name of the village "floats back into his mind . . . [seizing] him with restlessness." Deeply disturbed, the student is now caught up in the desire to return to the event of destruction he has managed to ignore all along. To recall Freud, he is now "developing the anxiety whose omission was the cause of the traumatic neurosis." Unable to control his anxiety, in the middle of the night he "roughly wakes [the Arab] and whispers the name of the village" (FF 101).

It is, of course, not merely scientific curiosity about the history of the place that motivates the student of history. His anxiety to have the name of the village reconfirmed proves that he has already intuitively made the connection between the destroyed village and the Arab. The whispered name is meant not only as factual verification but also as a confession of a secret knowledge that the Jew possesses. It is a sign that encourages the Arab because it implies the recognition of his story. Indeed, the response of the Arab—whose "expression of surprise, wonder and eagerness suffuses all his wrinkles" and who "jumps up . . . pointing fervently, hopelessly, at the forest" (FF 101)—initiates the process of transference. The insight into the Arab's past turns the student into the object of the Arab's desire. Through an acknowledgment of the Arab's losses, the student holds the power to restore dignity and self-respect to the defeated. The scene that follows the whispering episode reinforces the Arab's hopes. A mutual understanding that the forest needs to be burned down creates a moment of communion in which "the fire watcher spreads his palms over the flame and the Arab does likewise [and] their bodies press in on the fire" (FF 109).

Now it is possible to understand the Arab's angry response to the student's story of the Crusades. The focus of mutual understanding is the name of his village, for which he is listening so intently. The absence of the name in the student's lecture is significant in more than one sense. On one level it communicates to the Arab that the student's story does not relate to his story; the anxiety of betrayal and abandonment engenders resentment. In this respect the Arab's subsequent reenactment of his tragic story is meant to impress the memory of his trauma in the Jew's consciousness. On a deeper level, however, the absence of the name signifies the Jew's two-tiered ambivalence, to which the Arab responds intuitively. In one sense the story of the Crusades that he tells the Arab represents the student's desperate, rather naive attempt to deny the failure of his scholarly undertaking. In another, more complex way, however, the narrative of the

Crusades represents an equally naive attempt to displace another history he has just learned about, namely, the tragic history of this afforested place, which has shaken the student out of his usual equanimity.

The earlier pronouncement of the village's name created an affinity between the Jew and the Arab that the student would rather forget. While the whispered name of the village marked the student as possessor of the key to the restoration of the Arab's self-dignity, the Arab's confirmation of the name turned him into the holder of the key to the Jew's liberation from his lethargy, indifference, and passivity. The interdependence of the Arab and the Jew has been established. Paradoxically, the student's subsequent disingenuous disassociation from the Arab's story demonstrates the impossibility to undo this interdependence. His reluctance—or, more precisely, his apprehension—to recognize the bond attests to the inescapable realization of the responsibility for the destruction that, as an Israeli Jew, he shares with Israeli society.

The map that the student draws in the wake of the scene of "The Whispered Name" evinces recognition of the delayed traumatic knowledge, a recognition that subsequently requires a far-reaching transformation. On a historical level, the map that meticulously records the traces of the ruins of the village that he painstakingly located under the forest testifies to the committed atrocity. In a painstaking search of the area lasting several weeks, he produces a visual report of his findings: ruins, traces left by humans, and outlines of buildings intertwining with the trees. Ironically, it is not an innovative scientific study of the Crusades that allows the student to prove his mettle as a historian. Rather, by documenting concrete evidence of the Zionist conquest, he demonstrates his talents as a historian-cum-archeologist. On a personal level the episode of "The Map" signifies the student's self-reaffirmation. His new sense of self-importance is signaled in the decision to leave the map behind: "He will display it on this wall here for the benefit of his successors, that they may remember him. Look, he has signed his name already, signed it to begin with, lest he forget" (FF 104). With uncharacteristic decisiveness and earnestness, the student defines his intentions. This episode testifies to a twofold transformation, namely, that of the place and that of his sense of self. As his signature suggests, he takes full responsibility for the authenticity of both.

"The Map" episode presents a quite evident political-moral message. It provides evidence of behavior that proves—contrary to the
official position espousing the humanity of the Israeli Jewish soldiers—
the atrocities committed during the war. While the forest writes the
triumphalist history of the victors, the mapped out underside of the
forest discloses the history of the defeated, which, as the characterization of the student demonstrates, has been completely suppressed.
The covered traces of the destruction illustrate yet another of Benjamin's previously mentioned views, namely, that the history of victory
would wipe out *"even the dead,"* that is, even the ancestral history
of the defeated. The production of the map has turned the student
of history into the historian of the victims. In this sense "Facing the
Forests" corroborates the accounts of destruction, torture, and subjugation in "Hirbet Hizah" and *The Pessoptimist*. Recall the prediction
of Yizhar's narrator concerning the haunting shadows and silent cries
of the dispossessed. To a remarkable extent "Facing the Forests" has
fulfilled this prophesy of the silent cries emitted by the mutilated
Arab, whereas the map attests to the history of the destruction.

Unlike the narrator in "Hirbet Hizah," however, the student does
not stop at accusatory complaints and powerless exhortations. His
drawing defies the Zionist doctrine of Jewish rebirth in the "empty
land." It makes visually clear the extent to which the present of Israeli
Jews is, in the literal sense of the word, grounded in the history of the
Palestinian people. Despite its definitive military victory, the Zionist
enterprise cannot extricate itself from the Arab history of the place.
The forest draws it nourishment from the destroyed life of the Arab
village, whereas the traces of the village stubbornly delimit the Arab
territory among the trees. The site of the forest unequivocally belies
the exclusivity of the Zionist claim to the land. Consequently, the
student's field study produces an ironic commentary on the Zionist
enterprise, which, having uprooted itself from the Diaspora, has
rooted itself in the Arab history in the land. In a sense the map visually
represents the two-tiered consciousness of the Israeli Jew. As allegori-
cally represented by the forest, the outer tier embodies the faith and
adherence to the Zionist dogma of Jewish renewal. The partially hidden remnants of the destroyed village, whose name remains haunt-
ingly real, represent the inner tier of the repressed, which sporadically
pierces through ideological defenses.

On a psychoanalytical level, therefore, the Arab's plan to burn down the forest transforms him into the object of the student's desire. As a representative of the suppressed, "forgotten" history that needs to be remembered, the Arab is capable of liberating the Jew from the limbolike unself-conscious existence that turned him into the "eternal" student of a "wrong" history.

The fire that eliminates the forest reveals a complete picture of the "other" history that the student could only partially divine through his map work. The forest now gone, "the ruined village appears before his eyes, born anew in its basic outlines as an abstract drawing, as all things past and buried" (FF 114). The past cannot be undone; yet even though the village remains lifeless in its abstraction, the emerging consciousness dissolves the student's lethargic, sterile existence. His transformation into a concerned and caring individual, as evidenced by his protective attitude toward the Arab girl, attests to the student's inner liberation. The story provides an allegorical representation of this transformation. His recurring dream "of a few dry, twisted, or stunted trees, desert trees, alien and salty" that haunted him all along turn into a dream of "green forests [that] spring before his troubled eyes" (FF 116–17).

The psychological recuperation, however, does not bring forth social recognition. Like the proverbial prophet who is ignored in his own town, the message that the student brings from the wilderness to the city commands no attention. The enraged response of the forest manager to his loud and boldly expressed concern for the Arab child foretells the rejection of society at large. Thus, the police who investigate the fire "treat him toughly, [as if] something of the old man's hostility has stuck to them" (FF 116). The attitude of the city seems even more punitive. The old friends deny him reentry into their social circle. Disappointed with the failure of their reform scheme, the friends do not welcome the student who "drops in on them, on winter nights shivering with cold, begging for fire and light" (FF 116). Maliciously they chase him away with the disgruntled question "Well, what now?" (FF 117).

Interestingly, though uniformly treated as a failure, the student has a different opinion. He believes that "the solitude has proved a success. True, his notes have been burned along with the books, but if anyone thinks that he does not remember—he does" (FF 117). Remember what? Among all the other recollections, is it not the final triumphant countenance of the arrested Arab that seems most intriguingly memorable? Recall that during the investigation the student broke down, suggesting the Arab as "a possible clue." At that moment the Arab is handcuffed, arrested, and taken away in a police car. When the student last sees him, the Arab has a "gratified expression in his eyes, a sense of achievement, "a heroic feeling [*regesh g'vurah*]" (FF 116).

When considered in light of the interdependence that evolved between the two, this puzzling response to betrayal and arrest makes sense. From this perspective the sense of victory signifies the fulfillment of desire. Paradoxical as it may seem, in order for the Arab to regain self-dignity his act of rebellion must be recognized by the enemy. Because the Arab is mute, he has been unable to communicate with his interrogators. The student is the only one who knows and can tell the story. In view of this realization, the Arab's triumphant expression elucidates the student's "betrayal." In the context of their relations of transference, the student's incrimination of the Arab constitutes submission to the desire of the Arab: he releases the information that makes the Arab feel like a hero. As we have seen, the student had earlier refused to acknowledge the story of the Arab. One should note here that he refused to acknowledge the story for the second time when the forest was burning and the Arab "[was speaking] to him out of the fire, [wishing] to say everything, everything at once" (FF 112). Ironically, the interrogation conducted by the representatives of the Jewish state finally compels the student to grant the Arab the desired understanding and attention. Precisely at the moment when the Arab demonstrates his triumph, the student regains his confidence and boldly approaches the authorities in the interest of the child. Paradoxically, the empowerment of the Arab empowers the student as well, making him recognize and actively respond to his moral obligation.

The name of the village had initiated the student's encounter with the buried history, and his naming of the Arab in the police interrogation finalized the process of recognition of this history. The transferential relations between Jew and Arab brought a measure of redemption for both. The secret knowledge of the destruction that the Arab imparted to the Jew infused the latter with a sense of responsibility for the committed injustice. Ironically, the sense of humane concern for the other that the student finally gains results from his acknowledgment of culpability he shares with the Israeli mainstream. This new consciousness turns him into an exile in his own community, one that refuses to acknowledge the story he carries with him from the forest.

The Price of Suppressed Histories

Despite its dissenting theme, which elicited ingenious canonizing strategies on the part of critics, "Facing the Forests" carefully limits its vision of Jewish-Arab relations to personal interactions remote from the larger social scene. The limits are set by the secluded location of the forest, the eventual arrest of the Arab, and the final social exclusion of the student. In addition, both protagonists' verbal impediments limit the possibility of social interaction at large. Thus, the equal *subject-to-subject* relationship of transference between Jew and Arab is never allowed to enter the public arena. Because of its private confines, Yehoshua's story focuses on the psychological stratum of this one-to-one relationship. In contrast, Mansour's novel *In a New Light* stages the relations between Arabs and Jews in the public sphere of the kibbutz. The context of the collective affects the individual characters and the relations between them. To better understand the interaction between the Arab protagonist-narrator-confessor and the kibbutz community, I briefly wish to consider the dynamics of subject formation in a social setting.

The issue of subjectivity has been widely discussed for several decades, especially in the areas of philosophy, ethics, and critical theory. One major area of investigation concerns the decentered subject of the post-*cogito* era. This discussion of the subject focuses on the extent to which we are conscious of that which remains unconscious, of our "internal other." In other words, this type of investigation examines the nature of the relations of the individual to the self in view of the fact that the unconscious—a part of the self—always escapes full knowledge. Another principal question involving the subject concerns the relations between the individual and the world. To what extent is our self shaped by our relationships with the world? This question relates to the problem of the subject's identification with and disassociation from the "external other," that is, its social environment.[10] It is, of course, impossible to separate these two approaches on the issue of subjectivity. Both the "internal other" of the unconscious and the "external other" of the social setting indelibly affect the formation of the subject. However, in the following discussion of Yossi's interaction with Israeli society, as represented by the kibbutz, it is the social component of subjectivity that remains my main concern.

It is always useful to begin with Freud's observation of the effect of the social setting on the individual psychological makeup: "In the individual's mental life someone else is invariably involved, as a model, as an object, as a helper, as an opponent; and so from the very first *individual psychology*, in this extended but entirely justifiable sense of the words, is at the same time *social psychology* as well."[11] As Freud sees it, ineluctably the external world is part and parcel of the formation of the individual subjectivity. Although, as Mikkel Borch-Jacobsen informs us, Freud did not develop much further the notion that "[inscribes] the [social] other *in* the ego,"[12] others did. In his assessment of postmodern existentialist thought, Davis affirms the powerful impact of social influence. In fact, social context negates the uniqueness of the subject by divesting it of its freedom. Davis claims that "subjectivity is intersubjective: in reflecting on myself the first thing I confront is the massive presence of the other. We live in the midst of others with their beliefs and values, fears and conflicts . . . deeply embedded in us." Referring to Heidegger's concept of the "death of the subject," Davis claims that in this sense "individuality is a fallacy . . . beneath which lurks the generalized other of consensual validations . . . that keep 'other people' firmly in charge as the sovereign authors of our being." From this perspective the dominating presence of others leads to loss of subjectivity even before subjectivity can be shaped. Subjectivity thus must be forged through the conscious effort to overcome the influence of the other. The primary, overwhelming, inauthentic desire to be like everybody else must be constantly surmounted and opposed so that our authenticity may prevail.[13]

Derrida, on the other hand, emphasizes the positive aspect of the other, whose presence constitutes a primary and integral component of the subject. In a revealing interview Derrida affirmed the ahistorical, ethical values of the subject:

I would add something that remains required by both the definition of the classical subject and by these latter nonclassical motifs, namely, a certain *responsibility*. The singularity of the 'who' is not the individuality of a thing that would be identical to itself. . . . It is a singularity that dislocates or divides itself in gathering itself together to answer to the other, whose call somehow precedes its own identification with itself, for to this call I can *only* answer, have already answered. . . . Here, no doubt, begins the link with the *larger questions of ethical, juridicial, and political responsibility* around which the metaphysics of the subjectivity is constituted.[14]

This approach, which Derrida clearly inherited from Emmanuel Levinas's philosophy of ethics,[15] contends that preceding all ego interests and desires there is the presence of the other. This presence does not dominate but rather inscribes the value of caring responsibility for the other. In contrast to the above notion of the "death of the subject," Derrida maintains that empathic recognition of and involvement with the other shapes our authentic subjectivity. According to Derrida, this position of the subject vis-à-vis the other determines all aspects of social intercourse.

Though briefly sketched, the above models of subjectivity in relation to social environment help to define the limits imposed on the subject in "Facing the Forests" and the expansion of these limits in *In a New Light*. In one sense, the relations of transference that evolve between the adversarial protagonists in "Facing the Forests" widen the perspective of "Hirbet Hizah," where one noted the conspicuous absence of contact between the dissenting Jewish narrator and the Arab victims of the conquest. Yet I also noted that, though in "Facing the Forests" the rediscovered history initiates a new chapter in the history of Arab-Jewish relations, its lessons cannot be applied to the social scene. In the end, the memory of the decimated forest is reduced to contemptuous, mocking remarks that the community directs at the student. The evidence uncovered in the forest leaves no noticeable impact on the city, which resolutely ostracizes the bearer of the unwelcome truth. As represented in Yehoshua's story, Israeli society insists on its uniform, monolithic subjectivity, categorically rejecting its identification as a conqueror who effectively erased the past and the present of the conquered.

The avoidance of the public sphere in "Facing the Forests" sets into sharp relief the signification of the kibbutz, the meeting place of Arabs and Jews in *In a New Light*. Mansour placed his characters in the framework of the quintessential Zionist institution commonly perceived as a model Israeli society. The irony of this proposition is evident in the very location of the kibbutz. Unlike the concealed ruins of the Arab village in "Facing the Forests," here the past history of the land is by no means hidden; on the contrary, it is visible to all since the kibbutz is built on Arab ruins. Moreover, the kibbutz borders an Arab settlement of makeshift tents and huts, a miserable locus of the evicted and dispossessed inhabitants of the destroyed village. This geographic, historical, and sociological configuration locates the interaction between Arabs and Jews in the realia of the post-1948 war.

In "Facing the Forests" the subjectivity of both Jew and Arab is informed by the Jew's twofold emerging, hitherto suppressed consciousness, namely, that of the Arab history in the "empty land" and that of its destruction by the Israelis. *In a New Light* proceeds in the opposite direction. In Mansour's fiction Arab and Jewish characters attempt to construct their subjectivity on the basis of a deliberate, joint decision to suppress memory. Thus, Mansour's story line signals a movement neither toward a rediscovery of the forgotten nor toward a remembrance of the erased past. Unlike Yehoshua's story, which is predicated upon liberation from trauma and moral rehabilitation as a consequence of rediscovering history, Mansour's novel ironically suggests that social coexistence is conditioned upon a mutual consent to "forget." That is to say, the novel proposes that relations between Israeli Jews and Israeli Arabs are predicated upon a conscious deletion of national identities. Whereas the membership of Yossi is predicated upon suppression of his Arab identity, the membership of the "new" Jews in the Zionist movement is conditioned by the repudiation of the Diaspora Jews. As I will show in greater detail, the peaceful coexistence of Arab and Jew on the kibbutz is possible only so long as both parties consciously estrange themselves from their religious and cultural pasts.

It is, in fact, the moral issue of his estrangement from his national heritage that motivates Yossi to write his story. "My heart," he admits, "cries when I recall my lie. It's terrible, it's shameful, but am I wholly to blame? . . . No, the world must be at fault, too." Recall Freccero's codification of the autobiography as a story of conversion from character into author. Indeed, at the opening of the novel Yossi admits that his decision to become the author of his life story is the result of "having undergone a complete, irrevocable change."[16] The consciousness of the change is echoed in the sentence that opens and closes the narrative: "*I saw everything in a new light*" (INL 176; emphasis in English trans.), an amplification of the novel's title.

In one respect Yossi's conversion is signaled in the confession of his "terrible" and "shameful" lie. At the same time, the question "But am I wholly to blame?" as well as the generalization "I saw *everything* in a new light" indicate a conversion not only of his self-perception but also of his perception of the social environment. Yossi's rationalizations not only attest to self-justification but, more significantly, point to the mutual shaping of individual and society. Indeed, in Yossi's autobiographical, confessional account the kibbutz community plays a crucial role. In its critical depiction of the kibbutz, Yossi's story examines his own integrity in the context of his relationships with the kibbutz members, as well as the integrity of the members in the event of an encounter with an Arab.

The kibbutz, however, is represented not solely through the eyes of the Israeli Arab. As we shall see, Yossi's autobiographical narrative also includes an episode of another confessional narrative, that of an Israeli Jew. The following juxtaposition of these episodes, which I have called "The Bulldozer Scene" and "The Mosque Story," sheds light on the dynamic of the relations grounded in the suppression of the past.

Turning first to Yossi's internal monologue:

A bulldozer rakes up and clears away the ruins of the abandoned Arab village. *Such was my village, or rather my father's.* My own [the kibbutz] is quite different. Its houses are built far apart, meticulously planned. My father's village did not even have a master plan: people just built their houses to suit their needs. They wanted to live close to one another because they were afraid of drifting apart. My father, too, was afraid . . . but all his precautions were useless: he bled to death and his blood was red like the bulldozer which cleared the debris in the abandoned village. . . . Why did I have to remember all this? I had *no right to remember.* My father's blood stood for war and destruction, whereas *the bulldozer was a vehicle of peace and construction.* . . . I was beset with longings for my mother, just as the bulldozer's operation reminded me, for no apparent reason, of father's blood squirting out of his shirt. (*INL* 40; emphasis added)

Yossi's stream of consciousness represents an almost classic case of traumatic fixation. The concreteness of the disposal of the Arab past—the bulldozer actually transforms the history of the Arab presence in the land into rubble—triggers an inner upheaval of conscious struggle against the involuntary surge of traumatic reminiscences. The return of haunting, anxiety-provoking memories reinforces the desire to replace the old self, as defined by the paternal village, with a new self, as circumscribed by the kibbutz and its socialist ideology. In this double-bind situation, the fearful memories intensify the wish for a new self while simultaneously precluding its actualization. The naive, self-berating comment "I have no right to remember" underscores the ironic futility of Yossi's struggle to erase the terrible memory of his father's death. As Yossi's stream of consciousness demonstrates, this memory is far from erased; in fact, it is hardly repressed.

Yossi's response to the red color of the bulldozer, which he associates with his father's blood, illustrates with great accuracy the phenomenon of posttraumatic stress disorder. Caruth maintains that posttraumatic stress disorder "is not so much a symptom of the unconscious as it is a symptom of . . . an *impossible history* within [the traumatized]."[17] Caruth's observation draws attention to the historical significance of the task that the bulldozer is performing: it concretely eliminates the history of the defeated. What Yossi is witnessing when the unwanted memories of terror return is the ultimate elimination of a village "such as his." On the one hand, this instinctive recognition points to Yossi's persistent, though unwanted, association with his paternal community ("my village"). On the other hand, the immediate retraction—the village is not his but rather "my father's"—signals Yossi's conscious desire to detach himself from the community he considers vastly inferior to the community of the kibbutz. This interpenetration of involuntary memories and the desire to eliminate these memories demonstrates that, despite the adoption of a new home on the kibbutz, the continuing trauma of Yossi's orphanhood has not abated.

The association of the bulldozer with the "impossible history" of loss proves exceedingly menacing. It is precisely the resurgence of the terrible memories that drives Yossi away from his people to the society of victors. The fear of the past prevents Yossi from identifying the bulldozer for what it really is, namely, a tool for the ruthless Israeli dispossession of the Arabs. Yossi prefers to rationalize the scene of destruction by resorting to the truisms of the "bulldozer [as] a vehicle of peace and construction" (*INL* 40) and the kibbutz as the standard-bearer of the socialist future for humanity. The bulldozer scene conflates the traumatic underpinnings of Yossi's twofold losses—that of his murdered family and that of his nation's defeat.

In "The Mosque Story," by contrast, we are told about the Zionist intended suppression of Diaspora history. It is important to note that it is only after Yossi's Arab identity has become common knowledge that Shlomo, a leading kibbutz member and the epitome of the "new" Jew, addresses him with the following confession:

Look, it's all very distressing, but three years ago we arrived in Israel and were sent here to establish a settlement. You probably know there was a deserted Arab village here. We were told to demolish it but some of the boys said it wasn't fair to destroy the mosque. *So I went ahead and blew up the mosque.* I told them *this sanctimonious attitude didn't become a people who wanted to build their own country.* We had to build our State on lands that had already been settled by another nation. We had no alternative whatsoever, except to live out *rotten lives in Brooklyn.* . . . until the Americans decided to drown us in a sea of blood, the way it happened in Germany, Poland, Russia. . . . They demolished the Arabs' houses and built their own on the ruins, but they wanted to preserve the mosque. *What for?* (*INL* 123; emphasis added)

Despite its entirely different historical context, Shlomo's confession of the deliberate rejection of his Diaspora heritage corresponds with Yossi's confession of the deliberate refutation of his ancestral past. Recall that Yossi's forced justification of the bulldozer's destruction of the remnants of the Arab village reflects the fear of his people's suffering. In a similar way, Shlomo's justification of *his* destruction of the mosque reflects the fear of the persecutions of the Diaspora Jews. This terrible history, Shlomo claims, has created a potential danger for Jews everywhere, justifying the existence of a Jewish state.

As Shlomo sees it, the need to avoid further persecutions has given the Zionists the license to reject the option of living "rotten lives" as Jews in Brooklyn. It should be mentioned in passing—a point to which I shall return—that the particular semantic message of "rotten lives" with reference to the Jews living in Brooklyn—the location of many, mainly Orthodox, Jewish communities—communicates Shlomo's vehement rejection of the Jewish religion.

In a very real sense Shlomo's confession illustrates my earlier discussion in the first part of this study, which established the indelible connection between the deliberate Zionist erasure both of the Diaspora memory and of the presence of the Arab in the land. The destruction of the mosque reconfirms not only the tenet of "the empty land" but also signals a rejection of all religious faiths. Shlomo's destruction of the Arab house of prayer represents the elimination of Arab life in the land while at the same time representing the "birth" of the "new" Jew, who is strong, ruthless, and devoid of compassion, as well as unfettered by all religious bonds. In view of Shlomo's ideological convictions, it is possible to see how his contemptuous repudiation of the "rotten lives" of Orthodox Jews legitimizes his refusal to preserve the symbol of Arab religious life.

It is true that the content of Shlomo's confession sounds belligerent; however, both his choice of listener and the manner in which he ends his confession reveal an underlying vulnerability. Incongruously, Shlomo has chosen to confess to Yossi, who, prior to the disclosure of his Arab identity, he had mocked for his fear of blood and to whom he had admitted his dislike for the Arabs (*INL* 83). Perhaps even more surprising is the fact that Shlomo sincerely expects Yossi to respond to his story. When Yossi remains silent, Shlomo insists on getting his opinion. As Yossi notices, Shlomo speaks with "a strange, suppressed laugh . . . without merriment." Tormented by uncertainties about himself and his future, Yossi recognizes with some satisfaction that "at least he, too, was suffering." Yet he limits his response to telling Shlomo to drink his coffee, whereupon "it was difficult not to notice that [Shlomo] sounded relieved" (*INL* 123–24). It is obvious that Yossi's evasive response to the confession dispelled Shlomo's apprehension and eased his mind.

Shlomo's insistence on having Yossi hear his story as well as his need to have him react to his terrible deed indicates a relationship of transference. The Jew clearly searches out the Arab as listener, while eagerly assuming the part of teller. Curiously, the revelation of Yossi's true identity transformed him into Shlomo's "object of desire." In an ironic reversal, the Arab now appears to the intrepid "new" Jew as the possessor of "secret knowledge" capable of easing his mind and relieving him of the haunting memory of his unconscionable deed. Clearly, Shlomo's deferential attitude toward Yossi in the mosque scene highlights the importance that the Jew attributes to the Arab as the judge of his wrongdoings.

Shlomo's need to confess and his choice of Yossi as his confessor raises several questions. Why does the destruction of the mosque become for Shlomo, the "new" Jew par excellence, a traumatic experience that demands confession? Why does he wish to confess to Yossi, who is hardly an objective listener? Finally, why does he assume that Yossi's response might eliminate his traumatic memories?

In order to demonstrate the affinity with Yossi that Shlomo unconsciously senses, one must recall Yossi's torment in the bulldozer scene. It seems that Yossi's traumatic past and his ambivalence over his identity have positioned him as, in the words of Freud, a "positive transference" of a friendly, even empathically disposed, listener. In a paradoxical way, to become a Zionist kibbutz member exacted for the Arab the same price as it did for the Jew. Their new identities dispossessed both Arab and Jew of their national, cultural, and religious filiations. Motivated by fear of suffering and persecution, both Shlomo and Yossi have reneged on their historical roots. In this sense their conscious dissociation from their past has entailed the traumatic loss of parental history, while their rejection of identity has deprived them of their national traditions. The two characters interrelate through negation. It is therefore possible to view this situation as one of transference between Arab and Jew, each of whom possesses a personal history he expects the other to understand and condone.

This affinity between Arab and Jew is reinforced in the final scene involving the kibbutz assembly meeting. Ostensibly the assembly was organized to make "a historic decision" (*INL* 169) with respect to granting a kibbutz membership to an Arab. As things turned out, the meeting also represented a moment of self-reckoning for the kibbutz community. At one point some members claim that Yossi's birth places him with "his people," that is, the Arabs. Shlomo rises in

Yossi's defense, poignantly driving home the issue by confronting his friends with the question of their own identity: "Yossi is not an Arab. Perhaps he is not a Jew either, but then what kind of Jews are we? Does [*sic*] any of you, Comrades, know that tonight is the eve of the *Ninth of Ab?*[18] . . . Are we Jews? Well, I'll leave it at that. But you all know it isn't exactly true, and it's certainly even less true that Yossi is an Arab. . . . If we don't [admit him as a member] we shall not be able to go out of this room and look people in the eye" (*INL* 172).

It is worth noting that Shlomo does not choose to defend Yossi by means of an argument of socialist ideology stressing equality for all. What he implicitly refers to is his own rejection of the "rotten lives" of Jews in Brooklyn as well as Yossi's absence of condemnation of the destruction of the mosque. Both Yossi and the kibbutz members, Shlomo insists, are equally detached from their religious heritage. Thus, as Shlomo deduces, the refusal of Yossi's candidacy on the grounds that he should be with "his people" would undercut the raison d'être of the Zionists in severing their ties with "their people" in the Diaspora. The Zionists have adopted a new identity to escape persecution and subjugation. That is why, as bona fide Zionists, they cannot reject an Israeli Arab, who rejected his heritage for the same reason; like them he abandoned his people out of fear of suffering and subjugation, which, ironically, the "new" Jews inflicted upon the Arabs.

The kibbutz decides to accept Yossi as "one more member, neither Jew nor Arab" and "to keep the whole discussion confidential" (*INL* 175). This decision makes Yossi see *everything* in a new light. "I had won my fight," he realizes, "but this kind of victory left a bitter taste in my mouth." As he sees it, he will be "allowed to stay but only stealthily, like a thief in the night" (*INL* 176). And while everybody is praising the kibbutz secretary for having found the "Golden Path," a compromise acceptable to all, Yossi weeps at what he perceives not only as humiliation but also as a hypocritical departure from the socialist ideals that the kibbutz had thus far professed to implement. Indeed, the determination to avoid bad publicity before forthcoming elections underscores the hypocrisy of the kibbutz members' decision. However, a closer inspection of the resolution—which does not send Yossi back to "his people" and at the same time strips him of any national-ethnic identity by declaring him *"neither Jew nor Arab"*—points to the deeper signification of this decision.

What would it have meant to identify Yossi publicly as either *an Arab* or *a Jew*? In fact, the story elucidates the signification of each option in terms of the reality of the Zionist state. To begin with the first option, why not identify Yossi as an Arab and send him back to "his people"? Indeed, the nearby village of Nur-Allah provides concrete implications of this option. The parodic depiction of the relations between the kibbutz and the village collapses the socialist facade of the kibbutz. The kibbutz members are consistently represented as oppressors and exploiters of the Arab minority. Economically destitute, the inhabitants of the village are completely dependent on temporary construction jobs on the kibbutz. Deprived of political freedom, these Israeli citizens have become pawns in the corrupt political games of Israel's political parties.

Mahmud, a young, educated Arab, represents what life with his people would have been like for Yossi. Mahmud works as a driver for Ben-Tsedek (literally "Son of Justice"), a highly positioned bureaucrat in the Arabic department of the Israeli government. Ben-Tsedek's main function is to solicit Arab votes with empty promises. Mahmud, who also serves as Ben-Tsedek's translator, mispresents the Arabs' pleas for employment by attenuating their complaints and embellishing the translation with constant flattery of his boss. While Mahmud dutifully repeats Ben-Tsedek's catchphrase—"It's an Arab's duty to stay with his people and help them" (*INL* 166)—it is clear that Mahmud sees his duty as one of pleasing his employer in order to retain his job. To a remarkable extent Mahmud's characterization reminds us of Saeed, the narrator-protagonist in Habiby's novel *The Pessoptimist,* especially Saeed's obsequious behavior toward his Israeli bosses. Recall that, traumatized by the war, Saeed became an informer for the Israeli Secret Service. Not unlike Saeed, Mahmud has lost his freedom in the service of his master; in a sense he follows Saeed, who, suspended on a stake, belongs neither to his ruthless masters nor to his oppressed people. Would it therefore be possible to claim that had Yossi disclosed his Arab identity, he might have become another Mahmud or, worse, another Saeed, whose double life drove him to distraction and death?

These representations of Israeli Arabs as servants of Israeli Jews return us to Hegel's concept of the self-negation of the bondsman vis-à-vis the lord. The bondsman, fearful of his lord, effaces himself as a subject; his servitude has made him an object devoid of consciousness. Hegel sees the hope of inner liberation in the relationship that the bondsman creates with his work. "Through work the bondsman becomes conscious of what he truly is. . . . [I]n fashioning the thing, he becomes aware . . . that he himself exists essentially and actually in his own right."[19] In Mansour's representation, however, neither the villagers, who ingratiate themselves with a ruler who wields the power to employ them, nor Mahmud, who compromises his values to remain employed, are permitted such a redemptive attitude toward their work, which would restore their dignity. Like their masters they lead a life of deceit and corruption under the guise of the socialist ideal.

Thus, the decision not to send Yossi back to "his people" serves the interests of the kibbutz members. The scheme to ignore Yossi's Arab identity enables them to perpetuate their own identity as socialists. Sending a devoted comrade back to the Arab village would have presented the kibbutz members with an unacceptable self-image as colonizing exploiters. Even though Yossi may not register the irony of the situation, the erasure of his Arab identity indicates his official enlistment in a political and economic system built upon cheap Arab labor.

This realization leads to the second option, namely, that of Yossi as *a Jew*. Why not declare Yossi a Jew? Indeed, Yossi's efforts become assimilated into Jewish society are so successful that—to recall Bhabha's notion of the colonized as a "mimic"—he is able to "pass" for a Jew or a "colonizer" for quite a long time.[20] To escape the fate of the oppressed Arab minority, Yossi has chosen to become a member of the Zionist collective. Recall Davis's discussion of the loss of subjectivity as a result of conforming to social "consensual validation." Clearly, Yossi's lifelong desire has been to become "consensually validated." His former participation in Hevrat Noar and the *hakhsharah*[21] and his present self-dedication to the kibbutz (*INL* 99) have shown, beyond any doubt, the extraordinary extent of his motivation to integrate himself into the dominant society.

Furthermore, the extent to which he succeeds in obliterating his cultural origins underscores his desire to become another. Not only has he forgotten his mother tongue but he has also erased the earliest and most basic socialization lessons in Arab life. When a young Arab boy corrects Yossi, who has confused the appellations *Effendi* and *Hawadja,* Yossi realizes the enormous distance between himself and his native community: "I remembered now . . . *Hawadja* was reserved for Jews and Christians. *Hawadja* and *Effendi* were two different things, just as a Jew and a goy were different. From early childhood we learned to be different, and everybody repeated this fact to us a thousand times" (*INL* 106). Yossi's mistaken appellation reveals the extent of his cultural detachment; he has forgotten or, rather, deeply repressed the semantic markers of Arab social structure that had been inculcated in him since childhood.

Despite all his efforts to integrate himself into Zionist society, Yossi cannot become a bona fide "new" Jew. Indeed, Yossi admits to himself that the identity of the "new" Jew is beyond his reach. Interestingly, it is not religion that prevents him from achieving a complete sense of belonging. In the socialist setting of the kibbutz religious differentiation does not—or, at least, should not—present a problem. Thus, it is not conversion to the Jewish faith that precludes full integration into Jewish society but rather his failed transformation into an intrepid fighter: "If only I could take part in a war. . . . Perhaps I would still be somebody, would have some rights on my own. . . . [N]obody believed that I spent the war in the cookhouse. Perhaps it was better that way—somebody might still believe I was a fighter. But in my heart of hearts I knew the truth and it wasn't pleasant. As a matter of fact it hurt and rankled" (*INL* 69).[22]

In this sense it is possible to understand Yossi's desire to integrate himself into the kibbutz as a projection of his yearning for "secret knowledge"—a phrase that was used earlier in my discussion of transference—that the male kibbutz members seem to possess, namely, how to become a fighter. From this perspective one may see Yossi's love affair with Rivka, a kibbutz member, as a displacement of this desire rather than a representation of the optimistic and naive adage "amor vincit omnia." The characterization of Rivka's husband, Yehuda, a former U.S. marine now in charge of the kibbutz armory, whose name is associated with the fearless lion of Judah, illuminates the psychological significance of Yossi's sexual "conquest." To replace Yehuda as Rivka's husband would transfer the battlefield into the sexual arena, where Yossi has a better chance to restore his sense of potency. Such a victory would imply a vicariously obtained self-identification as a fighter. Despite his disappointment and bitterness, Yossi describes the debate over his kibbutz membership in military terms: it was a "fight" that he had won; it was his "victory." His acceptance into the kibbutz community makes him feel victorious. Indeed, while being embraced by Rivka Yossi takes a final look at the defeated husband and observes that Yehuda "stood by the door, silent and lonely" (*INL* 176).

This reading of *In a New Light* suggests mutual transference, which tends to deny rather than confront the repressed past. Yossi's noncommittal response to Shlomo's confession of his destruction of the mosque sanctions the Zionist "new" Jewish identity. At the same time, Yossi's conscious denial of his Arab identity and his desire to become a fighter attest to his compliance with the consensual norms determined by the dominant society. Thus, the function of the membership that the kibbutz extends to Yossi is twofold: not only does it erase Yossi's lies and deception but it also allows the kibbutz members to persist without qualms, to see themselves as a group of virtuous and noble individuals who represent the merits of Zionist socialism.

It is true that Yossi's autobiographical confession recounts the "conversion" that made him see *everything* in a new light, that is, through the lens of hypocrisy and deceit. Yet the fact that he remains on the kibbutz attests to his compliance rather than rebellion. By accepting the compromise, Yossi de facto conforms to the Zionist enterprise. Despite his disenchantment with the kibbutz and its distortion of the socialist idea, his decision to stay is at least partly due to his numerous ties to the kibbutz. It is not only his love affair with Rivka, which confirms his acceptance in a personal sense. I have already mentioned the extent of commonality in the transferential relationship between Shlomo and Yossi. This relationship emerges from the painful denial of parental legacy and—perhaps even more—from the painful tacit agreement to perpetuate this denial.

A response to traumatic events through denial rather than confrontation presents us with a case of what Eric Santner calls "narrative fetishism," which he defines as "the construction and deployment of a narrative consciously or unconsciously designed to expunge the traces of the trauma or loss that called that narrative in the first place."[23] The Candidesque aspect of the narrative in *The Pessoptimist* may be seen as a similar attempt to suppress the trauma of defeat through irony and laughter. As Saeed's letters show, this attempt failed. Saeed must tell the traumatic story even at the price of madness and death. The circumstances of memory suppression in Mansour's novel differ considerably. Here the compromise is predicated upon a common denial of the past, agreed upon by both winners and losers. As Dominick LaCapra explains, such an expedient denial of traumatic experiences indicates "a redemptive, fetishistic narrative that excludes or marginalizes trauma through a teleological story."[24] While Mansour's narrative ends on a note of an achieved status quo, his protagonist's bitterness, which permeates the entire story, underscores the sense of "unfinished business" that such a "fetishic," partial solution has engendered.

In *In a New Light* Mansour is conscious of the shortcomings of the solution he offers, yet the story does not altogether disqualify relationships grounded in the conscious suppression of truth. The child that is to be born of Arab-Jew loving relationships seems to imply some hope for a purer future, less tainted by ideologies and political interests. In the meantime the transference that recognizes the need of both sides for each other—even if it is in the problematic context of "fetishistic" national/religious/ethnic identity suppression—suggests the possibility of an imperfect coexistence.

Amos Oz's story "Nomad and Viper" (1963) dispels all hope for coexistence between Arabs and Jews and paints a horrific vision of the moral disintegration of Israeli society. The visceral hatred of the Arab, which supersedes all moral considerations, manifests itself in terrible acts of indiscriminate violence. Whereas in Mansour's novel one observed how the kibbutz members reveal some self-awareness of their hypocritical use or, rather, abuse of the Zionist socialist ideal, in "Nomad and Viper" there is a complete lack of self-awareness of the cynical abuse of the Zionist socialist ideal for the sake of aggressive domination. While "Facing the Forests" and *In a New Light* examine various *possibilities* of dialogic interaction—the former on a personal level in the seclusion of the forest and the latter in the public sphere of the kibbutz—"Nomad and Viper" demonstrates the *impossibility* of such a dialogue. The story examines the psychological mind-set of the "new" Jew, which precludes constructive relations with the Arab minority. The horrifying scene of barbaric violence at the conclusion of the story implies an unsparing self-examination as a precondition for any possible future interaction.

9

Descent into Barbarism

Amos Oz's "Nomad and Viper"

To begin with a brief plot synopsis of "Nomad and Viper," in a summer beset by drought Israeli military authorities allows a starving
Bedouin tribe to move to the southern part of Israel. The Arabs set
up their encampment in the vicinity of an unnamed kibbutz. The kibbutz, whose members have never been exposed to Israel's Arab minority, is completely unprepared for such an invasion of its territory.
Hostile relationships with the unwanted visitors develop. Though
they cannot find evidence to support their claims, the kibbutz members accuse the nomads of stealing items and damaging property. The
narrative centers on two encounters between Arabs and Jews. The
first involves a meeting between the head of the Bedouin tribe and
Etkin, the kibbutz secretary, during which the Bedouin admits to
some thefts and pays for them. Following the meeting, the young
members of the kibbutz decide on a punitive operation against the
tribe. The second encounter takes place between Geula, a respected
kibbutz member, and a young Bedouin shepherd. There is a hint of
erotic attraction between the two. Feeling rejected, Geula imagines
that the Arab tried to rape her. She lies on the grass and dies, bitten
by a poisonous snake. Meanwhile, the young kibbutz members are
setting out toward the encampment to attack the tribe.

According to the canonical interpretations of the Arab presence in
Israeli Jewish fiction, the Arab characters are either seen as allegorical
representations of general truths of victimization and suffering or as

reflections of Israel's existential anxieties and fears. This approach has not changed; in fact, it has been reiterated and reinforced in recent critical essays. Thus Yochai Oppenheimer claims that the Arab in the story "is identifiable only by external features, the result of a projection of Israeli fears and desires."[1] Hannan Hever focuses on the story's "linguistic deterritorialization," which spreads uncertainty and confusion in the Israeli camp. He identifies the failed "attempt to create a joint discourse of minority and majority." He ascribes this failure to the fact that the Arab in the story is used as a catalyst to set off the Oedipal rebellion of the kibbutz's sons against the founding fathers. The response to the Arabs, according to this critic, projects the Israeli majority's self-perception as a threatened minority.[2] Menakhem Perry stresses the aspect of menace in the story by claiming that, like other stories of the period, in "Nomad and Viper" the Arab is a reflection of the precarious psychological state of mind of the Israeli. Thus, "not only is the contact with the Arab an internal one but the contact with the 'Arab' within is an outburst of life resulting in death or disaster."[3]

My readings of "Hirbet Hizah" and "Facing the Forests" deviated from the canonical treatment of the Arab as an embodiment of Israeli existentialist concerns. I approached the Arab as a *character* rather than as an allegorization of a psychological component of the Israeli character. I showed that in these texts the Arab character acts as a *subject* in his interaction with the Jewish *subject*. The focus on intersubjectivity allowed me to trace patterns of interaction between Arabs and Jews that the canonical abstraction of the issue had ignored. My reading of "Nomad and Viper" similarly departs from the canonical interpretations. I continue to follow the theme of a possible empathic interaction between Jew and Arab that I first introduced in "Hirbet Hizah" and "Facing the Forests." In contrast to these stories, "Nomad and Viper" marks the end of any possibility of a binational dialogue. At the same time, the refusal of the Bedouin tribe to be coopted by the kibbutz signals defiance, a self-affirming stance on the part of the oppressed, who insist on their independence.

Thus, the following reading demonstrates that the Arabs in "Nomad and Viper" act as subjects rather than refractions of the Jewish characters. The undeniable subjectivity of the Arabs clearly emerges in their public and private meetings with the Jews. On these occasions the Arabs affirm their subjectivity in their rejection of Jewish attempts at co-optation and domination. Furthermore, the Arab refusal to comply affects the subjectivity of the Jew; the Arab's defiance of the Zionist "fetishistic narrative," which ignores the suffering of the victim, marks the breakup of the kibbutz members' self-image of moral and intellectual superiority. The "new" Jews' failure to subdue the "inferior" opponent results in a grave injury to the ego, which prompts violent retaliation.

Unlike Hever, I wish to argue that the kibbutz attackers do not act as a minority. On the contrary, they exhibit the enraged attitude of hitherto unchallenged dominators. They defend their territory, over which they have held unlimited authority and control against the unexpected appearance of the "other." As they see it, the very presence of the destitute tribe is an insult to their pride and potency. Thus, it is possible to argue that their violence feeds on egotistical and narcissistic needs, which preclude the recognition of others and their needs. Recall Walter Benjamin's thesis of barbaric acts of cruelty and victimization methodically erased from the annals of the victorious. These young "new" Jews are setting forth to silence the defeated, who, as Benjamin states, "call every victory in question."[4] Indeed, the conquest of Hirbet Hizah is replayed in the concluding scene in the story, which demonstrates how, infuriated by a devastating blow to their collective self-image, the young kibbutz members are about to reaffirm the triumphalist Zionist history. In other words, they are determined to punish the Arabs who dared to insist on their version of history and thus defy Israel's historical narrative of heroism and moral superiority.

The story ends with a description of the young kibbutz member venturing on their punitive mission against the defiant Bedouin tribe "She [Geula] watched the gang of youngsters crossing the lawn on their way to the fields and the wadi to even the score with the nomads. We were carrying short, thick sticks. Excitement was dilating our pupils. And the blood was drumming in our temples."[5]

The kibbutz's recourse to the most primitive level of aggression and the enthusiasm with which the destruction is to be carried out demonstrate the enormity of the narcissistic hurt inflicted by the Arabs. To gain a deeper insight into the implications of this ego injury, I wish to briefly examine Freud's concept of narcissism. Freud distinguishes between two narcissistic constructs, that of ego-libido and that of object-libido. He sees the former as "primary" or "infantile" narcissism. Ego-libido is marked by megalomania, which manifests itself in "an over-estimation of the power of . . . wishes and mental acts, the 'omnipotence of thoughts,' a belief in the thaumaturgic force of words, and a ['magical'] technique for dealing with the external world." As a result of an emerging conflict between the childish state of megalomania and the developing "cultural and ethical ideas," the individual constructs an ego ideal, the equivalent of Freud's later notion of the superego. In the process of departure from the state of infantile megalomaniacal narcissism, the subject also enters the stage of object-libido, directing his or her narcissism toward an object-choice, that is, the object of his loving attention. Since "a narcissistic object-choice is to be loved," the reorientation toward another means that "the person who loves has, so to speak, forfeited a part of his narcissism, and it can only be replaced by his being loved."[6]

In view of Freud's observations on narcissism—particularly his comments on ego-libido—it is possible to interpret the primeval, "cave-man" type of violence exhibited by the kibbutz members as the result of an injury to their "primary narcissism." One would expect these young people to be at the stage of ego-ideal rather than that of "infantile" or "primary" narcissism. But Freud had already observed that the transformation from one stage to another is by no means linearly progressive because the need to let go of the stage of "primary" narcissism often results in inner resistance. Emergence from primary narcissism elicits the dialectical wish to remain in the primary stage.[7] This wish to remain in a state of infantile omnipotence is confronted by another psychological development that Freud identifies as the evolution of conscience. As Freud sees it, ego ideal elucidates the notion of " 'conscience,' " which expresses itself in the feeling of "being *watched.*" The power of "watching, discovering and criticizing all our intentions . . . exists in every one of us in normal life." That is to say, the internalization of the ego ideal results in self-accountability, whereby the individual no longer feels omnipotent. Rather, having become conscious of one's social situation, one becomes the judge of one's actions.[8]

It is important to note that in his explanation of the role of conscience Freud links ego ideal with group psychology by maintaining that "in addition to its individual side . . . it is also the common ideal of a family, a class or a nation [and] the non-fulfillment of this ideal . . . is transformed into a sense of guilt (social anxiety). Originally, the sense of guilt was a fear of punishment by the parents. . . . [L]ater the parents are replaced by an infinite number of fellow-men."[9] From this perspective, individuals are not only accountable to themselves for satisfying the demands of ego ideal; out of a sense of guilt and fear of punishment, they must set the goal of the ego ideal in compliance with social norms.

This last observation of the power of society over the individual takes us back to the conclusion of "Nomad and Viper." As indicated by the shift from "I" to "we," the nameless narrator—who, despite his consistently prejudiced and xenophobic attitude toward the nomads, has opposed the use of force—submits to the collective will and joins the attackers. In contrast to the critical interpretation of the attack in terms of an Oedipal struggle with the kibbutz founders, I wish to argue that the Oedipal motive is at best of minor importance. The founding generation has become too unprincipled and weak to constitute a valid target for a youthful rebellion. Rather than rebellion, the old members elicit contempt. Their cynical abuse of the socialist ideals has not been lost on the younger generation. In fact, it is the older generation that, without too much resistance, yields to the young people. In a highly ironic reversal from the socialist ideal of humanism and equity upon which the institution of the kibbutz was founded, the elders' support of the attack demonstrates the totality of corruption. In light of the preceding discussion of narcissism, it is possible to view the situation in terms of collective psychology: the kibbutz seems to be arrested at the primary, infantile stage of narcissism, manifested here in a megalomaniacal show of force.

The disproportionate retaliation for relatively minor offenses, if any, is quite puzzling. Why should the presence of the physically harmless, economically destitute nomads prove so traumatic to the superior, incomparably more powerful, prosperous kibbutz? The moral implications of this savagery worthy of *Lord of the Flies* notwithstanding, from a psychological point of view the final scene evinces the kibbutz's regression to the primitive stage of ego development. The violent action against the Arab intruders demonstrates what Freud has called a "vigorous attempt" to recover the state of primary narcissism. Indeed, this argument is supported by Freud's astute observation: "In the undisguised antipathies and aversions which people feel toward strangers with whom they have to do we may recognize the expression of self-love—of narcissism. This self-love works for the preservation of the individual."[10] The hostility toward the intruder indicates the individual's desire to preserve the narcissistic, childlike sense of control over the external world. The recognition of the other implies an acknowledgment of the other as an independent subject who cannot be controlled and who, moreover, brings forth the sense of "being watched." In Freud's terms, therefore, the recognition of the other signifies a transformation from the mind-set of narcissistic independence to one that submits to the moral judgment of the other.

In "Nomad and Viper" the opportunity to enter such a relationship with the external world arises with the appearance of the starved Bedouin tribe. The physical appearance of the Arabs in the territory of the kibbutz is a concrete representation of the "call of the other," which, in effect, is a call upon the ego ideal. This call, as Derrida's discussion of subjectivity revealed, is the prerequisite to subject formation. Unlike the individual who blindly conforms to the collective, this subject "dislocates or divides itself in gathering itself together to answer the other." It could be argued that, according to Derrida, when answering the call of the other, the subject enters a process that splits its narcissistic self-loving image.[11] Note Derrida's complementation of Freud's view of transformation from primary narcissism to the stage of ego ideal. The ability to hear and respond to the call of the other is predicated upon the capacity to see oneself in a loving relationship with another rather than in one of self-love.

This Freudian-cum-Derridean perspective enables the reader to interpret the sudden appearance of the nomads on the kibbutz territory as a dire menace to the kibbutz's narcissistic self-image. Heeding the nomads' call would have evoked a sense of responsibility, and the awakened "conscience" would have effected the kibbutz's moral dependency upon the nomads' welfare. As Freud taught us, the development of the ego ideal entails the recognition of being watched, that is, being observed by others, a situation that bears the obligation of moral responsibility. One can now gain a deeper insight into the kibbutz's seemingly unfounded and incomprehensible hatred for the Bedouin tribe. To acknowledge the Arabs would have amounted to an acknowledgment of watching and, consequently, critically evaluating others. For the self-loving kibbutz members, arrested in the stage of primary narcissism, the position of being critically evaluated is psychologically unbearable. Thus, the "call of the other," who is weak, destitute, and starved, places the kibbutz in a predicament: its members must *hear* the call of the other, yet they are too self-loving to *heed* it.

This predicament results in a campaign of dehumanization—even demonization—of the Arabs. This strategy has as its goal to negate the nomads as civilized human beings. The exclusion of the Arabs from a normative society justifies not only the reluctance to respond to their call but also the hatred and violence of the "civilized" kibbutz members toward the tribe. The lengthy opening depiction of the Arabs' foreignness in the kibbutz's social reality ends with a portrayal of an unbridgeable social gap: "Some were half-blind, or perhaps feigned half-blindness from some vague alms-gathering motive. Inscrutable to the likes of you" (NV 120). The literal translation from the Hebrew of the final sentence—"[People] such as yourselves (kibbutz members) would never be able to fathom their (the nomads') [base] motives"—clearly communicates the strangers' complete incompatibility with the kibbutz's incomparably superior society. One should note in passing that the insinuation concerning the strangers' feigned half-blindness ironically draws attention to the kibbutz's complete blindness with regard to its self-deception.

The tendency to demonize the Arabs culminates in the episode where a kibbutz youth has "beaten senseless" an Arab shepherd. According to the narrator, the attack was totally justified in view of the individual's appearance: "He was blind in one eye, broken-nosed, drooling; and his mouth—on this the men responsible were unanimous—was set with long, curved fangs like a fox's. A man with such an appearance was capable of anything. And the Bedouins would certainly not forget this lesson [the beating]" (NV 121). In a tragically ironic historical reversal, the argument of the Israeli Jews echoes the centuries-long anti-Semitic search for signs of the diabolical in the Jew's physical appearance as evidence of Jewish inhumanity.[12] At the same time, the boast of having "successfully" beaten the Arab into a "better" behavior invokes one of Freud's definitions of narcissistic megalomania, namely, the belief in "a [magical] technique for dealing with the external world." The grotesque exaggeration of the shepherd's physical appearance reflects the enormity of the persecutors' desperation to recuperate the "magic" of their former omnipotence. The greater the inhumanity of the Arab, who is "capable of anything," the greater the victory of the "civilized" world. The demonization of the other enhances the heroic stature of the attackers, reassuring them that the intruder had to be eliminated. In a psychological sense, therefore, the insistence on robberies committed by the Arabs makes sense. The accusation reveals a displaced sense of loss: the infringement of the other has robbed the kibbutz of its narcissistic self-image of exclusivity and superiority.

It is important to note that the organized retaliation against the tribe at large is the result a meeting between the two leaders of the warring communities: the head of the Bedouin tribe, who remains nameless, and Etkin, the secretary of the kibbutz. The meeting opens with the Arab's admission, in "careful, formal Hebrew" (NV 122), of some thefts for which he pays right there. Then Etkin makes a speech in "broken Arabic" which dates from the "time of the [Arab] riots [1936] and the siege [of Jerusalem in 1948]." The association of Jewish-Arab militant hostilities in the past with Etkin's decision to speak in broken Arabic draws attention to the undertone of animosity and intimidation in his ostensibly peace-seeking speech. Etkin begins with a "statement about the brotherhood of nations—a cornerstone of our ideology" and continues with a long and detailed list "of thefts, damage, and sabotage" allegedly committed by the tribe. His speech ends with a proposition—which sounds more like an ultimatum—that "if the stolen property were returned and the vandalism stopped once and for all," plans for reciprocal children's visits would be made "in the interest of deepening mutual understanding." The guest, however, takes no notice of Etkin's final offer of building a relationship between the communities. After pointing out that his hosts would not be able to prove thefts other than those "he had already admitted and for which he had sought our forgiveness" (NV 123), he respectfully departs.

At this point the young members of the kibbutz start clamoring for an attack against the nomad encampment. The uncontrollable urge for a quasi-military operation against the tribe reflects the depth of the attacker's narcissistic frustration. The anger of the kibbutz members shows their dismay at having the vacuity of their claim exposed by the Arab, who, in their stereotypical view, must be dishonest, ignorant, and easy to fool. The dignified comportment of the Arab, his formal Hebrew, and, most significantly, his honest admission of the thefts, for which he takes full responsibility, combine to present the kibbutz with an unpleasant truth about themselves. It is impossible for them not to sense their inferiority vis-à-vis the Arab, whose manner is civilized, speech fluent, and offer honest.

From another point of view, it is the Arab's silence in response to Etkin's offer of friendly relations that probably offends them most. As noted, the Arab ignores completely Etkin's platitudes concerning a brotherhood of nations and mutual understanding, as well as his plan for children's meetings. Clearly, the Arab is not interested in any social relationships with the kibbutz. The absence of even perfunctory gratitude presents the kibbutz members with an unexpected refusal to comply. Against all odds, the Arab refuses to be co-opted. The reader will recall a similar strategy of co-optation in Mansour's novel *In a New Light*. There, too, as Yossi's painful experience demonstrated, the promises of socialist brotherhood proved devoid of meaning. Despite his frustration and disappointment, the Arab in Mansour's novel complies and joins the "fetishistic narrative" of the Zionist majority. In the case of Yossi, however, one noted a redeeming aspect in the emerging consciousness of the fallacy of the Zionist socialist idea of brotherhood. Recall how Shlomo, a Jewish kibbutz member, confronted the kibbutz members with the hypocrisy evident in their hesitation to grant an Arab membership. This act of sincere self-criticism by at least one member of the kibbutz promises some hope for an understanding between Arabs and Jews.

Not a single voice of self-critical candor is raised in "Nomad and Viper." Instead, there are repeated attempts to be rid of the Arabs, first by an act of terror, then by an ideological co-optation, and finally by a collective punishment of the tribe. The strategy of co-optation is of particular interest since it attempts to turn the Arabs into "mimics." To recall Bhabha, they are the colonized who are allowed to become like but "never quite the same" as the colonizer. To entice the Arab into the position of a "mimic," Etkin embarks on a two-step plan of deceit. First, he attempts to reform the "savages" by making them not only admit to but also pay for transgressions they did not commit. Second, he tries to persuade the Arabs to put their trust in his offer of "mutual understanding," which he calls "the cornerstone of our ideology." As the previous acts of violence have shown, these are but empty words. In terms of the narcissistic self-confidence that it projects, Etkin's speech illustrates what Freud described as a megalomaniacal "belief in the thaumaturgic force of words"; it is the narcissists' belief that they possess a magical language that will force the external world to submit to their will. Etkin attempts to silence the "call of the other" that the Bedouin tribe represents by merging it into the univocal chorus of the kibbutz. Etkin hopes that once tempted by the promise of equality, the Arabs will work toward perfecting their mimicry of the dominating power rather than becoming a watching and judging presence in the dominator's sphere.

Etkin's attempt fails due to the flaw of omission. He fails to reciprocate the Arab's admission of his young tribesmen's transgressions with an equally honest admission of the acts of brutality committed by his young people. This lack of integrity on the part of the secretary of the kibbutz speaks loudly of the lack of integrity of the kibbutz as a whole. In the words of Freud, an honest confession would have signaled the recognition of the "watching" presence of the other; it would have marked a progression from "primary narcissism" toward the stage of ego ideal, or conscience, which would have impelled the consciousness of the social environment. Instead, Etkin uses his authority disingenuously to preserve the kibbutz's narcissistic sense of exclusionary superiority. In contrast to the subject-to-subject relations in "Facing the Forests" and in *In a New Light,* Etkin is unable to see the Arab as his equal. On the contrary, Etkin's purpose is to manipulate the Arab's desire to become like the majority. In psychoanalytical terms, Etkin wishes the kibbutz to become the Arab's object-choice, that is, for the kibbutz to become the Arab's object of love.

To elucidate this last point, note that Freud distinguishes between two kinds of identification with the love object, namely, fascination and bondage. Whereas fascination signals reciprocal love that enriches the lover, bondage surrenders or enslaves the lover to his or her love object, creating a relationship of abject dependence. In the case of bondage, Freud claims that "*the object has been put in the place of the ego ideal.*"[13] That is to say, the inaccessible other has replaced the demands of conscience. To apply this to our story, using the strategy of threat and promise (stick and carrot), Etkin wishes to cow the Arab into a state of psychological "bondage" with regard to the kibbutz, the unattainable object of desire. Since the kibbutz members by no means intend to reciprocate this love, the Arab will be reduced to a helpless mimic of the dominant society. Had Etkin had his way, the Arabs would have entered the situation of Hegel's bondsman, whose frustrated desire for the lord's recognition deprives him of subjectivity.

The Arab, however, reveals no desire to enter any "bonding" situation involving unequal relations with the Jews. In other words, he shows no desire to compromise his conscience in order to satisfy the narcissistic will-to-power of his opponents. The man asserts his subjectivity not only as a "man of his word," who will not renege on his testimony, but also as a responsible leader of his tribe, committed to preserve the values of his tradition. "Boys will be boys" is how he explains to his hosts the reason for thefts his young people committed, adding that "the world was getting steadily worse." Nonetheless, despite the deterioration of the world at large, he acts on the belief that "stolen property fastens its teeth in the flesh of the thief, *as the proverb says*" (NV 122; emphasis added). As his reference to the proverb signifies, the leader of the Bedouin tribe is guided by the wisdom of his heritage. In contrast to Etkin's lip service to socialist ideals, the head of the Arab tribe has a firm sense of moral responsibility upon which he is determined to act. Thus, he assumes full responsibility for his tribal members' misdemeanors and pays for the transgressions.

The *mauvaise foi* of the Jewish contingent at the public meeting is echoed in the meeting between Geula and the Bedouin shepherd. Ostensibly the episode involves an awakening sexual attraction that comes to naught. Upon closer inspection it appears that sexual desire is but an expression of Geula's overriding desire for domination. Like the meeting between Etkin and the head of the tribe, the meeting between the young people ends in Geula's failure to impose her will on the shepherd. The sense of defeat engenders an irrational, vindictive, infantile urge to inflict suffering on the tribe at large. Imagining that the Arab has tried to rape her, Geula formulates the following silent wish: "Let's the boys [the young kibbutz members] go right away tonight to their [the Arabs'] camp and smash their black bones because of what they did to me" (NV 131). Like her male counterparts, who experience the refusal of the head of the tribe to comply with their demands as a devastating blow to their ego, Geula feels violated by the shepherd's refusal to enter a relationship of "bondage," one in which she positions herself as an unattainable object of desire.

Geula's desire to dominate becomes clear the moment her conversation with the shepherd is interrupted by the "languorous call" to prayer from the encampment. To offset the intrusive call, "Geula pursed her lips and whistled an old tune." Mesmerized for a moment, the Arab nonetheless turned away, knelt down, "touched the forehead on the ground, and began mumbling fervently." Having failed to get his attention, Geula resorts to more insidious means. She mockingly repeats his earlier confidence of not having had "a girl yet" (NV 128). She interrupts his prayer twice with a loud, contemptuous mimicry of his confession: "You're still too young . . . very young. Young. No girl for you. Too young." The man who had been speaking Hebrew "replied twice with a very long and solemn remark in his own language." This shift to Arabic elicits an enraged response: "Why are you talking to me in Arabic all of a sudden? What do you think I am? What do you want here anyway?"(NV 129–30).

The shepherd's shift to Arabic clearly expresses his offense, communicating his decision to end the meeting. He responds to her interruption during a moment of prayer, indicating a blatant lack of respect on her part for the Arab's religious observance. While it is true that Geula's mockery of the shepherd's sexual deprivation may reflect her own sexual needs, the religious context of her interruption is significant, indicating that Geula's wish to become the object of the Arab's desire has transcended her sexual interest. Her inconsiderate interruptions assume a political dimension. As a member of the ruling majority, Geula feels entitled to command the attention of the inferior minority member even during a moment of prayer.

The shepherd's response in Arabic, which remains incomprehensible to her, turns the tables, so to speak; it defies her superior position, creating a sphere of communication that she is unable to control. Thus, in its literal sense her question "What do you think I am?" communicates a new realization that deals a death blow to Geula's narcissistic ego. To recall Freud, she is affronted by the emerging awareness of "being watched" and judged by another. Even though she does not understand, what she hears cannot be ego enhancing. Indeed, the Arab provides an indirect answer to the question. Terrified, he withdraws from her "as though from a dying creature" (NV 130).

The image of "a dying creature" is not only terrifying but also prescient since, as already mentioned, Geula ends up dying soon after as a result of being bitten by a poisonous snake: "And the living thing slithering among the slivers of glass among the clods of earth was a snake, perhaps a venomous snake, perhaps a viper. It stuck out a forked tongue, and its triangular head was cold and erect. Its eyes were dark glass. It could never close them, because it had no eyelids" (NV 134). The association of the snake with the sexual aspect of the episode is so transparent that it implies yet another signification of the snake. I wish to suggest that the snake—especially its glassy, unseeing eyes—becomes an emblem of Geula's emotional blindness, her lack of psychological insight into herself and others. In a sense, Geula dies as a result of her narcissistic blindness, her inability to relinquish her self-love, to be able to love or hear the call of the other. In this sense the episode that precedes her death is revealing. Just before being bitten by the snake, she lies among the bushes. Her wish to avenge the insult has given way to a desire to forgive. Geula now longs "to make peace and *forgive* . . . to find him among the wadis and *forgive him* . . . [e]ven to sing to him" (NV 133; emphasis added).

Davis claims that "the most precarious thing in the narcissist's world is one's identity. . . . [T]he other must forever prop up a faltering sense of self."[14] Ironically, Geula's emerging noble sentiments attest to her pervasive narcissism. Having failed to appropriate the shepherd by means of aggressive intimidation, she fantasizes about dominating him through the munificence of her forgiveness. Geula's inability to recognize *her* abusive treatment of the shepherd and, consequently, her moral obligation to ask *his* forgiveness perpetuates her irredeemable entrapment in self-love, which eventually proves fatal. Engrossed in constructing an imaginary self-image of compassion and generosity of spirit, Geula fails to notice the viper. The circumstances of her oversight reiterate the impossibility of release from the primary, infantile stage of narcissistic megalomania. Her irredeemable excess of narcissism adds an ironic dimension to her name, Geula, which means "redemption."

The snake as a metaphoric representation of blindness and death unites the public and private sightlessness of the kibbutz and its members. Its "eyes [of] dark glass," which it "could never close," indicate a complete lack of insight since they can only peer out. The snake's inability to "close its eyes" in order to metaphorically look within suggests a connection with the blindness of the kibbutz members. While Geula's self-absorption prevents her from seeing the snake, the vengeful kibbutz members with "dilated pupils" blindly rush to attack the tribe. The destructiveness of the blind, poisonous snake illuminates the destructive behavior of a community blinded by its megalomaniacal sense of power and privilege.

In contrast to the previously explored possibilities of dialogical patterns between Arabs and Jews, the conclusion of "Nomad and Viper" communicates a foreboding termination of all social interaction between the two groups. In the other texts I have considered, Jewish and Arab protagonists—whether socially marginalized, mad, or even dead—manage to tell a story whose dissent from the dominating ideology implied recognition of the other as subject and even the possibility of a dialogue. The narrator in "Hirbet Hizah" disrupts the complacency of his community by reiterating the story of Arab dispossession and exile. In "Facing the Forests" the protagonist's discovery of the destroyed Arab village and the connection that he establishes with the victimized Arab antagonizes the monolithic Zionist mainstream. In *The Pessoptimist* Saeed, the protagonist-narrator, tells his story of bondage and attains a measure of inner liberation from his oppressors. Yossi, the protagonist-narrator of *In a New Light*, denounces the hypocrisy of the kibbutz and its distortion of the socialist ideal while simultaneously deploring his own weakness. In these narratives the protagonists on both sides of the political divide insist on transcending the ideological and cultural boundaries and asserting themselves as subjects through their personal story. On the one hand, the telling as an act of dissent allows them to gain an insight into their weaknesses and, on the other, suggests the possibility of a future rapprochement.

By contrast, the narrator in "Nomad and Viper" exhibits regression rather than deepening self-knowledge. Instead of initiating a dialogue, the ending of the story resounds with the horrible silence of death and unspeakable cruelty: the death of Geula, the Israeli character, and the suffering inflicted on the Arabs. When barbaric violence triumphs over "the call of the other," there is no room for stories of hope. Significantly, the telling, which represents a measure of self-searching, comes to an end when the teller joins the attackers. Words have been replaced by "thick, short sticks." The story, which presents the Jewish view of Arabs as "savages" and the Arab view of Jews as "dying creatures," spells the end of any hope for dialogic interaction.

Thematically "Nomad and Viper" centers on the blindness resulting from a lack of self-consciousness and the terrible effects due to an absence of self-knowledge. From this perspective, therefore, the story can be seen as a plea for a measure of introspection. The next chapter presents an answer to this plea in the form of an examination of two fictional autobiographies, Oz's *My Michael* and Habiby's *Saraya, Daughter of the Ghoul*. These are introspective narratives of characters split between a traumatic fixation on an idealized, pre-1948 childhood and the ideologies that inform their lives in a postwar state. While the public self adheres to the national telos, the private self experiences an unrelieved state of melancholia over the past destroyed by the war. Is it possible to detect affinities in the responses to the traumatic effects of the war on both sides of the political divide? If so, what do these affinities teach us about the psychological complexity of a possible interaction?

My analysis of *My Michael* and *Saraya* will suggests that an introspective exploration of the trauma of war may aid recovery from the moral disintegration that marks the dead-end conclusion in "Nomad and Viper." While the public and political life must go on, the memory of the tragic past and its losses can never be entirely suppressed nor ignored. In fact, as the two novels show, the irrepressible progress of life is incessantly disrupted by equally irrepressible memories and nightmares. Eventually the voices that mourn the atrocities of the war recede into silence. Nonetheless, each narrative completes an introspective tale, one that is disturbingly mournful and yet significant for the future. As the following examination of the two novels shows, it is only when the legitimacy of melancholy is recognized that the possibility of the dialogue may reemerge.

10

Melancholia and Telos

Amos Oz's *My Michael* and Emile Habiby's *Saraya, Daughter of the Ghoul*

Between a Historical Past and an Ideological End of History

The tension between the trauma of war and the ideological suppression of memory defines the theme of the texts selected for analysis. Arguably Oz's most celebrated novel, *My Michael* (1968) explores the fragmentation of the victorious Israeli Jewish self in post-1948 reality. *Saraya, Daughter of the Ghoul* (1993), Habiby's last work, focuses on the fragmented self of the defeated Israeli Arab. In the previously discussed works by Oz and Habiby the protagonists are confronted by their adversaries: "Nomad and Viper" places the kibbutz and the nomads in an antagonistic relation, while Habiby's *The Pessoptimist* depicts the subjugation of the Arab protagonist, who works for the Israeli Secret Service. In contrast, *My Michael* and *Saraya* do not center on the interaction between Arabs and Jews. Rather, the protagonist-narrators in these autobiographical fictional works set out on an introspective journey, an unsparing self-examination oppositional to the inexorably advancing political and ideological reality of the state.

My Michael takes place in the first decade of the state. The narrative is in the form of a journal kept by Hannah Gonen, a young woman who tells the story of her marriage to Michael Gonen, a doctoral candidate in geomorphology at the Hebrew University. Michael is a devoted son, husband, and father, a rational, task-oriented young man and a loyal citizen. He is intent on "making it" in the academic world and improving his family's socioeconomic status. Hannah is a Jerusalemite who previously studied literature. She escapes her unsatisfying married life by engaging in dreams and fantasies, all of which originate in her childhood memories of the Arab twins Halil and Aziz, who were her playmates in the pre-state days of the British Mandate. The 1948 war incontrovertibly cut the ties between Hannah and her childhood friends. In her dreamworld Hannah associates the twins with the juvenile literature she voraciously read as a child, especially with such heroic male figures as Michael Strogoff and Captain Nemo. Her fantasized adventures with powerful men demonstrate a partly suppressed sexual, sadomasochistic component that is combined with persistent fantasies of violence, terror, and war atrocities.

Saraya, Daughter of the Ghoul is told in two, often indistinguishable and mostly first-person voices belonging to the narrator and his imagined interlocutor, an alter-ego named Abd Allah. The story is a *khurfiyyah*, the literary form of a fabulous tale that, as the narrator tells us in the introductory paragraph, he borrowed from Arab folktale tradition. In his story, which blends the factual, the associative, and the imaginary, he returns to the pre-1948 Palestinian world that disappeared with the establishment of the state. A vision of a young girl on the shore of Akhziv (a place north of Acre) in 1983 brings back the recollection of Saraya, the girl he loved in his boyhood. This association triggers memories that take him back to his childhood, his family history, and especially his elusive uncle Ibrahim, who introduced him to the world of fantasy and the imagination. The recollections of the games he played with Saraya evoke dreamlike flashbacks of Carmel and nostalgic glimpses of Haifa, places the heartbroken, grieving narrator revisits in a futile search for his edenic childhood.

The magical landscape of the narrator's youth clashes with Habiby's thinly disguised fictional self-portrait as a public figure on Israel's political landscape. Like Habiby, the narrator, who devoted himself to the welfare of the Israeli Arab national minority, has served for almost fifty years as one of the leaders of the Israeli Communist party, is a Knesset member, and holds the position of editor at *al-Ittihad*, the Communist Arab newspaper. His prominent position in the public sphere and his preoccupation with political matters—especially his communist orientation—estranged him from family and friends, who have been living in exile; it also obliterated his childhood memory. Disillusioned with the public sphere, the narrator now denounces his public self and struggles to reconnect in memory and imagination with a life destroyed in war and with a long-forgotten past.

Despite the obvious differences between the two texts in terms of genre, content, and the nationalities of the protagonist-narrators, the above brief synopses highlight corresponding thematic strands. The texts evolve along similar trajectories. Each presents a construct of disjunction between, on the one hand, the traumatic eruption of the 1948 war and, on the other hand, the ongoing sociopolitical life of each national group, namely, Israeli Jews and Israeli Arabs. The characters live in a perennial state of melancholia over the world they lost, a state of mind that collides with the ideological telos of each national group. While the overriding national telos drives the collective forward into the future, inexorable recollections, dreams, and fantasies relentlessly draw the protagonist-narrators back to the past.

In this chapter I investigate the interaction between telos and melancholia, whose seemingly parallel tracks appear to exclude the possibility of contiguity. How can the melancholy retrospective mode simultaneously meet, illuminate, and, as we shall see, raise questions about the dominant teleology of progress? One is reminded of Benjamin's concept of history, which emphasizes the unacknowledged presence of suffering in every story of triumph. Benjamin's concept of a two-tiered history is further illuminated by his famous parable of the angel of history. I wish to suggests that Benjamin's perception of the angel provides a remarkably apt model for this discussion. The parable elucidates the points of convergence of the contradictory public and private trajectories in the texts before us.

Deeply affected by Paul Klee's *Angelus Novus*, Benjamin interpreted the painting as a metaphor of the tension between the forces of mournful retrospection and triumphalist social progression:

The angel is looking as though he is about to move away from something he is fixedly contemplating. His eyes are staring, his mouth is open, his wings are spread. This is how one pictures the angel of history. His face is turned toward the past. . . . [H]e sees one single catastrophe which keeps piling wreckage upon wreckage and hurls it in front of his feet. . . . The angel would like to stay, awaken the dead, and make whole what has been smashed. But the storm [that] is blowing from Paradise . . . got caught in his wings with such violence that the angel can no longer close them. The storm [that] irresistibly propels him into the future to which his back is turned . . . is what we call progress.[1]

While the angel insists on turning back to the past, the storm disempowers him, propelling him toward the future. With his wings pinned down, the angel is at the mercy of the wind, which propels him forward. All he can do is to stare at the devastation that progress leaves in its wake and internalize its disastrous effects. Thus, though physically powerless, the angel's contemplation of the past implies a certain degree of freedom as both a witness to the destruction and a keeper of its memory. In this sense he opposes the forces that consign the memory of destruction to oblivion. The portraiture of the angel and his vision—his fixation on the past and his impotent desire to undo the destruction—bespeak the mode of melancholia.[2]

Freud defined melancholia in the context of mourning. Mourning involves "reality-testing," which proves that "the loved object no longer exists" and demands "that all libido [be] withdrawn from its attachments to that object." In the case of melancholia, however, the individual refuses to abide by the reality principle. Here the libido establishes "an identification of the ego with the abandoned object." In other words, the loss is internalized or, as Freud says, "the shadow of the object fell upon the ego."[3] Melancholia reflects an inability to accept the trauma of a loss. The inability of the person to detach him- or herself from the loss manifests itself through loss of inhibition and withdrawal from the world. These phenomena produce conflictual relationships between the melancholic person and the social environment. In this sense, the concept of melancholia illuminates Benjamin's angel in its persistent contemplation of the past. In his melancholic fixation on the losses he would like to retrieve and the dead he would like to "awaken," the angel refuses what Freud calls "reality-testing," that is, the acceptance of the loss. In terms of our texts, the melancholy behavior of Benjamin's angel of history illuminates the narrator-protagonists' compulsive re-visioning of the world that they have lost. Their constant return to the past points to a melancholy state of mind that antagonizes the relentless progress of the national telos toward the future.

Paul Klee, *Angelus Novus*. © 2003 Artists Rights Society (ARS), New York/VG Bild-Kunst, Bonn.

Hannah and Michael's biographies delineate the parameters of melancholia and teleology in the novel. Hannah's fantasies represent elaborations on her memories of childhood games with the twins. She "used to wrestle with [the twins] furiously." She also "was in love with both of them." They were "[a] pair of strong, obedient seamen from Captain Nemo's crew. . . . They hardly ever spoke. . . . A pair of gray-brown wolves. . . . Wild and dark. Pirates."[4] Hannah's imaginary reenactments of her memories become increasingly aggressive and destructive; they feature violent sex, pillaged cities, natural disasters, mutinies, and brutal conquests. This inexorable aggression culminates in the concluding fantasy. Hannah tells herself, "I am still able to unfasten the heavy padlock. To part the iron gates. To set free two [sic] twin brothers, who will slip out into the vast night to do my bidding. I shall urge them on." In precise, concrete details she imagines the twins executing a large-scale terrorist attack in Israel's territory (*MM* 285–86). Hannah's extreme reaction to her loss illustrates what Freud sees as melancholic ambivalence between aggression and submission. Her self-representations as a ruthless ruler, a victorious commander, a princess who dominates her subjects, which alternate with her self-representations as a denigrated, violated, and dominated woman, are fantasized destructions of world and self. They indicate the emergence of what Freud calls "memory-traces" that engage her in "countless separate struggles . . . over the object, in which love and hate contend with each other."[5]

But it is not only the anger over the disappearance of the loved objects that seems to trigger the fantasies of violence and destruction. Chained, like Benjamin's angel, by the forward-thrusting social telos, Hannah feels deceived by the community, whose conformist weltanschauung has erased the tragic past. Indeed, toward the end of her story Hannah realizes the loneliness of her struggle against the "wind of progress." When Hadassah, her socially and financially successful friend, assures her that one day she and Michael will "also reach their goal," Hannah indignantly sums up the gulf that separates her from the rest of the world: "Was it possible that everyone except me had come to terms with time, with dedication, perseverance, effort, ambition, and achievement? . . . I feel depressed. Humiliated. There has been a deception" (*MM* 274). The deception lies with the world, which moves ahead, achieving its well-defined targets and—most terrible of all—a world that willingly makes the compromise of "coming to terms with time," which allows one to forget the past. Against the world of indifference and forgetting, Hannah sets herself free in her world of the imagination. There, unbridled, violent fantasies that emerge from the memories of the childhood world compensate for her social powerlessness and alienation. The motif of violence signals an ominous and destructive fixation on the losses. The relentless return of the past drives Hannah to the verge of insanity.

In contrast, Michael, whose life steadily evolves along the trajectory of the telos, remembers his childhood as that of a "little Jewish socialist." He was raised on the stories his idealistic Zionist father told him about "Hasmonean children, *shtetl* children, children of illegal immigrants, children on the kibbutzim." There were also stories with a universal socialist message of starving, wounded, heroic, exploited, and fighting children (*MM* 29). Hannah's imaginative associations of Captain Nemo and Michael Strogoff with the Arab twins communicates rebellion and freedom. Michael's unimaginative categorization posits his childhood heroes as paragons of virtue, self-sacrifice, and idealistic social behavior.

The model of his father shaped Michael's social orientation. Michael's father, an idealistic Zionist par excellence, was a *haluts* and a member of Hashomer, the first Jewish self-defense militia established to defend Zionist settlements against the Arabs. Michael's *Bildung* reflected his family's adherence to the Zionist weltanschauung. His scholarly and social achievements actualized more than just his father's expectation that he carry on the Zionist *maskilic* tradition of his paternal grandfather, who was of a nationalistic persuasion and had taught science in the Hebrew seminary in Grodno (*MM* 10). He also fulfilled both his aunts' pragmatic yet patriotic exhortation that he "work hard, study hard, and get on in the world . . . [to become] a doctor, helping his country and making a name for himself" (*MM* 29).

For Hannah Israel's independence signified a traumatic severance of her relationships with the twins, which condemned her to a lifelong state of melancholia. For Michael, however, the birth of the state signified his rebirth as a "new" Jew, a new beginning. On the day of the declaration of independence, his father endowed Michael with a new identity by changing the family name "from Ganz to Gonen"

(*MM* 29), thereby divesting the "new" Zionist Jew of his Diaspora connection. Because Michael always complied with his father's decisions, he objected neither to the change of name nor to its militant connotation.[6] Hannah notes Michael's passive acceptance of authority with a trace of irony: "[Michael] had inherited . . . from his father [the principle] of a fierce, proud loyalty to the laws of our state" (*MM* 64). She repeatedly observes Michael's uncanny resemblance to his father in terms of his appearance, demeanor, and speech (*MM* 49, 157, 264). Following in his father's footsteps and without a moment of hesitation, Michael has subscribed—one might say in body and spirit—to the Zionist telos.

Not unlike the contrasting configuration of Hannah and Michael, the inner split of Habiby's narrator reflects the contrasting obsession with mournful memories of losses and compulsive engagement in the service of *pro bono publico*. When betrayed by the public and political aspects of his life, the narrator immerses himself in melancholy recollections. In contrast to Hannah's increasingly violent fantasies, Habiby's narrator waxes nostalgic in his fantasy of the past. Yet, like Hannah's self-destructive tendencies, he experiences regret and grief over the irretrievable ideal past, leading to depression and a death wish. His dejection seems to illustrate Freud's observation that "in melancholia it is the ego itself" that has become poor and empty], since the person tends to see "his ego as worthless, incapable of any achievement and morally despicable."[7] Indeed, the narrator constantly blames himself for having forsaken Saraya, his first love, and his regret over his betrayal is mortifying. To the very end of the narrative—which, as we shall see, also marks the end of his life—he berates himself for having "imprisoned Saraya high up in a cloud of abandonment."[8]

Reminding us of Benjamin's angel and his futile wish to "awaken the dead," Habiby's narrator eventually realizes that the past cannot be undone. He recalls the childhood lesson he learned from an owner of a bicycle shop who refused to exchange a rented bicycle that had broken down. The refusal communicated clearly that life—or God, for that matter—does not offer second chances (*S* 169).[9] Now, at the conclusion of *khurfiyyah*, which marks the conclusion of his life story, the narrator finds himself enclosed in "a glass-roofed shell of the ending," which is also the "shell of genesis," that is, his mother's womb

(*S* 168). His desperate mood signals a belated traumatic effect, which causes him to constantly dwell on his losses. The narrator's melancholia over irrevocably missed chances seems as self-destructive as the desperate imaginary battles that Hannah wages against forgetting.

As the protagonist-narrator of *Saraya* sees it now, he missed his chance of happiness when he forsook his past to embrace the communist vision of the future. Thus, for fifty years he replaced Saraya's love—and his personal happiness on his native, magical Carmel—with Lenin's "parable of the swamp," which claimed humanity's need for redemption. As the narrator reminds us, following Plato's parable of the cave, Lenin repudiated the world's blindness to its own misery and predicted that redemption would come with the light of socialist progress toward equality and well-being for all (*S* 144–45). As long as he remained "wedded" to this ideological outlook, the narrator suppressed the memory of his defeated Palestinian heritage, devoting himself to building the national future of the Israeli Arab community. His faith in the communist ideal, which fueled his struggle to "provide a loaf of bread for himself and his people" (*S* 91) estranged him from family and friends in exile (*S* 158).

Rejection of past defeat and suffering combined with faith in a future renewal characterize both Zionist and communist ideologies. Louis Althusser's postulation that "ideology has no history"[10] encapsulates the denial of the past in both *My Michael* and *Saraya*. Davis elaborates on this notion, which counterpoises history and ideology, concluding that ideology "blinds us to history" by the production of consciousness. That is to say, ideology, which presents itself as the ultimate, unchangeable "essence," has as its aim to structure consciousness based on its values and beliefs.[11] In terms of similarities between communism and Zionism, both ideologies dissociated themselves from the past for the sake of transforming the individual into a new subject, a member of a new, homogeneous society. In this sense the adherents to both Zionism and communism were totally dedicated to building a reality oriented exclusively toward the future.

Recall Michael's obedient espousal of his father's Zionist orientation toward the future, symbolically represented by the discarding of the family name and the adoption of a new Hebrew name. The past has thus been rejected. In Hannah's poetic yet acerbic remark, Michael "regarded the present as a soft, shapeless substance from which one has to mold the future by dint of responsible hard work. . . . The past appeared to Michael like *a pile of orange peels* which must be disposed of. . . . [T]hey must be collected and destroyed. To be *free and unburdened*. To be responsible only to the plans which *have been set before him* for the *future*" (*MM* 260; emphasis added).

In *Saraya* the communist way of discarding the past is even more dramatic than a name change. Here the narrator identifies with Danko, the hero in a Maxim Gorki's parable that describes a group of fearless fighters who were trapped in a dense forest, in "*blinding darkness* and humidity, which extinguished their torch. They chose Danko . . . to lead them *out of the forest* to the *light they were yearning for*. . . . Danko tore out his heart, lit it, and held it above his comrades to illuminate their way. When the group had reached its destination, the bleeding Danko fell to the ground" (*S* 147; emphasis added).

The extent of the narrator's identification with the mission of creating a better future for his people is perhaps best illustrated in the poignant scene of his mother's departure. Strongly disapproving of her son's dedication to his political career, his mother decides to join Na'im, her other son, who is in exile. Ironically playing on the word *na'im* (literally "pleasant"), she tells her son the Communist, "One moment with my Na'im is worth to me all the pleasures [*ha-neyimot*] of your Eden." As the narrator well understands, the pun indicates his mother's deep displeasure with the "pleasures" of his "Eden of socialism" (*S* 102). Though profoundly pained by her departure, the narrator continues to dedicate himself to his ideological mission. Only later does he realize the extent to which, ironically, he was blinded by the light of communism.

The Dissenting Power of Melancholia

Hannah's image of the orange peels and Gorki's metaphor of the dark forest represent the ideological weltanschauungen of the Jewish Zionist majority and Communist Arab minority, both of which reject the past in order to focus solely on the future. Davis calls these uncritical espousals of ideology "productions of consciousness."[12] The question that such "productions" raise relates to the individual's position vis-à-vis the ideologically oriented community. What psychological mechanism prompts the individual to comply with the communal weltanschauung? What are the psychological strategies that the community employs to co-opt the individual?

Freud tells us that the desire to conform to the "group mind" lies in libidinal attachment. As he sees it, it is the power of "Eros" that privileges social convention over the particularity of the individual. The fact that "an individual gives up his distinctiveness in a group and lets his members influence him by suggestion . . . gives the impression that he does it because he feels the need of being in harmony with them rather than in opposition to them."[13] While Freud dwells on the *individual's* libidinal gratification in joining the consensus, Davis points to *society's* need for a consensual shaping of the individual. The ideological manipulation of the individual is intended to "determine the inwardness, identity, and self-consciousness" of the person.[14] Slavoj Žižek sees the social integration of the individual into the system in the impact of the ideological *"gaze" of the social system* upon the *narcissistic self-image* of the individual. The ideological gaze shapes the ego ideal or, as the critic calls it, the "imaginary identification" of the individual. Žižek claims that it is the point from which we are observed "which dominates and determines the image, the imaginary form in which we appear to ourselves likeable."[15]

While each emphasizes a specific angle of the process, all three thinkers—Freud, Davis, and Žižek—recognize the influence of the group and its ideological orientation on subject formation. Their approaches elucidate the conforming subject (Michael), or the conforming part of the self (the public persona of Habiby's narrator) in the two novels. The melancholy return of the past in the characterizations of Hannah and the private self of Habiby's narrator indicates a response dialectically opposed to the dominant outlook with respect to the future. The undeniably powerful influence of the collective consciousness shaped by the ideological telos highlights the phenomenon of melancholia as rebellious rejection of the norm. Why is melancholia, associated with passivity and depression, capable of defying the dominant ideology characterized by activism, energy, and "eros"? Why would melancholia, immersed in the memories of past losses, be capable of subverting the appropriating "gaze" of the dominating ideological consensus?

It seems that Jacques Lacan's discussion of subjectivity in terms of *meaning* and *being* may elucidate the seeming oxymoron of melancholic dissension. In his discussion of the "being of the subject, that which is there beneath the meaning," Lacan postulates that "if we choose being, the subject disappears, it eludes us, it falls into non-meaning. If we choose meaning, the meaning survives only deprived of that part of non-meaning that is, strictly speaking, that which constitutes in the realization of the subject, the unconscious."[16]

To further explain Lacan's important distinction, I refer the reader to Gilbert Chaitin's comment on the social implications of Lacan's view of meaning and being. Chaitin explains meaning as complete adherence to socio-ideological norms, an adherence that signifies identity loss. On the one hand, to choose meaning signifies "acceding blindly to the demand of the Other, [a choice that] turns you into something like an inanimate object, a pure universal rather than a subject." On the other hand, being signifies refusal of meaning and withdrawal from social intercourse, a withdrawal that signifies, first and foremost, the refusal of language. The rejection of communication denies social interaction. The absence of social interchange precludes recognition, and lack of recognition—here one should recall Hegel—eliminates subjectivity or self-consciousness. Chaitin reaches the conclusion that by choosing being "you refuse the social mandate contained in the meaning imposed upon you, exclude yourself from social life and . . . renounce subjecthood. The ultimate phase of this process is the complete alienation of psychosis."[17]

The notion of being as refusal of language and therefore rejection of society refers us back to the question concerning melancholia as dissension. How can the melancholy narrators, immersed in their world of dreams and fantasies, simultaneously be rebellious dissenters on the social scene? Indeed, Julia Kristeva's discussion of melancholia and its links to depression, implies connection between melancholia and the refusal of language.[18] "Melancholia," Kristeva tells us, "ends up in asymbolia, in loss of meaning: if I am no longer capable of translating or metaphorizing, I become silent and I die." Fortunately not all people prone to melancholy end in deadening silence. As Kristeva observes, "unlike what happens to psychotics . . . [who] are carried away into the solitude of mutism, depressed [melancholy] persons do not forget how to use signs." Kristeva claims that articulation through art establishes a particularly meaningful connection. The sublimation of the lost subject through art rescues the patient from psychotic silence since the work of art substitutes for the lost object the "ideal object that never disappoints the libido." Thus, "when we have been able to go through our melancholia to the point of becoming interested in the life signs," it is possible to embark on "imaginary discourses" of art. These "translations" or "metaphors" of the loss indicate a "shift from depression to possible meaning."[19]

Kristeva's observations attribute not only an aesthetic but also a therapeutic function to art. Art is both a translation of melancholia into metaphoric (that is, artistic) expression and, at the same time, an escape from the final stage of psychosis. This insight underscores the socially complex and mentally precarious position of our protagonist-narrators *as writers*. Where are they situated between the polar opposites of meaning and being, that is, between complete identification with social existence and the desire to escape from it? In what ways are they capable of avoiding, on the one hand, the pathological attraction of being and its danger of psychotic silence, and, on the other hand, the enticement of meaning and its danger of the loss of individuality through conformist patterns of articulation?

Concerning being, one notes in both Hannah and Habiby's narrator the dangerous inclination to withdraw into the "asymbolia" of "the loss of meaning." The characters constantly struggle against the silence of total alienation. It is true that, by virtue of their position as *narrators,* the protagonists speak and therefore necessarily defy silence. Nonetheless, the threat of silence is never remote. Feeling completely alienated from her husband and child, Hannah remarks, "I would suddenly observe in both of them, in all three of us, a quality which I can only call melancholy, because I do not know what other term to use" (*MM* 91).[20] "Melancholy" is the only word she finds to describe her situation; at the same time, the threat of silence emerges in her inability to find "other terms." The scarcity of words to describe her feelings signals Hannah's closeness to mutism. The lack of words as a reminder of the constant danger of withdrawing into silence is reemphasized in the physical aspect of her recurring sickness, which manifests itself in "painful constrictions of the throat" that cause her to occasionally lose her voice (*MM* 178). As a psychosomatic symptom, Hannah's inability to speak evinces her gradual sinking into the silence of psychotic alienation.

The silence of alienation threatens the world of *Saraya* as well. The construction of the novel as an imagined dialogue between the narrator and his invented alter-ego Abd Allah signals a reluctance to communicate with the world that betrayed him. On the social plane, the narrator's estrangement from his Communist comrades indicates, in the words of Chaitin, his refusal of the "social mandate." He also mistrusts his Jewish fishermen friends and keeps his vision of Saraya on the beach a secret. The narrator's facade of a feebleminded *ingénu* that he assumes vis-à-vis his friends and his silent endurance of their harmless yet condescending tricks highlight his social alienation (*S* 22–23). Only in their writing do both narrators confess their innermost memories, dreams, and fantasies of their lost loves.

Concurring with Kristeva, Anselm Havercamp points out that "the melancholy poet consciously digs his own grave, or, rather, in writing it he tries to escape it."[21] Havercamp seems to be saying that evasion of the deadening silence of melancholia is possible through writing about its imminence. In this sense writing becomes a precarious lifeline always on the verge of breaking. "I am writing this," Hannah begins, "because people I loved have died. I am writing this because when I was young I was full of the power of loving, and now that power of loving is dying. I do not want to die" (*MM* 3). The vanishing ability to love points to the growing impoverishment of Hannah's emotional resources. The traumatic loss of the twins she had loved, constantly reiterated in dreams and fantasies, has diminished her vitality. Writing keeps the narrator alive because it allows her to hold on to memories that relentlessly and inexorably recede into silence. The way to temporarily halt the onset of psychotic silence is to cultivate the inconsolable sense of loss, which, in an ironic paradox, is the primary cause of depression.

Thus, Hannah keeps a journal in order to write everything down (*MM* 103). Through writing she fights time, which, "menacing and prowling," threatens memory (*MM* 114). As she promises herself, "I cannot forget a thing. I refuse to surrender a crumb to the fingers of cold time. . . . A pretty, clever girl in a blue coat, a scaly kindergarten teacher with varicose veins, and in between the two a pane of glass which becomes more and more opaque, despite the frantic polishing" (*MM* 176–77). To lose the reflection of herself as the free girl she once was—inseparable from the twins, with whom she used to play and wrestle and whom she ruled and loved—would amount to losing herself. The image of herself fixed in the vanished, uninhibited relations with the twins has kept her captive in the long-lost world of childhood. "To forget," Hannah says, "means to die" (*MM* 59). In the end she inevitably loses the battle with time, realizing that "it is impossible to write everything. Most things slip away to *perish in silence*" (*MM* 256; emphasis added). The ineluctable loss of memory forebodes the deadening silence of madness.

Whereas Hannah writes to *retain* memory, Habiby's narrator engages in writing to *recapture* the forgotten past. Once his faith in social progress had crumbled, and his fellow Communists rejected him, the memory of his uncle Ibrahim, a "poet and writer" (*S* 148), "comes to rescue," reminding him that nobody can take his "heart and tongue" away from him (*S* 111). Thus, the narrator decides to record all that "arises in [his] memory so that the memory may not be lost and so that we won't get lost together with it" (*S* 78). Reclaiming memory from oblivion, however, proves a very difficult if not an impossible undertaking. The "sites of his youth," whose ruins he revisits, "turn away" from him, punishing him for his decades-long absence, which, he now understands, amounts to betrayal. The punishment proves painful since, as he well knows, his desertion of the world of childhood love and imagination cost him the inheritance of Ibrahim's cane, the "key to life." The loss of the cane signifies an irrevocable loss of the way back to his "first meeting with Saraya" (*S* 58–59), which, metaphorically speaking, would have restored him to the edenic innocence of his youth.

Incapable of retrieving his youth, the narrator must reconstruct the world of the past on his own. Writing becomes a tormented, tortuous process that forebodes failure. The hopelessness of the endeavor exacerbates his sense of guilt and worthlessness, instilling depression. Indeed, the images that the narrator uses to describe the act of writing are indicative of his emotional depletion, a sign of his melancholy state of mind. For example, he compares writing to digging "underground tunnels" of memory that invariably lead to a dead end (*S* 27). He likens writing to a falling stone—a metaphor to which

I will return—which, according to the "law of gravity . . . detaches itself from a peak of the Carmel, rolling down the wadi, sometimes following its intended course, oftentimes straying from it" (*S* 61–62). Above all, writing as a way to re-create the past becomes the narrator's *via dolorosa*, a path of excruciating pain resulting from guilt and regret (*S* 58, 60, 85, 103, 106). The association of his ordeal with the Passion and Crucifixion of Christ points to the immensity of suffering, which portends the silence of unrelieved depression.

To fend off the encroaching silence, the narrator resorts to fantasy. In his daydreams he recalls how, "half a century ago, Saraya used to take his hand, walking him up the 'lovers' wadi'" (*S* 37), how she used to feed him *jany* apples, the apples of mad infatuation and love, how she used to quench his thirst by allowing him to drink from her hidden spring on the Carmel (*S* 83). Not unlike Hannah's narcissistic fantasy of the uninhibited, unchecked freedom that marked her childhood attachment to the twins, the narrator constructs his fantasy of an idyllic love story with Saraya in the edenic landscape of the Carmel. Thus he naively and quite narcissistically deludes himself into believing that even though he has abandoned and forgotten *her,* his beloved will not abandon *him* in his search for his forgotten love. He imagines that Saraya will throw one of her braids down to help him climb out of the "hole of oblivion." She will pull him up to the rim, and he will take hold of her hand and will be saved from guilt and desperation (*S* 89).

While daydreams and fantasies may assuage the narrator's despair for a while, a "marvelously clear" dream that "recurs night after night" poignantly dispels his delusion. In his dream the narrator discovers that he can fly and soars over the sites of his youth. He flies over Acre, Haifa, the Carmel, finally finding himself above the roof of his family's house. Instead of coming down to return home, he finds to his dismay that he is unable to land and flies off to the sea. Next follows an even more dismaying epiphany, the realization that "if I truly wanted to descend, I could." Following this insight, unavoidable questions arise and he must finally deal with his ambivalence: "Why would I hesitate? Where would I descend? Why would I not continue to fly upward into the sky?" It is at this moment that Saraya's "Who is it?" brings his self-reckoning to an abrupt end, turning his dream into a nightmare. Upon hearing her voice, "I plunged like a bird hit by a hunter's bullet. Have you ever seen a bird hit by a hunter's bullet? . . . It drops in a straight line, like a stone that falls from the ends of the sky" (*S* 130).

Ironically, the dream is a ruthless awakening to a reality the narrator has long denied; it confronts him with his own ambivalence about his identity and sense of belonging. As his reluctance to return home demonstrates, his determination to retrieve the loss is not as powerful as he had imagined. The dream also confronts him with another, perhaps even more painful, truth he can no longer evade; it ends his naive, narcissistic fantasy that he will always be welcomed back. Saraya's question presents him with a truth that pierces him like a bullet. Her failure to recognize him confronts him with the truth he has tried to evade, namely, that his late return precludes the possibility of redemption.

The fact that the truth insists on reemerging in the narrator's dreamworld signals the dreamer's resistance to admit the irrevocable loss of love and innocence. Indeed, the eventual realization of having become a stranger to the world of his childhood love has a devastating effect. The image of himself as a free-falling dead bird communicates the deathly effect of the definitive crushing blow to his hopes. The dream of death foretells the imminent rupture of the lifeline of writing. In effect, the episode of the dream is followed by the final chapter, which opens with the premonition of an impending ending. The narrator confesses that the inevitably approaching conclusion of this tale has resulted in a depression incomparably deeper than the feelings of sadness that would accompany the "pangs of labor" of his previous stories. This realization makes him ponder whether the ending of this *khurfiyyah* signals the termination of his creative potency as a writer, or, as he calls it, the end of "story-birthing" (*S* 133). Recall that the narrator had previously associated the process of writing with a stone rolling off Mount Carmel. The motif of the stone reiterated in the image of the felled bird communicates the approaching abyss of deathly silence.

To return to the psychoanalytical differentiation between being and meaning, both Hannah and Habiby's narrators experience a depletion of creative and vital resources as they inexorably approach the silent pole of being. In this sense their losing struggle to communicate illustrates Kristeva's observation: "The artist consumed by melancholia is at the same time the most *relentless in his struggle against the symbolic abdication* that blankets him. . . . Until death strikes or suicide becomes imperative for those who view it as final triumph over the void of the lost object."[22]

It is, however, not only the pole of being that threatens the writer. The narrator-protagonists struggle against more than just their own desire to reject language and sink into the death of silence. As an act of resistance to the temptation of psychotic silence, writing places them in a complex situation with regard to the pole of meaning. Recall Lacan's notion of meaning, which "survives only [when] deprived of that part of non-meaning . . . the unconscious." To repeat, it is the unconscious that, unbeknownst to us, determines our unique subjectivity. In this sense the deprivation of the unconscious in the sphere of meaning, that is, in the prevailing ideological discourse, incurs the loss of the individual voice. In this sense submission to conformity precludes subjectivity. As Chaitin observes, when the subject "accepts meaning [which is language] . . . her individual being is crushed by the universalizing function of the signifier."[23] In other words, the writer's decision to express herself through commonly shared signs of communication signals the risk of losing her uniqueness in the sphere of meaning.

I began this discussion by noting the seeming incongruity of dissent in melancholia. Like Benjamin's angel, who insists on contemplating the destruction, the protagonist-narrators in *My Michael* and *Saraya* defy the telos of building a past-free future. In what way is their melancholia useful to counterpoise the appropriating power of the dominating ideological telos? In the second part of this study I raised the issue of the canonical neutralization of the fiction of dissent. Now I approach the issue of the double bind of literature that dissents from ideological conformity. To communicate its message clearly, dissension must be meaningfully articulated; a meaningful articulation of dissension, however, risks dissolution or neutralization of the message through ideological co-optation.

The problem of neutralization underscores the layered construction in *My Michael* and *Saraya* as a defense against co-optation. I wish to suggest that the texts seek ways to safeguard their dissenting messages against the reductive encroachment of the pole of meaning. The following analysis demonstrates how relentless grief over traumatic losses afforded the protagonist-narrators the ability to distance themselves from the pole of meaning while keeping the dissension meaningful.

As was already mentioned, each text presents us with a dual narrative that places the trajectory of melancholia alongside that of the ideological telos. Though contradictory, these trajectories are inseparable. The indelible connection is a matter of course in the case of Habiby's narrator, whose characterization demonstrates a self split between communist ideology and melancholy recollection. In the case of Michael and Hannah, the indissoluble tie between the two is symbolically represented by the marriage bond, which, as Hannah sees it, has turned them into "two travelers *consigned by fate* to adjacent seats on a long railway journey" (*MM* 67; emphasis added). Even though they pursue contrasting objectives, the couple is nonetheless destined—perhaps doomed—to keeping each other company on their life's journey.

The narrative perspective in each text highlights a complex, asymmetrical interaction between the disparate yet contiguous worldviews. As fictional autobiographies, the stories are told in their entirety from the viewpoint of the protagonist-narrators. The single point of view indicates that the trajectory of melancholia both *encompasses* and *subsumes* that of the telos. That is to say, the teleological stories of the ideological devotees—Michael in his identification with his father's Zionist adherence and the adherence of Habiby's narrator to the communist idea—are represented from the perspective *and* in the context of the protagonist-narrators' melancholy stories. It is important to note that the comprehensive perspective of the narrators endows them with a depth of awareness that conspicuously contrasts with the lack of insight and obtuseness of their counterparts. Recall Žižek's postulation that the self-image of the individual is always already shaped by the "gaze" of the dominant ideological beliefs. In the texts before us, however, the encompassing, overarching perspective of the dissenting narrators escapes and thus defies the ideological gaze. Not only do the devotees to the ideological telos fail to affect the melancholy tellers but, perhaps more important, the narrow vision of the devotees, confined to a single-minded ideological orientation, makes them unaware of the melancholy "gaze" that surreptitiously undermines *their* story.

Thus, in terms of the metaphorical representation of the Gonens' marriage as a train journey, Michael is "stuck" in the "seat" of social conformity. Even though he knows of Hannah's childhood friendship with the Arab twins, he comprehends neither her melancholy obsession with her losses nor the intensity of her longing for the lost childhood of freedom, imagination, and love. In Habiby's story one encounters an equally remarkable measure of self-unawareness. While conforming to the demands and expectations of the public office, Habiby's narrator obliterated the past by severing all ties with his childhood world, characterized by Saraya's love, Ibrahim's poetic imagination, and the magic of Carmel. In other words, the limited knowledge of the adherents to the ideological telos exposes their vulnerability and their shortsightedness—or even blindness. These weaknesses effectively strengthen the defiant standpoint of the protagonist-narrators. Consequently, the depth of the understanding and self-consciousness of the melancholy dissenter vis-à-vis the limited consciousness of the ideological conformist empowers the former. The ideological erasure of history, to recall Althusser, signals the deficiency of the ideological position. The negation of the past of the ideological proponents presents the possibility of dissension for those who possess an encompassing historical vision. By remaining fully conscious of the history of sustained losses, the protagonist-narrators in our texts fend off the neutralizing pole of meaning. Thus, they maintain a degree of freedom that allows them to question the social consensus.

The short scene involving Michael's reconstruction of the battle for Jerusalem (*MM* 249) is a case in point. Its two-tiered composition, consisting of Michael's explanation of the battle and Hannah's critical, corrective commentary on this explanation elucidates the subversivity of the melancholy trajectory. Hannah marvels at Michael's ability "to explain complicated things to Yair in a very simple language, using hardly any adjectives." She watches Michael's explanation of the battle "with the help of twigs and stones" and notes that the lesson is grounded strictly in "system and logic," whereby time is conceived "as a succession of equal squares on a sheet of graph paper." Though Hannah claims to know little about the battle, she remembers its tragic aftermath. She recalls that "the villa which belonged to Rashid Shahada, the twins' father," was confiscated and "handed over to the Health Organization which turned it into a pre- and postnatal clinic." She also remembers that "the Germans and the Greeks abandoned the German and Greek colonies," and that "new people moved to take their places." Hannah's recollection of the dispossessed and displaced victims presents the battle in a way that counteracts Michael's dispassionate, matter-of-fact explanation of the war as "a chess match."

Hannah's re-visioning of the historical events evolves simultaneously with the war game that Michael stages. Remembering the history of defeat amounts to combating time, which, as was previously mentioned, she sees as a "and prowling" destroyer of memory. Thus, against Michael's linear concept of time, one that divides history into symmetrical, emotionless units or "equal squares," Hannah recalls the human or, rather, the inhuman dimension of the war by invoking the fate of the defeated. Like Benjamin's angel, who witnesses the wreckage and the debris of the destroyed world, Hannah is the remembering witness of the suffering of the defeated non-Jewish ethnic populations of Jerusalem. Michael sees the victory as a fait accompli, a useful example for the historical study of Zionist triumphs. Hannah looks back at the injustice and destruction that has been forgotten and understands that the victory has not been conclusive. She foresees more battles over Jerusalem. In a fearful fantasy articulated in intensely poetic imagery, she describes how under the city "secret forces [are] relentlessly scheming, swelling and surging and bursting out through the surface" (*MM* 249).

In contrast to Hannah's imaginative, highly dramatic vision of impending destruction, Michael sees the battle in terms of universal, ahistorical "motives [that] were self-evident: conquest and domination." Michael's emphasis is on the telos of the war, that is, the intention to conquer and control. He presents the war with equanimity and self-assurance, reflecting his identification with the dominant ideological "gaze." Michael clearly identifies with the victors' historical perception. As Hannah observes, in his presentation of the battle he enthusiastically and seriously assumes the role of a "general" who devises a successful war campaign. At the same time, Hannah's observations of the limitations of Michael's language and his omission of adjectives point to a weakness that Michael is unable to acknowledge. His language, which conspicuously contrasts with the vivid and poetic language of her prophetic vision of the impending war, reflects his unconscious anxieties and fears, which he keeps at bay by limiting his language to mere technical expressions (*MM* 249).[24]

I might add that this notion of unconscious anxiety and unacknowledged fears is corroborated by the fact that the battle over Jerusalem in 1948 ended in the division of the city. The victory was by no means total and the goals of conquest and domination were not completely attained. The triumph of the winning Israeli forces is therefore qualified. Could it be that the meticulous reenactment of the past battle implies an unconscious preparation for another battle? Might the strategic planning of future victories serve as a way to alleviate the victors' anxiety over the unforeseeable future? In view of recent developments of the second intifada and the exacerbation of terror, Hannah's intuition about forthcoming eruptions of violence seems quite prophetic.

Presented from Hannah's overarching point of view, the scene illustrates a consciousness that refuses to enter the triumphalist national narrative. On one level Hannah's perspective, which brings forth the suppressed story of the defeated, exposes the limited view of ideologically shaped history. On another, deeper level her vision calls attention to the apocalyptic, literally earthshaking consequences of the triumphalist telos of "conquest and domination" as it emerges in Michael's representation of the battle. This scene—in which Hannah both interweaves and counterpoises two accounts of the battle and offers her own vision of the future—defies the ideological consensus. Her two-tiered narrative dissents against the moral blindness of the official, ideologically prescribed triumphalist view of history.

It is important to note that Hannah's dissent remains in the private sphere. Her opposition to the mainstream worldview is expressed only within the limits of the inner monologue of her secret journal, which reaches the outside world through the publication of *My Michael*. In the world of the novel, her resistance to the national normative discourse remains secret. Thus, while she escapes the universalizing tendencies of the pole of meaning, the private form of this escape determines the limits of her defiance.

A two-tiered reevaluation of the past in monologue form characterizes the episode of the "wing-clipped gypsy girl" in *Saraya*. Here the protagonist-narrator recalls an event that took place forty years earlier, at the high point of his involvement in public life. A gift from a little gypsy girl, a prototypical Saraya, was handed to him at the moment when he was composing a fiery editorial for his Communist newspaper *al-Ittihad*. He explains that in the early years of the state, the Israeli authorities considered all contacts with Palestinian refugees a security threat. Even the slightest suspicion of any connection with the Palestinian Diaspora could put the Israeli Arab community at risk. As the narrator recalls, "We would reprimand anybody who would do such a thing, accusing him of being blatantly irresponsible concerning the future of his people" (S 160). It is therefore out of fear and mistrust of "both lover and foe"—namely, both his Arab comrades and the Jewish authorities—that he decides to burn the gift. The burning of the gift symbolizes a conscious act of severing all emotional ties with the defeated and exiled Palestinian community. The elimination of the "gift," a voice from the past, also signals a single-minded determination on the part of the Israeli Arab political activist in the Arab Communist party to build a new life for the Israeli Arab community.

Now, forty years later, the protagonist-narrator, who refers to himself as "he," recalls how, after having destroyed the gift, he remained on the beach. It was then that he had a vision. He "*imagined* [*hu dima*] that he was seeing armed silhouettes dragging a little, beautiful, *wing-clipped* gypsy girl. He was standing there, as if paralyzed, at the edge of the slope, facing the blinding sunset. And he *imagined* that the armed silhouettes dragged the wing-clipped girl up the slope toward him; and he *imagined* that her eyes were growing wider as she was approaching . . . and she looked away from him, so that her eyes would not meet his. Or perhaps it was *he who averted his eyes and looked away*" (S 166; emphasis added).[25]

One notices the almost uncanny similarities between the wing-clipped gypsy girl and Benjamin' angel, whose wings are immobilized by the wind of progress. Like the staring eyes of Benjamin's angel, which mirror the destruction before him, the widening eyes of the gypsy girl reflect suffering and loss. Like Benjamin's wind of progress, which thrusts forward, oblivious of the ruins of the past, the narrator, blinded by his ambition—metaphorically reflected in the blinding light of the sun—is unable to face his own history, which is also the history of his people's defeat. His choice of the communist ideology, an avenue for the political progress of the Arabs who remained in Israel, impels him to repress the memory of those who went into exile.

As the repetition of the phrase "he imagined" indicates, the encounter with the arrested gypsy girl was no more than a fantasy, a figment of the narrator's imagination arising from unacknowledged regret and pangs of conscience. From a psychological point of view, this fantasy reveals his repression of the guilt of betrayal. Indeed, he "forgot" the incident for forty years. At the time of his political activism, the narrator was unable to admit his disloyalty even to himself. To maintain his position as a public figure on the Israeli political landscape, he had to disavow his past, his love, even his memories. The fact that the narrator admits his self-deception in this confessional *khurfiyyah* forty years later attests to his growing self-awareness. His current awareness of his former self-deception is an acknowledgment of the limited vision of his former political orientation. The third-person form of the recollection emphasizes this new awareness, reflecting the narrator's distance from his former self, which was blinded by ideological and political convictions.

Like Hannah's private journal, the confession of Habiby's narrator occurs in self-imposed isolation. In a situation similar to that of *My Michael*, the narrator of *Saraya* grieves over his errors and losses. Like Hannah, he keeps the story to himself. The distance from the world allows both protagonist-narrators to maintain, if only temporarily, a balance between the poles of being and meaning. The clandestine nature of the writing protects the message from blending with the ideologically uniform discourse of the external world. I have previously shown how, once published, the dissenting texts were co-opted into the literary canon. As long as it remains private, however, the story's dissent remains intact.

It is, of course, possible to argue that the private nature of the confession has produced an ineffectual defiance of the ruling system. A private melancholy dissension is ineffectual because it has no impact upon the discourse of the dominant telos that it opposes. It is also precarious since the silence of depression can be kept at bay only so long as the act of dissenting writing persists. Thus, the *finis* of the written text marks not just the end of a confessional narrative; the end of the story also communicates the depletion of the libidinal energy of the narrators, that is, the death of their creativity. The daydream that marks the end of Hannah's fantasy world indicates her death wish. The concluding imaginary act of terrorism that the twins perform at *her* bidding in the territory of *her* state signals the irresistible spell of self-destruction induced by the irrevocable loss of love. Recall the final scene in *Saraya,* where the narrator describes himself as sitting in a glass-domed shell, waiting to be launched into space or returned to his mother's womb. These images of seclusion, which conclude the *khurfiyyah,* spell the narrator's death wish. With their stories ended, both narrators withdraw to the death of silence. In this respect the narrators in *My Michael* and *Saraya* invoke Saeed and his secret epistolary narrative in *The Pessoptimist.* Once his letters are completed and sent out, Saeed disappears into the shadows of insanity and death. Although the narrators disappear, the narratives do not. As the next chapter will demonstrate, narratives of dissent do reemerge on the public scene.

The Return of the Repressed

"Repression," Freud postulates, "leaves *symptoms* behind it"; that is to say, it *manifests itself* through symptoms, which indicate "a *return of the repressed.*" Thus, the repressed can never be completely retrieved; it returns in the form of "symptoms" or "substitutive formations."[26] The preceding discussion has shown that the repressed past produces forbidding symptoms of melancholia and depression on both sides of the political divide. Clearly, there is no need to elaborate on the deplorable inequality between the dominating Jewish majority and the dominated Arab minority in all the texts I have studied; in a sociopolitical sense, any search for symmetry would be not only futile but morally flawed. Of interest, however, is the fact that both novels demonstrate how on each side the politics of memory erasure has effected the dialectics of a compulsive, albeit melancholy, return to history. In each of these fictional autobiographies I have noted dichotomous movements: the movement of retrospection, which strives to retrieve and relive the repressed history of the defeat, and the ideological movement forward, predicated upon the repression of this past.

The tension between melancholia and telos communicates the struggle of the suppressed memory to reinstate itself in the consciousness of the victor. It offers a vision whereby the reaffirmation of the story of the defeated will make Benjamin's angel of history face the powerful wind of progress and confront it with the denied history of destruction and suffering. Then the symptoms of the repressed history will reinsert themselves into the dominating field of vision. Once the "forgotten" history had been acknowledged, the hitherto parallel running trajectories of memory and progress would interlock. The conflation of the trajectories is bound to transform the relations of estrangement between those who intend to forget and deny and those who strive to remember and mourn.

The succeeding discussion of David Grossman's novel *The Smile of the Lamb* and Anton Shammas's *Arabesques* will show that the symptoms of the repressed history can no longer evade the social scene, nor can they remain in the private domain of the melancholy writer. In these novels the repressed memory of destruction and mourning emerges into the open. Published in the 1980s, the narratives are told from a post-1967 perspective. In view of the events of the war and of the ensuing occupation, in many respects a déjà vu situation recalling the 1948 period, history can no longer be denied. The reader is no longer positioned as the recipient of secret narratives of discovery of the repressed histories of defeat, such as "Hirbet Hiza," *The Pessoptimist, My Michael,* and *Saraya.* Nor is the reader the confessor of the shameful communal secret of suppressed identity, as we have seen in *In a New Light.* The reader has now become a spectator of a dramatic encounter between memory and telos that evolves conspicuously at the center of the narrative. Emerging from silence, the story of the loss asserts its presence in the social landscape of the novel, and its articulation signals the remote but nonetheless real possibility of a dialogue.

Focusing, in particular, on *The Smile of the Lamb,* Menakhem Perry maintains that in the 1980s Israeli fiction "personal and political—have collapsed." The critic claims that those characters in Grossman's novel who have attempted to oppose the world of lies and violence are forced to give in to a reality ruled by deception. They compromise their moral principles by assimilating strategies of dishonest manipulation they had previously rejected. Perry contends that the novel presents us with the absence of a "tangible solution" and leads to the conclusion that "the only tangible things left are the lies."[27] Indeed, as my discussion will show, in both *The Smile of the Lamb* and *Arabesques* the protagonists find themselves in a moral predicament that causes them to question their own truthfulness and integrity. At the same time, I demonstrate how the protagonists' reckoning with their moral weakness and confusion attests to an evolving self-critical self-consciousness. The hard-won, unsparing awareness of the compromises they have made in compliance with the ideological mainstream signals the possibility of an honest interaction.

Each novel presents characters, both Arab and Jewish, who struggle with their own ambivalence in a world that no longer presents them with essentialist, clear-cut choices between truth and lie. To some extent their predicament lies in the fact that the decisions they have to make are far from unambiguous. I will suggest that the message communicated in *The Smile of the Lamb* and in *Arabesques* lies neither in the optimism of personal or political redemption nor in the pessimism of the "collapsed lines of both personal and political response," as Perry sees it. Rather, the message emerges in the process of intersubjective formation of adversaries who can no longer remain distinct from each other. This interactive process arises from the growing awareness of the extent to which the reality of domination and oppression has affected the subjects on each side of the political divide. In both *The Smile of the Lamb* and *Arabesques* the departure from ideological conformity occurs as a result of a gradually evolving consciousness of the irreversible effects of war, domination, and oppression, and the complex yet inextricable bonding that has evolved in the face of these atrocities.

In both novels the consciousness of history, which cannot be undone yet must be acknowledged and confronted, takes the form of transgenerational transmission of the story that cuts across political and ethnic divides. As symptoms of repressed history, the stories of the fathers impress themselves upon the consciousness of the successors. It is with the unqualified awareness of the legacy with which they were entrusted that the successors attempt to enter a relationship with their political and social surroundings. The prospects of a dialogue lie in the interaction between the obligation to the message imposed by the past and the compromises required by the political reality of the present.

11

Tales That Ought to Be Told

David Grossman's *Smile of the Lamb* and Anton Shammas's *Arabesques*

The Paternal Legacy of Tales of Love

To demonstrate the centrality of the storytelling motif in both novels, I wish briefly to recapitulate the plots of each of these works. In *Arabesques* the two interweaving narratives are entitled "The Tale" and "The Teller." The connection between these narratives is forged by Uncle Yusuf, the narrator's uncle and the village storyteller. Among the stories he shares with his nephew, Anton Shammas, Yusuf tells the story of a cousin named Anton who allegedly died in infancy. Apparently Anton the narrator was named after the dead child. Uncle Yusuf is a Christian Arab who maintains friendly relations with Muslim Arabs. These friendships are certainly atypical of the long-term hatred and hostility that marked relationships between Arab Christians and Muslims. Indeed, Yusuf tells his stories over the course of years while waiting for his own son, Ameen, who ran away to Lebanon to join with Christian Arabs in their struggle against Muslim Arabs. Yusuf's stories prompt Anton to search for his namesake, the cousin who he believes is still alive. The search leads him to write "The Tale." This part of *Arabesques* presents the saga of the Shammas family, whose history extends from the Ottoman and British rule of Palestine, through the Israeli conquest in 1948, up to the Israeli

248

occupation of the West Bank and Gaza Strip in the wake of the 1967 Six-Day War. The story of the hostilities between Muslim and Christian Arabs merges with the story of the Israeli conquest of Fassuta and the transfer of some of its inhabitants to refugee camps. Episodes of war and violence intermingle with the story of the courtship and marriage of the narrator's parents and his nostalgic recollections of his childhood in the village.

The family saga intersects with segments of "The Teller," where the protagonist-narrator recounts his stay in Paris and his participation in the International Writing Program in Iowa City, Iowa. One of the many thematic strands of "The Teller" focuses on the narrator's ambivalent relationship with the Israeli Jewish writer Yehoshua Bar-On, who is planning to write a novel about an Israeli Arab. Another strand follows an unexpected development in Anton's search for his cousin. The ties between Anton, the narrator, and Michael Abyad—the adopted son of a Lebanese couple, who works for the Palestinian Center for Research in Beirut and who, presumably, is the other Anton—are reestablished in a dramatic meeting in Iowa City. Yet another thematic strand recounts the narrator's love affair with Shlomith, an Israeli Jewish woman married to an army officer, which ends abruptly. The narrator's love letters, written in Hebrew from Iowa City, recount the tale of his childhood. The interception of the letters by the husband ends all communication between the lovers. In an ironic and quite confusing plot twist, it turns out that the narrator's autobiographical tale, parts of which fell into the hands of the Israeli officer, was not written by Anton but appears to be a translated (by Anton) version of an autobiography written by Michael Abyad. In the course of his meeting with Anton, Michael, who denies being the first Anton but who nonetheless identifies with the dead child, admits to having written an autobiography in the narrator's name, which he (Michael) had entitled "Tale."

In *The Smile of the Lamb*, the importance of the storytelling motif is signaled by the refrain of the Arabic phrases "kan-ya-ma-kan" (once upon a time) and "tuta tuta khelset elkhaduta" (so ends the tale), which the protagonist, Uri, a young Israeli Jew of Iraqi origin, has learned from the Arab Khilmi, an estranged member of his community, a worldly wise fool, and a storyteller. Uri has befriended Khilmi in Andal, a village in the occupied territories, where he serves as an assistant to his Jewish friend Katzman, the military governor of the area. Khilmi, who lives in a cave above the village, has captivated Uri with his fantastic stories about his imaginary redeemer, the Greek hermit Darius, who came to console him after his father's suicide. Thanks to his tales of love, Darius taught Khilmi to live in a world of poetic fantasy, to disregard the mockery and degradation inflicted upon him by his village because of his strange lifestyle, his physical handicaps, and his illegitimate birth.

Katzman establishes his friendship with Uri through a completely different though perhaps no less fantastic story of his Holocaust experience. Katzman avoided deportation by hiding with his parents in a pit. There his father, a literary scholar, made him memorize his lost manuscript on the moral parallels in Ariosto's *Orlando Furioso* and Cervantes' *Don Quixote*. Through retelling the Ariosto epic, the father and son established bonds of love. Upon his arrival in Israel, Katzman deliberately detached himself from his past, assumed the identity of an Israeli-born Sabra, turned into a fearless fighter, eventually becoming a high-ranking officer in the Israeli army. By contrast, naive and gentle Uri was mocked and degraded at school and in the army. His beloved grandfather, Amram, died of shame after having been repudiated by Uri's father for his cowardly behavior in the 1948 war. The father, who returned from the war consumed by hatred of the Arabs, drove the grandfather into depression, silence, and ultimately death. During his service in the West Bank, Uri, an idealistic pacifist, wages a futile struggle to improve the living conditions of the Arabs. Meanwhile, Katzman has a love affair with Uri's wife, Shosh. When Yazdi, Khilmi's adopted son, who joined the PLO, is killed in a military action led by Katzman, Khilmi takes Uri hostage, presenting an ultimatum for the Israeli army's withdrawal from the occupied territories. Uri does not oppose Khilmi and neither does Katzman, who, tormented by doubt and guilt, goes up to the cave to free Uri and is killed by Khilmi.

Though far from complete, these synopses offer an insight into the multiple, intertwining story lines in the novels. These are complex narratives—partly first-person, partly third-person, partly stream-of-consciousness—whose inconclusiveness confounds the search for cohesive, clearly evolving plots. I wish to suggest that the portrayals of father-son relationships in the novels provide a key to this fictional maze. More specifically, the conspicuous motif of storytelling—the stories that fathers tell their sons—offers point of departure for an unraveling of these fictions. In this respect, it is possible to disentangle the narratives from the stories the father figures—Uncle Yusuf, Khilmi, and Katzman's father, all victims of persecutions—try to communicate to their sons. It is important to note that the stories the fathers tell are uniformly rejected by their biological sons Ameen, Yazdi, and Katzman. Eventually the stories become the legacy of the surrogate sons Anton and Uri. The latter are deeply affected—even transformed—by the messages they receive. I wish to argue that the construction of the novels revolves around two interrelated thematic strands, the first being the complex interaction between the protagonist-inheritors of the story and their surrogate fathers and the second the no less complex interaction between the surrogate sons and the world to which they reveal the stories they inherited. To illuminate the significance of the interrelations among the fathers, the surrogate sons, and the world, it is important to understand the basis upon which the biological sons rejected the story. What was the message that the sons refused to accept?

As was mentioned earlier, to escape the foreboding silence of melancholia, the memory of the loss must be communicated. To recall Benjamin's parable, the angel of history must face the wind of progress and confront the history of triumph with the testimony of the victims. The present texts, however, depart from Benjamin's paradigm, indicating that it is not necessarily the *story of destruction* that the dissenting angel might choose to tell. In these texts the persecutions endured by the fathers do not metamorphose into testimonies of victimization. Rather, they challenge the telos of victory and progress with testimonies of moral fortitude in the face of degradation, persecution, and terror. We shall see how, in the confinement of prison, the alienation of the cave, and the horror of the pit, the fathers counteracted hate, pain, and fear with the *poetry of love*. In the stories they tell, they rewrite the traumatic effects of defeat and dispossession (Uncle Yusuf), mental and physical abuse (Khilmi), and the Nazi decree of annihilation (Katzman's father) into stories aimed at forging relationships of love and trust. These tales teach neither submission nor violent opposition to oppression. Utilizing the universal voice of poetry, they teach us how to promote tolerance. The dissension encountered in these stories does not follow the usual course involving the denouncement of the victor and the latter's atrocities. Rather, it confronts the dominating system with a story of love and poetic imagination. It is this message of love that the heirs to the stories are meant to communicate to the victorious mainstream, nurtured by stories of militancy, war, and domination.

How relevant is the message that one generation transmits to the next? Unsurprisingly, Benjamin, who insists on remembering the past, asserts the binding obligation that the past imposes upon the present: "There is a secret agreement between past generations and the present one. Our coming was expected on earth. Like every generation that preceded us, we have been endowed with a *weak* Messianic power, a power to which the past has claim."[1] Jürgen Habermas identifies in Benjamin's postulation "*a drastic reversal* of the horizon of expectation and the space of experience. To all past epochs [Benjamin] ascribes a horizon, and to the future-oriented present he assigns the task of experiencing a corresponding past through remembering of unfulfilled expectations." Habermas sees the horizon of expectations exclusively in terms of remembering "the innocently suffered fate of past generations." As he puts it, "The anamnestic redemption of injustice, which cannot of course be undone . . . can at least be virtually reconciled through remembering."[2]

If, as Habermas sees it, the successors' sole responsibility is to remember, then the messianic power conferred upon them is weak indeed. In this respect, Habermas's interpretation of Benjamin's postulation underscores the degree to which the expectations of the fathers in the present texts exceed remembering. Here the "secret agreement" between the generations confers upon the successors a rather greater messianic power, and a claim bigger than "the anamnestic redemption of justice." The stories of the fathers in both novels communicate a request to address the reality of oppression with a story that proclaims a loving attitude toward the world despite experiences of brutality, hatred, and suffering. It is important to note that these lessons do not remain in the sphere of an abstract humanistic ideal. The fathers practice the ethics of love and tolerance they preach. To a remarkable extent they lead their lives according to the gospel of nonviolence and love for humanity they communicate in their stories.

As Anton recalls, "[I]n the early years of this century, he [Uncle Yusuf] and the other villagers of Fassuta were subject to persecutions and torture at the hand of the Muslim inhabitants of the nearby village. . . ." This experience did not prevent Yusuf from making friends with Muslim Arabs. In 1929, having been arrested for smuggling arak (a kind of hard liquor) together with his Muslim friend, Yusuf was sentenced to a prison term in Jerusalem. There, Anton tells us, "my uncle, an indefatigable wordsmith, composed poems of love and longing for Hagob [an Armenian who was sentenced for having tried to murder his Muslim girlfriend's brother]." These letters were smuggled out of the prison to the girlfriend, "but not before all the prisoners had memorized them." Years later Uncle Yusuf met Hagob's family in the Armenian quarter of Jerusalem, where the wife told him that "it was only because of his poems that she kept faith with Hagob" and eventually married him.[3] Uncle Yusuf's early experience of imprisonment among murderers inspired his poetry of love, which evidently transformed his listeners. The poetry not only imprinted itself in the memory of hardened criminals but also defused violent religious and ethnic intentions, paving the way for the marriage between an Armenian and a Muslim.

A formative experience of immense cruelty shaped Khilmi's antiviolent, peace-loving weltanschauung. The lesson of love that he communicates originated in his response to the people of Andal, who, as he recounts, "made me the butt of their jokes and called me Khilmi el Tartur, Khilmi Cap-and-Bells. . . . I, playing the fool, drank in their derision, knowing they were not to blame, for someone else was inscribing hatred in their flesh in order to dispatch great legions of pain into the world, but I fooled him according to the precepts of Darius, my patron and redeemer."[4] To thwart evil, Khilmi withdraws to his cave. There he attempts to overcome the power of hatred through the language of love and tenderness by spinning a "tale within a tale" (*SL* 115) about fantastic flying creatures, magicians, and the secrets of nature. By teaching how to love and how not to hate, Khilmi tries to prevent first Yazdi and then Uri, from morally surrendering to a world ruled by terror and violence. He preaches that it is not by means of a hateful reaction to the indignities of Israel's military domination that one wins the war against oppression and injustice but rather by passive resistance actualized in withdrawal into a world of dream and fantasy. There, through the redeeming powers of poetic language, one can weave the experience of suffering into a tapestry of magical stories. Khilmi believes that his stories of wondrous, exotic worlds liberate the victim from the reality of degradation. These stories are the "weapons" of passive resistance whose "stubborn patience and infinite weakness" will eventually break Israel's rule of domination (*SL* 36).

One should note Katzman's father's similar withdrawal into the world of the imagination. While in the pit, he sought relief from indignity and fear by immersing himself in the poetry of *Don Quixote* and *Orlando Furioso*. Poetry became a two-pronged way to defy the "final solution." On a symbolic level, the memorization of the classic works of European civilization and the study of their moral worldview reaffirmed the ideals of humanism against Europe's decline into the most barbaric chapter of its history. On the level of personal relations, Katzman's father's telling and teaching the old stories to his son transformed the degradation of the experience into one of love. Ariosto's and Cervantes' stories of magical exploits and fearless fighters filled the horrible confinement of the pit with words of poetry. The magic of their language created a bond of love between father and son: "Gradually a bond formed between [Katzman] and his father. . . . They conversed in lines of poetry. . . . They retired to a world where the language was Ariostic, where words and images . . . took on meaning and life, because thanks to them, he knew his father loved him" (*SL* 177).

Like Uncle Yusuf and Khilmi, Katzman's father saw poetry as a teacher of truth. He realized that, to recall Habermas, in view of the enormity of evil "new horizons of expectations" were emerging from old stories. In an act of "private resistance," he rewrote the stories of Cervantes and Ariosto, letting "Don Quixote defeat the windmills" and making "that fool Astolfo [who flew to the moon to retrieve Orlando's sanity] the hero of *Orlando Furioso*" (*SL* 179, 178). In a world governed by injustice and tyranny, the voice of madness is metamorphosed into the voice of reason and acts of insanity are redefined as acts of redemptive heroism. Like Yusuf's time in prison and Khilmi's self-imposed exile in the cave, the ordeal in the pit proved that injustice can—at least in the sphere of ethics—be defeated by means of poetry because the latter can rewrite and thereby imaginatively replace reality.

The Sons and the Legacy of Love

The sons—Ameen, Yazdi, and Katzman—rejected the teachings of the fathers; in Benjamin's terms, they renounced the "messianic power" the stories conferred upon them. Instead, the sons responded to another "messianic power"—that which speaks the language of hatred—by subscribing to national ideologies of militant aggression. Of course, in each case the target of aggression differs: Ameen fights Muslim Arabs, Yazdi fights Israelis, and Katzman oppresses the Palestinians. Nonetheless, the common objective of resolving ethnic, religious, and national conflicts with violence informs the sons' belief system. Their militant weltanschauung antagonizes the expectations of their fathers. The sons distance themselves from the sphere of poetic imagery, which transcends conflicts of faith, culture, and ethnicity. They replace their fathers' language of poetry with ideological slogans and catchphrases whose rhetoric promotes hatred and violence.

When Anton shows Ameen a picture of Michael Abyad looking compassionately at two corpses, victims of the slaughter in the Sabra camp, the ruthless and hateful rhetoric of Ameen's response demonstrates his distance from his father Yusuf, a friend of Muslims and "the indefatigable wordsmith" of the poetry of love and longing. Full of hatred, Ameen tells Anton, "For a hundred years, since the 1860s, they [the Christians] have been suffering at the hands of the Muslims and the Druse. And if this Michael Abyad, whose face looks so pitying, identifies with the Muslim corpses . . . it's better both for him and for us that we be not related" (*A* 230). The enemy's death has not lessened Ameen's hatred, which exceeds his affinity with family members. Ameen communicates a degree of implacable hate that not only eliminates the possibility of reconciliation but also establishes a value system that excludes those—even family members—who do not share it.

Like Ameen, who rejected his father's language of love, Yazdi moved away from the "infant tongue" of innocence (*SL* 39) and "the vegetal words of love and care and longing" (*SL* 29) that Khilmi had taught him. Instead, he adopted the violent language of radical freedom movements: "Tyranny will be met by force, the iron fist will be crushed by a leaden one" (*SL* 243). He lectures Khilmi about "blood and holy war and a popular uprising," telling him that "we have important things to do. . . . We have to fight. . . . They [the Israelis] understand only the language of power" (*SL* 30). Furthermore, Yazdi tells Khilmi that he considers the imaginary world Khilmi has created in his stories to be nothing but falsehood and deception. Even more important in terms of this discussion is Yazdi's accusation against Khilmi for having constructed an illusory world that condoned the community's loss of dignity and respect: "You speak shamelessly of *the rose air of freedom you breathed* as you glided over Andal like a bird, when all the while you were a slave among the slaves" (*SL* 235; emphasis added). It is when Yazdi denounces Khilmi's language of poetry that the latter finally understands the unbridgeable distance that separates him from his son: "[Yazdi] knows my thoughts and despises them. I will not see him again" (*SL* 36).

In Katzman's case, the rejection of his father's language of poetry and its ethics took place upon his arrival in Israel. In Eretz Israel Katzman swiftly detached himself from the intellectual European heritage that he received from his father, transforming himself "as quickly as possible from an obstinate Polish-speaking enigma . . . into a Sabra-boy, assimilating sunshine into muscle." The tenderness and love of the pit dissolved, replaced by "a hard core of muscle-bound self-sufficiency, with a wild and bitter fortitude verging on self-hatred, and a fine, detached perceptiveness" (*SL* 17, 18). To become a "new" Israeli Katzman had to repress the memory of denigration and impotence that he endured in the Diaspora—especially at the time of the Holocaust—and adopt the Zionist ideological tenet of the "negation of the Diaspora." The passivity and the powerlessness of the Arabs now threatens to release Katzman's repressed memories of *his* passivity and powerlessness in the pit. Thus, the fear of his own past prohibits him from seeing the suffering of the Arab population under his rule.

The need to feel powerful and self-sufficient subjugates Katzman to a system that idolizes might. The position of military governor empowers him and, paradoxically, enslaves him to a brutal system of oppression. In his last conversation with Uri, Katzman reiterates the Zionist rhetoric of contempt for the Arabs, who do not fight for their freedom: "I have no respect for the million or million and a half who live quiescently under the regime they don't want." Subsequently Katzman, whose "words spill with hatred," is driven, despite himself, to distort his own father's search for justice for the oppressed in the "madness" experienced by Ariosto's and Cervantes' poetic heroes. He reasserts his superiority as a fighting "new" Jew over the inferior Arabs, who passively endure their subjugation and who therefore are, in his words, "beneath contempt." Aware that he is betraying his father's struggle against the "windmills" of tyranny, oppression, and injustice, he tells Uri, "They [the Arabs] will never *breathe the rose air* of Ariosto" (*SL* 321; emphasis added).

The manner in which both Katzman and Yazdi negate their fathers' image of flight into the rosy empyrean—a metaphoric depiction of the freedom of fantasy and imagination—calls attention to the similarity of their perspectives. Both Katzman and Yazdi deny the liberating fragrance of rose air to "slaves," who are incapable of armed struggle against their dominators. This view is predicated on common ideological patterns that associate militancy with dignity and honor. Even though they belong to enemy camps, both Katzman and Yazdi subscribe to a worldview that cuts across political divides. Ironically, both Katzman, the "new" Zionist Jew and an "old" experienced officer, and Yazdi, the freshly recruited Palestinian guerrilla fighter, act in accordance with a belief system grounded in two interrelated convictions. The first ascribes supreme value to militant defense of national freedom, while the second denies human dignity to those who do not follow the first.

Both Katzman and Yazdi see their "new" identities—post-pit and post-cave, respectively—ineluctably determined by their loyalty to group ideology. This perception of subjectivity informed by the needs of a national collective refers back to the discussion of subjectivity formation and its social context. Recall Freud's observation of the close interrelations between individual and social psychology, a notion further developed to its extreme in Heidegger's concept of the "death of the subject." According to this perspective, the impact of social surroundings is perceived as so powerful that the loss of subjectivity is practically inevitable, unless one embarks on a conscious struggle against the overpowering influence of the social consensus. This view of subjectivity determined by the ideological collective highlights the opposite stance of the fathers, whose stories dissent from the social norm. Against the collective language of violence, the stories promulgate the language of poetic imagination. The fathers' conscious choice of the world of poetry, which placed an emotional and mental distance between them and the warring environment, enabled them to maintain their dissenting perspectives. In contrast to the sons' choice to join the militant, war-oriented collectives, the fathers refused to conform.

The notion of militancy as social norm is certainly not new. In fact, Yizhar's prototypical story "Hirbet Hizah" was the first to characterize the "new" Jews as ruthless conquerors. It will be recalled that the story takes place during the 1948 war and deals with the Israeli conquest of an Arab village and the expulsion of its inhabitants. Admiring the beauty of the place, one soldier remarks, "Ours [the Israelis] would have fought for this place to the very end, and these [the Arabs] run away, they won't even try to fight!" To which another soldier retorts, "C'mon, leave these *Arabushim* [pejorative epithet for Arabs] alone—they are not human beings" (HH 55). Note that the victorious Israelis in "Hirbet Hizah" do not just boast of their superior military skills and their courage, as opposed to the cowardice and weakness of their enemies. They go further, reasserting that their bravery in the battlefield defines them as proud human beings, while the enemies who cannot fight do not deserve to be called human. The contemptuous, dehumanizing perception of the enemy renders the defeated Arabs "invisible," allowing the victors to remain blind to the atrocities they commit in the battlefield. For the Israelis in "Hirbet Hizah," human dignity is defined first and foremost in terms of ruthless militancy.

Some forty years after Yizhar's story was published, Katzman's declaration of contempt for the Arabs' nonbelligerence reiterates the same negative perception of the Arabs, reinforcing the old Zionist notion of the "invisibility" of the native population. What has changed during the decades is the Arab response? Since the 1967 victory the Arabs have become conscious of the Israeli oppressor's contempt for the nonfighting opponent. As Yazdi puts it, in terms that uncannily echo the Israeli soldiers in "Hirbet Hizah," "to [the Israelis] we are no more than a kind of pest, mere shells of men" (*SL* 234). Ironically, Yazdi's subsequent decision to enlist in the guerilla forces reveals ways of thinking parallel to those propagated by the Israeli militant weltanschauung. In a doubly ironic twist, in order to gain self-respect Yazdi, the oppressed Arab, must earn the respect of the Israeli occupier as a dedicated and courageous fighter for his nation's freedom. This situation illustrates Hegel's notion that the bondsman's self-consciousness, or sense of self, is predicated upon his being recognized by the lord. . . . In this sense, paradoxically, the determination to take up armed struggle against the occupier reaffirms the dependency of Arab subjectivity upon the Israeli "gaze."

To gain recognition as a fighter, Yazdi develops the same attitude of contempt toward nonfighting Arabs as the Israeli occupier. To a remarkable extent, Yazdi's rejection of Khilmi's world of poetry and love resembles Katzman's rejection of his father's world. To join the elite of the militant Sabras, Katzman had to repress the language of love and imagination his father had taught him in the pit. To join the terrorist organization of freedom fighters, Yazdi repudiated the language of nature and magic that Khilmi had taught him in the cave. Both Katzman and Yazdi assume a collective identity that eliminates individuality and critical, independent evaluation of the world and self. The collective identity shapes a self-image grounded in communal solidarity *in* struggle. Readiness for a militant engagement with the enemy becomes a decisive and conclusive marker of camaraderie and collective national identity. Ironically, what emerges is an interdependency in terms of identity shaping; the self-definition and self-image of each side depends upon the extent to which its militant hostility would gain the other side's hateful recognition, preferably in the form of an admission of defeat. The state of militant aggression has shaped the indelibly intertwined Arab and Jewish identities.

The Surrogate Sons and the Fathers' Message to the World

The sons' rejection of their fathers' poetic legacy places the surrogate sons—the heirs by choice—at the center of this discussion. While Ameen, Katzman, and Yazdi become standard-bearers of the collective militant orientation of their social groups, Uri and Anton assume the role of caretakers and proponents of a paternal legacy, which proves to be a complex and difficult undertaking. The heirs face the problem of propounding a message of love to a society that has chosen to follow the path of hatred and violence. The fathers present their successors with a tale they told in different places under very different circumstances. Uncle Yusuf's love poetry, Khilmi's folk tales, and the world of chivalry and honor of Katzman's father— all forged out of the reality of suffering and terror—are imagined environments of love, magic, and poetry. In the enclosed space of the prison, the cave, and the pit, the story of love transformed the reality of hatred. But how is it possible to transfer the message from the private sphere, infused with fatherly love, into a social landscape dominated by militancy and aggression?

I have already mentioned the "weak messianic power" that, according to Benjamin, the preceding generation grants to the succeeding generation. The willingness to inherit the story signals an assignment that requires more than a "weak messianic power," or, as Habermas tells us, more than just the commitment to remember. Indeed, in view of the sons' rejection of the fathers' story of love in order to construct their own story of war, the undertaking of the surrogate sons assumes messianic proportions.

The obligation to carry out a legacy so difficult that it has been rejected by the next of kin presents the protagonists with a dilemma. Despite the obligation that they feel toward the fathers, the incongruity of the mission in the face of the political reality of hostilities and occupation creates a sense of uncertainty, doubt, and identity disorientation. It is impossible to disregard the tension inherent in the split between the collective consensus and the "call of the other." As Derrida has stated, the need to comply with the general consensus of the "gaze" of the dominant collective clashes with "a certain *responsibility* to answer to the other, whose call somehow precedes [the subject's] own identification with itself." The concept of the primary and overriding obligation to respond to the call of the other reconfirms Benjamin's insistence on the obligation to previous generations, whose claim to fulfill their expectations informs our sense of self.

What happens when the "secret agreement," as Benjamin calls the responsibility to previous generations, is exposed to a highly antagonistic public? What psychological and moral changes can we expect from exposure to a story whose poetry teaches love? How and to what extent does the delivery of the story to the world affect the protagonist and his sense of self? These questions naturally lead to a discussion of identity shifts of both bearers and recipients of the message of love and empathy.

The mutual impact of the protagonists, who speak the language of moral responsibility, and their counterparts, who speak the language of militancy and violence, raises questions about the potential for a dialogue. In the following discussion of *The Smile of the Lamb* and *Arabesques* I will explore the extent to which the meeting of the protagonists and the characters who represent the dominant collective has reshaped each other's sense of self and society. However, it is first necessary to understand the dynamics of the relations between the ethics of responsibility to which the protagonists feel morally obligated and the politics of social reality in which they participate as members of the community. To gain a better insight into the tension involved in the split identity of the subject as an individual and as a member of a social body, I will refer to Emmanuel Levinas's philosophical concepts being-for-the-other and the third party, as well as to Zygmunt Bauman's sociopsychological analysis of these concepts.

As Levinas sees it, the individual faces two contradictory demands, both of which must be accommodated. On the one hand, there is the demand of the "ethical anteriority of responsibility" to-be-for-the-other. The demand of responsibility for the other has no boundaries; it extends to the past, as "I am thrown back toward what has never been my fault or my deed . . . [and what] concerns me . . . [is] my participation in the past of others, who 'regard me.'"[5] The primordial sense of responsibility informs my subjectivity even before the emergence of the egotistical needs of well-being and self-preservation. This responsibility is beyond reciprocity; my obligation to be-for-the-other is not predicated upon the other's obligation toward me.

On the other hand, my unmediated closeness to the other is disrupted by "the third party," that is, "a human plurality." The presence of many others introduces the criterion of comparison, a situation that creates "the demand for justice,"[6] which signifies equality of all. The notion of justice introduces the element of objectivity. In this context, rather than being unequal through my responsibility to the other, whose needs always come before mine, I am equal to all others. Making a crucial distinction between the other and the third party, Levinas explains that while the relationship of responsibility is asymmetrical, "the relationship with the third party is an incessant correction of the asymmetry of proximity . . . the reverting of the *incomparable subject into a member of society.*"[7]

Levinas proposes to reconcile the contradictory demands of responsibility and justice, of moral inequality and social equality, through the principle of simultaneity. As Simon Critchley tells us, the two aspects of social relations create "a doubling of discourse" that presents the "simultaneity of ethics and politics."[8] Nonetheless, it is important to note that, according to Levinas, the coexistence, or simultaneity, of the two movements is sustained by an irreducible and unequivocal moral order that makes me unequal in my relations to the other. According to Levinas, the ethics of being-for-the-other precedes and, in fact, shapes the disposition of the third party since "justice remains justice *only* in a society where there is no distinction between those close and those far off, but in which there also remains the impossibility of passing by the closest."[9]

Whereas Levinas predicates a just social system upon an ethics of unmediated responsibility of being-for-the-other, Bauman takes the *seemingly* opposite view. From Bauman's perspective, the appearance of the "Third," which signifies the birth of society, spells the disintegration of the "exceedingly vulnerable togetherness of a 'moral party.'" The latter, as Bauman calls relations based on the ethics of responsibility, cannot survive in the reality governed by social order. According to Bauman, "Objectivity, the gift of the third, has delivered a mortal, and at least *potentially* terminal, blow to the affection which moved the moral partners." As Bauman sees it, the appearance of the "Many," who wear masks that hide the face, divested the moral party of an innocence that had permitted unqualified, face-to-face confidence in moral relationships. Because relations are now replaceable and exchangeable, the trust deriving from the uniqueness of the unmediated relations with the other has turned into uncertainty and mistrust. Bauman believes that while in one sense human relations must arise from unconditional affection, in another sense this affection is always mitigated by anxiety born of suspicion, since "we believe others to be trustworthy and suspect at the same time."[10]

While Bauman's view seems opposite to that of Levinas, the language of both thinkers implies a common aspect of indeterminacy of the relations between the "moral party" and the "third party." On the one hand, Levinas's postulation that justice can be maintained *only* when social equality coexists with ethical inequality indicates that the possibility of an unjust society devoid of moral stratification should by no means be ruled out. The danger of an unjust society is always there. On the other hand, Bauman's modification of a "mortal blow" to the moral party as "*potentially* terminal" is a concession that to a limited extent the strand of unconditionally trusting relations in the fabric of social relations is still viable. Indeed, we cannot exist without some belief in unconditional affection and moral responsibility for the other. I suggest that the attention Bauman draws to the coexistence of trustworthiness and suspicion in human relations attests to *his* belief in noticeable traces of the "moral party" in social relations among the "Many."

A brief analysis of the archetypal story of the biblical Fall may help elucidate the dual nature of human relations grounded both in the ethics of the "moral party" and the politics of the "Many." The appearance of the snake, the "third party," has incontrovertibly disrupted the perfect coexistence of Adam and Eve by insinuating suspicion, deception, and fraud into the hitherto trusting and innocent relationship. Nonetheless, the corruption ensuing from the appearance of the third party has been unable to obliterate the desire to reattain the purity and innocence of completely trusting relations between human beings, each of them unique. Whereas the state of perfection has been irrevocably lost, the memory or the consciousness of such a state underlies the ethical aspect of human relations. In this sense, the individual vacillates between two irreconcilable aspects of identity, one of a subject who is incomparable, that is, unique, and the other of a subject as a member of society. While the response to the call of the other determines the uniqueness of an individual's ethical subjectivity, social membership defines an individual's "sameness," that is, subject to the principle of equality, which underlies the social structure.

The above paradigm of the duality of social discourse defines the ways in which the protagonists and their counterparts in our texts affect and transform each other's weltanschauung. As the plots of *The Smile of the Lamb* and *Arabesques* evolve, the representatives of opposed social orientations appear to shift positions. In terms of the theories of Levinas and Bauman, in both texts there is a movement from the pole of ethics toward the pole of politics and vice versa. Specifically, the encounter with the pole of militancy and domination compels Uri and Anton, the protagonists, to adjust their message of love and trust to the social reality they wish to penetrate. At the same time, the encounter with the protagonists and their message affects the perception of characters, such as Katzman and, to a lesser extent, Bar-On, who adhere to the ideology of militant nationalism. Though corresponding in a general sense, these tendencies of shifting positions by no means follow similar trajectories in both texts. *The Smile of the Lamb* portrays a dramatic reversal of positions between Uri and Katzman. This drastic transformation ends in a tragic denouement that precludes meaningful interaction. *Arabesques,* by contrast, depicts the dialectic of the characters' evolving consciousness of self and other. Anton and Bar-On's growing awareness of interdependency seems to indicate a more hopeful, though extremely complex, progress toward mutual recognition. Even though the encounter ends on a note of missed opportunity, the sense of disappointment points to the possibility of further encounters.

In a sense, the fathers' adoption of the protagonists as the inheritors of their ethical legacy seems to have resolved the protagonists' identity issues. In fact, the "adoptions" by surrogate fathers mended the protagonists' disrupted or unfinished process of identity formation. Khilmi and Uncle Yusuf performed acts of parental bonding when they entrusted their adopted sons with the mission of opposing their visions of love to the present-day reality of injustice and oppression. The ensuing meeting with the world results in a complex situation. On the one hand, it exposes the fragility and inconsistency of the protagonists vis-à-vis the world. On the other hand, it reveals cracks in the ideological armor of the characters who represent the dominant society. Ironically, in its encounter with the world, the legacy of the love story instills ambivalence and hesitation in both the carriers entrusted with the story and its receivers.

Uri is certain to have achieved a closure to the disrupted story of his childhood in Khilmi's cave, where he rediscovers the sense of the home he lost when his grandfather died. Recall that his grandfather Amram's premature death was brought on by his son (yet another son who repudiates his father's legacy of nonviolence), a fanatical militant nationalist who banished Amram for his cowardice during the 1948 war and then banished his own son, Uri, to a boarding school. After Amram's death, the mattress in which he stuffed his notes was burned; thus, Uri never learned his grandfather's story. In fact, the "fragrant straw" in Khilmi's cave reminds Uri of "Grandfather Amram's mattress" (*SL* 56–57), whereas Khilmi's absolute rejection of armed struggle reiterates Amram's absolute terror of war. In this sense, Khilmi offers Uri a physical, emotional, and moral environment that bears a remarkable resemblance to his grandfather's senselessly destroyed legacy.

Uri's identification with Khilmi's withdrawal into the imaginary world of storytelling is further reinforced by his vicarious identification with the similarly imaginary retreat of Katzman's father at the time of the Holocaust. The story of the pit filled with the sounds of Ariosto's epic not only reconfirms poetry as an antidote to violence but also proclaims the power of poetry to bring together storytellers as different as Khilmi and Katzman's father. The image of the liberating flight in the fragrant air of roses indicates the connection between the two. As we have seen, this poetic image of air fragrant with roses is abused by Yazdi and Katzman, who use it to express their contempt for the passivity of the occupied population. For Uri, however, the image reflects a form of liberation through poetry. Uri acknowledges that Khilmi's story about his flight over the village—when he "soar[ed] like a bird and breathed the air of roses, the spirit of freedom"—is his "favorite story," one that makes him "feel happy." The feeling of happiness is a result of the connection that he makes between Katzman's story "about his father and Ariosto's epic about the fool who went to the moon in search of the hero's lost mind, where he, too, breathed the starry air of roses" (*SL* 135).[11]

This remarkable association through poetic imagery demonstrates to Uri the truthfulness of Khilmi's tale and obligates him to obey its message. To a remarkable degree, Uri's submission to Khilmi reflects Levinas's contention that the response to the need of the other is a responsibility that precedes all egotistical interests: "Subjectivity is being hostage. . . . [It posits] itself in abnegation, in sacrifice, in substitution that precedes the will."[12] When Khilmi tells Uri that he has been waiting for him to come, Uri, using Levinasian terminology, admits to having become a hostage to Khilmi's call. As he tells us, Khilmi's confession "gave me a funny feeling, as if I, Uri Laniado, had no reality apart from the force that had brought me here to him, the will that willed me here from afar" (*SL* 135).

Nonetheless, Uri ultimately fails to transform the legacy of love into a stepping stone enabling a dialogue between the warring parties. Nor is he capable of fulfilling the moral obligation of being-for-the-other. At the conclusion of the novel, with Uri literally having become Khilmi's hostage, Khilmi threatens to kill him if his ultimatum of Israeli withdrawal from the occupied territories is not met. Even though he feels ready to submit to this demand of ultimate self-sacrifice and become the proverbial "sacrificial lamb," Uri consciously misguides Katzman and causes him to die in his stead. In fact, Katzman is willing to sacrifice himself for Uri. Ironically, it is Katzman rather than Uri who literally fulfills Levinas's postulation that "it is the responsibility of a hostage which can be carried to the point of being substituted for the other person."[13] Shot by Khilmi, he dies, "fishing . . . out of his remotest depths, out of some forgotten abyss . . . a soft smile of surprise . . . a kind of promise . . . his eyes gazing at Uri with dead love . . . his hand fluttering inside his shirt like a heart bursting out of its rib cage or, perhaps, knocking on it" (*SL* 324–25). The tenderness and love that Katzman learned from his father in the "forgotten abyss" of the pit and has now rediscovered in his heart takes the ultimate form of being-for-the-other/Uri.

Katzman's self-sacrifice, expressed in his smile and gaze, fails to save Uri's idealistic innocence. Uri's physical transformation reflects an unmistakable defection to the vitiating world of politics. In Bauman's terms, this world of the "Many" is faceless; it presents itself through masks that can never entirely be trusted. Katzman's face— stripped of its masks of a "new" Jew, a dauntless fighter, and a ruthless military governor—communicates a truth rediscovered too late, a promise that cannot be kept. His gaze of love can no longer change anything, not only because it comes from the eyes of a dead man but because his dead eyes gaze at another who is also dead in a spiritual and moral sense. Katzman's eyes of love do not "look" at Uri's face but rather at a sinister mask of cruelty and evil, an empty shell that projects death. Just before being shot, Katzman observes with dismay how Uri's smile "isn't the smile of the lamb anymore, it's a grimacing mask of evil, a grim curse that Uri [wordlessly] hurls at him." His face has turned into "a cruel death-shell" and his eyes have "the malicious glare of the glassy jester's smile . . . a wolfish smile" (*SL* 323, 324). These diametrically opposed transformations of Uri and Katzman indicate the failure to establish some common ground between the world of ethics and politics.

The failure to bridge the distance between these worlds drastically reduces the possibility of a future dialogic interaction. The reason for failure may lie in the immutability of the opposing weltanschauungen: though the two characters have exchanged positions, the positions themselves have not changed. Now it is Katzman who takes on the role of being-for-the-other that costs him his life, whereas Uri's "wolfish smile," which is associated with the tenet "homo hominem lupus est," represents the ideological doctrine of self-preservation even at the cost of complete moral deterioration.

The difficulty of rapprochement between the two contradictory positions lies in the failure to construct a nonessentialist mode of coexistence or, in other words, to create a "script of relational positionality." This concept is borrowed from Susan Sanford Friedman's insightful discussion of feminist cultural narratives. Friedman calls for a "new geography of identity" that will acknowledge the relativity of identity construction in the particularity of a given social context. Identities shift in response to cultural, ethnic, religious, economic, or political aspects of social situations that confront the individual. Against the fixity of the binary, or essentialist, distinctions between the socially powerful and powerless, Friedman points to the changing aspects of identity of each side in different social encounters. She maintains that "identities are fluid states that can be understood differently depending on the vantage point of their formation and function."[14]

The following discussion of *Arabesques* demonstrates the extent to which both Anton, the Israeli Arab protagonist and first-person narrator, and his counterparts—especially Bar-On, the Israeli Jewish character—are capable of altering their identities and modifying their positions based on individual circumstances. In contrast, *The Smile of the Lamb* features a rigid modality of identities that encloses both

Uri and Katzman in a mind-set that permits only radical role reversals. In Katzman's case, he underwent a complete reversal of identity as originally shaped by his father at the time of the Holocaust. He rejects this earlier identity, grounded in love and poetry, when he turns into the "new" Jew and becomes a typical Israeli fighter. Katzman's complete identification with Zionist ideology marks the extent of his estrangement from the stories his father told him in the pit. The deliberate dissociation from the past exacts an enormous price. His love affair with Shosh, Uri's wife, reveals to Katzman the depth of his moral downfall. The unforgivable betrayal of his comrade's trust leads him to weigh the extent to which he has disgraced his father's legacy of love and truth. The process of unsparing self-examination leads him to condemn himself as a cynical and cruel oppressor of helpless others. Katzman's lack of relational perspective does not allow for a compromise, which might have offered the possibility of redemption; he turns into his own most severe judge and in a way sentences himself to death.

In contrast to Katzman's post-Holocaust subscription to the value of survival, which explains his cynical view of human nature, Uri's meekness and pacifism emerges from a belief in the universal goodness of all human beings. Uri is unable to accept the reality of relational responses to differing situations. Rather, his sense of trust and security is predicated upon the universal sameness of unrelated people and varying circumstances. I have already shown how Uri's association of his grandfather Amram with Khilmi makes possible his self-identification as Khilmi's surrogate son, a substitute for Yazdi. An even more striking example of Uri's tendency to seek commonality, a quality that precludes a sensitive approach to differing situations, is the connection he establishes between the history of the Holocaust and the occupation of the West Bank. Recall Uri's feeling of happiness upon discovering the affinity between Khilmi and Katzman's father, symbolized by the image of liberation toward a rose-scented realm. The similarity of the images allows him to see himself as a messenger of two legacies, namely, that of Katzman's father and that of Khilmi. From his perspective, these disparate legacies have become one.

It is perhaps in the association that Uri draws between Santa Anarella and Andal that his inability to differentiate among places and events manifests itself most clearly. As a volunteer in a rescue operation in Santa Anarella, an Italian village devastated by an earthquake, Uri experienced an enormous sense of gratification while unearthing people trapped under the ruins. There, he admits, he was "ecstatically happy" because he experienced "a kind of justice that swept [him] away." What made him happy was the sense of moral justice, of putting himself in danger out of love for suffering humanity. Andal, a village in the occupied West Bank, attracts him because it reminds him of Italy. Quite incongruously, this geographic association raises his hopes to relive his happiness in Santa Anarella (*SL* 5, 167, 180).

It is not just his narcissistic desire once again to act as an altruistic savior and redeemer of the suffering others that causes Uri to strive to relive the emotionally satisfying experience of Santa Anarella in the reality of Andal. More than anything, it is perhaps his determination "to reconstruct the Katzman [he] knew" there, that is, to hold on to the memory of Katzman, the person who talked of love among the ruins of the Italian village, and therefore the person irrevocably associated with "the lucid truth [he] experienced there" (*SL* 218). The Katzman of Santa Anarella, who talked about "the love between him and his father" born in the reality of the Holocaust made Uri "happy" because, as he says, Katzman's story awakened him to "a new love for the world and for [himself]." Not by coincidence, it would seem, it was then and there, while listening to Katzman's story of love amid the ruins of Santa Anarella, that Uri arrived at his epiphany, namely, that "there is an indivisible nucleus in each of us, a nucleus of love" (*SL* 180). The indivisible nucleus of love that, as Uri sees it, connects him with the rest of humanity—and especially with Katzman—is constitutive of Uri's identity. All along Uri wages a desperate battle to keep the nucleus of love intact. The new identity marked by the cruelty and horror of his wolfish smile and the "death-shell" of his transformed physiognomy demonstrate that the battle has been lost.

Uri's inability to grasp Katzman's transformation from the humanitarian in Santa Anarella to a ruthless military governor of the occupied territories demonstrates his lack of sophistication in terms of understanding and accepting what Friedman sees as fluid states of identity. This lack of insight into the psychological complexity of human behavior divests Uri of emotional defenses. When the nucleus of love, the core of his identity, is shattered, he feels himself no more than "a figment of other peoples' imaginations . . . impossible to know who Uri was or where his loyalties lay, or why he did what he did, and now Uri is just an *empty head* . . . a *receptacle* for other people's lies and Khilmi's madness" (*SL* 273; emphasis added). In this sense, the mask of evil—with its deathly, wolfish smile with which he reciprocates Katzman's final smile of hope—hides nothing but a depleted, empty self.

The ending of the novel, with Katzman's death and Uri's life-lessness, signals the failure of the paternal legacies of love. This message seems to corroborate Perry's pessimistic argument that *The Smile of the Lamb* ends with the realization that "the only tangible things left are the lies." In rejecting this conclusion, I wish to propose a reading that focuses on the characterization of Katzman. I will argue that even though tardy, Katzman's response of love suggests that change is possible, thereby undermining the definitiveness of Perry's conclusion. Katzman's change from survival at any cost to self-sacrifice as a signal of love points to the development of an ego ideal capable of hearing the "call of the other." In one sense the belatedness of Katzman's response to Uri's call, which articulates Khilmi's teachings, communicates the tragic result of Katzman's lack of sensitivity and attention to the other's needs. The belated attention turns the oppressor *of* others into a self-sacrificial lamb *for* another, an irreversible transformation ending in his death. At the same time, even though it is late, the ability to change indicates that redemption is still possible. Katzman's consciousness of his self-sacrifice indicates the truthfulness of his emotional and mental conversion. Applying the terminology of Levinas and Bauman, Katzman's conscious act of atonement represents a belated attempt to exit from the "third party" and establish a "moral party" with Uri.

In this sense, it is possible to redefine the novel's ending as a conceptual failure rather than an irrevocable disintegration of all values. The failure emerges in the insistence of both Katzman and Uri to see the world in essentialist categories of good and evil, right and wrong. Whereas Uri declares his unshaken devotion to the values of universal humanism, Katzman devotes his life to the cultivation of the exclusionary Zionist ideology that sees the world as an implacable enemy of the Jewish people. In view of these binary and irreconcilable weltanschauungen, it is possible to see the reason for the tragic events that conclude *The Smile of the Lamb* in the protagonists' mental and emotional blindness. In this sense, the ending of the novel becomes the beginning of rethinking and reconsideration, a process that reveals the dangers of an absolutist—be it universalist or nationalist—ideology. The awareness of a relational approach to the world suggests a degree of tolerance that might lead to a dialogic interaction between the warring parties.

My previous discussion of Levinas and Bauman in terms of the difficulty in accommodating ethics and politics inclines me to a reading that sees in *The Smile of the Lamb* a call for a more nuanced conception of right and wrong. For instance, Uri fails to accept and internalize the reality that the victims of domination, such as the inhabitants of Andal, are also Khilmi's ruthless victimizers; nor can he comprehend that survivors of the Holocaust, such as Katzman, are capable of both saving the victims of an earthquake and inflicting suffering and brutal humiliation. Rather, Uri compulsively tries to transplant the one-on-one intimacy of total trust and affinity with Khilmi, the "moral party," as Bauman calls it, to the context of the "third party," that is, to the oppressive militant society as represented by Katzman. Since Uri can identify only with binary sets of values, the failure to transform the "third party" into the "moral party" results in his emotional and moral disintegration.

Bauman observes that in the social setting it is "the mask [and not the face] which determines who I am dealing with and what my responses ought to be."[15] Since the mask may disguise both truth and deceit, I can never be certain whether the mask of the person in front of me represents a truthful state of mind. As a result, I can never be sure whether my response to the mask of the other is adequately mis/trustful. According to Bauman's reasoning, since my response is determined by the role the other assumes toward me, I also put on a mask to assume a role that is expected of me. Therefore I cannot entirely trust myself either.

Bauman's argument about the adaptability of social relations returns us to the issue of the fathers' legacies, which the sons are expected to present to the world. How are they supposed to bring the message of love to a world full of animosity, hatred, and violence? Khilmi tries to resolve the problem by unsuccessfully attempting to keep his heirs within the seclusion of the cave. His failure first with Yazdi and then with Uri communicates the impossibility of shutting out the reality of war and oppression outside the cave. Uncle Yusuf, the storyteller in *Arabesques,* takes a different approach. It is significant that Yusuf tells Anton the story of his (Anton's) name on "the enchanted boulder," which blocks "the entrance to the cave." According to local legend, this cave not only provided shelter for the villagers at the time of the religious wars in Lebanon in the 1860s but also contains a "golden treasure" hidden there by the Crusaders (*A* 13). The inaccessibility of the cave suggests that it is no longer possible to remain in the private world of imagination and poetry. The tale must seek its meaning in an engagement with the world of politics.

Right from the start Uncle Yusuf reveals to Anton that his name is the name of another, a piece of information that undermines the absolute sense of the self and instills the desire to search for his namesake. Furthermore, Uncle Yusuf equips his heir and messenger with "all the tools necessary for a weaver of tales," sending him "out into the world with many stories in [his] pack to keep people awake nights" (*A* 228). Thus, he undoes the ties that bind the "moral party" of two and releases his narrator into the world not to transform it in any drastic measure but rather to keep the story of the victim in the consciousness of the conqueror. Recall here Habiby's novel *The Pessoptimist* and the letters Saeed sends to the world. Unlike the latter, who disappears once the letters are sent, Anton will remain in the world as a teller and writer, thus keeping the consciousness of the past alive.

Unlike Khilmi, who believes in the power of the story to resolve the situation of oppression through passive resistance, Uncle Yusuf no longer attributes political power to his stories. He knows that to place the minority story of victimization in the space of the ruling majority exposes the story of powerlessness vis-à-vis the triumphalist history of conquest.[16] It is true that in 1929 his poetry of love, composed in the confinement of prison, was powerful enough to join ethnic and religious enemies in bonds of love and marriage. He realizes, however, that in the reality of the 1948 defeat the story has lost its power. Anton tells us that Uncle Yusuf "was well aware that his being was flawed and incomplete, like my own, and [that] the tale . . . [no longer had] sufficient power to restore the earth pulled from under our feet" (*A* 228). Unlike Khilmi, who retreats to his cave to dream up stories that will ensure future victory, Yusuf sends Anton into the world of the victorious rulers with a story of the powerlessness of the defeated, a story whose reflection of cruelty and injustice will haunt the victors.

As heir to the legacy of national loss and dispersion, Anton is therefore attuned to the fissured reality of life after defeat. Even his name, supposedly also the name of his cousin, represents the Israeli Arab's split identity in a divided world. As an Israeli Arab, he is a member of a minority in the Israeli Jewish mainstream. At the same time, his Israeli identity confronts him with the complexity of his position vis-à-vis the Palestinian Arabs in exile. The world into which Uncle Yusuf's tutelage sends him presents him with a number of discrete realities, each of which demands and elicits a different attitude and behavior and questions his sense of identity. This complex interaction with the world evolves in three simultaneous, intertwining main narratives, namely, Anton's love affair with Shlomith, his search for Michael Abyad, and his relationship with Yehoshua Bar-On.

Before turning to Anton's search for identity, it is important to note the pattern whereby in each of the three narratives Anton's position shifts from the center to the periphery. Anton is purposely placed in the center of the narrative, only to be dismissed and marginalized. First, in the narrative of his relationship with Shlomith, Anton's letters fall into the hands of the husband, an army officer. This unfortunate occurrence removes Anton from his lover's life. Second, the "Tale," which the reader is led to believe is Anton's autobiographical story, turns out to be Michael Abyad's text, in which Michael pretends to be Anton. At the end of the "Tale," Michael hands Anton the story with the words, "Translate it, adapt it, add or subtract. But leave me in" (*A* 259). Thus, shifting from the central role of author-narrator-protagonist, Anton has been relegated to the position of translator and editor of his own life story. Moreover, since the autobiographical story of Anton was imagined and written by Michael, Anton's story cannot be entirely Anton's;

paradoxically, Anton appears in his own story in the secondary role of translator and editor. Finally, one discerns the same pattern in the third narrative strand, that of Yehoshua Bar-On, who intends to write about an "educated Arab" who "speaks and writes excellent Hebrew" (*A* 91, 92). The model will be Anton. But Anton is marginalized once again when Bar-On changes his mind, replacing his character with the character of a Palestinian Arab from the occupied territories.

The transformations of his identities as the lover of a Jewish woman, author of his own life story, and central fictional character in a Jewish writer's story result in Anton's growing ambivalence, anxiety, and fear. Though he becomes delusional about Shlomith's red hair, which "entangled him, strangled him, stranded him in the strands of her life" (*A* 77), we never hear him respond to her telegram, in which she tells him of the stolen letters and challenges him by suggesting, "Shall we fight it [our misfortune]?" (*A* 176). In fact, as he tells Bar-On, he plans to do nothing about the situation, feeling that "it's all over with" (*A* 252). Intimidated by the legal and political repercussions of the affair, Anton eschews the fight.

An even greater sense of Anton's ambivalence and anxiety emerges at the meeting with Michael Abyad, allegedly the child after whom Anton was named, and, as Anton sees him, "half of his identity" (*A* 227). When the long-awaited meeting finally takes place, Anton is filled with regret and fearful hesitation. Afraid that Bar-On might suspect him of collaboration with Abyad, a former member of a terrorist organization, Anton panics. Even though Abyad reassures Anton that "the worst that can happen is that they [the Secret Service] could ask you a few questions" (*A* 257), Anton remains uncertain and insecure. On the one hand, fearful of the possible repercussions and concerned about his safety, he wishes to end the meeting, while, on the other, he feels ashamed of his cowardice and berates himself for "having allowed Bar-On to invade my life once more" (*A* 257). Anton's apprehension at being accused of belonging to an illegal organization is quite understandable in view of the fact that Israeli Arabs have always been viewed as suspects by Israeli authorities. At the same time, however, one must stress that his concern over a possible encounter with the Israeli Secret Service is not the only reason for Anton's ambivalence.

Other reasons for the ambivalence of a split identity have already manifested themselves in the initial stages of Anton's search for Michael. By a fortunate coincidence, Anton has located a woman who most probably knew Michael in pre-1948 Beirut. Laylah Khoury, who allegedly worked as a maid for the Abyad family, was expelled from Fassuta at the time of the war. A lifelong refugee, the reader learns that she lives in the village of Silwad in the occupied territories. Even though Anton can obtain easy access to the village with the help an Israeli Jewish friend, he hesitates. One reason is his reluctance to reawaken Laylah's traumatic memories of her dispossession. "I was concerned," he confesses, "about maintaining *my own ignorance.* . . . [W]hy should I let myself open *the diaspora of a past* already sealed by forgetfulness?" He admits that the forgotten past of the victimized young girl "was nothing but the tip of primal knowledge that had taken root in my consciousness. . . . [S]omething of this anguished soul had seeped into my consciousness all these years and had formed *relics of doubt, forbidden to the touch*" (*A* 34–35; emphasis added).

What are those forbidden relics of doubt that Anton would have preferred not to touch? In terms of Freud's concept of the return of the repressed, what is the repressed knowledge, now emerging through the symptoms of anxiety and ambivalence? In contrast to Uri, who, it will be recalled, shows little insight with respect to himself or the world, Anton is capable of a critical assessment of his inner conflict. He not only understands but is also honest enough to admit openly his unwillingness to recall the past—specifically, the disaster of the 1948 war. In a sense, Anton's confession coalesces with that of the narrator in *Saraya*, especially in the episode of the gift, where he recalls his conscious disavowal of the past to promote his career as an Israeli Arab politician. Both Habiby's narrator and Anton consciously suppress the tragedy that befell their people. In this sense, Uncle Yusuf's disclosure of the history of Anton's name sets Anton on a search that traces the repressed "half" of his Palestinian identity. The imposed search for national identity is disturbing because it clashes with this aspect of Anton's identity, which seeks to integrate itself into the intellectual milieu of the Israeli mainstream.

Anton's ambivalence is reconfirmed in his attitude toward "Paco," whom Anton ironically describes as "a charming fellow from Nablus" (*A* 146). Paco is the derisory nickname by which Anton refers to a Palestinian fellow writer at the Writers' Workshop in Iowa City. Seemingly innocuous, the nickname mocks the Palestinian's excessive use of a popular aftershave lotion. Since Anton identifies the other fellow writers by their private names, the omission of Paco's real name is significant. Paco's namelessness signals Anton's desire to distance himself from Palestinians at large. He clearly does not wish to be identified with his people—certainly not with the exiled Palestinians. He rationalizes his reluctance to befriend Paco by finding fault with the latter's lack of refinement and sophistication. This negative view of his compatriot is reaffirmed in the episode involving the trip to the lake, which proves the Palestinian's maladaptation to Western civilization. Paco disrupts the group's moment of nature worship by tossing a beer can into the lake (*A* 253). This act demonstrates utter insensitivity to the beauty and serenity of the place as well as complete ignorance of ecological concerns.

Anton's snobbish and derogatory characterization of Paco reveals more than just his desire to deny his bonds with the national tragedy of defeat. On another level Anton's dismissive attitude toward his compatriot also marks his bitterness at having been replaced by Paco as the protagonist in Bar-On's as yet unwritten novel. The latter's seemingly jocular declaration to Anton—"[Y]ou are henceforth released from the fear of my open notebook, because I've found a new hero"—is a devastating blow to Anton's ego, an injury he openly admits: "Instead of being happy about my freedom [from Bar-On's ubiquitous note taking], I was feeling let down. To put it precisely, I *was* feeling betrayed" (*A* 168, 169). Anton's exclusion from Bar-On's story signals his banishment from the mainstream Israeli Jewish writer's consciousness. To Anton this rejection represents the Israeli Jew's refusal to admit him in the dominant mainstream culture.

Ironically, upon closer examination, Bar-On's rejection of Anton as his character model reveals quite a remarkable degree of interdependence between the Jew and the Arab. The complex nature of this closeness emerges in the reasons for Bar-On's choice of the Palestinian over Anton, his fellow citizen Israeli Arab, from beyond the "green line." Bar-On's choice of Paco implies a shortsighted attempt on the part of the Israeli writer to evade the necessary confrontation between Israeli Jewish and Israeli Arab coexistence. As Bar-On explains, his preferred new hero "forces me to *take a stand* toward him [because] he is still a *pure* Palestinian, whose strength resides in his *simplicity* and lack of cynicism." By contrast, "my former hero [Anton] does not define himself as my enemy, at least *not in the accepted sense of the word*. And that makes it *hard* for me. On the other hand, I feel much *closer* to the problems of *this* Palestinian." (*A* 168; emphasis added except final instance).

Bar-On finds the complex nature of his relations with the Israeli Arab frustrating. The clear-cut position of the Palestinian as an enemy, which allows for a straightforward understanding of Israeli-Palestinian relations, elicits a sense of relief. The closeness that Bar-On feels for the Palestinian lies precisely in the *conflict of interest* that clearly defines their identities as each other's enemy. As an Israeli Jew, Bar-On is capable of understanding the Palestinian feelings of enmity toward him over the land. At the same time, Anton, who lives within Israel's borders and who is an Israeli citizen, causes Bar-On a considerable degree of uneasiness. Furthermore, being an Israeli Hebrew writer, Anton embodies a measure of cultural rivalry and competition, further complicated by a sense of cultural familiarity that is a bit too close for comfort.

What clearly frightens and confuses Bar-On is the proximity of the Israeli Arab. Levinas, it will be recalled, claims that proximity places the relationship in a situation that avoids symmetry and evinces a sense of responsibility for the other. In this sense, the Palestinian, as a representative of a "pure" and "simple" enemy *collective*, frees Bar-On from any and all responsibility. Thus, a Jew tries to evade a face-to-face encounter with an Arab who defies the definition of an enemy and whose presence evokes a sense of affinity that the Israeli victor is reluctant to acknowledge. The Israeli Arab on Israel's territory presents the Israeli Jew with a proximity that makes personal involvement unavoidable. As the "third party," per Bauman, Paco is expected to shift the relations from the threatening context of ethics into the realm of politics. In the realm of the "third party" the masks of enemies turn the relations into a well-defined and, above all, well-rehearsed and long-standing script of political conflict and militant hostility between Jews and Arabs.

Bar-On's scheme to circumvent ethical demands, signified by

Anton's presence, partly fails as a result of Paco's "barbaric" behavior at the lake. The uncouth toss of the beer can demonstrates a degree of Palestinian "simplicity" that Bar-On is not prepared to accept and endure. Paco is thus disqualified as Bar-On's protagonist (*A* 202). To a large extent, however, the failure of the scheme may be attributed to Bar-On's own barbaric behavior, which discredits him in the community of his peers and causes him to cut short his stay in Iowa City. In a fit of jealousy, Bar-On publicly assaults Amira, a fellow writer he suspects is having an affair with Anton. While Bar-On is on the verge of strangling Amira, it is Anton who comes to the rescue. As he recounts the incident, "With a strength I didn't know I had, I grabbed both his hands and pushed him back to his chair" (*A* 204).

Ironically, both episodes of "barbaric" behavior—that of Paco at the lake and that of Bar-On's assault of Amira—preclude Bar-On's plan to eliminate Anton from his life and his work. In the end, Bar-On assuages Anton's ego by admitting that by relinquishing him as his protagonist he has "given up on a really terrific story" (*A* 253). While a Palestinian's blunder returns the Israeli Arab to the sphere of Bar-On's literary interests, it is Bar-On's blunder that places the Arab in a direct physical confrontation with the Jew. The dramatic physical closeness of the assailant (the Jew) and the rescuer (the Arab) demonstrates an engagement of the two at the most primal, instinctive stage of male rivalry over a female. Ironically, the moment of wrestling abolishes the sociopolitical inequality of the contenders.

On a political level, the incident inverts the roles of victor and victim. Anton, the Israeli Arab who has won the friendship of Amira, a half-Arab, half-Jewish woman, finds out that he has both the physical strength and the daring to fight and subdue Bar-On, an Israeli Jew. This incident recalls a similar motif of Arab empowerment in Mansour's *In a New Light*, specifically the story of Yossi's love affair with Rivka. There Yossi's romantic "conquest" of the wife of Yehuda, the prototypical "new" Jew, permits a vicarious identification of the Arab with/as a dauntless Israeli fighter. Here the rivalry of two men over a woman highlights the basic human desires that override national, political, and ethnic differences. In an ironic twist, the common denominator of sexual interest places the opponents in a physical contact that—at least for a moment—bridges the distance between the two. Paradoxically, the violent encounter between Jew and Arab implies mutual recognition.

The Diminishing Distance

The incident involving Amira represents a climactic point in the engagement between the Arab and the Jew. A closer look at their relationship before this incident demonstrates a growing proximity that, though very complex, seems to efface or at least diminish the emotional distance between the two. I begin with a consideration of Bar-On's portrayal of the Arab/Anton as his literary model. While planning his novel, the seemingly self-assured and condescending Bar-On conceptualizes his protagonist as an "educated Arab [who] speaks and writes excellent Hebrew." The protagonist, as Bar-On envisions things, will be allowed to enter his Israeli Jewish "plot," but only "within the boundaries of the permissible," where he is doomed to suffer "the loneliness of the Palestinian Arab Israeli, which is the greatest loneliness of all" (*A* 91, 93).

Bar-On's thoughts, however, shed quite a different light on this patronizing projection of his Arab protagonist. Significantly, Bar-On himself reveals the connection between the planned fiction and his own sudden humiliating and painful downfall. We learn that his wife had recently left him and that his son had been arrested. Bar-On's own "plot" has turned into, in his words, "a metaphor for the new loneliness." From this point of view, a novel about the Arab represents Bar-On's attempt to infuse some meaning into his suddenly empty life. It is interesting to note that while contemplating his future novel it occurs to Bar-On that the subject ought to deal with his family crisis, the key to which may lie in his son's poems and a story he found after the son's arrest. However, the father instantly rejects this idea, affirming that he has no interest in pursuing the topic of his relations with his son (*A* 92). He is rather determined to make the Arab the focus of his story.

The guiding motif of the sons' obligations to the legacy of the fathers highlights Bar-On's situation. We have seen how the biological sons rejected their fathers' stories, and how the stories were eventually adopted by the surrogate sons. In Bar-On's narrative, it is the father who consciously refuses the legacy that his son has left behind him in "the drawers," which, as he admits, "I never even knew existed." Bar-On's acknowledgment of his ignorance of his son's life further illuminates his decision to focus on a plot that would place the Arab on the Israeli "plot," or territory. This decision is significant in two respects. First, the decision to write a story about an Arab—or about anybody else, for that matter—reflects a desire to leave the "drawers" of his failings as father and husband unopened. His choice allows him to exercise an unquestioned fatherly authority over the protagonist he will author. Second, the choice of the Arab, a minority group member, seems particularly suitable in the case of the Israeli Jew who needs to reaffirm his potency. Such a displacement of his personal problems reaffirms his identity as a member of the ruling majority.

The arrogant tone of superiority in Bar-On's blueprint for his novel *seems* to reinforce his sense of authorial empowerment. In his plot, Bar-On plans to limit his Arab protagonist's freedom to the "boundaries of the permissible."[17] Furthermore, the Arab protagonist's state of loneliness reflects the breakup of his love affair with a Jewish woman, an "army officer's redhead." The "initial premise" of the novel is that "when the forbidden fruit is revealed," the husband will explode and the love "will never be realized." The trial over the woman's child will end in the decree "that everyone must return to his or her place" (*A* 92–93). This *seems* like a clear case of a stereotypical representation of an Arab by a Jew, except for the fact that this is not just Bar-On's story. As was mentioned earlier, the story of the love affair between Anton and Shlomith is also one of *Anton's* narratives. Indeed, Anton does not keep his love affair a secret from Bar-On. When the latter discloses to Anton his plan to cast him as his protagonist, Anton decides to "prepare an imaginary autobiography" for Bar-On's new novel. In this invented autobiographical story, Anton chronicles his "love for the redhead wife of an army officer, who was in throes of a legal battle with him over the fate of their son" (*A* 137). When the invented story turns out to be real, as attested by Shlomith's telegram, Anton once again shares his misfortune with Bar-On. Now he tells him about his letters to Shlomith, which fell into the hands of her husband, and about his loss of all hope for a reunion with his lover.

The baffling, winding, and unresolved trajectory of the love affair narrative raises a question that Shammas's fiction never answers: Is it the Israeli Jewish writer or, rather, the Israeli Arab writer who fathered the story about an illicit relationship between an Israeli Arab man and a Jewish woman? This question directs us to a similar unanswered question about the authorship of another narrative strand in the novel: Is it Michael Abyad or, rather, Anton who is the author of the "Tale"? It will be recalled that the "Tale" is Michael Abyad's "fictitious autobiography," which Michael wrote in Anton's name and which he hands over to Anton. Anton received from Michael the license to "*translate it,* adapt it, *add* or subtract" as he sees fit (*A* 259; emphasis added). If so, how much of the "Tale" can be attributed to Michael and how much of it is Anton's?

While never answered, these questions draw attention to Anton's fourfold role. He is both the protagonist and a coauthor of Michael's story, as well as both the prospective protagonist and the prospective coauthor of Bar-On's planned novel. The multiplicity of the roles demonstrates Anton's relational identity. As an Arab he could not have regained his Palestinian identity, which he had repressed all along, without the reemergence of Michael, his alter-ego and exiled Palestinian. Not could he have shaped his Israeli identity without the presence of Bar-On, the Israeli Jew who, as a Hebrew fellow writer, is in some respect also Anton's alter-ego. In the case of Michael's narrative, the collaborative authorship of the "Tale" indicates Anton's acceptance of the forgotten, Palestinian "half of his identity." Anton's final conjecture that Michael might have concluded the "Tale" with a paraphrase from Borges—"Which of the two of us has written this book I do not know" (*A* 259)—is particularly illuminating. It indicates that Anton, the translator and editor of his own story written in his name by an exiled Palestinian, has finally acknowledged the national identity he shares with the Palestinian dispersion.

An even more complicated picture emerges in the narrative strand involving the interaction between Anton and Bar-On. In contrast to Anton's and Michael's narrative, which ends in an awareness of the shared story/history of national identity, the relationship of Bar-On and Anton ends on a note of disjunction. Bar-On's story of the "educated" Arab does not materialize. In addition, his disgraceful behavior in Iowa City makes him return to his Israeli reality, which, as we have seen, is now marked by the terrible loneliness following his family's complete breakup. Surprisingly similar motifs characterize Anton's story. His relationship with Shlomith ends and the breakup restores Anton to his previous state of loneliness as an Israeli Arab, which Bar-On defines as "the greatest loneliness of all."

The parallel patterns of the stories of the Arab and the Jew end on a note of separation and alienation. The closure precludes the protagonists' mutual recognition of loneliness. Nonetheless, the fact that an interaction, however imperfect, unfriendly, and unfruitful, did take place cannot be denied. When one looks closely at the story of suspicion, mistrust, and rivalry, one discovers hopeful traces of ambivalence and regret over lost opportunities. Hardly satisfying our desire for a definite and optimistic closure, these hints nonetheless indicate a tenuous probability for an Arab-Jewish rapprochement.

I will conclude with a consideration of two brief episodes that may hold out some hope for the future. Has there ever been a time of openness and trust between the two characters? In light of the preceding discussion, it would be quite impossible to answer this question in the affirmative. Nevertheless, I suggest that the episode where Anton describes his feelings of rejection—he has been replaced by Paco as Bar-On's protagonist—is echoed in the episode of Bar-On's apology for his rejection of Anton as his protagonist.

Anton's sense of betrayal involves more than just a deep blow to his ego. The description of his feelings as that of *betrayal* also implies a breach of trust that Anton believed existed between him, an Israeli Arab, and Bar-On, an Israeli Jew. At the unique moment when he bares his soul, Bar-On admits that he has been deeply disturbed about the way he rejected Anton as his protagonist. Recall that he explained his rejection on the grounds of his inability to define Anton as his enemy, "at least not in the accepted sense of the word" (*A* 168). Bar-On confesses to Anton that "he thought a great deal about what he had said . . . [that] he feels bad about it . . . [and that] apparently he had touched upon an essential matter in the depths of his soul, which his conscience needed to clarify." Angry and suspicious, Anton does not allow this moment of openness to continue. While admitting to his own "lugubrious thoughts . . . in the wake of the incident," he cuts Bar-On short, telling him that "it looks as if each of us will have to deal with the problem separately, from his own point of view" (*A* 170).

Unfortunately, Anton's prediction proves true and, as already noted, each of the characters experiences separation and loneliness. It is, however, not without a sense of regret and ambivalence that they separate. A hitherto unacknowledged desire for affinity emerges in Anton's ambivalence about Bar-On's departure. Despite his triumph over Bar-On, Anton cannot rejoice. While admitting his deep dislike of Bar-On—"the bitter taste" that he left "in [his] mouth"— Anton cannot help feeling that a great opportunity has been lost: "I felt *as if I had missed something,* and even felt a few mild pangs of conscience, for perhaps I should have gotten closer to him—*however unlikely that was*—instead of spending my time trying to match my life with that of Michael Abyad" (*A* 202–3; emphasis added).[18]

"Unlikely" but not impossible. This remarkably insightful confession not only reminds us of Anton's relational identity both as a Palestinian Arab and as an Israeli minority citizen; it also emphasizes the indelible connection between the two. Anton's comment positions him not only in relation to Michael; it also makes him a connecting link between Michael and Bar-On. One must not forget that Anton has been given the ultimate editorial authority over Michael's story, which establishes him as a coauthor of this autobiographical story. This authority allows him to *translate* and *add* to the text on condition that Michael remain in the story. Thus, it is *Anton's* translation of Michael's story *into Hebrew* that determines its Israeli Jewish readership. At the same time, Anton *adds* the narrative of his failed interaction with Bar-On, which Michael could not have written. This narrative presents the Israeli Jewish readership with the complexity of the Israeli-Arab-Palestinian identity. At the same time, it presents the same readership with the missed—and therefore *possible*—opportunity of a dialogic interaction of an Israeli Arab with an Israeli Jew. In this sense, the likelihood of a future narrative of rapprochement of Israeli Jews and Israeli Arabs has not been entirely lost.

Epilogue

Longing for Hope

This study was conceived at the time of the Oslo Agreements, when hopes for peace were high. At its completion, however, the second Palestinian uprising, the intifada known as Al Aqsa, was raging and the failure of the meeting became tragically evident. The Israeli government, headed by Ariel Sharon, who was known for his intransigence and belligerence, watched as Palestinian suicide bombers killed innocent Jewish and Arab Israelis. The Israeli army retaliated by closing off Palestinian towns. A high-level commission was established to investigate the killings of thirteen Israeli Arabs by the Israeli police. As I watched all this with growing dismay, all prospects for peace were collapsing in the face of unspeakable aggression and hostility. It was the unabated hatred and brutality on both sides that affected me the most: the killing of the little Arab boy in his father's arms; the lynching of Israeli soldiers; the young Arabs hurling stones at Israelis and being shot at; funerals turning into riots of unbridled violence; Arab suicide terrorists detonating bombs on crowded buses and in packed restaurants; and Jewish settlers ferociously attacking the Palestinian population. Such scenarios were impossible to predict.

The reality of violence and destruction made it hard, if not impossible, to make a clear distinction between feelings of distress and pain at the political situation and the need for rational objectivity in scholarly research. The frustration over missed opportunities for peace and the dismay at the growing suffering of innocent people on both sides exacerbated my sense of futility with regard to this study. The acts of savagery seemed to be divesting it of meaning and validity. The reality that confronted me seemed to be answering in the negative the initial query that prompted my investigation: Can literature affect the political culture in which it has been produced? Specifically, in terms of the context of this study: What is the use of showing how literature attempted to counter the half century of conflict between Jews and Arabs? Can my search for dialogue in literature be meaningful in view of attacks, military actions, retaliations, and, above all, overwhelming irrational hatred for each other? How relevant is it to follow the protagonists, figments of the writers' imagination, as they endeavor to listen to the other in a reality whose brutality seems to belie even a semblance of rational thought?

The manifestations of unrestrained aggression raised the unavoidable question: Why, despite so many diplomatic efforts, has violence prevailed? Reasons and speculations of a *political* and *military* nature were discussed and analyzed ad infinitum in the media and other forums. There were other views, however, that projected a different perspective. These voices talked about the conflict as a manifestation of *psychological* patterns deeply embedded in the mind-sets of the adversaries. They argued that only when each side stopped seeing the other as an implacable enemy bent on its destruction could the acts of violence, hostility, and hatred possibly metamorphose into the language of peace negotiations. That is, only when each side understood *empathically* the fears of the other would it be possible to consider a relationship based on trust. The search for resolution in the psychological aspects of the conflict suggested to me that perhaps my quest for a dialogic connection in the literatures produced by the two peoples was of some merit after all. Was it possible that some people understood the importance of *listening* to the other that literature had been trying to communicate all along?

The willingness to listen to the other may yet transform the negative bonding of mistrust and hatred between Arabs and Jews. It suggests the possibility of breaking out of old patterns of thinking, moving forward, and abandoning deep-rooted stereotypical thinking. But how can such a transformation be accomplished? This is precisely the question that preoccupies the works of fiction I have examined. As I have shown, both Israeli Jewish and Israeli Arab literatures defied the Zionist politics of hostility toward the Arab by offering an alternative dialogue to the Zionist ideology of separation and its politics of domination.

The doctrine of the "negation of the Diaspora" projected deep fears that the Zionists tried to eliminate through the "poster image" of the "new" Jew—the *haluts* redeeming the "empty land." As history has shown, this politics of disavowal and suppression of the Arab presence in the land by no means made the fear and anxiety of annihilation disappear. If anything, the propagation of denial was exacerbated in wake of the 1967 war, manifesting itself in the rule of oppression in the occupied territories. Fueled by fear and hostility, the Israeli regime of domination evoked fears and hostility in the Arab population. As demonstrated in manifold acts of terrorism and the two intifadas, these feelings engendered horrific acts of aggression.

As this study has shown, literature foresaw the conflict at its embryonic stage. Suffice it to mention here Ahad Ha'Am's "Truth from Eretz Israel," Buber's *A Land of Two Peoples,* and Brenner's "From the Notebook." These texts, discussed in the first part of this study, astutely analyzed the reasons for the Zionist politics of domination toward the Arab in the land and accurately predicted the tragic implications of such politics. These predictions were corroborated by later Israeli Jewish fiction, such as Yizhar's "Hirbet Hizah," followed by the literature of the "new wave" writers. The Jewish literary perspective was reaffirmed in Israeli Arab texts, whose protagonists' existence under Israeli rule was shaped and distorted by fear, uncertainty, and suspicion. While characters like Saeed in Habiby's *The Pessoptimist,* Yossi in Mansour's *In a New Light,* and Anton in *Arabesques* chose to comply with the dominating regime at a terrible cost to their self-esteem, Arab characters like Walaa, Saeed's son in *The Pessoptimist,* Michael Abyad in *Arabesques,* and Yazdi in *The Smile of the Lamb* opted to struggle against fear and degradation.

Paradoxically, the fear that Jews and Arabs have engendered in each other produced an equalizing power of hatred that has allowed the Jewish oppressor to claim the status of victims, a claim that turned the oppressed Arab into a victimizer and thereby created a situation that justified the Jewish claim to victimhood. It is this vicious cycle of fear-generating-violence-generating-fear that the literature I have analyzed attempts to halt. The way out is predicated upon the recognition of the other's fears. In this sense, it is possible to argue that the emerging realization of the need for a psychological transformation, as expressed by some during ongoing crises (alongside unceasing declarations of belligerence and continual violence on both sides), was long ago anticipated in fiction. The fiction of both Jews and Arabs has taught us that although it entails an extremely complex process, breaking out of the cycle of violence is nonetheless possible. The readiness to *tell* one's story and to *listen* to the story of the other signifies mutual recognition, which alleviates fear. Attention to the story of the other signals the ability to transform the knot of violence into a dialogic interaction.

What, then, is the validity of *this* study of *these* literatures in the face of the reality of ongoing violence between Jews and Arabs? Its merit, I believe, lies not only in showing that these literatures have demonstrated a proleptic—perhaps even prophetic—capacity to anticipate history but in raising our consciousness concerning what these literatures wish to teach us about ourselves. They tell us not only about the potential to transform bonds of fear into bonds of peace but also that the responsibility to actualize this potential is ours.

A corroboration of these frail hopes came from an unexpected source following the completion of this study. Upon my arrival in Israel in the summer of 2002, I learned about a new book whose title and and whose authors' familiar names made me rush to purchase it. It was *The Stand Tall Generation: The Palestinian Citizens of Israel Today,* by Dan Rabinowitz and Khawla Abu Baker. The first part of the book tells the tragic story of the Israeli Arabs and describes the growing need of the younger generation to confront the situation and engage in social and political action for equality and justice. It is, however, the second part, entitled "The Story of Two Families," that presents a factual, "real-life" reaffirmation of my study. Here the two writers—Dan Rabinowitz, an Israeli Jew, and Khawla Abu Baker, an Israeli Arab—tell their respective life stories. The families of both writers settled in Haifa, where they were raised. Because the authors are about the same age and both families have lived in Haifa since the 1920s, the commonalities as well as the discrepancies between the two narratives are inescapable. The stories intertwine and complete each other by sharing the painful experiences of 1948, the suffering of Khawla's family, the prosperity of Dan's family, as well as both authors' growing consciousness of the continuing acts of injustice toward Arab Israeli citizens.

Implementing in "real" life the literary attempts to interact in a dialogue that I have examined in this study, Dan and Khawla confide in each other, and the confidence that they grant each other attests to the need for each other's empathic understanding. Like this study, their dialogue concludes on a very cautious note of optimism. Conscious of the worsening political situation, the authors admit, "The final lines of this book are being written with deep and disturbing insecurity. . . . The two communities which are bonded with each other's blood and soul have not yet digested [the recent developments]. . . . We conclude the book with longings for hope, but not knowing where to look for it."[1] Will the longing for hope transform into a realistically hopeful expectation for the future? Perhaps the attention that the two adversaries-friends pay to each other's story signals that the possibility of a dialogue between the warring societies still remains in the domain of the real.

Notes

Bibliography

Index

Notes

Prologue

1. I realize that some Israeli Arabs prefer to be called Palestinians, or Palestinian Arabs, while Israeli Jews call themselves Israelis. I chose to call the national groups Israeli Arabs and Israeli Jews to signal their common Israeli citizenship as members of the two ethnic groups—as opposed to Diaspora Jews and Palestinians who are not Israeli citizens—that reside in the State of Israel.

2. There are, of course, Israeli authors, both Jewish and non-Jewish, who write in languages other than Hebrew, such as Arabic, Polish, Russian, and Rumanian. I wish to thank Margalit Matitiahu, general secretary of the Israeli Federation of Writers' Union, for bringing these national literatures to my attention.

3. Stephen Greenblatt, "Culture," in *Critical Terms for Literary Study,* ed. Frank Lentricchia and Thomas McLaughlin (Chicago: University of Chicago Press, 1995), 227.

4. Yehoshua, Oz, and Grossman were born in Jerusalem; Yizhar was born in the agricultural colony of Rehovot.

5. Mansour was born in the Galilean village of Jish, Shammas was born in the Galilean village of Fassuta, and Habiby was born in Haifa.

6. There are other cases of ideological suppression. For the feminist aspect, see Naomi B. Sokoloff, "Gender Studies and Modern Hebrew Literature," in *Gender and Text in Modern Hebrew and Yiddish Literature,* ed. Naomi B. Sokoloff, Anne Lapidus Lerner, and Anita Norich (New York: Jewish Theological Seminary, 1992), 257–65; Sokoloff provides a comprehensive annotated bibliographical listing of literature. Yael Feldman treats the subject of women's Israeli literature and its struggle with the Zionist male chauvinist orientation in her book *No Room of Their Own: Gender*

291

and Nation in Israeli Jewish Fiction (New York: Columbia University Press, 1999). For the suppressed story of the Iraqi Jews who emigrated to Israel, see Nancy E. Berg, *Exile from Exile: Israeli Writers from Iraq* (Albany: State University of New York Press, 1996), and Ammiel Alcalay, *After Jews and Arabs: Remaking Levantine Culture* (Minneapolis: University of Minnesota Press, 1993). For cinematic mispresentations of the Sephardi Jews, see Ella Shohat, *Israeli Cinema: East/West and the Politics of Representation* (Austin: University of Texas Press, 1987). See also the critique of the "Zionist narrative" in the study by Yosefa Loshitzky, *Identity Politics on the Israeli Screen* (Austin: University of Texas Press, 2000).

7. Some scholars prefer the more "positive," perhaps less judgmental terms "Exile" or "Dispersion" in place of "Diaspora." I have borrowed the phrase "the negation of the Diaspora" from Ahad Ha'Am's 1909 essay "The Negation of the Diaspora," in which he presciently claims—contrary to the political Zionists—that the Diaspora will never disappear but that its national life "must be strengthened . . . by the creation of a fixed center for our national life in the land of its birth." In Arthur Herzberg, ed., *The Zionist Idea: A Historical Analysis and Reader* (New York: Atheneum, 1986), 276. I discuss Ahad Ha'Am's essay and his idea of the land as a cultural center in the first part of the study.

8. The slogan was invented by Anthony Ashley-Cooper, seventh earl of Shaftesbury in 1851 and was later popularized by Israel Zangwill. See Adam Garfinkle, *Politics and Society in Modern Israel: Myths and Realities* (Armonk, N.Y.: M. E. Sharpe, 1997), 44.

9. G. W. F. Hegel, *Phenomenology of Spirit,* trans. A. V. Miller (Oxford: Oxford University Press, 1977), 111.

10. My discussion does not include the fiction of Israeli Arabs written in Arabic, nor do I discuss the Israeli Druse writer and poet Naim Araydi, who writes in Hebrew. Araydi's only novel, *Tevilah katlanit* [A fatal christening] (Tel Aviv: Bitan, 1992), focuses on the problem of Druse-Christian intermarriage. Araydi does not touch on issues concerning Jews, Arabs, and Zionism, topics that are the main interest of this study. Since the completion of the present study, Sayed Qushu, an Israeli Arab, has published *Dancing Arabs* (Modan: Moshav Ben Shemen, 2002) in Hebrew.

Part 1. Zionism and the Discourses of Negation, Introduction

1. See especially chapter 10 in Chelouche's memoir *Parashat hayayi* [The story of my life], *1870–1930* (Tel Aviv: Strud and Sons, 1930), where he describes the founding of Tel Aviv and the enormous difficulties and complications encountered.

2. Adi Ophir, *Working for the Present: Essays on Contemporary Israeli Culture* (in Hebrew) (Tel Aviv: Hakibbutz Hameuchad, 2001), 259, 276.

3. Tom Segev, *The Seventh Million*, trans. Haim Watzman (New York: Hill & Wang, 1993); Benny Morris, *The Birth of the Palestinian Refugee Problem* (Cambridge: Cambridge University Press, 1988). See also: Boas Evron, *Jewish State or Israeli Nation* (Bloomington: Indiana University Press, 1995); Uri Ram, *The Changing Agenda of Israeli Sociology: Theory, Ideology, and Identity* (Albany: State University of New York Press, 1995); and Gershon Shafir, *Land, Labor and the Origins of the Israeli-Palestinian Conflict, 1882–1914* (Berkeley: University of California Press, 1996). Lawrence J. Silberstein's study *The Postzionism Debates: Knowledge and Power in Israeli Culture* (New York: Routledge, 1999) offers a summation of post-Zionist writing.

4. See, for example, the section "Zionist Dialectics" in *Israel Studies* 1, no. 1 (1996): 196–295, and the continuation of the debate in vol. 1, no. 2 (1996): 170–267. See also: Benny Morris, "The Eel and History: A Reply to Shabtai Teveth," *Tikkun* 5, no. 1 (March–April 1990): 19–22, 79–86; Shabtai Teveth's vituperative response to Segev's *The Seventh Million in Ben Gurion and the Holocaust* (New York: Harcourt Brace, 1966). Lastly, for Anita Shapira's view of the new trends as basically immature, see her "Politics and the Collective Memory: The Debate over the 'New Historians' in Israel," *History and Memory* 7, no. 1 (1995): 9–41. These are just a few examples of journalistic and academic polemical writings relating to the post-Zionist trend.

5. Ophir, *Working for the Present*, 261.

6. Criticism of post-Zionist scholars and their scholarship abounds. For example, noted veteran historian Jacob Katz has criticized the "new historians" in his essay "Historia v'historionim, hadashim kh'yeshanim" [History and historians, like new like old], *Alpayim* 12 (1996): 9–35. In the same issue of *Alpayim* Gershon Shaked denounces the new orientation of Israeli literary criticism in his review (51–73) of *Anu khotvim otakh moledet* [Narratives with no natives] by Yitzhak Laor (Tel Aviv: Hakibbutz Hameuchad, 1995). For criticism of new approaches in sociology, see Moshe Lissak, " 'Critical' Sociology and 'Establishment' Sociology in the Israeli Academic Community: Ideological Struggles or Academic Discourse?" *Israel Studies* 1, no. 1 (1996): 247–95.

7. One notable example—most of which emphasized the revisionist trend in Israel—was the series on Israel that appeared in the *New York Times* from 6 April 1998 to 30 April 1998. See especially the article published on 10 April 1998 entitled "Israel's History, Viewed Candidly, Starts a Storm: TV Series Shakes Myths of Founders."

8. To take one example, Anita Shapira has on many occasions dealt with the revision of Zionist representations of history. She claims that the critical approach to Israel's response to the Holocaust by such revisionist historians as Tom Segev, Idith Zartal, Amnon Raz-Krakotskin, Ilan Pappe, and Dany Rabinowitz "was to become one of the battering rams in attacks on the

Israeli entity," and that their criticism "tried to undermine the very legitimacy of the state." "The Holocaust: Private Memories, Public Memory," *Jewish Social Studies: History, Culture, and Society* 4, no. 2 (1998): 40, 54. In her earlier essay on the "new historians" she presents a more balanced view of "post-Zionism" in relation to the state, claiming that post-Zionism extends "from regarding [Israel] as a positive and even important phenomenon in Jewish history and human history in general . . . to a view, which, although accepting the fact that Israel exists, grants it no intrinsic value." "Politics and the Collective Memory," 11.

9. See, for instance, the appreciation of Benny Morris's balanced analysis of the 1948 war in Philip Mendes's article "Benny Morris, the Refugees, and Peace," *Response* 68 (fall 1997–winter 1998): 198–224. Mendes claims that Morris debunks the myth of the forcible exodus of the Palestinian refugees inflicted by the Israelis by insisting it was propagated by the Arabs (201). Conversely, again according to Morris as interpreted by Mendes, the myth of the voluntary exodus of the Palestinians instigated by the Arab states was actually propagated by the Israelis. At the same time, Morris never negates the legitimacy of the Zionist idea. His "position," Mendes emphasizes, "is essentially of moral relativism. The underlying assumption appears to be that the creation of a Jewish state in Palestine was a morally just objective irrespective of its impact on the Palestinian Arabs" (206).

10. My understanding gains support from Ilan Pappe, who claims that "in the scholarly world, the terms *anti-Zionist* and *Zionist* are largely a matter of self-definition. Among this group, the works of those who declare themselves Zionists are generally as antagonistic toward Zionism as those of authors openly calling themselves anti-Zionists." "Post-Zionist Critique on Israel and the Palestinians—Part 1: The Academic Debate," *Journal of Palestine Studies* 26, no. 2 (1997): 30.

11. Ophir claims that there are very few scholars in Israel whose post-Zionism means rejection of the Zionist vision and the Jewish state. *Working for the Present*, 258.

12. Eliezer Schweid, "Beyond All That—Modernism, Zionism, Judaism," *Israel Studies* 1, no. 1 (1966): 231–32, 224.

13. Schweid, "Beyond All That," 225.

14. Schweid is here referring to the Canaanite movement, established in the 1940s, which completely rejected Jewish tradition and claimed roots in the pre-biblical Canaan and its Hebrew heritage. Even though the Canaanites failed as a political movement, their ideological position influenced the formation of the native Israeli.

15. Eliezer Schweid, *Ha-tsionut she-aharei ha-tsionut* [Zionism in a post-modernistic era] (Jerusalem: Hassifria Haziyonit, 1996), 102.

16. See the following articles by Schweid on Zionism and its destiny today: "Meah sh'not 'tsionut m'dinit' u'ma hal'a?" [A hundred years of Zionism and what next?] *Hadoar* 77, no. 3 (12 December 1997): 5–7, and

77, no. 4 (26 December 1997): 5–7. "Ha'tsionut kh'tsurat z'khut yehudit b'zmanenu" [Zionism as a form of Jewish identity in our time], *Kivunim* 11–12 (1997): 29–35.

17. See, for instance, a recent article by Gad Ya'akobi, Israel's onetime ambassador to the United Nations and a former minister in several Israeli governments, entitled "Mitrahakim v'holkhim" (Getting further apart) *Hadoar* 77, no. 17 (10 July 1998): 4. Ya'akobi deplores the estrangement of Israeli Jews from the American Diaspora: "Instead of dialogic relationships and mutual respect, in Israel we hear statements addressed to American Jews such as 'We don't need your favors' and 'Make aliyah and the rest is your business,' which cause further estrangement."

18. For instance, as a Polish-Jewish magazine reported, on his recent visit to Poland to celebrate the fiftieth anniversary of the state, Israel's prime minister Benjamin Netanyahu told members of the Jewish community that Poland was dead for the Jews, and that their place was in Israel. "Netanyahu's Visit" (Polish) *Midrasz* 5 (May 1998): 29.

19. Quoted in *The Jew and the Modern World: A Documentary History*, ed. Paul Mendes-Flohr and Jehuda Reinharz (New York: Oxford University Press, 1995), 560–61.

1. Zionist Voices of Dissent

1. Indeed, this assumption is confirmed in an essay by Allan Arkush ("The Jewish State and Its Internal Enemies: Yoram Hazony Versus Martin Buber and His 'Ideological Children,'" *Jewish Social Studies* 7, no. 2 [2001]: 169–91) that appeared after the present study had been completed. The essay is a response to Hazony's book *The Jewish State* (New York: Basic Books, 2001). Hazony indicts Buber, Gershom Sholem, and other Brith Shalom intellectuals as the "fathers" of the post-Zionists who preach antinationalism, universalism, pluralism. According to Hazony, they are anti-Zionists. Though Arkush places himself in the camp of "old-style Zionists," he does not accept Hazony's argument against Buber and his fellow intellectuals. While he dismisses Hazony on the grounds of faulty and shallow reasoning, Arkush admits that "the adaptation of a century-old doctrine to new circumstances" is absolutely needed. This statement obviously refers to the emergence of post-Zionism, which, according to Arkush, draws upon Herzl's universalism, cosmopolitanism, and rejection of the Jewish tradition. If I understand Arkush correctly, he is claiming that in order to save Zionism we need to defend it against post-Zionists, who, according to him, are the followers of Herzl, the visionary founder of the Zionist state. It seems to me that this convoluted argumentation derives from an arbitrary categorization into old-time Zionists and post-Zionists. This unhealthy and damaging typology precludes a constructive debate regarding the burning issue of the Jewish state as a democracy.

2. See Anita Shapira's argument to this effect in "Politics and the Collective Memory," 28.

3. As Anita Shapira contends in "Ahad Ha'Am: ha-politika shel sublimatsia" [Ahad Ha'Am: the politics of sublimation], *Yehudim Hadashim Yehudim Yeshanim* [New Jews, old Jews] (Tel Aviv: Am Oved, 1997), it is not a coincidence that three biographies of Ahad Ha'Am have been published in the last decade. Shapira refers to Yosef Goldstein's *Ahad Ha'Am* (Jerusalem: Keter, 1992), Alfred Gottshalk's *Ahad Ha'Am v'ha-ruach ha-leumi* [Ahad Ha'Am and the national spirit] (Jerusalem: National Library, 1992), and Steven Zipperstein's *Elusive Prophet: Ahad Ha'am and the Origins of Zionism* (Berkeley: University of California Press, 1993). No less discussed are Buber and the cofounders of the Brith Shalom and Ichud movements. For current considerations of Buber and Brith Shalom see Tomis Kapitan, "Historical Introduction to Philosophical Issues," in *Philosophical Perspectives on the Israeli-Palestinian Conflict,* ed. Tomis Kapitan (Armonk, N.Y.: M. E. Sharpe, 1997); see also Gideon Shimoni, *The Zionist Ideology* (Hanover, N.H.: Brandeis University Press, 1995). Concerning Eliezer Schweid's ambivalence vis-à-vis post-Zionism, it is important to note his recourse to Brith Shalom as an example of a constructive critical approach to the Zionist movement. Schweid claims—with little justification—that unlike the post-Zionist dissension, Brith Shalom's opposition to the Zionist political line stayed within the confines of the classic Zionist ideology: "All the views that pointed to the solution of the external and internal problems in the implementation of the Zionist idea developed within the Zionist framework and not outside it. This is also true of the most extreme positions of Brith Shalom regarding the attitude of Zionism toward the Arabs." "L'mahuta u'l'reka shel ha-post tsionut" [Concerning the essence and background of post-Zionism], in *Post-Zionism and the Holocaust: The Role of the Holocaust in Public Debate on Post-Zionism in Israel, 1993–1996* (in Hebrew), ed. Dan Michman (Ramat Gan: Bar Ilan University, 1997), 289.

4. Quoted in *The Zionist Idea: A Historical Analysis and Reader,* ed. Arthur Herzberg (New York: Atheneum, 1968), 268; emphasis added.

5. The partition plan divided Palestine into a Jewish state, an Arab state, and an internationalized sector. The resolution, which passed in the United Nations despite the opposition of Arab countries, recognized the legitimacy of the Jewish state.

6. Quoted in Martin Buber, "Two Peoples in Palestine," *A Land of Two Peoples: Martin Buber on Jews and Arabs,* ed. Paul R. Mendes-Flohr (Gloucester, Mass.: Peter Smith, 1994), 195, 197, 199; emphasis added.

7. It is important to mention the eminent literary critic Baruch Kurzweil's (1907–1972) opposition to the Zionist desire to become a "nation like all nations." Despite his criticism of the secularism of Ahad Ha'Am, of Gershom Scholem, and especially of Buber, who was his teacher, Kurzweil agreed with these thinkers' resistance to the absorption of the Jewish nation into the

larger historical picture, or, as he called it, the historicization of the existence of Israel: "At the root of [Zionist] deeds and aspirations there is the desire to assimilate the life of the Jewish people to the life of all other nations. They have not noticed that it is precisely the pluralism of our anomalousness that is the source of our national life." *B'ma'avak al erkei ha-yahadut* [The struggle over Jewish values] (Tel Aviv: Schocken, 1969), 207.

8. Herzberg, *The Zionist Idea,* 268.

9. Ibid., 267.

10. Ibid., 276.

11. Menachem Brinker, *Narrative Art and Social Thought in H. Y. Brenner's Work* (in Hebrew) (Tel Aviv: Am Oved, 1990), 172.

12. Berdyczewski was quite aware of his predicament when he deplored the negative power of Jewish tradition, while at the same time recognizing its greatness: "When we defeat the past, it is we ourselves who are defeated. But if the past conquers, it is we, and our sons, and the sons of our sons, who are conquered. . . . Elixir and poison in one and the same substance." Quoted in Herzberg, ed., *The Zionist Idea,* 301.

13. Avner Holtzman, *Essays on Micha Yosef Berdyczewski* (in Hebrew) (Tel Aviv: Reshafim, 1993), 166.

14. Herzberg, *The Zionist Idea,* 295.

15. Berdyczewski describes the Jews as "yehudim mufshatim" (lit. "abstract Jews"). He seems to perceive the Jew as the proverbial luftmensch (lit. "man of air"), a Yiddish expression that captures the uprootedness of the Jews and their uncertain, "suspended," unproductive existence in the Diaspora.

16. I translate "yehudim ivrim" literally as "Hebrew Jews," an expression interchangeable with "new Jews" or "new Hebrews." These expressions are usually employed to depict the Zionist rebirth of the Jewish individual and to mark the contrast between the *haluts* and the "Diaspora Jew."

17. Berdyczewski, as quoted in Kurzweil, *B'ma'vak al erkei ha-yahadut,* 209–10.

18. On this point see Avner Holzman's essay, which concludes that although the Nietzschean component is present in Berdyczewski's thought, Nietzsche's concepts constituted only one element in a larger, independent vision of the Jewish future. "Hashpa'at Nietzsche b'yetsirato shel Micha Joseph Berdyczewski" [The influence of Nietzsche in the oeuvre of Micha Yoseph Berdyczewski], *Nietzsche, Zionism, and Hebrew Culture* (in Hebrew), ed. Jacob Golomb (Jerusalem: Hebrew University/Magnes Press, 2002), 173–79.

19. See Herzberg, *The Zionist Idea,* 295.

20. Menahem Brinker maintains that Ahad Ha'Am was ready to accept the Nietzschean notion of the superman "on condition that the progress of the individual will be measured by his achievements in the area of science and ethics, but not in the area of art and/or physical or military prowess."

"Nietzsche v'ha-sofrim ha-ivriim: nisaion l'q'r'iah khollelet" [Nietzsche and the Hebrew writers: Toward a global overview], in Golomb, *Nietzshe, Zionism, and Hebrew Culture,* 136.

21. Ahad Ha'Am, "The Transvaluation of Values," in *Nationalism and the Jewish Ethic: Basic Writings of Ahad Ha'Am,* ed. Hans Kohn (New York: Schocken, 1962), 173, 176, 178.

22. Ibid., 187.

23. Ahad Ha'Am, "Emet m'eretz Israel" [Truth from Eretz Israel], trans. Alan Dowty, *Israel Studies* 5, no. 2 (2000): 175–76.

24. Alan Dowty, "Much Ado about Little: Ahad Ha'am's 'Truth from Eretz Israel,' Zionism, and the Arabs" *Israel Studies* 5, no. 2 (2000): 157.

25. Buber, "A Letter to Hugo Bergman," in *A Land of Two Peoples,* 37.

26. Buber, "A Letter to Ghandi," in *A Land of Two Peoples,* 111–30.

27. See Paul Mendes-Flohr, "The Politics of Convenantal Responsibility: Martin Buber and Hebrew Humanism," in *Dialogue: The Essence of Buber,* ed. Joshua Stampfer (New York: J. Stampfer, 1988), 24–25.

28. Buber, "Nationalism," in *A Land of Two Peoples,* 54.

29. Ibid., 56.

30. In 1939 Buber berated himself for not having been even more pragmatic in publicizing his plan. The following quote proves how serious he was about the actual implementation of dialogic cooperation with the Arabs: "Everything I say here has already been said by me twenty years ago. . . . Nothing has been done. Today I accuse myself for having been deceived then by prejudice against publicity. . . . We held the decree of Zionist discipline higher than that of our own political understanding. That has proven to be a grave error." Buber, "Concerning Our Politics," in *A Land of Two Peoples,* 141.

31. Buber, "The Children of Amos," in *A Land of Two Peoples,* 253–54.

32. See for instance, Buber's letters to Ben-Gurion and Levi Eshkol, which he wrote in his old age, in which he argues for Arab rights, "Letter to Ben-Gurion on the Arab Refugees," in *A Land of Two Peoples,* 294–304.

33. See, for instance, Mark Tessler, who claims that the "the importance of Brith Shalom and other, smaller groups should not be overemphasized. . . . [T]he movement never struck a responsive chord among the Zionist public and remained a small and peripheral movement of opinion." *A History of the Israeli-Palestinian Conflict* (Bloomington: Indiana University Press, 1994), 182–83. Amos Elon concurs when he says that "the bi-national state was rejected by most Jews as it was by practically all Arabs." *The Israelis: Founders and Sons* (New York: Holt, Rinehart and Winston, 1971), 179.

34. See Gershon Shafir, "Ideological Politics or the Politics of Demography: The Aftermath of the Six-Day War," in *Critical Essays on Israeli Society, Politics, and Culture: Books on Israel,* vol. 2, ed. Ian S. Lustick and Barry Rubin (Albany: State University of New York Press, 1988): 44–45. See also the informative essay by Shalom Ratzbi, "Immigration and Majority in the Thought of the Central European Members of Brith Shalom" (in Hebrew), in *Ingathering of Exiles, Immigration to Eretz Israel: Myth and Reality* (in Hebrew), ed. Dvora Hacohen (Jerusalem: Zalman Shazar Center, 1997), 165–93. The essay discusses the politics of "majority" versus "many" that preoccupied the Yishuv. While Brith Shalom and Ihud claimed that the number of Jews in Eretz Israel should be determined in accordance with the Arab population, the Zionist authorities, represented by Ben-Gurion, aimed for majority of Jews in accordance with their plans for Jewish statehood.

35. Mendes-Flohr, "The Politics of Covenantal Responsibility," 24–26.

36. Take, for example, Buber's own admission in 1929 of the difficulties that he encountered due to his unpopular political views regarding the Arabs: "My opinion . . . on our relations with the Arab people has not changed. This is not a consistency that gives me joy; rather it causes me great anguish. Therefore I feel compelled to refute the charge of opportunism." "The National Home: A National Policy in Palestine," in *A Land of Two Peoples,* 83.

37. Buber, "Two Peoples in Palestine," 196.

38. Buber, "The National Home: A National Policy in Palestine," 84–86.

39. Yigal Zalmona, "Introduction," *To the East: Orientalism in the Arts in Israel,* (Jerusalem: Israel Museum, 1998), vi.

40. Quoted in Joel Greenberg, "Israel's History, Viewed Candidly, Starts a Storm," *New York Times,* 10 April 1998, 8. See also Ilan Pappe's review essay "Israeli Television's Fiftieth Anniversary 'T'kumma' Series: A Post-Zionist View?" *Journal of Palestine Studies* 26, no. 4 (1998): 99–105. In view of the outbreak of Intifada Al-Aqsa, Caspi seems to have become less liberal when he claims that the Israeli Arabs "joined the war against us. . . . [T]he conclusion to be drawn is . . . even today the Arabs are not willing to compromise on our existence here." *Jerusalem Report,* 6 November 2000, 14.

41. Buber, "The National Home: a National Policy in Palestine," 82.

42. Ibid., 86, 87.

43. Buber, "Hebrew Humanism," quoted in Herzberg, ed., *The Zionist Idea,* 460.

44. Buber, "At this Late Hour," in *A Land of Two Peoples,* 91.

45. Martin Buber, *The Knowledge of Man,* trans. Maurice Friedman and Ronald G. Smith (London: George Allen, 1965), 85.

46. Baruch Kimmerling, "Al da'at ha-maqom . . . al historia hevratit

v'al antropologia ha- m'gayeset-atzma shel Israel" [On the knowledge of the place . . . About social history and about Israel's propagandist anthropology] *Alpayim* 6 (1992): 65; emphasis added.

47. Buber, "The National Home: A National Policy in Palestine," 89–90.

48. Ibid., 88.

49. Buber, "A Proposed Resolution on the Arab Question," in *A Land of Two Peoples,* 61.

50. Gershon Shafir, "Zionism and Colonialism: A Comparative Approach," *Israel in Comparative Perspective: Challenging the Conventional Wisdom,* ed. Michael N. Barnett (Albany: State University of New York Press, 1996), 230, 233. According to Shafir, the threefold aim of a pure settlement colony was "control of land, employment that ensured an [*sic*] European standard of living, and massive immigration," 235.

51. Shafir, *Land, Labor,* 218.

52. Jay Y. Gonen, *Psycho-History of Zionism* (New York: New American Library, 1975), 180.

53. Susan Slymovics, *The Object of Memory: Arab and Jew Narrate the Palestinian Village* (Philadelphia: University of Pennsylvania Press, 1998), 30.

54. Barbara J. Smith, *The Roots of Separatism in Palestine: British Economic Policy, 1920–1929* (Albany, N.Y.: Syracuse University Press, 1993), 13–14, 181. Smith's findings regarding the British preference for the Jews are also applicable on the administrative level. As Adam Garfinkle maintains, "For at least the first ten years of the British Mandate, government policies greatly favored the Zionist enterprise. . . . Zionists populated the British administration at nearly every level. The country's infrastructure improved markedly, which helped the Zionists who were building a nationwide movement." *Politics and Society in Modern Israel,* 46. Tom Segev reaches similar conclusions in his study *One Palestine, Complete: Jews and Arabs under the British Mandate,* trans. Haim Watzman (New York: Metropolitan Books, 2000).

55. Buber, "Concerning Our Politics," 138–39.

56. Ibid., 138, 141; emphasis added.

57. Ibid., 139; emphasis added.

58. Suffice it to recall here the 1956 Sinai Campaign when Israel joined France and Britain in the capturing of the Suez Canal. I discuss this event in more detail later.

59. Maxime Rodison, *Israel: A Colonial-Settler State* (New York: Monad, 1973), 91. An even more vituperative criticism of Zionism as an imperialist agent is expressed by Abdelwahab M. Elmessiri, who calls Israel "a vassal Jewish state" and claims that "in implanting and backing white settlers in South Africa and Zionist settlers in Palestine, the British Empire was founding two little pockets of settler-colonists who would owe allegiance to

the imperial metropolis and would serve as bases of operation when the need arose." *The Land of Promise: A Critique of Political Zionism* (New Brunswick, N.J.: North American, 1977), 101.

60. Edward W. Said, *The Question of Palestine* (New York: Vintage, 1979), 60.

61. Ibid., 69.

62. Ibid., 87.

63. Ibid., 72; emphasis added.

64. Ibid., 81–82. The notion of the "empty land" is indeed a colonial concept widely accepted by nineteenth-century historians, who tended to disregard the native peoples of the colonized lands. For example, eliminating the native peoples from his picture of America, Frederick Jackson Turner saw the place as "virgin soil," an "unexploited wilderness," and an "unoccupied territory." "Western State-Making in the Revolutionary Era," *American Historical Review* 1 (October 1985): 70–72.

65. Prov. 30:22.

66. Hegel, *Phenomenology of Spirit,* trans. A. V. Miller (Oxford: Oxford University Press, 1977), 113. I discuss Hegel's concept of the interaction between lord and bondsman more fully in the third part of this study.

67. Buber, "Concerning Our Politics," 140.

2. The Zionists

1. See Ben-Gurion's speech "The Imperatives of the Jewish Revolution," in Herzberg, ed., *The Zionist Idea,* 606–19.

2. Ben-Gurion, "On the Arab Question" (January 7, 1937), in Mendes-Flohr and Reinharz, eds., 604, 605.

3. Ibid., 604.

4. Ibid., 607–8.

5. Ze'ev Tzahor, "David Ben-Gurion's Attitude Toward the *Gola* (Diaspora) and Aliyah" (in Hebrew), in Hacohen, ed., *Ingathering of Exiles,* 139.

6. Homi K. Bhabha claims that "colonial mimicry is the desire for a reformed, recognizable Other," that is, the desire to turn the colonized into "the same but not quite." This ambivalence turns the colonial subject into a partial or incomplete presence. *The Location of Culture* (London: Routledge, 1994), 86.

7. Bhabha's concept of mimicry further develops Albert Memmi's classic definition of the colonized-colonizer relationships. Memmi refers specifically to the Diaspora Jews, whom he sees as the colonized and who, he claims, "endeavor to resemble the colonizer in the frank hope that he may cease to consider them [the Jews] different from him. Hence their efforts to forget the past, to change the collective habits, and their enthusiastic adoption of Western language, culture and customs. But if the colonizer does not always openly discourage their aspiration to develop that resemblance, he never

permits to attain it either." *The Colonizer and the Colonized,* trans. Howard Greenfeld (Boston: Beacon Press, 1991), 15. In a sense Bhabha's and Memmi's views complement each other; the former presents the incomplete process of assimilation of the colonized from the colonizer's point of view, whereas the latter describes the incessant and ultimately unsatisfying pursuit of assimilation on the part of the colonized.

8. Bhabha, *The Location of Culture,* 86.

9. Jacques Kornberg reminds us that "by the fifteenth century [Jews] were the only non-Christian people living in Europe." *Theodor Herzl: From Assimilation to Zionism* (Bloomington: Indiana University Press, 1993), 18.

10. For an insightful historical analysis of Jewish adherence to the concept of *Bildung,* see George L. Mosse, *German Jews Beyond Judaism* (Bloomington: Indiana University Press, 1985). On the same subject, see the analysis of *Bildung* and cultural Zionism in Paul Mendes-Flohr, "Cultural Zionism's Image of the Educated Jew: Reflections on Creating a Secular Jewish Culture," *Modern Judaism* 18, no. 3 (1998): 227–41.

11. According to Sandor L. Gilman, "Even as one distances oneself from . . . oneself, there is always the voice of the power group saying, Under the skin you are really like them anyhow. The fragmentation of identity that results is the articulation of self-hatred." *Jewish Self-Hatred: Anti-Semitism and the Hidden Language of the Jews* (Baltimore: Johns Hopkins University Press, 1986), 3.

12. For instance, in 1937 Henri Bergson wrote: "My reflections have led me closer and closer to Catholicism, in which I see the complete fulfillment of Judaism." Bergson did not convert because of his sense of solidarity with the Jewish people in view of the increasing threat of the Nazi persecution. Quoted in Jacob C. Agus, *Jewish Identity in an Age of Ideologies* (New York: Frederick Ungar, 1978), 235. Of special interest in this context is Herzl's pre-*Judenstaadt* proposals of intermarriage and of Jewish mass conversion to end the anti-Semitic treatment of Jews and liberate them from their inferior status. See Kornberg, *Theodor Herzl,* 24.

13. The Damascus affair brought home to Western Jews the need for communal solidarity, leading to the establishment of the Alliance Israelite Universelle. This show of solidarity gave impetus to the innovative ideas of Rabbis Yehuda Alkalai and Zvi Hirsch Kalisher, the precursors of Zionism, centering on a return to the Jewish homeland. (Shimoni, *The Zionist Ideology,* 76). The pogroms of 1881 changed Leo Pinsker's view of the future. Abandoning his hope to russify the Jews, he concluded that Jews needed a place of their own. Pinsker expressed his ideological conversion to Jewish nationalism in the pamphlet *Auto-Emancipation* (1882), the first important Zionist statement, and eventually became the leader of the Hovevei Tsion movement, chairing its founding conference in 1884. Though anecdotal, the story about Herzl's conversion to Zionism while covering the Dreyfus trial

is nonetheless instructive. While historians have demonstrated that Herzl was preoccupied with Jewish nationalism long before the Dreyfus trial (see Shimoni, *The Zionist Ideology,* 89; Kornberg, *Theodor Herzl,* 2–3), the radicalism of the controversy that split France as a result of the trial galvanized Jewish public opinion and paved the way for Herzl's Zionism. The Kishinev pogroms furthered the consolidation of the Zionist movement. Hayyim Nahman Bialik's famous poem "In the City of Slaughter," a powerful indictment of Jewish passivity and submission to anti-Semitic persecutions, raised public awareness of the Jewish plight and contributed to the establishment of Hashomer, the first Jewish self-defense organization. See Mendes-Flohr and Reinharz, eds., *The Jew and the Modern World,* 411.

14. For the history of the Bund, see Calvin Goldscheider and Alan S. Zuckerman, *The Transformation of the Jews* (Chicago: University of Chicago Press, 1984), 129–33.

15. These days the term "transfer" is used in Israel quite often. It designates the wishful thinking of right-wing Jewish Israelis to get rid of the Arab population by "transferring" it from the occupied territories to some unspecified destinations.

16. See the firsthand testimonies of Zionist officials who were involved in purchasing the land—and their ingenious and not always straightforward methods of making the Arabs sell the land—in Hadara Lazar, *In and Out of Palestine* (in Hebrew) (Jerusalem: Keter, 1990), 74ff.

17. Zeev Sternhell sees the "hatred of the Diaspora as one of the building blocks of Zionist thought. . . . No one could have possibly surpassed the founding fathers in their excessive repugnance toward their people, their contempt for the latter's weaknesses and way of life. . . . These tough people did not wallow in self-pity. Their depictions of the Diaspora were often as bad as those of the worst anti-Semites." *Nation Building or a New Society? The Zionist Labor Movement [1904–1940] and the Origins of Israel* (in Hebrew) (Tel Aviv: Am Oved, 1995), 62.

18. Theodor Herzl, *The Jewish State* (New York: Dover, 1988), 92.

19. In Herzberg, ed., *The Zionist Idea,* 350. The idea of Jews as "the Christ among nations" was accepted at the time. As Hedva Ben-Israel notes, Hans Kohn maintained that the Jewish people were chosen to suffer, as did Buber and Christian Zionists. "Reflections on Zionist History," in *The Age of Zionism* (in Hebrew), ed. Anita Shapira, Jehuda Reinharz, and Jay Harris (Jerusalem: Zalman Shazar Center for Jewish History, 2000), 27.

20. In Herzberg, ed., *The Zionist Idea,* 612.

21. David Vital, "Zionism as Revolution? Zionism as Rebellion?" *Modern Judaism* 18, no. 3 (October 1998): 211.

22. Herzl, *The Jewish State,* 85.

23. In Herzberg, ed., *The Zionist Idea,* 235.

24. Herzl, *The Jewish State,* 83, 157.

25. Ibid., 86.

26. Ibid., 135.

27. Michael Gluzman offers an analysis of Herzl's utopian novel about the Jewish state wherein he demonstrates that the national project of the Jewish state was, to a large extent, an attempt to turn the melancholic and effeminate Jew into a "truly" manly figure. Gluzman shows that the Jew Loewenberg was able to attach himself to a young woman in Palestine only after he had succeeded in creating a long-lasting and close relationship with Kingscourt, a Viennese aristocrat and former officer. This friendship enables him to grow into a "real" man. "Longing for Heterosexuality: Zionism and Sexuality in Herzl's *Altneuland*" (in Hebrew), *Theory and Criticism: An Israeli Forum* 11 (1997): 145–63.

28. Kornberg, *Theodor Herzl,* 182.

29. Theodor Herzl, *Altneuland: Old-New Land,* trans. Paula Arnold (Haifa: Haifa Publishing Co., 1960), 80.

30. As Boyarin sees it, Herzl's utopia demonstrates "the logic of Zionism, which contends that if the Jews succeed in proving their virility to the Germans by turning into colonialists, the Germans will accept the equality of Jews." "Colonial Drug: Zionism, Gender, and Mimicry" (in Hebrew), *Theory and Criticism* 11 (1997): 139.

31. Herzl, *Altneuland,* 217.

32. Shlomo Avineri, "Darkho shel Herzl l'gibush toda'ah leumit yehudit" [Herzl's way toward consolidation of Jewish national consciousness] *Alpayim* 15 (1997): 256.

33. All quotations are from Yosef Haim Brenner, *Khol khitvei Y. H. Brenner* [Complete works of Y. H. Brenner] (Tel Aviv: Ha-Kibbutz Hameuchad, 1960), 212. Translations from the Hebrew are partly mine and partly based on the translation provided by Ariel Hirschfeld in his essay "My Peace unto You, My Friend," *Palestine-Israel Journal* 2 (1994): 112–18.

34. See, for instance, Yaacov Shavit, *The Hebrew Nation: A Study in Israeli Heresy and Fantasy* (London: Frank Cass, 1987), 123.

35. From Hirschfeld, "My Peace Unto You," 113.

36. Ibid., 113–14.

37. Ibid., 114.

38. Ibid.

39. In a paper entitled "Ideology, Authorized Reading and Translation: The Case of Brenner's 'From a Notebook,'" presented at the International Conference on Hebrew Language, Literature and Culture, Ben-Gurion University of the Negev, Beer Sheva, July 2–4, 2002, Dr. Rivka Maoz sums up the earlier interpretations of the text. She claims that by sanctifying Brenner as the martyr of implacable Arab hatred, these interpretations reflect an ideological appropriation of Brenner.

40. Edna Amir Coffin, "The Image of the Arab in Modern Hebrew Literature," *Michigan Quarterly Review* 21 (1982): 323.

41. Waren Bargad, "The Image of the Arab in Israeli Literature," *Hebrew Annual Review* 1 (1977): 54.

42. Hirschfeld, "My Peace Unto You," 118.

43. In the third part of the present study I discuss more fully other aspects of transference in Freud and Lacan. Here I limit myself to repetition and remembrance.

44. Sigmund Freud, "Further Recommendation in the Technique of Psychoanalysis: Recollection, Repetition and Working Through," *Therapy and Technique,* ed. Philip Rieff (1914; reprint, New York: Collier, 1963), 161, 162, 164.

45. Quoted in Brinker, *Narrative Art and Social Thought,* 157.

46. In Herzberg, ed., *The Zionist Idea,* 307, 311.

47. Shavit, *The Hebrew Nation,* 10, 6.

48. James S. Diamond, *Homeland or Holy Land? The Canaanite Critique of Israel* (Bloomington: Indiana University Press, 1986), 6.

49. The manifesto of the Canaanite movement, which did not conceal its utmost contempt for the Diaspora Jew, was published in 1944, when the atrocity of the Holocaust had been revealed to all. See Shavit, *The Hebrew Nation,* 1.

50. Ibid., 121, 125.

51. As Boas Evron explains, the Canaanite leaders criticized the Israeli government for not extending the 1948 war to densely populated Arab areas. They believed that the Hebrew nation "would be achieved not by cultural influence and propaganda but by war and conquest, in the wake of which the Hebrew nation would forcibly impose Hebrew culture and nationhood on all the peoples of the Land of Kedem." *Jewish State or Israeli Nation?* 215.

52. Shavit, *The Hebrew Nation,* 124.

53. Quoted in Diamond, *Homeland or Holy Land?,* 67; emphasis added.

54. Quoted in Shavit, *The Hebrew Nation,* 124.

55. Shimoni, *The Zionist Ideology,* 318.

56. For a concise description of the inferior status of Israeli Arab citizens, see Rebecca Kook, "Between Uniqueness and Exclusion: The Politics of Identity," in Barnett, ed., *Israel in Comparative Perspective,* 199–227.

57. Michael Berkowitz, *Zionist Culture and West European Jewry before the First World War* (Cambridge: Cambridge University Press, 1993), 47.

58. Quoted in Amnon Rubinstein, *The Zionist Dream Revisited: From Herzl to Gush Emunim and Back* (New York: Schocken, 1984), 4. "Yid" is an extremely pejorative, anti-Semitic slur for an eastern European Jew.

59. Max Nordau, "Jewry of Muscle," in Mendes-Flohr and Reinharz, eds., *The Jew in the Modern World,* 547–58. Bar Kochba (the leader of the last revolt against the Romans in 135 B.C.E.) was the name of the Jewish gymnastics club founded in Berlin in 1898.

60. For the cultivation of the Bar Kokhba myth in the Yishuv and, later, in the state, see Yael Zerubavel, *Recovered Roots: Collective Memory and the Making of Israeli National Tradition* (Chicago: University of Chicago Press, 1995).

61. Berkowitz, *Zionist Culture,* 107.

62. *Mauschel* is a pejorative nickname for Moses, a common anti-Semitic description of the Jewish businessman. In his 1897 article "*Mauschel*" Herzl attacked anti-Zionists while resorting to the worst anti-Semitic tradition. See Theodor Herzl, *Zionist Writings: Essays and Addresses,* trans. Harry Zohn (New York: Herzl Press, 1973), 163–65.

3. The Land as Homeland?

1. Zali Gurevitch and Gideon Aran, "Al ha-maqom (antropologia israe-lit)" [About the Place: Israeli Anthropology], *Alpayim* 4 (1991): 22, 11, 9. This controversial essay tries to show that "even in the Zionist era . . . the distance between the Israeli and the land did not diminish. The distance is internal—a kind of reluctance to integrate totally in the land." The notion that the Jewish people are inherently nomadic and that even Zionism was not capable of effacing the sense of ambivalence about permanent location elicited criticism, most notably from Baruch Kimmerling, who emphasized the concreteness of the land and its Arab inhabitants. For a cogent summary of this discussion, see Risa Domb, *Home Thoughts from Abroad: Distant Visions of Israel in Contemporary Hebrew Fiction* (London: Valentine Mitchell, 1995), 7–8, 15 n. 25.

2. Hannah Naveh, *Men and Women Travellers: Travel Narratives in Modern Hebrew Literature* (in Hebrew) (Tel Aviv, Israel: Ministry of Defense, 2002), 53, 58, 60.

3. Amnon Raz-Krakotzkin, "Exile within Sovereignty: Toward a Critique of the 'Negation of Exile' in Israeli Culture" (in Hebrew), *Theory and Criticism* 4 (1993): 46.

4. For a comprehensive discussion of these writers, see Gila Ramraz-Rauch, *The Arab in Israeli Literature* (Bloomington: Indiana University Press, 1989).

5. See A. D. Gordon and his philosophy of the "religion of labor," which emphasized farming as indispensable to the organic connection between the Jewish people and the land. Some of his writings are reprinted in Herzberg, ed., *The Zionist Idea,* 369–86.

Part 2. Dissenting Literatures and the Literary Canon, Introduction

1. Avner Holtzman, "Hebrew Literature and the 'Culture of Controversy' in the Zionist Movement, 1897–1902," in Shapira, Reinharz, and Harris, eds., *The Age of Zionism,* 160, 162, 165.

2. A. B. Yehoshua, *The Terrible Power of a Minor Guilt* (in Hebrew) (Tel Aviv: Yediot Aharonot, 1998), 182. The lectures include the biblical story of Cain and Abel, Euripides, Camus, Dostoevsky, Faulkner, and Carver; the Hebrew writers include Brenner and Agnon.

3. Ran Edelist, "Sifrut u'musar: al sifro he-hadash shel A. B. Yehoshua, *Khoha ha-Nora shel ashma k'tana*" [Literature and morality: About the new book by A. B. Yehoshua, The terrible power of a minor guilt] *Moznaim* 73, no. 6 (March 1999): 58.

4. It is obvious that in his indictment of Yehoshua and other Israeli Jewish writers Edelist is not referring to the phrase as Julien Benda intended in his famous treatise *La Trahison des clercs* (1972), in which he criticized the intellectuals for getting involved in the realm of politics. Rather, the critic uses the term in the same way as Buber, who claimed that Benda's contention is the true betrayal of the function that an intellectual must play in society: "The betrayal of the intellectuals cannot be atoned for by the intellect's retreating into itself, but only by proffering to reality true service in place of false." Buber, *The Land of Two Peoples*, 103. In a not altogether different context Edward Said calls the "trahison des clercs" the "ideology of difference," that is, the attitude of Western intellectuals toward the Israeli-Palestinian conflict, which legitimizes Israel's politics of oppression. Said sees the betrayal of the intellectuals in their biased position, which precludes objectivity. See his article "An Ideology of Difference," *Critical Inquiry* 12 (1985): 38–58. It is worth mentioning here Mahmoud Darwish's definition of the role of the intellectual with regard to the Israeli-Palestinian conflict. Darwish distinguishes three conceptions that should guide the intellectual. The first is knowledge of self and other. The second is the dialogue that must develop, since Israel and Palestine "have a shared future." The third is normalization, which, as Darwish sees it, is not possible so long as the "the Palestinian land and some Arab lands are still occupied." "Palestine: The Imaginary and the Real," in *Innovation in Palestinian Literature: Testimonies of Palestinian Poets and Writers,* trans. Abdul-Fattah Jabr (London: Ogarit Centre for Publication and Translation, 2000), 25, 6.

5. In his socio-psychological study of Herzl, Jacques Kornberg shows that, although Herzl was convinced of Dreyfus's innocence quite early, Herzl's dramatic revelation in 1899 that the trial converted him to Zionism intended to construct the prophetic image that he wished to project. According to Kornberg, Herzl's Zionism resulted from years of inner struggle and ambivalence much before the trial (Kornberg, *Theodor Herzl,* 190–200). Nonetheless, I would suggest that, even if only a legend, Herzl's affirmation of his "conversion" as a result of the Dreyfus trial indicates his affinity with social revolutionaries, such as Zola. The Zionist enterprise clearly identifies Herzl as an intellectual who changed history.

6. Max Likin, "Rights of Man, Reasons of State: Emile Zola and Theodor Herzl in Historical Perspective," *Jewish Social Studies* 8, no. 1 (2000): 145.

4. Israeli Jewish Fiction of Dissent

1. For critical discussions of the representations of the Arab in Israeli literature, see Ramraz-Rauch, *The Arab in Israeli Literature,* and Risa Domb, *The Arab in Hebrew Prose, 1911–1948* (London: Vallentine, Mitchell, 1982); for theatrical dramatizations of the Palestinian issue, see Dan Urian, *The Arab in Israeli Theatre* (in Hebrew) (Tel Aviv: Or-Am, 1996); for cinematic treatments see Shohat, *Israeli Cinema,* and Loshitzky, *Identity Politics on the Israeli Screen.* See also the following articles: Gershon Shaked, "The Arab in Israeli Fiction," *Ariel* 54 (1983): 74–85; Shimon Levi, "Sh'vuyim b'bidion: ha-aravim B'sifrut ha-ivrit he-hadashah" [Hostages of fiction: Arabs in Israeli modern fiction] *Moznaim* 57 (October–November 1983): 70–73; Gilead Morahg, "New Images of Arabs in Israeli Fiction," *Prooftexts* 6 (1986): 147–62; Edna Amir Coffin, "The Image of the Arab in Modern Hebrew Literature."

2. The rich body of critical literature on this fiction includes: Nurith Gertz, *Captive of a Dream: National Myths in Israeli Culture* (in Hebrew) (Tel Aviv: Am Oved, 1988); Gershon Shaked, *A New Wave in Israeli Fiction* (in Hebrew) (Merhavia and Tel Aviv: Sifriat HaPoalim, 1970); Avraham Balaban, *Between God and Beast: An Examination of Amos Oz's Prose* (University Park: Pennsylvania State University Press, 1986); Yair Mazor, *Somber Lust: The Art of Amos Oz,* trans. Margaret Weinberger-Rotman (Albany: State University of New York Press, 2002); and Ibrahim Taha, *The Smile of an Opsimistic Lover: A Comparative Reading of the Hebrew and Palestinian Novel in Israel* (in Hebrew) (Tel Aviv: Hakibbutz Hameuchad, 1999).

3. With the exception of Yehoshua's novel *The Lover,* these texts are compared with the Arab texts in the third part of the present study. *The Lover* is discussed in this second part in terms of its canonical reception.

4. Hannan Hever, a noted literary scholar, has analyzed Yehoshua's "Facing the Forests," Oz's "Nomad and Viper," and Amalia Kahana-Carmon's "Heart of Summer, Heart of Light." Hever claims that these works belong to "the literary canon—that group of literary texts which has risen to a special eminence in the particular culture. . . . They are officially promulgated by the establishment; they can count on an automatic endorsement, or at least a certificate of legitimacy, from prestige literary criticism; and of course they dominate our high school and university curricula." See his article "Minority Discourse of a National Majority: Israeli Fiction of the Early Sixties," *Prooftexts* 10 (1990): 129–47. While he refers to only two of the writers I discuss, his definition of the canon undoubtedly extends to Grossman as well. In my discussion of Yehoshua and Oz in the third part of this study I show how Hever's view of these authors complies with the patterns of canonization. For the problems of canonization of Hebrew literature see also, Michael Gluzman, *The Politics of Canonicity: Lines of Resis-*

tance in Modernist Hebrew Poetry (Stanford, Calif.: Stanford University Press, 2003). Gluzman's study was published after my book was completed. Gluzman examines the issue of exclusion from the canon, whereas I focus on the politics of inclusion.

5. See Ben-Gurion, "The Imperatives of the Jewish Revolution," in Herzberg, ed., *The Zionist Idea,* 613.

6. Yosef Gorni, "Hirhurim al ha-tsionut kh'ideologia utopit" [Thoughts on Zionism as a utopian ideology], *Alpayim* 18 (1999): 201.

7. On this point see Yaffah Berlovitz's study *Inventing a Land, Inventing a People* (in Hebrew) (Tel Aviv: Hakibbutz Hameuchad, 1996). Focusing on the cultural and literary patterns of the first *alyiah* (1881–82), it argues that the exclusionary characteristics of the "new man," the "new people," and the "new land" were established by the literature of the first pioneering settlers. On the struggle for the domination of the Hebrew language, the search for a "new" Jewish culture, and the rejection of the cultural tradition of the Diaspora, see in particular the chapter "M'd'fusei ha-Sifrut l'd'fusei ha-tarbut" [From literary patterns to patterns of culture], 199–234.

8. Fredric Jameson, *The Political Unconscious: Narrative as a Socially Symbolic Act* (Ithaca, N.Y.: Cornell University Press, 1981), 9, 10.

9. Derek Attridge, "Oppressive Silence: J. M. Coetzee's *Foe* and the Politics of Canon," in *Decolonizing Tradition: New Views of Twentieth-Century "British" Literary Canons,* ed. Karen R. Lawrence (Urbana: University of Illinois Press, 1992), 215, 117.

10. Ibid., 216.

11. Not everybody would agree with this differentiating statement. See, for instance, Edward Said's sarcastic comment: "All liberals, and even most 'radicals,' have been unable to overcome the Zionist maneuver of equating anti-Zionism with anti-Semitism. Any well-meaning person can thus oppose South African or American racism and tacitly support Zionist racial presentation of non-Jews in Palestine." "Zionism from the Standpoint of Its Victims," *Dangerous Liaisons: Gender, Nation, and Postcolonial Perspectives,* ed. Anne McClintock, Aamir Mufti, and Ella Shohat (Minneapolis: University of Minnesota Press, 1997), 19. See also the poster by Uri Davis, an Israeli Jewish artist, which reads "Israel: An Apartheid State," reproduced in Dan Rabinowitz, "Uri Davis" (in Hebrew) [special issue: "Fifty to Forty-eight: Critical Moments in the History of the State of Israel"] *Theory and Criticism* 12–13 (1999): 171.

12. If the designation "Jewish" sounds redundant, one should remember that certain Christian groups see themselves as Zionists, in that they support the Jewish Zionist settlement in the Holy Land as a harbinger of the Second Coming. The additional distinction of "Israeli" is necessary because Christians or, for that matter, Jews who see themselves as Zionists are not necessarily Israeli citizens.

13. Ziva Shamir, "Diokan ha-historion shel ha-sifrut kh'bore m'tsiut"

[Portrait of the historian of literature as a creator of reality] *Moznaim* 73.11 (August 1999) 5, 6; parentheses in original; emphasis added.

14. Gershon Shaked, *Literature Then, Here and Now* (in Hebrew) (Tel Aviv: Zemora-Bitan, 1993), 50, 53.

15. Shaked, *A New Wave in Israeli Fiction,* 196.

16. Ibid.

17. Ibid., 187.

18. Menakhem Perry, "The Israeli-Palestinian Conflict: A Metaphor in Recent Israeli Fiction," *Poetics Today* 7, no. 4 (1986): 605, 609.

19. Gershon Shaked, *Wave after Wave in Hebrew Narrative Fiction* (in Hebrew) (Jerusalem: Keter, 1985), 181.

20. Ibid., 185.

21. Shaked, *A New Wave in Hebrew Fiction,* 140.

22. Gershon Shaked, *No Other Place: On Literature and Society* (in Hebrew) (Tel Aviv: Hakibbutz Hameuchad, 1988), 77.

23. I discuss Shaked's historical periodization of Israeli literature in more detail in the third part of this study, especially the period he calls "te Palmach generation," in my reading of S. Yizhar's "Hirbet Hizah." Here I focus on the period of the "new wave" generation.

24. Nurith Gertz, *Captive of a Dream,* 122, 123, 125.

25. Nurith Gertz, "Olam l'lo g'vulot: ha-z'hut ha-ivrit v'ha-z'hut ha-aravit b'yetsirot sifrutiyot v'kolnoyiot b'shnot ha-sh'monim" [A world without borders: The Hebrew and Arabic identity in literary and cinematic works in the 1980s], in *Independence—The First Fifty Years: Collected Essays* (in Hebrew), ed. Anita Shapira (Jerusalem: Zalman Shazar Center, 1998), 518.

26. Ibid., 520.

27. Attridge, "Oppressive Silence," 220.

28. In her review Shamir credits Shaked with the fact that the "new wave" writers are certainly not "garret poets" and mentions the especially comfortable situation of Yehoshua and Oz. Shamir, "Portrait of the Historian of Literature," 6.

29. Yitzhak Laor relates to this issue in his harsh criticism of major figures in Israeli literature. He denounces the critics Shaked and Gertz, as well as the writers Yehoshua and Oz, among others, as representatives of Zionism, which he sees as a colonially oppressive movement. While he makes some astute observations about the reflections of the history of Zionist domination in Israeli literary and critical writings, Laor's relentless offensive, absence of critical methodology, and repetitive argumentation detract from the credibility of his interpretation. *Narratives with No Natives: Essays on Israeli Literature* (in Hebrew) (Tel Aviv: Ha-Kibbutz Hameuchad, 1995), 77–78. In terms of the present discussion, I wish to mention Shaked's long and vituperative review of Laor's book. At the end of his response Shaked identifies Laor as a representative of a group "which tries to undermine some of the fundamentals that justify my life here and now." Shaked ends his re-

sponse with the following declaration: "I still believe in the will to exist and in the need for the existence of the Jews. I also believe that literary texts carry great weight in the confrontation with the questions that this existence has raised. . . . Whoever wants to live needs to believe in a certain justice— even if it is not perfect—his justice and the justice of the groups to which he belongs." Shaked, review of "The Other" by Itzhak Laor, 72.

30. This report was first published in the weekly *Khoteret rashit* [The headline] on the twentieth anniversary of the Six-Day War and attained instant publicity. David Grossman, *The Yellow Wind* [1987], trans. Haim Watzman (New York: Delta, 1988). The quotation appears on page v of the introduction Grossman wrote for the English edition.

31. Amos Oz, *All Our Hopes: Essays on the Israeli Condition* (in Hebrew) (Jerusalem: Keter, 1998) 112–13, 114. Peace Now is the Israeli left-wing movement favoring a peace agreement with the Arabs. Israel Kings Square is a central location in Tel Aviv where Peace Now holds its rallies. After the assassination of Itzhak Rabin, which occurred there, it was renamed Rabin Square.

32. A. B. Yehoshua, "The Next Fifty Years," *Azure* [special issue: The Jewish State: The Next Fifty Years] 6 (1999), 227, 228, 229; emphasis added.

33. For a discussion of Grossman's Western existentialist framework in *The Yellow Wind,* see Rachel Feldhay Brenner, "The Anatomy of the Israeli-Palestinian Conflict: Universalism and Particularism in David Grossman's *The Yellow Wind,*" *Shofar* 8, no. 3 (spring 1990): 30–38.

34. Grossman, *The Yellow Wind,* 216.

35. Yehoshua, "The Next Fifty Years," 226. Yehoshua reads the charter as an endorsement by the State of Israel that it is the solution to the Jewish problem. This reading is clearly incorrect. The charter states: "In the appraisal of the Palestine question, it be accepted as incontrovertible that any solution for Palestine cannot be considered as a solution of the Jewish problem in general. . . . It is . . . most improbable that there could be settled in Palestine all the Jews who may wish to leave their present domiciles, for reasons of immediate displacement or distress, or actual or anticipated anti-Jewish attitudes in the countries in which they now reside." United Nations, Special Committee on Palestine: Recommendations to the General Assembly, A/364, 12 September 1947. See http://www.mfa.gov.il/mfa/go.asp? MFAH017x03.

36. David Grossman, *Sleeping on a Wire: Conversations with Palestinians in Israel,* trans. Haim Watzman (New York: Picador, 1993) 309, 21, 111. The original title of the book can be literally translated as "Present Absentees," which, as Grossman explains in the book, refers to those Arabs whose land was confiscated by the state according to the Absentee Property Law. The latter defined absentee Arabs as those who were not physically present on their land by November 1948. Those who returned after that

date and could not recover their land were designated "present absentees" (82–83).

37. Perhaps the most outstanding example of the growing political consciousness of Israeli Arabs was Azmi Bishara's candidacy for the position of prime minister in the Israeli elections. It was a symbolic gesture to assert the importance of the Israeli Arab minority on Israel's political scene. Since then, Bishara's anti-Israeli pronouncements have cost him his legal immunity as a Knesset [Parliament] member. The tragic events in the Israeli Arab sector at the time—in October 2000 thirteen Israeli Arabs were killed by Israeli police during a demonstration—reflect the frustration of the Arab minority at their discriminatory treatment by the Israeli government.

38. Amos Oz, *In the Land of Israel* (1983), trans. Maurie Goldberg-Bartura (San Diego, Calif.: Harcourt Brace, 1993), 166, 168–89.

39. Muhammad Ali Taha, quoted in Mishael Maswari Caspi and Jerome David Weltsch, *From Slumber to Awakening: Culture and Identity of Arab Israeli Literati* (Lanham, Md.: University Press of America, 1998), 155. Though badly edited, this book includes some interesting interviews with Israeli Arab and Israeli Jewish intellectuals.

40. Quoted in Caspi and Weltsch, *From Slumber to Awakening*, 55, 154.

41. Bernard Horn, *Facing the Fires: Conversations with A. B. Yehoshua* (Syracuse, N.Y.: Syracuse University Press, 1997), 74–75.

42. Grossman, *Sleeping on a Wire*, 55, 56.

43. The book was written initially as doctoral thesis under the supervision of Professors Miron and Balas.

44. Taha, *The Smile of an Opsimistic Lover*, 84, 83.

45. Quoted in Horn, *Facing the Fires*, 74.

46. Anton Shammas, *Arabesques* (in Hebrew) (Tel Aviv: Am Oved, 1986). Translated into English as *Arabesques* by Vivian Eden (New York: Harper & Row, 1988).

47. Quoted in Horn, *Facing the Fires*, 74.

48. Ibid., 75.

5. Israeli Arab Fiction and the Mainstream

1. Not all Israeli Arab fiction in Hebrew focuses on the confrontation between the Zionist hegemony and the Arab minority in Israel. I have already mentioned Naim Arayidi's Hebrew novel *A Fatal Christening*, which focuses on the problem of intermarriage between a Druse and a Christian.

2. The London-based Lebanese newspaper *Al-Hayat* published the reactions of twenty-five Arab intellectuals, who demanded that Habiby return the prize. See the brief note "B'ad v'neged" [For and against], in the Israeli paper *Ha-ir*, 1 May 1992, 29. Among the very few Arab intellectuals who supported Habiby were Egyptian novelist and Nobel laureate Nagib Mhfouz, Palestinian spokesperson Dr. Hanan Ashrawi, and Egyptian politi-

cal writer Fat'hi Ghanem. Nonetheless, the condemnation of his close friend Mahmoud Darwish and the lack of support from Yasir Arafat affected the writer most profoundly. See Habiby's interview with Dalia Karfel, "Yesh am Palestini v'yesh lo sifrut" [There is a Palestinian people and it has a literature], *Ha-ir*, 1 May 1992, 26–29.

3. For instance, Muhammad Ali Taha, a writer, educator, and former Communist party member, claimed that the prize had been given to Habiby as a reward for having quit the Communist party. The prize, Taha claims, was given "for changing his ideas, not for the book." Samih al-Kasim, a prominent Israeli Arab poet, is of the opinion that by accepting the prize Habiby let down not only the Palestinian cause but also the Israeli supporters of this cause. See Caspi and Weltsch, *From Slumber to Awakening*, 161, 164.

4. Yuval Ne'man, a well-known scientist and a right-wing politician, returned his Israel Prize for physics and walked out of the ceremony in protest. See Yerach Tal, "Ha-pras magi'a l'Habiby: al m'cha'ato shel Yuval Ne'man al ha'anakat pras Israel l'Emile Habiby" [Habiby deserves the prize: On Yuval Ne'man's protest against awarding the Israel Prize to Emile Habiby"], *Ha'Aretz*, 10 May 1992, 10.

5. Interview with Dalia Karfel, "Emile v'ha-mashmitsim" ["Emile and the slanderers"], *Kol ha-ir*, 1 May 1992, 34.

6. *London Sunday Times*, 15 June 1969, 12.

7. Sandra Khandra Jayysi, ed., *Anthology of Modern Palestinian Literature* (New York: Columbia University Press, 1992); Ami Elad-Bouskila, *Modern Palestinian Literature and Culture* (London: Frank Cass, 1999).

8. Quoted in Patrick McGee, "Texts between Worlds: African Fiction as Political Allegory," in *Decolonizing Tradition: New Views of Twentieth-Century "British" Literary Canons*, ed. Karen R. Lawrence (Urbana: University of Illinois Press, 1992), 251, 250.

9. Ngũgĩ wa Thiong'o, *Devil on the Cross* (London: Heinemann, 1982).

10. McGee, "Texts between Worlds," 256, 250.

11. This does not mean that Israeli Arab population does not know Hebrew. On the contrary, Hebrew is taught in Arab schools and many Arabs speak excellent Hebrew. Proficiency in Hebrew, however, did not facilitate Arab entry into the Israeli cultural milieu. See for instance a fairly recent study by Salim Abu-Rabia entitled "The Learning of Hebrew by Israeli Arab Students." The study investigated "the relationship between the attitudes and cultural backgrounds of Israeli Arab students and their reading comprehension of Jewish and Arab stories." The results showed that "the motivation of the Arab students to learn Hebrew was primarily instrumental rather than integrative." It also showed that "the participants evaluated Jewish characters and their roles more negatively than they evaluated Arab characters in both the Jewish and Arab stories." *Journal of Social Psychology* 138, no. 3 (June 1998): Electronic Collection A 20615250. I thank Cynthia Miller for drawing my attention to this article.

12. Quoted by Giora Behor, "Habiby—natun l'hatslafot ha-Shot" [Habiby—subject to whipping], *Ha'Aretz,* 14 April 1992, 35.

13. Mahmoud Darwish, "An Interview with Hilit Yeshurun in Rabat Amon on 7 February 1996" (in Hebrew), *Hadarim* 12 (1996): 194–95. Darwish was born in 1942 and fled with his family to Lebanon in 1948. He returned to the state too late to obtain identity papers. In 1971 he left Israel for Cairo, and in 1973 he joined the Palestinian Liberation Organization in Paris, where he also became president of the Union of Palestinian Writers and Journalists. Until the Oslo Agreement in 1993, Darwish was a member of the PLO Executive Committee. Darwish was a close friend of Habiby; his public condemnation of the latter's acceptance of the Israel Prize was a very heavy personal blow to Habiby.

14. See, for instance, Habiby's interviews with the following: Dalia Karfel in *Ha-ir* (nn. 2 and 5); Yotam Reuveni, "Ha-khol over, Habiby" [Everything passes, Habiby], *Yediot Aharonot,* 20 May 1993, 12; and Michal Adam, *Kol Bo* 3 September 1993, 77.

15. Emile Habiby, *The Secret Life of Saeed, the Pessoptimist,* trans. Salma Khadra Jayyusi and Trevor LeGassick (London: Zed Books, 1985), 124.

16. Emile Habiby, *Ikhtayyeh,* Hebrew trans. by Anton Shammas (Tel Aviv: Am Oved, 1988), 22.

17. Emile Habiby, *Saraya, Daughter of the Ghoul,* Hebrew trans. by Anton Shammas (Tel Aviv: Hakibbutz Hameuchad, 1993), 13.

18. Shammas, *Arabesques,* 228.

19. Jacques Derrida, *Acts of Literature,* ed. Derek Attridge (New York: Routledge, 1992) 37, 38; emphasis added.

20. M.D., "Tsalash l'Shammas" [A medal for Shammas], *Ma'ariv,* 9 December 1988, 15.

21. Yael Lotan, "Likrat sifrut Israelit" [Towards an Israeli literature], *Al ha-Mishmar,* 4 July 1986, 15.

22. Heda Boshas, "Al ma holmim ha-aravim?" ["What do the Arabs dream about?"], *Ha'Aretz,* 28 April 1986, 25.

23. Dan Laor, "Ha-Fassutaim: ha-sipur sh'lo nigmar" [The Fassutans: the story that never ends], *Ha'Aretz,* 31 May 1986, 6–7.

24. S. Yael Feldman, "Postcolonial Memory, Postmodern Intertextuality: Anton Shammas's *Arabesques* Revisited," *PMLA* 114 (1999): 385.

25. Hannan Hever, "Hebrew in an Israeli Arab Hand: Six Miniatures on Anton Shammas's *Arabesques,*" *Cultural Critique* [special issue: "The Nature and Context of Minority Discourse," ed. Abdul R. JanMohamed and David Lloyd] 7 (1987): 74, 76.

26. Ibid., 73.

27. Dan Miron, "La'ant ha-shanim sh'adayin lo ukhla" [The years of bitterness that have not disappeared], *Ha-olam ha-ze,* 9 July 1986, 26.

28. Quoted in Avner Bernheimer, "Mi ata Emile Habibi?" [Who are you, Emile Habiby?] *Ha-shavua,* 20 May 1992, 50.

29. Quoted in Orly Toren, "Matsavo ha-ishi, matsavo ha-politi, matsavo ha-sifruti: Emile Habibi, sofer Arvi Palestini nehshav, b'avar haver Knesset komunist, humlatz l'pras Israel l'sifrut. Ma omrim al khach anshei sifrut?" [His personal situation, his political situation, his literary situation: Emile Habiby, an important Arab Palestinian writer, a past Knesset member, was recommended for Israel Prize for literature. What do literary experts say?], *Yediot Aharonot,* 13 March 1992, 24.

30. Shulamith Hareven, "Absurd hu ir prazot" [Absurd is an open city], *Yediot Aharonot,* 19 June 1992, 14.

31. Hannan Hever, " 'Ha-p'litot la-p'litim': Emile Habiby v'kanon ha-sifrut ha-ivrit" [The refugee women to the refugees: Emile Habiby and the canon of Hebrew literature in Israel], *Ha-mizrah He-hadash* 35 (1993): 114, 105, 113, 106–7.

32. Habiby, *The Secret Life of Saeed, the Pessoptimist,* 16–17.

33. Atallah Mansour, *Waiting for the Dawn* (London: Secker & Warburg, 1975), 95.

34. Yona Bahir, "S'nunit" [A swallow], *Ha'Aretz,* 18 March 1966, 10.

35. Ora Ardon, "Israel b'or hadash" [Israel in a new light], *La-merhav,* 22 April 1966, 15.

36. Iza Perlis, "Tsair arvi b'kibbutz" [A young Arab on a kibbutz], *Ma'ariv,* 25 March 1966, 22.

6. The Canon and the "True Heart of Europe"

1. Anton Shammas, "Kitsch 22: On the Problems of the Relations Between Majority and Minority Cultures in Israel," *Tikkun* 2, no. 4 (September–October 1987): 22.

2. Ibid., 22, 26.

Part 3. Discourses of Bonding, Introduction

1. Walter Benjamin, "Theses on the Philosophy of History," *Illuminations,* trans. Harry Zohn (New York: Shocken, 1973), 255.

2. Neil Lazarus, "Modernism and Modernity: T. W. Adorno and the Contemporary White South African Literature," *Cultural Critique* 5 (winter 1986–87): 135.

3. Nadine Gordimer talks about "the branding as traitor, or, at least, turned backside of indifference that await the white [dissenting writer] from the white establishment." "The Essential Gesture: Writers and Responsibility," *Granta* 15 (spring 1985): 145.

4. Lazarus, "Modernism and Modernity," 134.

5. I have already discussed the strategies of canonical neutralization of the works in the criticism of Shaked and Gertz. Other critics were less inclined to see Yehoshua's "Facing the Forests" as a reflection of Western existentialist and nihilistic trends. Mordechai Shalev has accused Yehoshua of destroying the Zionist dream by using the Arab as a representation of his Oedipal complex. "Ha-aravim kh'pitaron sifruti," [The Arabs as a literary solution] *Ha'Aretz,* 30 September 1970. In a more recent and more positive previously mentioned article ("Minority Discourse of a National Majority") Hannan Hever examines Yehoshua's "Facing the Forests," Oz's "Nomad and Viper," and Amalia Kahana-Carmon's "Heart of Summer, Heart of Light" in terms of Israeli self-identity. Hever finds in all three stories— "whose *canonical* status is not in doubt"—a similar motif of the Jewish majority acting and reacting as a minority. The focus is once again on the Israeli Jew and the search for identity with the help of the Arab as the marginal other.

6. Azmi Bishara, ed. *Beyin ha-ani l'anahnu: havnaiat z'huiot v'z'hut Israelit* [Between "I" and "We": The construction of identities and Israeli identity] (Jerusalem: Hakibbutz Hameuchad, 1999): 13–14.

7. Isabel Kershner, "Blue-and-White Palestinians," *Jerusalem Report* 10, no. 13 (25 October 1999): 14, 18.

8. For a detailed account of this painful event and its aftermath, see Dan Rabinowitz and Khawla Abu Baker, *The Stand Tall Generation: The Palestinian Citizens of Israel Today* (in Hebrew) (Jerusalem: Keter, 2002), a collaborative study by an Israeli Jew and an Israeli Palestinian.

9. Maurice Halbwachs, *On Collective Memory,* trans. Lewis A. Coser (Chicago: University of Chicago Press, 1992), 188.

10. Zerubavel claims that "followers of Zionism shared some fundamental views about the Jewish past and the present: they regarded Jewish life in exile as inherently regressive and repressive, and believed in the need to promote some form of revival of Jewish national life as experienced in Antiquity." *Recovered Roots,* 14.

11. Benjamin, "Theses," 256.

12. This is, of course, a common motif in literature. Suffice it to mention Shakespeare's *Macbeth* and Dostoevsky's *Crime and Punishment*. In both cases the dead victims of the crime become an increasingly powerful presence in the life of the murderer.

13. Sigmund Freud, *Totem and Taboo,* trans. James Strachey (New York: Norton, 1950), 142. Emphasis added.

14. Mikkel Borch-Jacobsen, "The Freudian Subject, from Politics to Ethics," in *Who Comes After the Subject?,* ed. Eduardo Cadava, Peter Connor and Jean-Luc Nancy (New York: Routledge, 1991), 62, 76.

15. S. Yizhar, "Hirbet Hizah," *Arba'a sipurim* [Four stories] (Tel Aviv: Hakibbutz Hameuchad, 1968).

16. Ramraz-Rauch, *The Arab in Israeli Literature*, 67. Some points in my analysis of "Hirbet Hizah" were inspired by Ramraz-Rauch's insightful interpretation of the story.

17. Anita Shapira, "Hirbet Hizah: Between Remembrance and Forgetting," *Jewish Social Studies: History, Culture, and Society* 7, no. 1 (2000): 55.

18. Quoted in Rubik Rosenthal and Hed Sela, "Ze ha-okyianus ha-bilti noda, u-ma she-tsarikh hu lo lehacknis bo mey shopkhin" [This is an unknowable ocean and we need not pour sewer water into it] *Panim: Quarterly for Society, Culture and Education* 10 (summer 1999): 55.

19. Quoted in Ramras-Rauch, *The Arab in Israeli Literature*, 73.

20. Ibid.

21. Palmach is the acronym for Plugot Mahatz (assault companies). These were the elite commando units of the Hagana in Palestine and, later, the shock battalions of the Israel Defense forces. The Palmach Generation is also called the 1948 generation, that is, the generation who fought in the 1948 War of Independence.

22. Shaked, *Literature Then, Here and Now*, 22–23.

23. On periodization, see Shaked, *A New Wave in Hebrew Fiction*, 53; see also Nurith Gertz, *Generational Shift in Literary History: Hebrew Narrative Fiction in the Sixties* (in Hebrew) (Tel Aviv: Porter Institute, 1983).

24. Mention should be made here of the humanistic, universalist approach to the story that Amos Oz adopted in his 1978 critique. As Anita Shapira notes, "In Oz's view, the basic point of Yizhar's story is not the Arabs and their fate, but the psychological turmoil of the narrator, who assimilated the best of the humanistic and nationalistic values he was brought up on, and then found himself faced with a rupture between those two value systems." Shapira, "Hirbet Hizah," 40.

25. Moshe Shamir, *He Walked in the Fields* (in Hebrew) (Tel Aviv: Sifriat Ha-poalim, 1948); *With His Own Hands* (in Hebrew) (Tel Aviv: Sifriat Ha-poalim, 1951).

26. See Ramraz-Rauch, *The Arab in Israeli Literature*, 88.

7. The Traumas of Victory and Defeat

1. John Freccero, "Autobiography and Narrative," in *Reconstructing Individualism: Autonomy, Individuality, and the Self in Western Thought*, ed. Thomas C. Heller, Morton Sosna, and David E. Wellbery (Stanford, Calif.: Stanford University Press, 1986), 17.

2. Interview with Rochelle Furstenberg, quoted in Ramraz-Rauch, *The Arab in Israeli Literature*, 69; emphasis added. More recently Yizhar reiterated his position during an interview with Moshe Granot. Referring to "Hirbet Hizah," he confided: "With the naiveté of those days, I thought then

that there are things a Jew should not do—because he is a Jew. Clearly this is nonsense, rather sentimental nonsense. I accepted the idea innocently and with no due innocence it shattered. You must see as I do that Jews are like everybody else." "Hashavti lomar al khlum et ha-khol" [I intended to say everything about nothing], *Moznaim* 75, no. 1 (January 2001): 17.

3. Sigmund Freud, *Beyond the Pleasure Principle,* ed. and trans. James Strachey (New York: Norton: 1989), 29.

4. Sigmund Freud, "Fixation upon Traumas: The Unconscious," in *A General Introduction to Psycho-Analysis,* trans. Joan Riviere (New York: Simon and Schuster, 1963), 243.

5. Cathy Carouth, "Introduction," *Trauma: Explorations in Memory,* ed. by Cathy Carouth (Baltimore: Johns Hopkins University Press, 1995), 5.

6. S. Yizhar, "Hirbet Hizah," 43; emphasis added. Unless otherwise indicated, all translations are mine. Subsequent page numbers in the text are preceded by HH.

7. Ronnie Janoff-Bulman, *Shattered Assumptions: Toward a New Psychology of Trauma* (New York: Free Press, 1992), 51–52.

8. Robert Jay Lifton, *The Broken Connection: On Death and the Continuity of Life.* 2nd ed. (New York: Basic Books, 1983), 169.

9. Yochai Oppenheimer, "The Image of the Arab in Israeli Fiction," *Prooftexts* 19, no. 3 (1999): 207.

10. Quoted in Ramraz-Rauch, *The Arab in Israeli Literature,* 73; emphasis added.

11. See, for instance, Ramraz-Rauch, *The Arab in Israeli Literature,* 69–71; and Shapira, "Hirbet Hizah," 11–34.

12. Yaira Genosar, "'Ha-b'riha' v'ha-'neshek' shel Emile Habiby" [The "escape" and the "weapons" of Emile Habiby], *Iton* 77, no. 237 (November 1999): 19.

13. Quoted in Ramraz-Rauch, *The Arab in Israeli Literature,* 74.

14. Habiby, *The Pessoptimist,* 73. Subsequent page numbers in the text are preceded by P.

15. James C. Scott, *Domination and the Arts of Resistance: Hidden Transcripts* (New Haven, Conn.: Yale University Press, 1990), 14.

16. Cathy Carouth, "An Interview with Robert Jay Lifton," in Carouth, *Trauma,* 137.

17. Walter A. Davis, *Inwardness and Existence: Subjectivity in/and Hegel, Heidegger, Marx, and Freud* (Madison: University of Wisconsin Press, 1989), 259, 262–63.

18. Hegel, *Phenomenology of Spirit,* 117.

19. Ibid., 111.

20. Davis, *Inwardness and Existence,* 41.

21. Ibid., 39.

8. Bonds of Confession

1. Freud, *Beyond the Pleasure Principle,* 18:32.

2. Eric L. Santner, *Stranded Objects: Mourning, Memory, and Film in Postwar Germany* (Ithaca, N.Y.: Cornell University Press, 1990), 25.

3. Dominick LaCapra, *Representing the Holocaust: History, Theory, Trauma* (Ithaca, N.Y.: Cornell University Press, 1994), 199.

4. Carouth, "Introduction," 10.

5. Carouth, "Interview with Robert Jay Lifton," 143.

6. Freud, "Recommendations to Physicians Practicing Psycho-Analysis," in *Therapy and Technique,* 111; emphasis added.

7. Jacques Lacan, *The Four Fundamental Concepts of Psycho-Analysis,* trans. Alan Sheridan (London: Penguin, 1994), 232, 233; emphasis added.

8. A. B. Yehoshua, "Facing the Forests," in *Sleepwalkers and Other Stories: The Arab in Hebrew Fiction,* ed. Ehud Ben-Ezer (Boulder, Colo.: Lynn Rienner, 1999), 115–16. Subsequent page numbers in the text are preceded by FF.

9. In the first part of this study I discussed transference in terms of repetition and remembering. Here I focus on the "secret" knowledge that would restore the traumatic losses that the teller and the listener attribute, or transfer, to each other.

10. See, for instance, Cadava, Connor, and Nancy, eds., *Who Comes after the Subject?;* Linda Marie Brooks, ed., *Alternative Identities: The Self in Literature, History, Theory* (New York: Garland, 1995); Thomas C. Heller, Morton Sosna, and David E. Wellbery, eds., *Reconstructing Individualism: Autonomy, Individuality, and the Self in Western Thought* (New York: Garland, 1995). For an insightful overview of the issue from the feminist point of view, see Feldman, *No Room of Their Own,* 10–13.

11. Sigmund Freud, *Group Psychology and the Analysis of the Ego,* in vol. 18 (1920–1922) of the Standard Edition of the Complete Psychological Works, ed. and trans. James Strachey. (London: Hogarth Press, 1955), xviii, 69; emphasis added.

12. Mikkel Borch-Jacobsen, "The Freudian Subject, from Politics to Ethics," in Cadava, Connor, and Nancy, *Who Comes after the Subject?* 68.

13. Davis, *Inwardness and Existence,* 115.

14. Jacques Derrida, " 'Eating Well,' or the Calculation of the Subject: An Interview with Jacques Derrida," by Jean-Luc Nancy, in Cadava, Connor, and Nancy, *Who Comes after the Subject?* 100–101; latter emphasis added.

15. Derrida comes close to Levinas, who argues that "in the 'prehistory' of the ego posited for itself speaks a responsibility. The self is . . . a hostage, older than the ego. . . .What is at stake for the self, in its being, is not to be" but rather to be for others. Emmanuel Levinas, "Substitution," in *The*

Levinas Reader, ed. Sean Hand (Oxford: Basil Blackwell, 1989), 107. I discuss Levinas's concept of the other in more detail in the last chapter.

16. Atallah Mansour, *In a New Light,* trans. from the Hebrew by Abraham Birman (London: Vallentine, Mitchell, 1969), 11. Subsequent page numbers in the text are preceded by *INL.*

17. Carouth, "Introduction," 5; emphasis added.

18. *Tish'a b'av,* literally the ninth day of the month of av, involves fasting to commemorate the destruction of both temples.

19. Hegel, *Phenomenology of Spirit,* 118.

20. Bhabha's notion of "mimicking" provided the framework for my discussion of the Zionists as European mimics in the first part one of this study.

21. Hevrat Noar is the Zionist Youth Movement; *hakhsharah* was the collective name for the camps that trained Israeli youth for life on a kibbutz.

22. Today one observes an opposite phenomenon on the Israeli scene. Many non-Jewish Israeli citizens join the army. When they die in battle, they are buried in a special area, outside the cemetery.

23. Eric L. Santner, "History beyond the Pleasure Principle: Some Thoughts on the Representation of Trauma," in *Probing the Limits of Representation: Nazism and the "Final Solution,"* ed. Saul Friedlander (Cambridge, Mass.: Harvard University Press, 1992), 144.

24. LaCapra, *Representing the Holocaust,* 192.

9. Descent into Barbarism

1. Oppenheimer, "The Image of the Arab in Israeli Fiction," 229.

2. Hever, "Minority Discourse of a National Majority," 137.

3. Perry, "The Israeli-Palestinian Conflict," 607.

4. Benjamin, "Theses on the Philosophy of History," 255.

5. Amos Oz, "Nomad and Viper," in *Sleepwalker and Other Stories: The Arab in Hebrew Fiction,* ed. Ehud Ben-Ezer (Boulder, Colo.: Lynn Rienner, 1999), 133. Subsequent page numbers in the text are preceded by NV.

6. Sigmund Freud, *On Narcissism,* vol. 14 (1914–1916) of the Standard Edition of the Complete Psychological Works, ed. and trans. James Strachey (London: Hogarth Press, 1957), 75.

7. Ibid., 94.

8. Ibid., 95.

9. Ibid., 101–2.

10. Freud, *Group Psychology and the Analysis of the Ego,* 18:102.

11. Derrida, "Eating Well," 101–2.

12. See, for instance, Sandor L. Gilman, *The Jew's Body* (New York: Routledge, 1991).

13. Freud, *Group Psychology and the Analysis of the Ego,* 18:113.

14. Davis, *Inwardness and Existence,* 74.

10. Melancholia and Telos

1. Benjamin, "Theses on the Philosophy of History," 257–58.

2. Benjamin dealt with the issue of mourning and melancholy in his discussion of "Trauerspiel" (play of mourning) in his *Origin of German Tragic Drama*. As Anselm Havercamp maintains, "it is the melancholy constitution of the world rather than the successful adaptation to reality that provokes Benjamin's 'theory of mourning.'" This theory of mourning, according to Benjamin, "can only be developed in the description of the [death world] that reveals itself to the eye of the melancholy man." "Mourning Becomes Melancholia—A Muse Deconstructed: Keats's *Ode on Melancholy*," *New Literary History* 21, no. 3 (spring 1990): 694.

3. Sigmund Freud, *Mourning and Melancholia*, vol. 14 of The Standard Edition of the Complete Psychological Works, ed. and trans. James Strachey (London: Hogarth Press, 1914–16), 244, 247.

4. Amos Oz, *My Michael*, trans. Nicholas de Lange (New York: Alfred A. Knopf, 1972), 28. Subsequent page numbers in the text and notes are preceded by *MM*.

5. Freud, "Mourning and Melancholia," 14:256.

6. The names are meaningful. The original name "Ganz" is a German as well as a Yiddish word meaning "whole," or "complete." The Hebrew name "Gonen" has the connotation of "defender." In the reality of Israel's constant wars, the "wholeness" of the nation associates with the need for defense. Note Slavoj Žižek's reference to the Lacanian theory of family name: "The family name comes from the father—it designates the Name-of-the-Father, a point of symbolic identification, the agency through which we observe and judge ourselves." *The Sublime Object of Ideology* (London: Verso, 1989), 108. In the present context I observe the aspect of the symbolic identification that makes Michael's father accommodate the Name-of-the-Father, represented by the Zionist doctrine, by *changing* his own father's name. He thus subordinated himself to the ego-ideal of the Zionist symbolic order, which eliminated the ego-ideal of the Diaspora.

7. Freud, "Mourning and Melancholia," 14:246.

8. Emile Habiby, *Saraya, Daughter of the Ghoul*, trans. Anton Shammas (Tel Aviv: Hakibbutz Hameuchad, 1933), 169. Subsequent page numbers in the text and notes are preceded by *S*. Unless otherwise noted, all translations from the Hebrew version of *Saraya* are mine.

9. This is the second version of the episode of the rented bicycle, which broke before getting the narrator to his destination. In the first version, when he asked the owner of the bicycle store to "cancel the first deal and give him another opportunity for the same penny, the man said, 'God Almighty does not do such silly things, how do you expect me to do it?'" (*S* 133–34).

10. Quoted in Davis, *Inwardness and Existence*, 204.

11. Davis, *Inwardness and Existence*, 204.

12. Ibid.

13. Freud, *Group Psychology and the Analysis of the Ego,* 18:90, 92.

14. Davis, *Inwardness and Existence,* 204.

15. Žižek, *The Sublime Object of Ideology,* 108.

16. Lacan, *The Four Fundamental Concepts of Psycho-Analysis,* 211.

17. Gilbert D. Chaitin, *Rhetoric and Culture in Lacan* (Cambridge: Cambridge University Press, 1996), 184.

18. Julia Kristeva, *Black Sun: Depression and Melancholia,* trans. Leon S. Roudiez (New York: Columbia University Press, 1989), 10–11.

19. Ibid., 42, 47, 98, 99, 100.

20. In this sentence, the term "melancholy" is used in the Hebrew text. "Melancholy" in the phrase "a melancholy dream" on p. 282 in the English translation does not appear in the Hebrew original.

21. Havercamp, "Mourning Becomes Melancholia," 701.

22. Kristeva, *Black Sun,* 9; emphasis added.

23. Chaitin, *Rhetoric and Culture in Lacan,* 187.

24. It is interesting to compare Michael's explanation of the battle with his explanation of geomorphology. When Hannah comments on the "dry" style of his research, Michael admits, "I myself conscientiously avoid using the striking phrases [and] vague expression. . . . There is a very slender dividing line between a scientific description and a fairy tale. . . . I make every effort to avoid crossing this line" (*MM* 136–37). His clearly expressed consciousness of the world of imagination and fantasy, which he deliberately avoids by means of a rational treatment of the language, communicates unacknowledged fears of the irrational.

25. The narrator's reluctance to confront suffering in the scene with the gypsy girl is reiterated in the motif of the "hesitation to take the final leap" (*S* 143–44, 167). The narrator describes his experience in 1940, when he refused to listen to Ibrahim's order to leap boldly into the world of the imagination. His hesitation cost him the miraculous cane of the three circles, the key to knowledge. Like Michael's reluctance to see the poetry of geomorphology and to talk about it in an imaginative way, the refusal of Habiby's narrator to confront the world of the imagination and his choice of the "world of reality" communicate the vulnerability of his ideological defenses.

26. Freud, "Repression," 14:154.

27. Perry, "The Israeli-Palestinian Conflict," 619.

11. Tales That Ought to Be Told

1. Benjamin, "Theses," 254.

2. Jürgen Habermas, *The Philosophical Discourse of Modernity: Twelve Lectures,* trans. Frederick G. Lawrence (Cambridge, Mass.: MIT Press, 1993), 14, 15. "Anamnesis" is defined as "a remembering, especially of a supposed life before life."

3. Anton Shammas, *Arabesques,* trans. Vivian Eden (New York: Harper and Row, 1988), 11, 235. Subsequent page numbers appear in the text preceded by *A.*

4. David Grossman, *The Smile of the Lamb,* trans. Betsy Rosenberg (New York: Farrar, Straus & Giroux, 1990), 111–12. Subsequent page numbers appear in the text preceded by *SL.*

5. Emmanuel Levinas, *Time and the Other,* trans. Richard A. Cohen (Pittsburgh, Pa.: Duquesne University Press, 1987), 111.

6. Levinas, *Time and the Other,* 106.

7. Emmanuel Levinas, *Otherwise Than Being or Beyond Essence,* trans. Alphonso Lingis (Pittsburgh, Pa.: Duquesne University Press, 1999), 157, 158; emphasis added.

8. Simon Critchley, *The Ethics of Deconstruction: Derrida and Levinas,* 2nd ed. (West Lafayette, Pa.: Purdue University Press, 1999), 227, 226.

9. Levinas, *Otherwise Than Being,* 159; emphasis added.

10. Zygmunt Bauman, *Postmodern Ethics* (Oxford: Basil Blackwell, 1993), 112–16; emphasis added.

11. It should be noted that Grossman reinterprets the original reference to the smell of flowers, which, in the epic, is meant to demonstrate transitoriness and decline. When touring the moon on the way to recover Orlando's wits, Astolfo and his companion, John the Evangelist, "passed a heap of flowers which once filled / The air with perfume but turned putrid soon." Ludovico Ariosto, *Orlando Furioso,* vol. 2, trans. Barbara Reynolds (London: Penguin, 1977), 332.

12. Levinas, *Otherwise Than Being,* 127.

13. Levinas, "Ethics and First Philosophy," *The Levinas Reader,* 84.

14. Susan Sanford Friedman, "Beyond White and Other: Relationality and Narratives of Race in Feminist Discourse," *Signs* 21, no.1 (1995): 7, 18.

15. Bauman, *Postmodern Ethics,* 115.

16. For an illuminating interpretation of the spaces in the novel and their connection to language and writing, see the insightful article by Christian Szyska, "Geographies of the Self: Text and Space in Anton Shammas's *Arabesques,*" in *Narrated Space in Literatures of the Islamic World,* ed. Roxane Haag-Higuchi and Christian Szyska (Wiesbaden: Harrassowitz, 2001), 217–32.

17. For a particularly apt analysis of the language boundaries that Bar-On imposes on "his" Arab, see Szyska, "Geographies of the Self," 217–32.

18. In the Hebrew original the literal translation of "as if I had missed something" is "a great lost opportunity" (hahmatsa g'dolah).

Epilogue

1. Rabinowitz and Baker, *The Stand Tall Generation,* 179.

Bibliography

Abu-Rabia, Salim. "The Learning of Hebrew by Israeli Arab Students." *Journal of Social Psychology* 138, no. 3 (1998): Electronic collection: A20615250; RN: A20615250.

Agus, Jacob C. *Jewish Identity in an Age of Ideologies*. New York: Frederick Ungar, 1978.

Ahad Ha'Am. "Emet m'eretz Israel" [Truth from Eretz Yisrael]. Trans. Alan Dowty. *Israel Studies* 5, no. 2 (2000): 160–82.

———. *Nationalism and the Jewish Ethic: Basic Writings of Ahad Ha 'Am*. Ed. Hans Kohn. New York: Schocken, 1962.

Alcalay, Ammiel. *After Jews and Arabs: Remaking Levantine Culture*. Minneapolis: University of Minnesota Press, 1993.

Araydi, Naim. *Tevilah qatlanit* [A fatal christening]. Tel Aviv: Bitan, 1992.

Ardon, Ora. "Israel b'or hadash" [Israel in a new light]. *La-merhav*, 22 April 1966, 15.

Ariosto, Ludovico. *Orlando Furioso*. Trans. Barbara Reynolds. London: Penguin, 1977.

Arkush, Allan. "The Jewish State and Its Internal Enemies: Yoram Hazony Versus Martin Buber and His 'Ideological Children.'" *Jewish Social Studies* 7, no. 2 (2001): 169–91.

Attridge, Derek. "Oppressive Silence: J. M. Coetzee's Foe and the Politics of Canon." In *Decolonizing Tradition: New Views of Twentieth-Century "British" Literary Canons*, ed. Karen R. Lawrence. 218–38. Urbana: University of Illinois Press, 1992.

Avineri, Shlomo. "Darkho shel Herzl l'gibush toda'ah leumit yehudit" [Herzl's way toward consolidation of Jewish national consciousness]. *Alpayim* 15 (1997): 254–88.

"B'ad v'neged" ["For and against"]. *Ha-ir*, 1 May 1992, 29.

Bahir, Yona. "S'nunit" [A swallow]. *Ha'Aretz*, 18 March 1966, 10.

Balaban, Avraham. *Between God and Beast: An Examination of Amos Oz's Prose.* University Park: Pennsylvannia State University Press, 1986.

Bargad, Warren. "The Image of the Arab in Israeli Literature." *Hebrew Annual Review* 1 (1977): 53–65.

Barnett, Michael N., ed. *Israel in Comparative Perspective: Challenging the Conventional Wisdom.* Albany: State University of New York Press, 1996.

Bauman, Zygmunt. *Postmodern Ethics.* Oxford: Basil Blackwell, 1993.

Behor, Giora. "Habiby—natun l'hatslafot ha-Shot" [Habiby—subject to whipping] *Ha'Aretz,* 14 April 1992, 35.

Benda, Julien. *La Trahison des clercs.* Paris: J.-J. Pauvert, 1972.

Benjamin, Walter, "Theses on the Philosophy of History." In Walter Benjamin, *Illuminations,* trans. and ed. Harry Zohn, 253–65. New York: Shocken, 1973,

Berg, Nancy E. *Exile from Exile: Israeli Writers from Iraq.* Albany: State University of New York Press, 1996.

Berkowitz, Michael. *Zionist Culture and West European Jewry before the First World War.* Cambridge: Cambridge University Press, 1993.

Berlovitz, Yaffah. *Inventing a Land, Inventing a People* (in Hebrew). Tel Aviv: Hakibbutz Hameuchad, 1996.

Bernheimer, Avner. "Mi ata Emile Habibi?" [Who are you, Emile Habiby?] *Ha-shavua,* 20 May 1992: 50.

Bhabha, K. Homi. *The Location of Culture.* London: Routledge, 1994.

Bishara, Azmi, ed. *Beyin ha-ani l'anahnu: havnaiat z'huiot v'z'hut Israelit* [Between "I" and "We": The construction of identities and Israeli identity]. Jerusalem: Hakibbutz Hameuchad, 1999.

Boshas, Heda. "Al ma holmim ha-aravim?" [What Do the Arabs Dream About?]. *Ha'Aretz,* 28 April, 1986, 25.

Boyarin, Daniel. "Colonial Drug: Zionism, Gender, and Mimicry" (in Hebrew). *Theory and Criticism* 11 (1997): 123–45.

Brenner, Rachel Feldhay. "The Anatomy of the Israeli-Palestinian Conflict: Universalism and Particularism in David Grossman's *The Yellow Wind.*" *Shofar* 8, no. 3 (Spring 1990): 30–38.

———. "'Hidden Transcripts' Made Public: Israeli Arab Fiction and Its Reception." *Critical Inquiry* 26 (Autumn 1999): 85–108.

———. "In Search of Identity: The Israeli Arab Artist in Anton Shammas's *Arabesques.*" *PMLA* 108, no. 3 (May 1993): 431–45.

Brenner, Yosef Haim. *Khol khitvei Y. H. Brenner.* [Complete works of Y. H. Brenner]. Tel Aviv: Hakibbutz Ha-meuchad, 1960.

Brinker, Menachem. *Narrative Art and Social Thought in H. Y. Brenner's Work* (in Hebrew). Tel Aviv: Am Oved, 1990.

Brooks, Linda Marie, ed. *Alternative Identities: The Self in Literature, History, Theory.* New York: Garland, 1995.

Buber, Martin. *The Knowledge of Man.* Trans. Maurice Friedman and Ronald Gregor Smith. London: George Allen, 1965.

———. *A Land of Two Peoples: Martin Buber on Jews and Arabs.* Ed. Paul R. Mendes-Flohr. 1983. Gloucester, Mass.: Peter Smith, 1994.

Cadava, Eduardo, Peter Connor, and Jean-Luc Nancy, eds. *Who Comes After the Subject?* New York: Routledge, 1991.

Carouth, Cathy, ed. *Trauma: Explorations in Memory.* Baltimore: John Hopkins University Press, 1995.

Caspi, Mishael Maswari, and Jerome David Weltsch. *From Slumber to Awakening: Culture and Identity of Arab Israeli Literati.* Lanham, N.Y.: University Press of America, 1998.

Chaitin, Gilbert D. *Rhetoric and Culture in Lacan.* Cambridge: Cambridge University Press, 1996.

Chelouche, Yosef Eliahu. *Parashat hayayi, 1870–1930* [The story of my life, 1870–1930]. Tel Aviv: Strud and Sons, 1930.

Coffin, Edna Amir. "The Image of the Arab in Modern Hebrew Literature." *Michigan Quarterly Review* 21 (1982): 319–41.

Critchley, Simon. *The Ethics of Deconstruction: Derrida and Levinas.* West Lafayette, Ind.: Purdue University Press, 1999.

Darwish, Mahmoud. "Ha-galut kho khakh hazaka b'tokhi, ulai avi ota art-zah" [The exile is so strong in me-perhaps I'll take it with me to the (mother)land]. An Interview with Hilit Yeshurun. *Hadarim* 12 (1996): 172–98.

———. "A Love Story Between an Arab Poet and His Land." *Journal of Palestinian Studies* 31, no. 3 (2002): 67–90.

———. "Palestine: The Imaginary and the Real." In *Innovation in Palestinian Literature: Testimonies of Palestinian Poets and Writers,* trans. Dr. Abdul-Fattah Jabr, 19–32. London: Ogarit Centre for Publication and Translation, 2000.

Davis, Walter A. *Inwardness and Existence: Subjectivity in/and Hegel, Heidegger, Marx, and Freud.* Madison: University of Wisconsin Press, 1989.

Derrida, Jacques. *Acts of Literature.* Ed. Derek Attridge. New York: Routledge, 1992.

Diamond, James S. *Homeland or Holy Land? The Canaanite Critique of Israel.* Bloomington: Indiana University Press, 1986.

Domb, Risa. *The Arab in Hebrew Prose, 1911–1948.* London: Vallentine, Mitchell, 1982.

———. *Home Thoughts from Abroad: Distant Visions of Israel in Contemporary Hebrew Fiction.* London: Vallentine, Mitchell, 1995.

Dowty, Alan. "Much Ado about Little: Ahad Ha'am's 'Truth from Eretz Israel,' Zionism, and the Arabs." *Israel Studies* 5, no. 2 (2000): 154–59.

Edelist, Ran. Rev. "Sifrut u'musar: al sifro he'hadash shel A. B. Yehoshua

Khoha ha-nora shel ashma k'tana" [Literature and morality: About the new book by A. B. Yehoshua, *The Terrible Power of Minor Guilt*]. *Moznaim* 73, no. 6 (March 1999): 57–58.

Elad-Bouskila, Ami. *Modern Palestinian Literature and Culture.* London: Frank Cass, 1999.

Elmessiri, Abdelwahab M. *The Land of Promise: A Critique of Political Zionism.* New Brunswick, N.J.: North American, 1977.

Elon, Amos. *The Israelis: Founders and Sons.* New York: Holt, Rinehart and Winston, 1971.

Evron, Boas. *Jewish State or Israeli Nation?* Bloomington: Indiana University Press, 1995.

Feldman, S. Yael. *No Room of Their Own: Gender and Nation in Israeli Jewish Fiction.* New York: Columbia University Press, 1999.

———. "Postcolonial Memory, Postmodern Intertextuality: Anton Shammas's *Arabesques* Revisited." PMLA 114 (1999): 373–89.

Freccero, John. "Autobiography and Narrative." In *Reconstructing Individualism: Autonomy, Individuality, and the Self in Western Thought,* ed. Thomas C. Heller, Morton Sosna, and David E. Wellbery, 16–30. Stanford, Calif.: Stanford University Press, 1986.

Freud, Sigmund. *Beyond the Pleasure Principle.* Ed. and trans. James Strachey. New York: Norton: 1989.

———. "Fixation upon Traumas: The Unconscious." In *A General Introduction to Psycho-Analysis,* trans. Joan Riviere, 242–53. New York: Simon and Schuster, 1963.

———. *Group Psychology and the Analysis of the Ego.* In Vol. 18 (1920–1922) of the Standard Edition of the Complete Psychological Works. Ed. and trans. James Strachey. London: Hogarth Press, 1955.

———. *Mourning and Melancholia.* In Vol. 14 (1914–1916) of the Standard Edition of the Complete Psychological Works. Ed. and trans. James Strachey. London: Hogarth Press 1957.

———. *On Narcissism.* In Vol. 14 (1914–1916) of the Standard Edition of the Complete Psychological Works. Ed. and trans. James Strachey London: Hogarth Press, 1957.

———. *Therapy and Technique.* Ed. Philip Rieff. New York: Collier Books, 1963.

———. *Totem and Taboo.* Trans. James Strachey. New York: Norton, 1950.

Friedlander, Saul, ed. *Probing the Limits of Representation: Nazism and the "Final Solution."* Cambridge, Mass.: Harvard University Press, 1992.

Friedman, Susan Sanford. "Beyond White and Other: Relationality and Narratives of Race in Feminist Discourse." *Signs* 21, no. 1 (1995): 1–50.

Garfinkle, Adam. *Politics and Society in Modern Israel: Myths and Realities.* Armonk, N.Y.: M. E. Sharpe, 1997.

Genosar, Yaira. "'Ha-b'riha' v'ha-'neshek' shel Emile Habiby" [The "escape" and the "weapons" of Emile Habiby]. *Iton 77,* no. 237 (November 1999): 17–22.

Gertz, Nurith. *Generational Shift in Literary History: Hebrew Narrative Fiction in the Sixties* (in Hebrew).Tel Aviv: Porter Institute, 1983.

―――. *Sh'vuyia b'haloma: mitosim b'sifrut ha-israelit* [Captive of a dream: National myths in Israeli culture]. Tel Aviv: Am Oved, 1988.

Gilman, Sandor L. *Jewish Self-Hatred: Anti-Semitism and the Hidden Language of the Jews.* Baltimore: Johns Hopkins University Press, 1986.

―――. *The Jew's Body.* New York: Routledge, 1991.

Gluzman, Michael. "Longing for Heterosexuality: Zionism and Sexuality in Herzl's *Altneuland*" (in Hebrew). *Theory and Criticism: An Israeli Forum* 11 (1997): 145–63.

―――. *The Politics of Canonicity: Lines of Resistance in Modernist Hebrew Poetry.* Stanford, Calif.: Stanford University Press, 2003.

Goldscheider, Calvin, and Alan S. Zuckerman. *The Transformation of the Jews.* Chicago: University of Chicago Press, 1984.

Goldstein, Yosef. *Ahad Ha'Am* (in Hebrew). Jerusalem: Keter, 1992.

Golomb, Jacob, ed. *Nietzsche, Zionism and Hebrew Culture* (in Hebrew). Jerusalem: The Hebrew University/Magnes, 2002.

Gonen, Jay Y. *Psycho-History of Zionism.* New York: New American Library, 1975.

Gordimer, Nadine. "The Essential Gesture: Writers and Responsibility." *Granita* 15 (1985): 137–51.

Gorni, Yosef. "Hirhurim al ha-tsionut kh'ideologia utopit" [Thoughts on Zionism as a utopian ideology]. *Alpayim* 18 (1999): 200–209.

Gottshalk, Alfred. *Ahad Ha'Am v'ha-ruach ha-leumi* [Ahad Ha'Am and the national spirit]. Jerusalem: Zionist Library, 1992.

Greenberg, Joel. "Israel's History, Viewed Candidly, Starts a Storm." *New York Times,* 10 April 1998, 8.

Greenblatt, Stephen. "Culture." In *Critical Terms for Literary Study,* ed. Frank Lentricchia and Thomas McLaughlin, 231. Chicago: University of Chicago Press, 1995.

Grossman, David. *Sleeping on a Wire: Conversations with Palestinians in Israel.* Trans. Haim Watzman. New York: Picador, 1993.

―――. *The Smile of the Lamb.* Trans. Betsy Rosenberg. New York: Farrar, Straus & Giroux, 1990.

―――. *The Yellow Wind.* Trans. Haim Watzman. New York: Delta, 1988.

Gurevitch, Zaki, and Gideon Aran. "Al ha'maqom (Antropologia Israelit)" [About the place (Israeli anthropology)], *Alpayim* 4 (1991): 9–45.

Habermas, Jürgen. *The Philosophical Discourse of Modernity: Twelve Lectures.* Trans. Frederick G. Lawrence. Cambridge, Mass.: MIT Press, 1993.

Habiby, Emile. "Emile v'ha-mashmitsim" [Emile and the slanderers]. Interview with Dalia Karfel. *Kol ha-ir,* 1 May 1992, 34.

———. "Ha'khol over, Habiby" [Everything passes, Habiby]. Interview with Yotam Reuveni. *Yediot Aharonot,* 20 May 1993, 12.

———. *Ikhtayyeh.* Hebrew trans. Anton Shammas. Tel Aviv: Am Oved, 1988.

———. Interview with Michal Adam (in Hebrew). *Kol bo,* 3 September 1993, 77.

———. *Saraya, bat ha-shed ha-ra* [Saraya, Daughter of the Ghoul]. Hebrew trans. Anton Shammas. Tel Aviv: Hakibbutz Hameuchad, 1993.

———. *The Secret Life of Saeed, the Pessoptimist.* Trans. Salma Khadra Jayyusi and Trevor LeGassick. London: Zed Books, 1985.

———. "Yesh am Palestini v'yesh lo sifrut" ["There is a Palestinian people and it has a literature"]. Interview with Dalia Karfel. *Kol Ha-ir,* 1 May 1992, 26–29.

Hacohen, Dvora, ed. *Ingathering of Exiles, Immigration to Eretz Israel: Myth and Reality* (in Hebrew). Jerusalem: Merkhaz Zalman Shazar, 1997.

Halbwachs, Maurice. *On Collective Memory.* Trans. Lewis A. Coser. Chicago: University of Chicago Press, 1992.

Hareven, Shulamith. "Absurd hu ir prazot" [Absurd is an open city]. *Yediot Aharonot,* 19 June 1992, 14.

Havercamp, Anselm. "Mourning Becomes Melancholia—A Muse Deconstructed: Keats's *Ode on Melancholy.*" *New Literary History* 21, no. 3 (Spring 1990): 693–705.

Hegel, G. W. F. *Phenomenology of Spirit.* Trans. A. V. Miller. Oxford: Oxford University Press, 1977.

Herzberg, Arthur, ed. *The Zionist Idea: A Historical Analysis and Reader.* New York: Atheneum, 1986.

Herzl, Theodor. *Altneuland: Old-New Land.* Trans. Paula Arnold. Haifa: Haifa Publishing Co., 1960.

———. *The Jewish State.* New York: Dover, 1988.

Hever, Hannan. "'Ha'p'litot la-p'litim:' Emile Habiby v'kanon ha-sifrut ha-ivrit" [The refugee women to the refugees: Emile Habiby and the canon of Hebrew literature in Israel], *Ha-mizrah He-hadash* 35 (1993): 102–14.

———. "Minority Discourse of a National Majority: Israeli Fiction of the Early Sixties." *Prooftexts* 10 (1990): 129–47.

———. "Hebrew in an Israeli Arab Hand: Six Miniatures on Anton Shammas's *Arabesques.*" *Cultural Critique* [special issue: "The Nature and Context of Minority Discourse," ed. Abdul R. JanMohamed and David Lloyd.] 7 (1987): 47–76.

Hirschfeld, Ariel. "My Peace unto You, My Friend." *Palestine-Israel Journal* 2 (1994): 112–18.

Holtzman, Avner. *Hakharat panim: masot al Mikha Yosef Berdyczewski* [Essays on Micha Yosef Berdyczewski]. Tel Aviv: Reshafim, 1993.

Horn, Bernard. *Facing the Fires: Conversations with A. B. Yehoshua.* Syracuse, N.Y.: Syracuse University Press, 1997.

Jameson, Fredric. *The Political Unconscious: Narrative as a Socially Symbolic Act.* Ithaca, N.Y.: Cornell University Press, 1981.

Janoff-Bulman, Ronnie. *Shattered Assumptions: Toward a New Psychology of Trauma.* New York: Free Press, 1992.

Jayysi, Sandra Khandra, ed. *Anthology of Modern Palestinian Literature.* New York: Columbia University Press, 1992.

Kapitan, Tomis. "Historical Introduction to Philosophical Issues." In *Philosophical Perspectives on the Israeli-Palestinian Conflict,* ed. Tomis Kapitan, 3–36. Armonk, N.Y.: M. E. Sharpe, 1997.

Katz, Jacob. "Historia v'historionim, hadashim kh'yeshanim" [History and historian: Like new, like old]. *Alpayim* 12 (1996): 9–35.

Kershner, Isabel. "Blue-and-White Palestinians." *Jerusalem Report* 10, no. 13, 25 October 1999,14–18.

Kimmerling, Baruch. "Al da'at ha-makom . . . Al historia hevratit v'al antropologia ha-m'gayeset-atzma shel Israel" [On the understanding of the place: About social history and about Israel's self-propagandist anthropology]. *Alpayim* 6 (1992): 57–69.

Kornberg, Jacques. *Theodor Herzl: From Assismilation to Zionism.* Bloomington: Indiana University Press, 1993.

Kristeva, Julia. *Black Sun: Depression and Melancholia.* Trans. Leon S. Roudiez. New York: Columbia University Press, 1989.

Kurzweil, Baruch. *B'ma'avak al erkei ha-yahadut* [The struggle over Jewish values]. Tel Aviv: Schocken, 1969.

Lacan, Jacques. *The Four Fundamental Concepts of Psycho-Analysis.* Trans. Alan Sheridan. London: Penguin, 1994.

LaCapra, Dominick. *Representing the Holocaust: History, Theory, Trauma.* Ithaca, N.Y.: Cornell University Press, 1994.

Laor, Dan. "Ha-Fassutaim: ha-sipur sh'lo nigmar" [The Fassutans: The story that never ends]. *Ha'Aretz,* 31 May 1986, 6–7.

Laor, Yitzhak. *Narratives with No Natives: Essays on Israeli Literature* (in Hebrew). Tel Aviv: Hakibbutz Hameuchad, 1995.

Lazar, Hadara. *In and Out of Palestine* (in Hebrew). Jerusalem: Keter, 1990.

Lazarus, Neil. "Modernism and Modernity: T. W. Adorno and the Contemporary White South African Literature." *Cultural Critique* 5 (winter 1986–87): 131–55.

Lentricchia, Frank, and Thomas McLaughlin., eds. *Critical Terms for Literary Study.* Chicago: University of Chicago Press, 1995.

Levi, Shimon. "Sh'vuyim b'bidion: ha-aravim B'sifrut ha'ivrit he'hadashah" [Hostages of fiction: Arabs in Israeli modem fiction]. *Moznaim* 57 (October–November 1983): 70–73.

Levinas, Emmanuel. *The Levinas Reader.* Ed. Sean Hand. Oxford: Basil Blackwell, 1989.

———. *Time and the Other.* Trans. Richard A. Cohen. Pittsburgh, Pa.: Duquesne University Press, 1987.

———. *Otherwise Than Being or Beyond Essence.* Trans. Alphonso Lingis. Pittsburgh, Pa.: Duquesne University Press, 1999.

Lifton, Robert Jay. *The Broken Connection: On Death and the Continuity of Life.* Second edition. New York: Basic Books, 1983.

Likin, Max "Rights of Man, Reasons of State: Emile Zola and Theodor Herzl in Historical Perspective." *Jewish Social Studies* 8, no. 1 (2000): 126–53.

Lissak, Moshe. "'Critical' Sociology and 'Establishment' Sociology in the Israeli Academic Community: Ideological Struggles or Academic Discourse?" *Israel Studies* 1, no. l (spring 1996): 247–95.

Loshitzky, Yosefa. *Identity Politics on the Israeli Screen.* Austin: University of Texas Press, 2000.

Lotan, Yael. "Likrat sifrut Israelit" [Towards an Israeli literature]. *Al ha-Mishmar,* 4 July 1986, 15, 18.

M.D. "Tsalash l'Shammas" [A medal for Shammas]. *Ma'ariv,* 9 December 1988, 15.

Mansour, Atallah. *In a New Light.* Trans. Abraham Birman. London: Vallentine, Mitchell, 1969.

———. *Waiting for the Dawn.* London: Secker & Warburg, 1975.

Mazor, Yair. *Somber Lust: The Art of Amos Oz* (in Hebrew). Trans. Margaret Weinberger-Rotman. Albany: State University of New York Press, 2002.

McGee, Patrick. "Texts between Worlds: African Fiction as Political Allegory." In *Decolonizing Tradition: New Views of Twentieth-Century "British" Literary Canons,* ed. Karen R. Lawrence, 239–60. Urbana: University of Illinois Press, 1992.

Memmi, Albert. *The Colonizer and the Colonized.* Trans. Howard Greenfeld. Boston: Beacon Press, 1991.

Mendes, Philip. "Benny Morris, the Refugees, and Peace," *Response* 68 (fall 1997–winter 1998): 198–224.

Mendes-Flohr, Paul, and Jehuda Reinhartz, eds. *The Jew and the Modern World: A Documentary History.* New York: Oxford University Press, 1995.

Miron, Dan. "La'ant ha-shanim sh'adayin lo ukhla" [The years of bitterness that have not disappeared]. *Ha-olam ha-ze,* 9 July 1986, 26.

Morahg, Gilead. "New Images of Arabs in Israeli Fiction." *Prooftexts* 6 (1986): 147–62.

Morris, Benny. *The Birth of the Palestinian Refugee Problem.* Cambridge: Cambridge University Press, 1988.

———. "The Eel and History: A Reply to Shabtai Teveth." *Tikkun* 5, no. 1 (March–April 1990): 19–22, 79–86.

Mosse, George L. *German Jews Beyond Judaism*. Bloomington: Indiana University Press., 1985.

Naveh, Hannah. *Men and Women Travellers: Travel Narratives in Modern Hebrew Literature* (in Hebrew). Tel Aviv, Israel: Ministry of Defense, 2002.

Ophir, Adi. *Working for the Present: Essays on Contemporary Israeli Culture* (in Hebrew). Tel Aviv: Hakibbuz Hameuchad, 2001.

Oppenheimer, Yochai. "The Image of the Arab in Israeli Fiction." *Prooftexts* 19, no. 3 (1999): 205–35.

Oz, Amos. *All Our Hopes: Essays on the Israeli Condition* (in Hebrew). Jerusalem: Keter, 1998.

———. *In the Land of Israel*. 1983. Trans. Maurie Goldberg-Bartura. San Diego, Calif.: Harcourt Brace Jovanovich, 1993.

———. *My Michael*. Trans. Nicholas de Lange. New York: Alfred A. Knopf, 1972.

———. "Nomad and Viper." In *"Sleepwalker" and Other Stories: The Arab in Hebrew Fiction,* ed. Ehud Ben-Ezer. Boulder, Colo.: Lynn Rienner, 1999.

Pappe, Ilan. "Israeli Television's Fiftieth-Anniversary 'Tekumma' Series: A Post-Zionist View?" *Journal of Palestine Studies* 25, no. 4 (1998): 99–105.

———. "Post-Zionist Critique on Israel and the Palestinians—Part 1: The Academic Debate." *Journal of Palestine Studies* 26, no. 2 (1997): 29–41.

Perlis, Iza. "Tsair aravi b'kibbutz" [A young Arab on a kibbutz]. *Ma' ariv,* 25 March 1966, 22.

Perry, Menakhem. "The Israeli-Palestinian Conflict: A Metaphor in Recent Israeli Fiction." *Poetics Today* 7, no. 4 (1986): 603–19.

Qushu, Sayed. *Dancing Arabs*. Moshav Ben Shemen, Israel: Modan, 2002.

Rabinowitz, Dan. "Uri Davis" (in Hebrew) *Theory and Criticism* [special issue: "Fifty to Forty Eight: Critical Moments in the History of the State of Israel"] 12–13 (1999): 169–71.

Rabinowitz, Dan, and Khawla Abu Baker. *The Stand Tall Generation: The Palestinian Citizens of Israel Today* (in Hebrew). Jerusalem: Keter, 2002.

Ram, Uri. *The Changing Agenda of Israeli Sociology: Theory, Ideology, and Identity*. Albany: State University of New York Press, 1995.

Ramraz-Rauch, Gila. *The Arab in Israeli Literature*. Bloomington: Indiana University Press, 1989.

Raz-Krakotzkin, Amnon. "Exile within Sovereignty: Toward a Critique of the 'Negation of Exile' in Israeli Culture" (in Hebrew). *Theory and Criticism* 4 (1993): 46.

Rodison, Maxime. Israel: *A Colonial-Settler State.* New York: Monad, 1973.

Rubinstein, Amnon. *The Zionist Dream Revisited: From Herzl to Gush Emunim and Back.* New York: Schocken, 1984.

Said, Edward. "An Ideology of Difference." *Critical Inquiry* 12 (1985): 38–58.

———. *The Question of Palestine.* New York: Vintage. 1992.

———. "Zionism from the Standpoint of Its Victims." In *Dangerous Liaisons: Gender, Nation, and Postcolonial Perspectives,* ed. Anne McClintock, Aamir Mufti, and Ella Shohat, 15–38. Minneapolis: University of Minnesota Press, 1997.

Santner, Eric L. Stranded Objects: *Mourning, Memory, and Film in Postwar Germany.* Ithaca, N.Y.: Cornell University Press, 1990.

Schweid, Eliezer. "Beyond All That—Modernism, Zionism, Judaism." *Israel Studies* 1, no. 1 (1966): 224–47.

———. "Ha'tsionut kh'tsurat z'khut yehudit b'zmanenu" [Zionism as a form of Jewish identity in our time]. *Kivunim* 11–12 (1997): 29–35.

———. *Ha-tsionut she'aharei ha'tsionut* [Zionism in a post-modernistic era]. Jerusalem: Hassifria Haziyonit, 1996.

———. "L'mahuta u'l'reka shel ha'post tsionut" [Concerning the essence and the background of post-Zionism]. In *Post-Tsionut v'Shoah* [Post-Zionism and the Holocaust: The Role of the Holocaust in the Public Debate on Post-Zionism in Israel, 1993–1996], ed. Dan Michman, 282–90. Ramat Gan: Bar Ilan University, 1997.

———. "Meah sh'not 'tsionut m'dinit' u'ma hal'a?" [A hundred years of Zionism and what next?]. *Hadoar* 77, no. 3 (12 December 1997): 5–7; 77, no. 4. (26 December 1997): 5–7.

Scott, James C. *Domination and the Arts of Resistance: Hidden Transcripts.* New Haven, Conn.: Yale University Press, 1990.

Segev, Tom. *One Palestine, Complete: Jews and Arabs under the British Mandate.* Trans. Haim Watzman. New York: Metropolitan Books, 2000.

———. *The Seventh Million.* Trans. Haim Watzman. New York: Hill & Wang, 1993.

Shafir, Gershon. "Ideological Politics or the Politics of Demography? The Aftermath of the Six-Day War." In *Critical Essays on Israeli Society, Politics, and Culture: Books on Israel,* Vol. 2, ed. Ian S. Lustick and Barry Rubin. Albany: State University of New York Press, 1988.

———. *Land, Labor and the Origins of the Israeli-Palestinian Conflict, 1882–1914.* Berkeley: University of California Press, 1996.

Shaked, Gershon. "Aher—al anu khotvim otakh moledet m'et Itzhak Laor" [Review of *The Other*: About narratives with no natives, by Itzhak Laor]. *Alpayim* 12 (1996): 51–73.

———. "The Arab in Israeli Fiction." *Ariel* 54 (1983): 74–85.

———. *A New Wave in Israeli Fiction* (in Hebrew). Merhaviah and Tel Aviv: Sifriat Ha'Poalim, 1970.

———. *Literature Then, Here and Now* (in Hebrew). Tel Aviv: Zemora-Bitan, 1993.

———. *No Other Place: On Literature and Society* (in Hebrew). Tel Aviv: Hakibbutz Hameuchad, 1988.

———. *Wave After Wave in Hebrew Narrative Fiction* (in Hebrew). Jerusalem: Keter, 1985.

Shalev, Mordechai. "Ha-aravim kh'pitaron sifruti" [The Arabs as a literary solution]. *Ha'Aretz,* 30 September 1970.

Shamir, Ziva. "Diokan ha-historion shel ha-sifrut kh'bore m'tsiut" [Portrait of the historian of literature as a creator of reality]. *Moznaim* 73 (August 1999): 4–6.

Shammas, Anton. *Arabesques.* Trans. Vivian Eden. New York: Harper, 1988.

———. "Kitsch 22: On the Problems of the Relations Between Majority and Minority Cultures in Israel." *Tikkun* 2, no. 4. (September–October 1987): 22–26.

Shapira, Anita. "Hirbet Hizah: Between Remembrance and Forgetting," *Jewish Social Studies: History, Culture, and Society* 7, no. 1 (2000): 9–57.

———. "The Holocaust: Private Memories, Public Memory," *Jewish Social Studies: History, Culture, and Society* 4, no. 2 (1998): 40–59.

———. "Politics and the Collective Memory: The Debate over the 'New Historians' in Israel." *History and Memory* 7, no. 1 (1995): 9–41.

———. *Yehudim Hadashim Yehudim Yeshanim* [New Jews, Old Jews]. Tel Aviv: Am Oved, 1997.

———., ed. *Independence—The First Fifty Years: Collected Essays* (in Hebrew). Jerusalem: Zalman Shazar Center for Jewish History, 1998.

Shapira, Anita, Jehuda Reinharz and Jay Harris, eds., *The Age of Zionism* (in Hebrew). Jerusalem: Zalman Shazar Center for Jewish History, 2000. 19–37.

Shavit, Yaacov, *The Hebrew Nation: A Study in Israeli Heresy and Fantasy.* London: Frank Cass, 1987.

Shimoni, Gideon. *The Zionist Ideology.* Hanover, N.H.: Brandeis University Press, 1995.

Shohat, Ella. *Israeli Cinema: East/West and the Politics of Representation.* Austin: University of Texas Press, 1989.

Silberstein, Lawrence J. *The Post-Zionism Debates: Knowledge and Power in Israeli Culture.* New York: Routledge, 1999.

Slymovic, Susan. *The Object of Memory: Arab and Jew Narrate the Palestinian Village.* Philadelphia: University of Pennsylvania Press, 1998.

Smith, Barbara J. *The Roots of Separatism in Palestine: British Economic Policy, 1920–1929.* Albany, N.Y.: Syracuse University Press, 1993.

Snir, Reuven. "'Hebrew as the Language of Grace:' Arab-Palestinian Writers in Hebrew." *Prooftexts* 15, no. 2 (1995): 163–85.

————. " 'Postcards in the Morning': Palestinian Writing in Hebrew." *Hebrew Studies* 42 (2001): 197–225.

Sokoloff, Naomi B., Anne Lapidus Lerner, and Anita Norich, eds. *Gender and Text in Modern Hebrew and Yiddish Literature*. New York: Jewish Theological Seminary, 1992.

Stampfer, Joshua, ed. *Dialogue: The Essence of Buber*. New York: J. Stampfer, 1988.

Sternhell, Zeev. *Nation Building or a New Society? The Zionist Labor Movement (1904–1940) and the Origins of Israel* (in Hebrew). Tel Aviv: Am Oved, 1995.

Szyska, Christian. "Geographies of the Self: Text and Space in Anton Shammas's *Arabesques*." In *Narrated Space in the Literature of the Islamic World*, ed. Roxane Haag-Higuchi and Christian Szyska, 217–32. Wiesbaden: Harrassowitz, 2001.

Taha, Ibrahim. *The Smile of an Opsimistic Lover: A Comparative Reading of the Hebrew and Palestinian Novel in Israel* (in Hebrew). Tel Aviv: Hakibbutz Hameuchad, 1999.

Tal, Yerach. "Ha-pras magi'a l'Habiby: al m'cha'ato shel Yuval Ne'man al ha'anakat pras Israel l'Emile Habiby" [Habiby deserves the prize: On Yuval Ne'man's protest against awarding the Israel Prize to Emile Habiby"]. *Ha'Aretz*, 10 May 1992, 10.

Teveth, Shabtai, *Ben Gurion and the Holocaust*. New York: Harcourt Brace, 1966,

Tessler, Mark. *A History of the Israeli-Palestinian Conflict*. Bloomington: Indiana University Press, 1994.

Toren, Orly. "Matsavo ha-ishi, matsavo ha-politi, matsavo ha-sifruti: Emile Habibi, sofer Arvi Palestini nehshav, b'avar haver Knesset komunist, humlatz l'pras Israel l'sifrut. Ma omrim al khakh anshei sifrut?" [His personal situation, his political situation, his literary situation: Emile Habiby, an important Arab Palestinian writer, a past Knesset member, was recommended for the Israel Prize for literature. What do men and women of letters Say?]. *Yediot Aharonot*, 13 March 1992, 24.

Turner, Frederick Jackson. "Western State-Making in the Revolutionary Era." *American Historical Review* 1, no. 1 (October 1985): 70–72.

United Nations, *Special Committee on Palestine: Recommendations to the General Assembly*. A/364. 6 September 1947. <*http://www.mfa.gov.il/mfa/go.asp?MFAH017x03*>.

Urian, Dan. *The Arab in Israeli Theatre* (in Hebrew). Tel Aviv: Or-Am, 1996.

Vital, David. "Zionism as Revolution? Zionism as Rebellion?" *Modern Judaism* 18, no. 3 (October 1998): 205–17.

Ya'akobi, Gad. "Mitrahakim v'holkhim" [Getting Farther Apart]. *Hadoar*, 77, no. 17, 10 July 1998, 4.

Yehoshua, A. B. "Facing the Forests." In *"Sleepwalkers" and Other Stories:*

The Arab in Hebrew Fiction, ed. Ehud Ben-Ezer. Boulder, Colo.: Lynn Rienner, 1999.

———. *Khoha ha-nora shel ashma k'tana* [The terrible power of a minor guilt]. Tel Aviv: Yediot Aharonot, 1998.

———. "The Next Fifty Years." *Azure* [special issue: "The Jewish State: The Next Fifty Years"] 6 (1999): 226–32.

Yizhar, S. "Hashavti lomar al khlum et ha-khol" [I intended to say everything about nothing]. Interview with Moshe Granot. *Moznaim* 75, no. 1. (January 2001): 15–18.

———. "Hirbet Hizah." *Arba'a sipurim* [Four stories]. Tel Aviv: Hakibbutz Hameuchad, 1968.

———. "Ze ha-okyianus ha-bilti noda, u-ma she-tsarikh hu lo lehacknis bo mey shopkhin." [This is an unknowable ocean and we need not pour sewer water into it]. Interview with Rubik Rosenthal and Hed Sela. *Panim: Quarterly for Society, Culture and Education* 10 (summer 1999): 52–57.

Zalmona, Yigal. "Introduction." *To the East: Orientalism in the Arts in Israel* [exhib. cat.] Jerusalem: Israel Museum, Jerusalem, 1998, vi–vii.

Zerubavel, Yael. *Recovered Roots: Collective Memory and the Making of Israeli National Tradition.* Chicago: University of Chicago Press, 1995.

Zipperstein, Steven. *Elusive Prophet: Ahad Ha'am and the Origins of Zionism.* Berkeley: University of California Press, 1993.

"Zionist Dialectics." *Israel Studies* 1, no. 1 (1996): 196–295; 1, no. 2 (1996): 170–267.

Žižek, Slavoj. *The Sublime Object of Ideology.* London: Verso, 1989.

Index

African literature, 92–93, 113–14, 141
Agreement, Oslo, 102–3, 284
Ahad Ha'Am: Berdyczewski and, 30–32; concerns expressed by, 28–30, 33–36; critique of Zionism by, 20; Eretz Israel as spiritual entity, 29–30; Herzl and, 56; morality and ethics, political Zionism and, 27–29; resistance to tenets of exclusion, 25–26; Zionism and, 83
aliyah, settler's experiences, 61–67
Alon, Yig'al, 113
Althusser, Louis, 229, 240
Altneuland (Herzl), 7, 67
angel of history, 223–25, 238, 243–44
Angelus Novus (Klee), 223–25
anti-Semitism, 55, 58–59; attributed to Arabs, 62, 64–65, 212–13; the Crusades and, 181; Jews as anti-Semitic, 72
apartheid, 141
Arabesques (Shammas), 109, 112, 120–21; authorial empowerment, 280; authorship ambiguities, 253, 273–74, 281; autobiographical form in, 273–74, 281; critical reception of works, 124–28; dialogic interactions, 261, 282–83; identity in, 248, 261, 267–68, 274–77, 281; multiple roles in, 281; names, 248, 276; narrative structure of, 248–49; parallel story patterns in, 282; reader as spectator, 246; rejection of the father's legacy, 255; split identity in, 274–75, 281; synopsis of, 248–49; Zionist identity in, 267–68

Arabic: as forgotten language, 202; Habiby's use of, 128–29
Arabs: as anti-Semitic, 62, 64–65, 212–13; as ghosts, 148; identification of Zionists with native Arabs, 75–76; identity of Israeli Arabs, 106, 273, 283; incorporation into Hebrew identity, 70; as objects of desire, 188, 216–18; as Other, 142; resistance to ideological cooptation, 208, 214; romanticized or sentimentalized, 76; as thieves, 75, 213; as threat to Zionist "return," 140. *See also* Arabs, as fictional characters; Arabs, negation of; Israeli Arab writers
Arabs, as fictional characters, 60, 286; in *Arabesques*, 274, 275–76, 279–81; demonized and dehumanized, 212–13, 258; in *In a New Light*, 200–201; as metaphors of Jewish psyche, 97, 99–100, 206–7; as mirror of identity, 65; the mute in "Facing the Forests," 178–79, 183; as servile, 200–201, 257; in *The Smile of the Lamb*, 249–50; subjectivity of, 207; as universalized victim, 97, 141–42, 143, 206; in Yehoshua's works, 107–8, 109, 142
Arabs, negation of, 19; by *aliya* pioneers, 35; Alon on Palestinian literature, 113; in *Arabesques*, 275–76; "empty land" and, 79; in "Hirbet Hizah," 258; Meir on Palestinians, 113; in *The Smile of the Lamb*, 258. *See also* "empty land" concept; invisibility of the Arab